THE
NEW TESTAMENT
SPEAKS

THE
NEW TESTAMENT
SPEAKS

GLENN W. BARKER

WILLIAM L. LANE

J. RAMSEY MICHAELS

1817

HARPER & ROW, PUBLISHERS

New York, Hagerstown, San Francisco, London

LIBRARY OF CONGRESS CATALOG CARD NUMBER: 69-10477

✳

This book is dedicated to our parents—

Mr. and Mrs. Wesley T. Barker
Mr. and Mrs. William J. Lane
Mrs. Ethel M. Michaels

*—as an expression of deep respect
and enduring affection*

CONTENTS

❋

CONTENTS

PREFACE

THIS VOLUME is neither a critical introduction to the New Testament nor an attempt at a biblical theology. It is an exposition of the New Testament message, written from an evangelical perspective. It is designed first for the university student but then for any others, laity or clergy, who desire a framework by which to strengthen their grasp of the biblical material. Critical questions are treated only as they bear upon the message of the various books. The bibliographies are not intended to be exhaustive or overly critical but simply to be useful to the student in pursuing topics of special interest to him. Although we have given attention to problems of history and tradition when necessary, our primary focus is upon the New Testament documents in their present form. Thus, in "The Story of Jesus" it will at once be obvious to the advanced student that we are less interested in the Jesus of the historians than in the Christ of the Gospels. Our purpose has been to focus attention on the message of the New Testament itself in order to make it plain and understandable.

In structuring the material for the book we have approached our task from the students' perspective and have attempted to do something new. The treatment of the books of the New Testament in an almost mechanical fashion has inevitably obscured the spontaneity of their message. The more a book is placed in its distinctive setting as a living word of the past, the more it tends to become a living word in the present. We determined that the reconstruction of the life situation of the several documents should be the dominant consideration in our presentation. The significant elements in the life setting—place, situation, the persons addressed—differ from book to book. But the question of the purpose of each book remains the crucial consideration, since purpose shapes the form and content of the message.

Although this book is the joint responsibility of its three authors, each has labored primarily in his own specific areas and is responsible in a more direct way than the others for particular chapters. Professor Barker's work laid the basis for the first two chapters as well as chapters four, five, and eighteen. Professor Lane is responsible for chapter three on the background to the New Testament, except for three sections, "The Maccabean Revolt," "An Independent State," and "The Story Told and Retold," which were the work of Professor Michaels. In addition, Professor Lane wrote chapters six through sixteen and chapter nineteen. Professor Michaels contributed chapter seventeen, and chapters twenty through twenty-five. The three of us have freely edited and revised one another's work in an effort to achieve unity of style and thought. It is our hope that the book will afford to some readers a small fraction of the enjoyment and satisfaction it has given to us.

Most of the Scripture quotations are from the Revised Standard Version of the Bible, copyrighted 1946 and 1952 by the Division of the Christian Education of the National Council of Churches, and used by permission. When we have substituted a translation of our own, this fact is indicated by an asterisk (*). Passages from Josephus, the apostolic fathers, Eusebius, Suetonius, and Tacitus have been taken from the Loeb edition and are reprinted by permission of the publishers, the Harvard University Press and the Loeb Classical Library.

To acknowledge the assistance received from others is a pleasant task. Our classes in the Divinity School as well as Professor Lane's experience of teaching the basic course in New Testament to underclassmen at Gordon College have been, as we indicated, a laboratory in which our approaches to the material could be tested and sharpened. We therefore express our appreciation to the administration at Gordon and to our students. The encouragements of our faculty colleagues has also meant a great deal to us and contributed immensely to our work. The task of deciphering three different scripts when typing the first draft was cheerfully undertaken by Miss Linda Dyer; the final draft was prepared by Mrs. Carrol Farrell and Mrs. Leah Tarnor. We would be remiss if we did not acknowledge the patience and understanding of our wives when "the book" consumed an excessive amount of our family time, and of our children, who provided that necessary goad with the innocent, but barbed question: "How many pages did you do today, Dad?" Finally, it is appropriate to acknowledge our debt to those who have preceded us in the task of seeking to introduce the message of the New Testament to a contemporary generation. We have rediscovered the truth of the encouragement which Jesus gave to his disciples, "I have sent you to reap that for which you did not labor; others have labored, and you have entered into their labor" (John 4:38).

G.W.B.
W.L.L.
J.R.M.

THE
NEW TESTAMENT
SPEAKS

I

THE NEW TESTAMENT SPEAKS

THE title of this volume, *The New Testament Speaks,* expresses concisely both the conviction and the personal experience of the authors. That is, that the authority of the New Testament is not to be located in its value as a source for unique religious ideas, nor in the excellence of its moral imperative, even less as a commentary on history or a norm for social ethics or political philosophy. Rather, the New Testament is that which speaks, which addresses man as man, in all his frailty and confusion. It speaks to let man know who he is, exposing his limitations and showing him what is his hope and glory.

But if it is asserted that the New Testament or the Scripture speaks, is not this in fact an enigma? How can any book or writing speak? Would it not be more correct to say that some early Christians wrote, or that what is recorded in the New Testament is the testimony of the early church, witnessing to its own faith and religious experience? Of course, all of this is true; but this is precisely what we do not have in mind. He who asserts that the Scripture speaks affirms that God speaks. Moreover, he declares that God speaks here, sovereignly in this very place, and that he speaks in and through the language of men.

If Scripture is the vehicle through which God speaks, then it is apparent what our relationship to the New Testament must be. To say that God speaks is also to say that man must hear, that God can and does in fact make known his purpose for man, that by his words God discloses himself, making himself open to man's knowledge and entering into relationship with man. Consequently, man's concern with respect to Scripture is equally clear. As God is the Discloser, so before the word of God man becomes the listener. He must listen to God's voice—God's word. For man this poses no small responsibility. To become the listener means that he is to be no less involved with Scripture than is God himself. Man is summoned by the word of God into a relationship; for him to hear God means that he must stand before God not passively or as object, but as the thinking, deciding, acting creature that he is. All his being now becomes channeled toward one possibility, the hearing of God.

Yet how will he hear God? Will he hear God as he overhears his neighbor across the backyard fence? This kind of hearing is probably of small merit. Rather, he must prepare himself for a special kind of listening, a kind of hearing different from any past experience. He who hears the New Testament speak will be one who has learned to listen with the heart, who has bared his very soul to God and been willing to experience God's grace.

One does not hear God's word of grace in the Scriptures unless he has decided that this is the word he really needs and wants to hear. He must decide that as he hears he is prepared to submit to the voice of God, to be judged by it and to have it challenge all that he knows and intends. He must understand that what he hears the Bible say can change his very life. Therefore, he cannot come to the New Testament as the disputer, the wise man, the judge over the word of God. He can come only as the child who needs to be made wise by the Wisdom of God (1 Cor. 1:18–31).

PRINCIPLES GOVERNING METHODS

How, then, may we recognize the word of God? Is it magical—to be known only in some mysterious fashion? Does it come as something outside the text of Scripture, prompted by the language of Scripture yet wholly different and apart from it? The answer to this question involves the setting forth of the first principle governing our methodology: *The word of God is none other than this word of Scripture.* This is, of course, a direct corollary of the fact that Scripture is God speaking. His words constitute a rational phenomenon. Language is the process through which one person communicates with another. As such, it is a rational activity. Accordingly, there can be only one approach to Scripture: in order to determine what God *says,* that which in fact God *said* must first be established. The process by which we determine the exact meaning of any given statement is called exegesis. Although the term is traditionally associated with biblical studies, it should not be assumed that its practice is peculiar to this discipline. On the contrary, a similar approach is employed whenever an important document is examined, whether the material is an archaeological find from the site of an ancient civilization or the latest pronouncement from the Kremlin. In either instance, the relative importance of the document will dictate the care with which it is examined. If its content is of sufficient importance, strict attention will be paid to the nuance of each word, phrase, and sentence. The whole communication will be read and reread against the known background in which it took form. Every scrap of evidence will be used to elucidate the intention of the author. Every effort will be made to penetrate its true and total intent. In such an activity the validity of the interpretation of a given text will depend upon the interpreter's ability to reconstruct the circumstances out of which the document came.

The written word of God is surely a most important document. The biblical text confronts us with God's communication to man. The process whereby we come to understand it must be similar to that employed in discerning other verbal utterances. Ultimately the extent to which we hear the word will be relative to our understanding of each historical utterance; it is precisely through historical utterances given once for all that God continues to address man. The hearing of the word thus involves a two-fold tension. On the one hand, it requires a willingness to allow God's word to become contemporaneous with our circumstances—not to historicize it so that it remains inoperative before us. On the other hand, it demands of us the quality of empathy, that is, a willingness on our part to become contemporaneous with the historical occurrence of the word. This means that we must allow it to be truly historical. In the very experience of our *being there* before God's word, God's word also *becomes here* before us.

There is an important fact in God's communication which we have yet to consider: *The Scriptures are not God's direct disclosure, but rather God's speaking through human instruments.* This remains true whether we have to do with a spoken proclamation in the name of God or the record of historical movements in the life of Israel or the human race in general. Each of the biblical writers, as a member of a given race of people, living in a particular place and time, is inevitably caught up in the tension of his own existence. In one moment he may be involved in the struggle of his people for survival against hostile forces from without. In another, he may be attempting to resist the corrosive forces of wickedness and rebellion from within. At still another time all events may be reduced to the level of his own spiritual awareness, his personal struggle for obedience to the righteous will of God and striving after the truth of God. It is within these tensions that God's Spirit so activates the life of the author that what he thinks, observes, and finally writes becomes the means by which God makes known his truth. It must never be forgotten that the written word of God is a word addressed first of all to the writer's own contemporaries.

Consequently, when we seek to interpret God's revelation in Scripture, we are inevitably committed to search out every detail of a given author's experience. It must be determined in each context precisely what the human author is saying. What factual information or knowledge does he convey to us? What external circumstances call forth his remarks? What categories are open to him by which he can express his thought? What limitations are placed upon him by the life situation of his first readers? Where does the author stand in relation to the unfolding of God's redemptive activity? What peculiar limitations or advantages accrue to him because of his present situation and past experience?

These are but a few of the questions that the student who seeks to know the word of God must attempt to answer. As listener he must always bear in mind that the divine word is this specific historical word. Only to the extent that he lays hold of the historical word does the living, eternal word become open to his understanding and he in turn to its relevance for him. Every tool of historical, linguistic, and critical analysis must be brought to bear fully upon the pursuit of biblical truth To do less is to dishonor the written word of God.

If the student of God's word must commit himself to a thorough investigation, even an interrogation of Scripture, by what principle shall he distinguish the word of God from all the peripheral elements surrounding it? Does not the New Testament contain thousands of details and incidents which are not germane to the main subject? Does not the study of these materials represent largely a waste of time and energy? The posing of this question leads to the statement of the second principle which governs our methodology: *The whole Bible, every word in the Scripture, participates in the miracle of God's word.* Study of the New Testament does not involve the reduction of its several elements to a single uniform phenomenon that can be isolated from the rest and be called the word of God. Rather it demands the broadest base conceivable in order that God's word should appear in its totality. It is not as if the word were entrapped within a wider verbiage of ideas which then must be culled in order to separate the wheat from the chaff. The word is not buried somehow within Scripture, waiting to be rescued by the cleverness of the scholar's mind and the ingenuity of his method. The word is God's sovereign expression of his own mind and purpose. He has chosen to express his will to us in the *totality* of what we know as Holy Scripture. We have no independent knowledge of what the word is which we can take to Scripture in order to find correspondence. Rather, we go to the Scripture in order to find what the word is. The whole of Scripture participates in this presentation. Human reason, within the church or without, should never be allowed to become a screen through which the eternal truth of God is processed. Whenever this rule has been violated, however meritorious the motives, the result has always been tragically the same: The truth of God has become distorted by the weakness and fallibility of man.

An important question, however, must be raised: Does not the Scripture in fact say many different things? Are there not vast differences within the teachings of Scripture? Do there not loom large areas of disagreement between Old and New Testaments? Even within the New Testament are there not sharp distinctions between the various books, both in form and content? Such problems necessitate a clear statement of a third principle: *The word of God is one word, not many words.* Every individual statement of Scripture finds its ultimate meaning as it is related to this one word. We can see this principle in operation with reference to Jesus Christ. He, the Incarnate Word, draws to himself the witness of Scripture. For the New Testament writers he is the clearest expression of the mind of God and the utterance of God as it appears in man's history. Thus in the fourth Gospel Jesus says, "Search the scriptures . . . it is they that bear witness to me" (John 5:39). The writer of the Epistle to the Hebrews says it this way: "In many and various ways God spoke of old to our fathers by the prophets; but in these last days he has spoken to us by his Son"* (Heb. 1:1-2). Martin Luther reduced this centrality of Jesus in the New Testament to a hermeneutical principle: The word of God is that which proclaims Christ.

Although this unifying principle makes a valid point, it must be safeguarded properly, for its converse is also true: What actually is proclaimed in Christ can only be known through the Scriptures. That is why so many of the noteworthy events in the life of Jesus are interpreted by him to the disciples or the multitudes in terms of the Scripture. Even his own inner experiences, in the few instances that they are recorded for us, are understood in the same way. This is presented in the Gospels, where the principle is accentuated, as a fulfillment motif. The concept is no less present in the rest of the New Testament: through Christ we understand Scripture, and through the Scripture we understand Christ.

Even though the word of God is one word, no writer of Scripture has grasped this word in its entirety. Accordingly, one statement of the word should not be chosen to the exclusion or neglect of any other. Luther appears to have fallen into this error by seizing upon the Pauline statement of the word, while giving little if any place to the word in James or Revelation. The history of the church has been marked by such choices. It has often chosen to emphasize John's life of Jesus over that of the synoptics, Paul's teaching over that of James or Hebrews. What happens under such circumstances is that the word of God tends to become reduced to those dogmatic terms which are most acceptable to a particular age and situation; other concepts, which may be equally important, are set aside. Whole church traditions have developed through such a process, and misunderstanding, division, and incomplete truth become the legacy. It must be restated in the strongest terms possible that our concern is to hear the whole of God's witness in the New Testament. We must discipline ourselves to listen to what the Spirit says through each writer. We must not hear John through Pauline ears, nor Mark through Matthean ears, nor Luke through Johannine ears. Rather we must commit ourselves to the faithful, radical hearing of each witness, fully convinced that since God has chosen to set forth his total word to us in this way, no individual word must be allowed to slip away.

But what of the form of God's word? Is it not true that the Scripture is marked by the inadequacies and weaknesses of its human authors? Do they not use in their presentations an approach to the material which is inconsistent with our own high standards of historical research? Do they not depend on literary devices no longer acceptable to our modern age? Do they not perpetuate archaic world views long ago discarded by informed men as relics of a prescientific culture? How then can Scripture be the word of God and wholly authoritative for man if its presentation is marked by such obvious inadequacies?

These questions lead us to the statement of our fourth principle: *Although the word of God is wholly divine in its origin, the form in which it is written is wholly human.* The church has at times had difficulty with this principle. Precisely because it knew the Scriptures as God's own word and desired that the divine character of the word should be acknowledged by all, it sometimes either neglected or suppressed in its statements the human character of Scripture. This is not very different from the problem the church faces in interpreting the nature of Jesus' life in the flesh. Knowing the Son of God for what he was in truth, it was difficult to acknowledge any limitation to Jesus' knowledge, power, or understanding, even as a growing boy. True weakness of the flesh, anguish of spirit, and trial of faith were denied to the Son of God. In Christology this development is known as Docetism, a heresy finally condemned by the great councils of the church. Docetic tendencies have continued to afflict the church, bringing about a parallel unwillingness to recognize the human quality in the Bible. For instance, the men who wrote the New Testament are not allowed to be really human, to think as men of their times would think, to experience any inadequacies of method or expression, to grasp the truth of God only in fragments or with limitations. Such views historically have tended to restrict the student of Scripture in his use of the critical method. They have forced him in some instances to deny obvious problems in the text, and have pushed him into peculiar "harmonistic" exegetical patterns so as to make him either deny the explicit statement of God's word or to caricature it beyond recognition.

Such tendencies the church has ultimately resisted, though it has had to contend in some cases against great pressure. Nonetheless, its greatest teachers have expressed themselves unequivocally at this point. Augustine, a strong defender of the divine nature of Scripture, stated very clearly the human limitation of its authors:

> For to speak of the matter as it is, who is able? I venture to say, my brethren perhaps not John himself spoke of the matter as it is, but even he, only as he was able; for it was a man that spoke of God, inspired indeeed by God, but still man. Because he was inspired, he said something; if he had not been inspired, he would have said nothing; but because a man inspired, he spoke not the whole, but what a man could, he spoke.[1]

The father of Reformed theology, John Calvin, was no less aware of the limitation which the human form placed on God's utterance. He saw this not as weakness but as necessity. God could speak only through inadequate human language if he truly desired to be heard. Calvin wrote:

> Let us therefore remember that our Lord has not spoken according to His nature. For if He would speak His (own) language, would He be understood by moral creature? Alas, no. But how has He spoken to us in Holy Scripture? He has stammered . . . so then God as it were resigned; for as much as we would not comprehend what He would say, if He did not condescend to us. There you have the reason why in Holy Scripture one sees Him like a nurse rather than that one hears of His high and infinite majesty.[2]

This insight must be incorporated methodologically into our approach to Scripture. We are not in any way to deny the human character of the form of Holy Scripture, as if somehow it were unworthy of God. Rather we must let it be seen and heard in all its different forms. We will not expect of any writer standards of expression that are any different from the culture and history he represents. We will expect a Jew of Palestine to think and write like a Jew, sharing that knowledge of the world that a Jew of the first century enjoyed. His ability to understand will be limited to some extent by his inner capacities; his efforts will necessarily take place within the framework of human comprehension and memory. This will be true also for a Jew of the Hellenistic world or for a Greek. Each one will come to his task as a man of his time, with the idiosyncrasies that are common to us all. Nevertheless, each one, as directed by God's Spirit, will speak the word of God.

Sometimes we will find that the truth of God will be presented in parallel themes that can be compared and recognized as supplementary to one another. On other occasions we will discover what appear to be contrasting and opposing presentations. When this happens, we must recognize that the truth of God is to be grasped in tension. We will not expect a writer in all cases to understand both sides of the tension, but we will permit him to express that aspect of the truth which God has allowed him to know and share. In this sense we will treat the writer as a truly historical figure, writing as a man under God's directive but nonetheless within his own possibilities. How could it be otherwise? We will expect to encounter every literary form, all uses of sources, abridgment, and reinterpretation acceptable in the common practice of the age. We will not prejudice what any author might do or condemn any man for what he in fact did. Rather, we will always stand in the confidence that God himself has chosen the time, the place, and the method for the event of Scripture. To the one who wills to hear, the word of God comes in power, in glory, and in divine transcendence; and if it comes to us in a frail human form, it comes in this way that the excellency of the word may prove to be of God and not of us.

NOTES

1. Augustine, *Homily on John* *1:1*. This and the following quotations are included in a helpful chapter on the human form of Scripture by K. Runia, *Karl Barth's Doctrine of Holy Scripture* (1962), pp. 57–80.
2. John Calvin, *Sermons on Deuteronomy* (Corpus Reformatorum, XXVI,

col. 387). Two quotations from Dutch Reformed theologians of the modern era may be compared with those of Calvin and Augustine. The same careful attempt to safeguard the human factor in Scripture is to be observed. Both authorities quoted locate the mystery of the human form of the word within the total condescension of God manifested in the incarnation. First, Abraham Kuyper, *Principles of Sacred Theology* (1954), pp. 478 f.:

> The divine factor of the Holy Spirit clothes itself in the garment of our form of thought, and holds itself to our human reality. . . . As the Logos has not appeared *in the form of glory* but in the form of a servant, joining himself to the reality of our nature, as this had come to be through the results of sin, so also, for the revelation of His Logos. God the Lord accepts *our* consciousness, our human life as it is. . . . The forms or types are marred by want and sin. The "shadows" remain humanly imperfect, far beneath their ideal content. The "spoken words," however much aglow with the Holy Ghost, remain bound to the limitation of our language, disturbed as it is by anomalies. As a product of writing the Holy Scriptures also bears on its forehead the mark of the form of a servant.

Then, H. Bavinck, *Gereformeerde Dogmatiek* (1928), Vol. I, p. 405; cf. p. 352:

> In the doctrine of Holy Scripture the doctrine of organic inspiration is the working out and application of the central fact of the revelation, the Incarnation. The LOGOS became SARX, and the Word became Scripture. These two facts not only run parallel to each other, but are very intimately connected with each other. Christ became flesh, a servant without form or comeliness . . . obedient unto death of the cross. Likewise the revelation of God entered into the forms of creation, into the life and history of men and nations, into all human forms of dream and vision, etc., even into that which is weak and despised; the Word became writing, and as a piece of writing it subjected itself to the fate of all writing. All this happened, that the exceeding greatness of the power, also of the power of Holy Scripture, may be of God and not from ourselves (I Cor. 4:7).

A fine treatment by a Roman Catholic on the same subject is provided by Jean Levie, *The Bible: Word of God in Words of Men* (1961).

II

✳

THE NEW TESTAMENT CANON

THE New Testament canon is the New Testament thought of as a rule of faith which possesses divine authority over the church. As canonical writings the twenty-seven books constitute the definitive witness to Jesus Christ as Lord, and are regarded by Christians as the infallible rule of Christian faith and life, the inspired deposit of God's revelation. Two questions in particular may be raised concerning the canon of the New Testament: 1. Historically, how early may we trace the origin of the canon? 2. Theologically, what does the collection and recognition of the authoritative character of the several books mean?

1. THE ORIGIN AND DEVELOPMENT OF THE CANON

In the one-hundred-year period extending roughly from A.D. 50 to 150 a number of documents began to circulate among the churches. These included epistles, gospels, acts, apocalypses, homilies, and collections of teachings. While some of these documents were apostolic in origin, others drew upon the tradition the apostles and ministers of the word had utilized in their individual missions. Still others represented a summation of the teaching entrusted to a particular church center. Several of these writings sought to extend, interpret, and apply apostolic teaching to meet the needs of Christians in a given locality.

From the beginning it was expected that certain of these documents would be read in the public gatherings of the church. The final instruction in Paul's earliest epistle is a solemn admonition to see that "this letter be read to all the brethren" (1 Thess. 5:27), while to the Colossians he wrote, "When this letter has been read among you, have it read also in the church of the Laodiceans" (Col. 4:16). The opening verses of the Book of Revelation envision the churches gathered in worship: "Blessed is he who reads aloud the words of the prophecy, and blessed are those who hear, and who keep what is written therein" (Rev. 1:3). Frequently a document demanded its wide circulation, as in the case of Galatians ("to the churches of Galatia") or Second Corinthians ("to the church of God which is at Corinth, with all the saints who are in the whole of Achaia"). The churches increasingly found it profitable to share their literary holdings with one another, with the result that copies of the earliest writings began to circulate among the several centers of Christendom.

As the amount of the materials circulating increased, it was inevitable that similar materials should be collected together in order to protect against loss as well as to make them more available for study and use within the churches. There appears to be some evidence that the first formal collection consisted of ten of Paul's letters which were bound together and published as a single corpus sometime prior to A.D. 100.[1]

Not long after, the Gospels were also collected and published as a single corpus.[2] The consequence of this action was to prove an even greater benefit to the church than had the publication of the Pauline corpus. Prior to this event, each of the Gospels had been identified with a particular geographical region: Mark with Rome, Matthew with Antioch and Syria, John with Ephesus and Asia, and Luke with Paul's churches in Greece. The differences among them were freely acknowledged, but only when the Gospels began to circulate beyond their own immediate environment were these differences accentuated.[3] This invited not only comparison but even choice among them, as some groups preferred one Gospel and some another. The collection of the four Gospels into a single corpus, and its publication as the fourfold *Gospel* of the church, preserved all four documents for the life and edification of each church. No longer required to compete for their existence, the Gospels were now allowed to complement each other.[4]

These two collections of material served as the solid core for a new body of literature which began to take its place alongside the Old Testament Scriptures. Very early the Book of Acts, First Peter, First John, and Revelation were added to this core. In individual regions additional writings were also included, not all of which finally achieved canonical status. Such documents as Clement's letter to Corinth continued to be read in that church until the fifth century[5]; there was extensive use of the *Didache* in Syria, of the *Epistle of Barnabas* in Alexandria, of the *Shepherd of Hermas* in Carthage, and of the *Apocalypse of Peter* in Rome. None of these documents, however, succeeded in establishing its authority over the larger church. They were seen to be examples of edifying literature which had proven useful for a time but which lacked the permanent validity of the apostolic writings.

It was probably the rise of heretics—especially Marcion, who adopted as his canon a truncated form of Luke and Paul's ten letters to churches —which forced the church to declare itself regarding the relative authority of the documents currently read in the churches. This new body of Christian literature only gradually imposed its authority on the church. In spite of the practice of publicly reading from the newer documents in services of worship, there is no clear, early evidence that they were considered to be equal in authority to the scriptures of the Old Covenant. If the term "Scripture" could be applied to Paul's letters (2 Peter 3:16) or later to the Gospels (II Clement, Justin), not until the end of the second century were the expressions "inspired writings," "Scriptures of the Lord," and "the Scriptures" used indiscriminately of both the Old Testament and the core of the New. At this time the designation "the New Testament" made its appearance and ultimately displaced all earlier names for the collection of the new books. Henceforth it was no longer a question of the nature of the canon, but only of its extent.

By A.D. 200, twenty-one of the books of the New Testament had a secure position in the canon. In the course of discussion it was possible to group a book according to one of three categories: (1) the *homologoumena* or universally accepted writings; (2) the *antilegomena* or disputed books, accepted by some churches but challenged by others; and (3) the *notha* or clearly spurious documents. During the third century, James, Jude, Second and Third John, Second Peter, and Hebrews were frankly disputed in different sectors of the church, so that Origen and Eusebius classified them among the *antilegomena*.[6] Revelation had enjoyed wide acceptance at the beginning of the century, but in the ensuing years it was subjected to challenge and discrimination. The dispute over questions of authorship, authenticity, style, and doctrine subsided by the middle of the fourth century, and these documents also took their place in the lists of books accepted by the bishops of the church. The church fathers Jerome and Augustine acknowledged the entire twenty-seven books of the canon, as did the councils of Hippo in 393 and Carthage in 397. By the end of the fourth century the limits of the New Testament canon were irrevocably settled in both the Greek and the Latin churches. Only in the churches of Syria and elsewhere in the East did the question continue to be debated. Even here all of the books accepted elsewhere in the church finally achieved recognition.

The fact that substantially the whole church came to recognize the same twenty-seven books as canonical is remarkable when it is remembered that the result was not contrived. All that the several churches throughout the Empire could do was to witness to their own experience with the documents and share whatever knowledge they might have about their origin and character. When consideration is given to the diversity in cultural backgrounds and in orientation to the essentials of the Christian faith within the churches, their common agreement about which books belonged to the New Testament serves to suggest that this final decision did not originate solely at the human level.

No less remarkable is the way in which this fourth-century conclusion continued to be vindicated and maintained throughout the history of the church. The canon of twenty-seven books endured the schisms of the fifth century, the division of the church into East and West in the ninth century, and the violent rupture occasioned by the Reformation in the sixteenth century. When diverse elements within the church found it impossible to find or maintain agreement on any other subject, they continued to honor the same canon.

The significance of this fact to the important dialogues which are taking place in our own generation can scarcely be overestimated. F. W. Beare has aptly said:

> In our own time, hopes of reunion could hardly be entertained, and the ecumenical movement would be all but inconceivable, were it not that all the churches concerned are in substantial agreement in recognizing the unique authority of the same twenty-seven books as constituting the canon of the New Testament, in employing them constantly in public and private devotions, and in appealing to them for guidance in faith and order.[7]

2. THE MEANING OF THE CANON

The question regarding the meaning of the canon is far more complex than questions of origin and development. It focuses primarily on the process by which the several books were collected and recognized as authoritative and inquires concerning the relative validity of that process. Ultimately it seeks to know the "truth" of the canon. Is the existence of a New Testament canon the intention of sacred history or a fortuitous accident within it?

Although ultimate answers concerning the "truth" of the canon cannot be found from its history, several factors can be examined which help create confidence in that history. First among these is the character of Scripture itself. The concept of "sacred Scripture" did not originate in the early church, but was already an essential part of the Jewish heritage. Moreover, the attitude which the Christians developed toward Scripture was drawn directly from Jesus, who confirmed to his disciples its character as the divine truth. He established the divine authority of Scripture by identifying the Old Testament with the word of his Father. He further demonstrated the divine nature of Scripture insofar as the effect of his coming was to realize its fulfillment. Jesus entered history as the Messiah promised according to the revelation the Father had given to Israel through Moses and the prophets. The implication which this had for the Christians was twofold: (1) It established the place and the function of the Old Testament in the life of the church; (2) It prepared the way for a new word of Scripture. If it was proper and necessary that God's word revealed to Moses and the prophets should be preserved and recorded, how much more important was it that the word given through the Son and proclaimed by the apostles should be preserved by the same process?

A second factor which has direct bearing on the meaning of a New Testament canon concerns the function of the church with regard to sacred documents. The church did not act to "commission," or "authorize," the writing of any materials. Holy Scripture remained the prerogative of God. The precedent was already established in Israel's history. The nation was never authorized to create its own prophets; prophecy owed its origin not to human desire but to the impulse of the Holy Spirit of God (cf. 2 Peter 1:19–21). Similarly, God by his Spirit raised up unknown prophets and teachers to accomplish his will in the church. Among those whom God selected as writers of the New Testament documents no more than three were immediate disciples of Jesus. The initiative to call men to this task remained God's; the function of the church was to receive what God had given to the community of faith. He selected the time, the circumstances, and the human instrument through whom the divine word of revelation should find written expression.

A third factor concerned the criteria which the churches apparently employed in recognizing the inspired character of the New Testament writings. While caution is necessary due to an insufficiency of evidence, it seems that subject matter, authorship, and evidence of continued use within the churches all contributed to the ultimate recognition of a document. In subject matter, was that which was written a genuine witness to Christ and from Christ? Did it conform to the words of Jesus and the apostolic tradition preserved within the church by prophets and teachers? Any document purporting to have been written by an apostle or by one who had labored closely with an apostle had a presumption in its favor that it was true to the received tradition. But the mere presence of a claim to trusted authorship was not sufficient to win enduring approval for a writing. The existence of the tradition in oral form provided the basis for testing such claims and resulted in the discrimination between authentic and spurious documents. The church was confident that if a document were genuinely inspired it would conform to the truth which God had revealed through tested witnesses. Finally, documents which imposed their authority upon the churches and continued to reflect use by the Spirit of God were acknowledged to be inspired. Thus writings such as Hebrews and James proved their worth in the daily life of the church and were recognized as canonical even though they could not with certainty be identified with apostolic authorship.

When one therefore examines the criteria used by the church and sees the care with which they were applied and the time alloted for decision, the confidence which he has in the results is strengthened. Ultimately, of course, one's confidence rests not in the process but in him who gives the Scripture to his church. For whatever weakness might be involved in the procedures of man, it is not such that it can set aside the firm intention of God.

PERTINENT DATA ON THE NEW TESTAMENT BOOKS

Due to the nature of the New Testament material, the matter of authorship, date, and place of origin is necessarily tentative and conjectural. Books which treat this material in a more extensive form include Feine-Behm-Kümmel, *An Introduction to the New Testament* (Protestant Liberal); D. Guthrie, *New Testament Introduction,* 3 vols. (Protestant Conservative); and A. Wikenhauser, *New Testament Introduction* (Roman Catholic). Our suggestions are as follows:

	AUTHORSHIP	DATE	PLACE OF ORIGIN
Matthew	Apostle Matthew	75–85	Antioch
Mark	John Mark	67–72	Rome
Luke	Luke	75–90	Greece(?)
John	Apostle John	90–100	Asia Minor
Acts	Luke	75–90	Greece(?)
Romans	Apostle Paul	55–56	Corinth

1 Corinthians	Paul	54–55	Ephesus
2 Corinthians	Paul	55	Macedonia
Galatians	Paul	55	Ephesus(?)
Ephesians	Paul	60–62	Rome
Philippians	Paul	60–62	Rome
Colossians	Paul	60–62	Rome
1 Thessalonians	Paul	50–51	Corinth
2 Thessalonians	Paul	50–51	Corinth
1 Timothy	Paul	62–64	Macedonia
2 Timothy	Paul	64–68	Rome
Titus	Paul	62–64	Macedonia
Philemon	Paul	60–62	Rome
Hebrews	Anonymous	62–66	Asia Minor(?)
James	James, the brother of Jesus	50–60(?)	Unknown
1 Peter	Apostle Peter	63–64	Rome
2 Peter	[Apostle Peter]	80–90(?)	Unknown
1 John	Apostle John	90–100	Asia Minor
2 John	Apostle John	90–100	Asia Minor
3 John	Apostle John	90–100	Asia Minor
Jude	Jude, the brother of Jesus	70–90(?)	Unknown
Revelation	Apostle John	96	Asia Minor

NOTES

1. Cf. G. Zuntz, *The Text of the Epistles: A Disquisition upon the Corpus Paulinum* (1953), pp. 14–17, 276–83. Zuntz argues on the basis of textual features that the ten Pauline letters to the churches existed as an entity known and used by Ignatius and Polycarp, demonstrating the existence of the Pauline corpus by A.D. 100. The fact that *I Clement,* written A.D. 96, refers to Romans and First Corinthians but not to the other epistles suggests that the corpus may have come into existence around the turn of the century.

2. E. J. Goodspeed dates this collection A.D. 115–125 (see *An Introduction to the New Testament* [1937], p. 314). Floyd V. Filson, *A New Testament History* (1964), p. 391, suggests A.D. 125.

3. Cf. the language of the *Muratorian Fragment* (late second century): "And therefore, though various beginnings are taught in the several books of the Gospels, it makes no difference to the faith of believers, since by one guiding Spirit all things are declared in all of them." For the complete text, see D. J. Theron, *Evidence of Tradition* (1958), pp. 107–13.

4. See Oscar Cullmann, "The Plurality of the Gospels as a Theological Problem in Antiquity," in *The Early Church* (1956), pp. 39–54.

5. Cf. the letter of Dionysius of Corinth (cf. 167–170) to the Romans under
their bishop, Soter: "To-day we observed the holy day of the Lord, and read
out your letter, which we shall continue to read from time to time for our
admonition, as we do with that which was formerly sent to us through Clement"
(Eusebius, *Hist. Eccl.* IV, xxiii, 11).

6. Eusebius, *Hist. Eccl.* III, xxv, 1–4; VI, xxv, 3 ff.

7. "Canon of the New Testament," *Interpreter's Dictionary of the Bible,* Vol.
I (1962), p. 520.

SELECTED READING

Aland, K., *The Problem of the New Testament Canon.* London: A. R. Mowbray, 1962.

Blackman, E. C., *Marcion and His Influence.* London: S.P.C.K., 1948.

Filson, F. V., *Which Books Belong to the Bible? A Study of the Canon.* Philadelphia: Westminster, 1957.

Knox, J., *Marcion and the New Testament: An Essay in the Early History of the
Canon.* Chicago: University of Chicago, 1942.

Moule, C. F. D., *The Birth of the New Testament.* New York: Harper & Row,
1962.

Ridderbos, H. N., *The Authority of the New Testament Scriptures.* Philadelphia:
Presbyterian and Reformed, 1963.

Sparks, H. F. D., *The Formation of the New Testament.* London: S.C.M., 1952.

Stonehouse, N. B., "The Authority of the New Testament," in *The Infallible
Word,* P. Woolley, ed. Philadelphia: Presbyterian and Reformed, 1945. Pp.
88–136.

Wikenhauser, A., "The Canon of the New Testament" in *New Testament Introduction.* New York: Herder & Herder, 1958. Pp. 18–61.

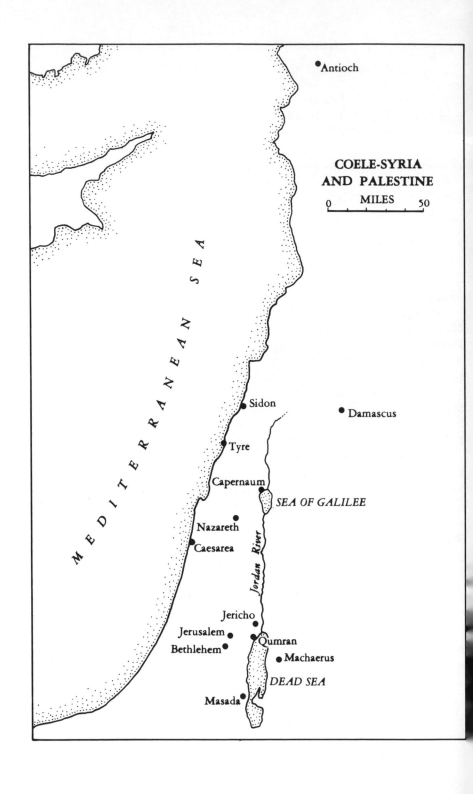

COELE-SYRIA
AND PALESTINE

0   MILES   50

III

✳

FROM PROLOGUE TO EPILOGUE—
THE DRAMA OF HISTORY

OUR first impression when we open the New Testament may be that very little has changed since the close of the Old Testament with Ezra, Nehemiah, and the latter prophets, Haggai, Zechariah, and Malachi. The first major figure that we meet, John the Baptist, seems wholly familiar to us. He is a prophet in Israel. The garb he wears is like that of Elijah. His message, marked by the language of Isaiah and Malachi, and his actions in calling the people to repentance remind us of the ancient prophets. Even the arena of interest, the wilderness of Judea and the Jordan River, is well known to us from the Old Testament.

How wrong we would be if we accepted this initial impression at face value. Everything we know of Israel, except the topography of the land itself, has undergone profound change in the intervening years. The small and indefensible city-state of Ezra and Nehemiah, consisting of a few acres of ground and a handful of people under priestly leadership, has been replaced by a nation whose people number two million, occupying a territory of 6,000 square miles, populated by great and refined cities of Greek and Roman origin. At the center of the nation stands a magnificent capital, immense in size and great in strength, whose priceless jewel is one of the finest temples in the Eastern world.

No longer is the ordinary Jew a keeper of camels, a leader of flocks, a tiller of the soil. Such tasks, of course, continue but are now primarily the occupation of a peasant class. The typical Jew is now an urban dweller, literate, prosperous, exposed to the luxuries and influences of a great new Hellenistic and Roman world. Even if the Jew should deliberately oppose and reject this world, he cannot say he has not been informed and molded by its existence.

The changes in Jewish life have been by no means the sequence of a normal or simple evolution of a people working out their own destiny. It has been both the glory and the burden of Israel to have been the pawn of empires, the buffer between hostile states. Influences from Persia, from the Macedonian empires of Alexander, the Ptolemies, and the Seleucids, and from Rome enter into the complex shaping of faith and practice, of language, concept, and culture within Israel. It is necessary to trace these events and their impact upon the nation in order to understand the degree of change to which nearly every aspect of life has been subjected when one turns from the prophecy of Malachi to Matthew's Gospel.

1. OUT OF EXILE

The years between the Old Testament and the New Testament are "years of silence" with respect to any authoritative new revelation from God. The first segment of this intertestamental era, the Persian period, is an age of relative silence even as far as useful historical evidence is concerned. Aside from the later books of the Old Testament[1] and the few testimonies to Jewish life in Mesopotamia and Egypt provided by Aramaic inscriptions, commercial tablets, and papyri, there are no documents available to illustrate the history of this period. Even Josephus, who had access to much traditional material concerning the Jewish people, can add nothing to these scanty sources. One significant fact, however, appears to emerge when the literary texts are scrutinized and the archaeological evidence is sifted: There was no devastation of Palestine by war or invasion during the two-hundred-year period of Persian domination. Persia was involved in both foreign and civil conflicts, but none occurred on Palestinian soil. Two centuries of unbroken peace was a rare phenomenon and must have contributed much to a climate in which Israel could mature and develop from a small Aramaic-speaking agrarian state to a province prepared for the encounter with Hellenism.

While historical and cultural information on Judea in the Persian period is sparse, certain important religious developments can be traced. Of primary importance was the displacement of the house of David from the political and religious scene and the consequent growth of the role of the high priest. This had not been accomplished by the Exile. The postexilic leader, Zerubbabel, was a lineal descendant of the royal house and would have been heir to David's throne had the country not been under foreign domination. Nevertheless, leadership ceased from the Davidic line. The Persians may have insisted that no one from the Judean royal family be allowed a continuing part in the government of the province. So complete was the obscurity into which the house of David fell that by the time of the New Testament, the heir to the throne is a village carpenter no longer resident in Judea. Even during the brief period when the Jewish people achieved independence under the Hasmoneans they displayed no inclination to remember the covenant God had made with the line of David, but satisfied themselves with other leaders.

With the disappearance of Davidic rule, political power was delegated to the high priest. The extent of the power vested in him may be estimated from what is known of Ezra, a priest who was made governor of Judea with authority to appoint judges, to instruct the people, and to exercise the powers of confiscation, imprisonment, and capital punishment over those who disobeyed the laws of God or the king (Ezra 7:11–26). The conferment of similar authority upon the high priest by the later kings of Persia was sustained in the Hellenistic period by both the Ptolemies of Egypt and the Seleucids of Syria. From the time of the restoration of the Jews exiled in Babylon until the period of the successors of Alexander the Great, the high priest functioned as religious and civil head both for the Jews of Judea and for the scattered Jewish communities outside of Palestine. It was inevitable that political interests should increasingly command his attention. His office became decidedly secular in orientation. The elevation of the high priesthood to a position of political supremacy explains why later, within the context of a crucial power struggle, the question emerges: Which is the legitimate high-priestly line?

Another significant religious development within the Persian period is the concern for law, both oral and written. The exigencies of exile in an alien land and culture had demanded a concern for the law of God and for its application to situations vastly different from those which had prevailed in Judea under the monarchy. The returning exiles brought with them the foundations for oral law that had been worked out in Babylon, and upon this base were erected the first levels of what would become a vast and complex system. The oral law fulfilled two purposes: (1) It provided for the application of the canonical law to new situations; (2) It served to keep the people a safe distance from transgressing the revealed will of God.

Concern for law derives from the priestly emphasis of this period, and is expressed in the biblical account of Ezra reading the law to the people, supplying an interpretation in the (Aramaic) vernacular of the people (Neh. 8:8). In this period Mosaic laws and other writings were collected into a body of canonical Scripture, recognized as divinely authoritative. The Scriptures, and especially the Mosaic law, became the chief characteristic and most prized possession of the Jewish people. Shortly after the close of the Persian era the Pentateuch began to be translated into Greek, in the version designated the Septuagint.

Finally, it is in the Persian period that the Samaritan schism takes place.[2] Shechem was one of the most venerable religious sites in the land. In all probability it had continued from antiquity to be a place of worship, with a priesthood of its own and a service of worship similar to that in Jerusalem, but lacking a temple. These facts took on a more serious complexion when the claim was made that Gerizim, and not Zion, was the place God had chosen for his habitation, the only place in the land where sacrifice was legitimately offered, vows absolved, and festivals observed. It is this claim, not the mere building of the temple at Shechem, which constitutes the Samaritan schism. The tension between the Judeans and the Samaritans persisted throughout the Persian period and into the Hellenistic and Roman eras as well. The hostility of the Jerusalemites was deep and lasting. A Jew writing near the beginning of the second century B.C. says: "With two nations my soul is vexed, and the third is no nation: those who live on Mount Seir, and the Philistines, and the foolish people that dwell in Shechem" (Sir. 50:25–26).

The startling note of offense in the New Testament can be understood when, in the account of the healing of ten lepers after which only one of whom returned to thank Jesus, it is noted that "he was a Samaritan" (Luke 17:16). When the Jews reject Jesus with the words: "Are we not right in saying that you are a Samaritan and have a demon?" (John 8:48), a resentment nursed for over four centuries toward a neighboring people comes to bitter expression.

2. ALEXANDER, APOSTLE OF A GREAT SOCIETY

Alexander has been called the Apostle of Hellenism.[3] Under Alexander the Greeks regarded it as their mission to spread their civilization, and they regarded language as a primary factor in culture. Both convictions were entirely new in the history of ideas. Himself a former pupil of Aristotle, Alexander attached to his general staff a number of Greek scholars and scientists whom Aristotle had trained. It was inevitable that the culture of Greece should make a deep impression on the peoples reached by the armies of Alexander.[4] Nevertheless, there was much to admire in Egypt and the Near East, particularly the great works of art and the mysterious wisdom and lore of ancient lands. The fusion of Greek thought with elements of culture from the East produced what is called the Hellenistic, as distinguished from the Hellenic, world.

The people of Egypt and western Asia, and especially those in the upper strata of society, were greatly attracted to Greek ways of life, especially when civilian Greeks, following the armies, settled in their midst. Many of the conquered peoples hastened to speak broken Greek, wear Greek attire, and participate in Greek sports. They erected gymnasiums, baths, and theaters, being fascinated by Hellenic fashions and luxuries. These imitators of the Greeks became known as Hellenists, from the verb *hellenizein,* which Plato in the fifth century used with the sense "to speak good Greek," but which came to have a derived meaning, "to imitate the ways of the Greeks." The typical Greek city, a flourishing center of commerce and culture, proved to be the standard bearer for Hellenization. Plutarch states that Alexander founded more than seventy cities (*Alexandri Magni fortuna* I. 5), the most important of which was Alexandria in Egypt. Such centers of Greek life proved to be at the same time both the strength and the weakness of Hellenism in Asia. The greatest among them—capitals of kingdoms like Alexandria, Pergamum, Antioch, and Seleucia—attracted the finest minds for government service and for the development of the arts and sciences. They became centers of learning to which pupils flocked and from which Greek culture was able to spread elsewhere. But Hellenism tended to prevail only in the cities and primarily among the upper classes of the native populations. The countryside, where rural folk retained their ancestral language and customs, was scarcely affected. Nevertheless, by introducing Greek culture into Syria and Egypt, Alexander had probably more influence on the development of Judaism than any one individual who was not a Jew by birth. As the Jewish writer of First Maccabees put it, Alexander "advanced to the ends of the earth, and took spoils from many peoples, and the earth was quiet before him" (1 Macc. 1:3).

3. JUDAISM IN THE HELLENISTIC AGE

Alexander's empire, the largest the world had known to that time, was rapidly built. At his death in 323 B.C. it disintegrated even more quickly. In the struggles between his generals to secure sections of the empire for themselves, Palestine fell to Ptolemy I Soter, who also controlled Egypt and the Mediterranean Sea. Syria and the eastern portions of the empire were seized by Seleucus I. Throughout the Hellenistic period Egypt remained Ptolemaic while Syria became the center of the Seleucid empire.[5]

Both the Ptolemaic and the Seleucid rulers were anxious to control Palestine as a buffer zone to protect their respective kingdoms from aggression. To secure this end there were almost constant intrigues and hostilities between the two kingdoms. For more than a century (323–198 B.C.) Palestine remained under Ptolemaic control.

The Ptolemies pursued a deliberate policy of not introducing any revolutionary changes in government or customs in Judea. For this reason Judaism could encounter Hellenism within a tolerant context. Evidence is provided by a book of the Apocrypha, written originally in Hebrew about 190 B.C., known as Sirach, or Ecclesiasticus. The author of this work was Jesus the son of Sirach (Sir. 50:27). He writes his collection of proverbs and counsel out of years of experience as a student and teacher of wisdom. He was a scribe who had instructed young men of the upper classes in Jerusalem in his academy (51:23), lecturing on Scripture, jurisprudence, ethics, and social grace. Sirach combines an awareness of Israel's distinctive position and role among the nations with a broad and tolerant appreciation of life in all its expressions. He had traveled much and benefited from his experiences in other lands (34:9–12). Sirach is typical of the cultured, liberal-spirited Jew who thought seriously about the greater and lesser questions of his day. His sound piety is mixed with a thorough knowledge of human nature, both its strengths and its weaknesses, and with a frank appreciation for the amenities of the social life that Hellenism had encouraged. It is likely that in his work has been preserved a monument of the "Oniad"[6] piety current at the close of the third century B.C., a piety characterized not only by a cosmopolitan spirit of moderation, but also by an opposition to any radical Hellenization of Judaism. The impact of Hellenism on Palestinian Judaism was in fact moderate throughout the Ptolemaic era.

Following a decisive battle in 198 B.C. Judea passed from the hands of the Ptolemies to Seleucid control. For the first thirty years there was no outward indication that this would mean any real change in the life and thought of Judaism. Moderate Hellenization of Judean life and manners continued to be evident, especially among the upper classes. Though segments of the Jewish population looked on this trend with disapproval, only later would it be seen that with the coming of Seleucid rule forces had been unleashed that would soon result in open conflict between Judaism and Hellenism. Looking back on these events after the conflict was over, the author of 1 Maccabees sees their sinister character with clarity:

> In those days lawless men came forth from Israel and misled many, saying, "Let us go and make a covenant with the Gentiles round about us, for since

we separated from them many evils have come upon us." This proposal pleased them, and some of the people eagerly went to the king [Antiochus IV]. He authorized them to observe the ordinances of the Gentiles. (1:11–13.)

But while they were taking place, these happenings seemed no different in character than what had occurred earlier under the Ptolemies. That they were to be the prelude to a struggle for the life or death of Judaism and biblical faith could not yet have been known.

4. THE MACCABEAN REVOLT

The conflict between Judaism and Hellenism in Palestine came to a head during the reign of Antiochus IV Epiphanes.[7] While Antiochus was a violent man and a fanatic for Hellenism, other factors besides his personal temperament contributed to the crisis of 167 B.C. The initiative for a more pervasive Hellenization came from "lawless men" among the Jews themselves who built a Greek gymnasium in Jerusalem and repudiated circumcision and the covenant (1 Macc. 1:14–15). There was at the same time a bitter and shameless struggle between two rival claimants to the high priesthood. This Antiochus interpreted as open revolt against his rule. In 167 he sacked Jerusalem and stripped the temple of its golden altar and candlesticks. Jewish worship and circumcision were forbidden; idolatry was commanded and all known copies of the law were burned (1 Macc. 1:41–64). Upon the altar of burnt offerings was erected a smaller heathen altar regarded by the Jews as an "abomination of desolation" (1 Macc. 1:54; cf. Dan. 9:27; 11:31; 12:11). All who continued to practice Judaism were slaughtered without mercy.

The reaction of loyal Jews to these blasphemies was not long in coming. It began to take shape at the small town of Modin, northwest of Jerusalem. There a priest named Mattathias defied the king's emissaries by refusing to sacrifice to idols and by killing the first Jew who started to comply with the royal edict. Mattathias then fled to the mountains with his five sons. Under the leadership of the eldest son, Judas the Maccabee, this family began to wage a guerrilla warfare that paid quick and rich dividends. At this point those Jews who were zealous for their traditions[8] faced a struggle with conscience: should they disobey the law in order to resist its total defilement by heathen hands? What place had the sword in lives dedicated to piety? In the early days a thousand were killed because they refused to defend themselves on the Sabbath (1 Macc. 2:29–38). Soon, however, their pacifism gave way to the ancient concept of holy war. A contemporary observer whose description of these events is contained in the pseudepigraphical *Book of Enoch* put it in symbolic language: "I saw till horns grew upon those lambs, and the ravens cast down their horns; and I saw till there sprouted a great horn of one of those sheep, and their eyes were opened" (Enoch 90:9). The "great horn" was Judas, celebrated in 1 Maccabees as being "like a lion in his deeds," one who "pursued the lawless" and "turned away wrath" from Israel (3:1–9). The early successes of the Maccabees were indeed spectacular. By 165, Judas and his outnumbered army had won a series of victories over the Seleucid forces, regained Mount Zion, and restored and rededicated the temple. The edict proscribing Judaism was rescinded; religious freedom had been regained; the initial purposes of the revolt had been achieved.

5. AN INDEPENDENT STATE

Religious freedom was one thing, political independence quite another. In spite of the victory that had been won, most of Judea was still under Seleucid rule and the Jews were a persecuted minority in many cities. Even in Jerusalem, Antiochus' citadel known as the Acra, manned with Seleucid troops, stood over against the temple as a symbol of Gentile domination, "a place to lie in wait against the sanctuary, and an evil adversary to Israel continually"* (1 Macc. 1:36). And so the war to throw off the heathen yoke continued, under the leadership of Judas and later of his brothers Jonathan and Simon.

Independence was achieved in 142 when Simon finally captured the Acra (1 Macc. 13:50 ff.), but the triumph was not without cost. Jonathan and Simon had advanced their cause at crucial points by alliances with certain pretenders to the Seleucid throne. These entanglements in the internal politics of the Seleucid empire savored less of a "holy war" than of the intrigues and maneuvering of any typically ambitious, petty Hellenistic prince. Once the Maccabees had established themselves with a degree of military and political power, rival claimants to the Seleucid crown began to outbid one another for their friendship. In 153 Jonathan had even received from a Greek pretender named Alexander Balas the appointment as high priest in Jerusalem! (1 Macc. 10:20). When independence came in 142, the grateful people of Israel conferred the high priesthood upon Simon, last surviving son of Mattathias (1 Macc. 14:35 ff.). It was decreed that he was to be "their leader and high-priest for ever, until a faithful prophet should arise; and that he should be a captain over them . . . and that he should be obeyed by all" (14:41 ff.). The decree tacitly recognized that Simon was not of the old Zadokite line of legitimate high priests; that line would presumably be restored when the "faithful prophet" came (cf. 1 Macc. 4:46; Deut. 18: 15 ff.). But for an indefinite future, the descendants of Mattathias, now known as the Hasmoneans, were to exercise both religious and political sovereignty in Israel. The reference to the "faithful prophet" appears to have been no more than a useful fiction designed to satisfy the purists and traditionalists while validating for all practical purposes Simon's absolute authority. The die was cast. Instead of a religious community centering exclusively in the law and the temple, Israel was for a time at least to be a nation among the nations. Of Simon it was said: "He established peace in the land, and Israel rejoiced with great joy. Each man sat under his vine and his fig tree and there was none to make them afraid" (1 Macc. 14:11 f.).

Under Simon's son John Hyrcanus (135–104 B.C.) the new independent state of Israel attained the height of its political power and geographical extent. John subdued the Samaritans, capturing Shechem and the temple on Mt. Gerizim. He also conquered the neighboring Idumeans and forced them to adopt Judaism. At the end of his reign the Hasmonean state almost equalled in extent the original kingdom of David and Solomon.

Simon's move in the direction of uniting sacral and civic leadership in one person was hardened into a fixed policy and a fact of life in the Hasmonean era. Once having laid hold of this dual authority, John and his successors were unwilling to give it up. The biblical injunctions against priest-kings[9] were all but forgotten. Like Melchizedek, the unique priest-king of Salem (Gen. 14), the Hasmoneans were called "priest of the Most High God" (Josephus, *Antiquities of the Jews* XVI, § 163; cf. *Assumption of Moses* 6:1), and may even have pointed to Melchizedek as justification for their practice. Josephus tells us that Hyrcanus' son Aristobulus was the first actually to assume the title of king (*Antiquities,* XIII, § 301), but the practice was continued by his brother and successor, Alexander Jannaeus. The latter's reign was marked by more wars of expansion, together with internal uprisings which Jannaeus ruthlessly suppressed.

The last years of the Hasmonean dynasty brought an end to the expansionist policy and a measure of peace and stability to the land. Jannaeus' widow, Salome Alexandra, reigned as queen for nine years while her son, Hyrcanus II, served as high priest without civil authority. As it turned out, her days were merely a brief respite prior to another major turning point in Jewish history. The cloud upon the horizon was Rome; the outcome of the new crisis was to be political collapse. In all, the life of the independent state of Israel was fewer than eighty years.

6. THE STORY TOLD AND RETOLD

The importance of most historical events lies not only in their immediate causes and effects but also in the ways they are regarded by subsequent generations. So it is with the Maccabean revolution and the achievement of Jewish independence. The end of the Hasmonean era is a good vantage point from which to look back, through the eyes of various groups in Israel, at what had took place during the preceding century. Two partially conflicting interpretations of the revolt itself are reflected in our two chief sources, First and Second Maccabees.

A fine piece of historical writing and our most reliable account of the war for independence, 1 Maccabees appears to be the work of a Hasmonean court historian writing midway through the reign of John Hyrcanus. Although he has written a remarkably objective account by the standards of the time, the author makes no secret of his firm allegiance to the Hasmonean house. He believes that the war for independence was an unambiguous conflict between good and evil. The trouble that came upon Israel in 167 was entirely the fault of the "sinful men." Moreover, Mattathias and his sons are presented as God's unique instruments, the only ones by whom Israel can be saved. When two of Judas' lieutenants attack the Gentiles on their own initiative, the author attributes their failure to the fact that "they did not belong to the family of those men through whom deliverance was given to Israel" (5:62). Simon especially, the founder of the Hasmonean dynasty and "father" of his people, is to be obeyed without question (2:65; 14:43). Frequent emphasis is laid upon the continuity between the Maccabees and the great biblical heroes of Israel's past (see, e.g., 2:26, 49–61; 7:41). First Maccabees is written out of a strong conviction that the God of the Old Testament is still at work and that the Hasmoneans were just as certainly his chosen vessels in putting down his enemies as Moses and Joshua had been.

Another example of how Jewish writers could glorify the Hasmonean priest-kings is seen in the composite document known as the *Testaments of the Twelve Patriarchs*. The famous eighteenth chapter of the *Testament of Levi* may well be overlaid with later messianic teaching and even with Christian interpolations attempting to connect the passage with Jesus Christ. It is generally agreed, however, that the original inspiration for this eloquent hymn was John Hyrcanus. If even part of it refers to John or his Hasmonean successors it witnesses remarkably to the hopes aroused by the appearance in Israel of a line of priestly monarchs:

Then shall the Lord raise up a new priest.
And to him all the words of the Lord shall be revealed;
And he shall execute a righteous judgment over the earth for a multitude of
    days.
And his star shall arise in heaven as of a king,
Lighting up the light of knowledge as the sun the day.
And he shall be magnified in the world.
He shall shine forth as the sun in the earth,
And shall remove all darkness from under heaven,
And there shall be peace in all the earth.
The heavens shall exult in his days,
And the earth shall be glad,
And the clouds shall rejoice. . . .
The heavens shall be opened,
And from the temple of glory shall come upon him sanctification,
With the Father's voice as from Abraham to Isaac.
And the glory of the Most High shall be uttered over him,
And the spirit of understanding and sanctification shall rest upon him. . . .
For he shall give the majesty of the Lord to his sons in truth for evermore;
And there shall none succeed him for all generations for ever . . . (*Test. Levi*
    18:2–8).

Second Maccabees, though less reliable historically, is of more theological interest than First Maccabees. The document purports to be an
epitome of a five-part history by an otherwise unknown writer named
Jason of Cyrene (2 Macc. 2:23) and probably dates from the late second
or early first century B.C.

The author (or else Jason, his predecessor) provides a somewhat more
complex interpretation of the revolt than can be found in 1 Maccabees.
The cause of Israel's trouble in the beginning was not simply the wickedness of the Gentiles; it was the sin of God's people themselves. A section
unparalleled in 1 Maccabees tells of a threat to the temple from a certain
Heliodorus several years prior to the pogrom of Antiochus Epiphanes.
This attack was crushed by immediate and supernatural divine intervention (2 Macc. 3:1–39). Then in some detail the bitter internal struggles
in Jerusalem for the high priesthood are depicted (3:40–4:50). The author
comments:

Antiochus was elated in spirit, and did not perceive that the Lord was angered
for a little while because of the sins of those who dwelt in the city. . . . But
if it had not happened that they were involved in many sins, this man would

have been scourged and turned back from his rash act . . . just as Heliodorus was (5:17–18).

But though the temple was "forsaken in the wrath of the Almighty, [it] was restored again in all its glory when the great Lord became reconciled" (5:20). The reconciliation comes through the deaths of the Jewish martyrs, typified by a mother and her seven sons. The last of the sons to die tells his tormentors: "We are suffering because of our own sins. And if our living Lord is angry for a little while, to rebuke and discipline us, he will again be reconciled with his own servants" (7:32–33). He intends to "bring to an end the wrath of the Almighty which has justly fallen on our whole nation" by giving up his life for the law (7:38). Immediately in chapter 8 Judas begins his resistance, and "the Gentiles could not withstand him for the wrath of the Lord had turned to mercy" (8:5). Thus 2 Maccabees is concerned less with the iniquity of the heathen and the glory of the Hasmonean house than with the theological problem of sin and its remedy.

Nevertheless, the author does accept the fight for independence as an accomplished fact. In retrospect he assures himself that the "holy war" was a necessity and that the Maccabees had indeed been chosen of God to wage it. This point becomes remarkably clear in his account of a vision that Judas had seen in a time of crisis. "Jeremiah the prophet of God" had appeared and "stretched out his right hand and gave to Judas a golden sword, and as he gave it he addressed him thus: Take this holy sword, a gift from God, with which you will strike down your adversaries" (15:14 ff.). To appreciate the irony of this scene one must remember that Jeremiah was the prophet who had stressed more than all others the futility of putting trust in sword or rider or bow. The heathen should not be resisted, for they were God's means of chastising his own people for their sins. In fact, Jeremiah's interpretation of the Exile parallels 2 Maccabees' own interpretation of the disasters inflicted by Antiochus. But in the account of Judas' vision the author is saying that, despite all this, even Jeremiah would have counseled the use of force against the ruthless provocations of Antiochus and his men. Behind this scene lie traces of the same struggle with conscience that had faced the pious Israelites from the very beginnings of the revolt.

Because it had been successful the war for independence could be accepted as the will of God, yet for the most part the militant nationalism of the first book of Maccabees is lacking in the second. A reasonable conjecture is that the latter work comes from the circle of the Pharisees, a group that emerges into the light of history during the reign of John Hyrcanus and becomes dominant for a time under Salome Alexandra (Josephus, *Antiquities* XIII, §§ 288–98, 400 ff.). The roots of Pharisaism go back at least to the fierce pietism of the Hasidim who had fought alongside Judas in the early days of the revolt. The Pharisees' later relationships to the Hasmonean regime are best described as checkered, ranging from qualified approval to outright antagonism. Second Maccabees exemplifies the former attitude and probably dates from the days of Salome, when the fortunes of the Pharisees and of the Hasmonean house coincided. Later Pharisaism did not hesitate to take a more negative view, interpreting the Roman conquest that shortly followed Salome's reign as a judgment of God. As in the days of Antiochus, the heathen had triumphed for a season "because the sons of Jerusalem had defiled the holy things of the Lord, had profaned with iniquities the offerings of God" (*Psalms of Solomon* 2:3). Fifty years later, an unknown author could represent Moses as prophesying of the Hasmoneans: "Then there shall be raised up unto them kings bearing rule, and they shall call themselves priests of the Most High God: they shall assuredly work iniquity in the holy of holies" (*Assumption of Moses* 6:1).

These voices of Pharisaism were raised in protest at what they regarded as a perversion of the originally lofty goals of the revolution. The torch of freedom has been lighted at the first by zeal for the law, but it seemed that with the establishment of political power, faithful Torah observance had become a thing of the past. The regulations concerning priesthood and kingship had been set aside; violence had become for some of those in power a way of life; even common morality seemed to have been forgotten. Still, military triumph spoke more loudly and eloquently even to most Pharisees than did their lingering moral reservations. The bitter memories of certain aspects of the Hasmonean age could not efface the deeds of valor by which Mattathias and his sons had liberated their people against fantastic odds. This was why, less than two centuries later, even the political quietists were willing to put aside their doubts and take up the sword once more to resist the heathen oppressors—but with disastrous results.

A third interpretation of the Maccabean age is reflected in the sectarian writings of the Essenes. The so-called *Zadokite,* or *Damascus, Document* (CD), discovered in 1896 in the storeroom of a Cairo synagogue and published in 1910, remained an enigma and a more or less isolated phenomenon until the discovery in 1947 of the now famous scrolls from Qumran, near the Dead Sea. This collection of biblical texts and commentaries, monastic rules of life, hymns, and apocalyptic writings attests the existence of a priestly sect that withdrew into the wilderness of Judea in the late second or early first century B.C.

For a time these people had been a part of the struggle for independence. Like the Pharisees, they may have been among the Ḥasidim who allied themselves with Judas. But the secularization of the priesthood under Jonathan, Simon, and the Hasmonean rulers was more than these pietists were willing to endure. The authors of the *Damascus Document* looked back upon the alliance with the Maccabees as twenty years of groping in darkness (CD i.9). What the freedom fighters had thought of as an opening of the eyes (cf. *Enoch* 90:9, see above, p. 42) was to the sectarians of Qumran a time of blindness and confusion. But God had raised up for them a "Legitimate Teacher" to lead them in straight paths (CD i.11). This anonymous figure appears to have been the founder of the Qumran community as we know it. It was expected that forty years after his death the powers of wickedness would be overthrown (CD, ms. B, ii.14 f.) and that at the end of days another Legitimate Teacher (or possibly the same one) would come to initiate a new age of blessedness (CD vi.11).

Over against the elect community stands a figure variously identified in the Qumran literature as the Man of Mockery, the Man of Lies, the Prophet of Lies, or most often, the Wicked Priest. He is most clearly delineated in the sect's brief commentary on the Book of Habakkuk (1 Qp Hab). Habakkuk's general reference to "the wicked" (Hab. 1:4) is specifically interpreted as the Wicked Priest (1 Qp Hab i.13). Though he was "called by the name of truth at the beginning of his coming," yet, "when he commanded over Israel, his heart rose up and he abandoned God and betrayed the precepts because of riches, and . . . followed the ways of abomination in every kind of unclean defilement" (1 Qp Hab viii.9, 12). Some identify this individual with Jonathan; some with Simon; some with John Hyrcanus or Alexander Jannaeus; but it is now widely agreed that in any case he is one of the priestly monarchs of the Hasmonean dynasty. In fact, since many of the Qumran writings view his activities from a later perspective, he may be a composite figure built up out of memories of more than one of these priest-kings.

Being essentially a lay group, the Pharisees could tolerate, even if they did not approve, the creation of a new priestly line and the usurpation by this priesthood of royal functions. The Essenes could not do this since they were themselves largely a priestly group. Therefore a break was inevitable. The Essenes regarded themselves as the "sons of Zadok" (CD iv.1 ff.), the true priesthood that Jonathan had set aside in practice (1 Macc. 10:20 f.) and the fate of which Simon had sealed by public decree (1 Macc. 14:41–49). For them the Hasmonean house meant not liberation but apostasy. This is why they withdrew into the desert to "prepare the way for God." The community's rule of order, or *Manual of Discipline* (1QS) quotes the same text that the early Christians were later to apply to the ministry of John the Baptist, Isa. 40:3: A voice cries: "In the wilderness prepare the way of the Lord, Make straight in the desert a highway for our God" (1 QS viii. 13 f.; cf. Matt. 3:3). The task of the wilderness community was the faithful study of the Law until that day when God would intervene to punish the wicked and establish the sectarians as the true priesthood and the true Israel.

Even in their violent reaction against the Hasmoneans, however, the Qumran group themselves bore some imprints of the events that had occurred in Jerusalem. Although their messianic expectations were exceedingly complex, or even confused, it seems clear that they gave priority to a messiah (i.e., an anointed future leader) who would also be a priest. Some texts speak of "an anointed one," others of "anointed ones" of "Aaron and Israel." An appendix to the *Manual of Discipline* (1QSa) describes a future messianic assembly and common meal in which "the Priest" takes precedence over "the Messiah of Israel" (1QSa ii.12 ff., 19 ff.). Thus, even though they denied the legitimacy of the Hasmonean priesthood and insisted that the functions of king and priest be separated, the Qumran sectarians agreed with their Hasmonean antagonists that the final authority should rest with priests. Whether the Essenes expected one messiah, or two, or more, an important fact is that their eschatology in some respects corresponds to the ideals of the Maccabean age, purified and projected into the future. Even the idea of holy war lived on at Qumran in an imaginative description of a great future battle between the "Sons of Light" and the "Sons of Darkness" (1QM). The Sons of Light were the Qumran sectarians themselves, while the Sons of Darkness, or *Kittim,* were the forces of the heathen. Detailed descriptions of both armies, their standards, their weapons, their formations, and of the final victory of the Sons of Light testify to the preservation of some Maccabean values even among those who reacted most violently against Jonathan, Simon, and their successors. In the century preceding Jesus of Nazareth and even well into the New Testament period, few in Israel could forget the valor of the sons of Mattathias. Through them God had given his people a sword to throw off the yoke of wickedness. An oppressed community had for eighty years maintained itself as a respected nation among the nations. It had happened once; if the provocation were ever as great again and if the time were ripe, who was there to say it could not happen again?

7. RETURN TO BONDAGE

Civil war between the two sons of Queen Salome Alexandra, Aristobulus II and Hyrcanus II, invited Roman intervention in the affairs of Judea. Rome had gradually extended its reach eastward so that Asia, North Africa, and the entire Mediterranean Sea had been brought under its control. When Antiochus IV Epiphanes had sought to annex the Ptolemaic empire in Egypt, Rome had intervened and frustrated his plans with nearly disastrous results for Judea. In the conflict with Syria when Jonathan was high priest, Judea had entered into alliance with Rome (1 Macc. 12:1). It may have been in view of this alliance that Rome intervened in Judean affairs once more.

The conflict between the two brothers in Judea attracted the attention of Pompey, chief of the Roman forces in the Near East.[10] In the spring of 63 B.C. he came to Damascus and heard the pleas of both Aristobulus and Hyrcanus. He also listened to a delegation of the Jewish people who were weary with civil strife and pleaded for the abolition of the monarchy and a return to rule by the high priest. Pompey made no decision at this time. He promised to settle the dispute when his current campaign against the Nabateans was completed. Meanwhile he would dispatch to Jerusalem a legion under one of his generals to represent Rome's interest in Judean affairs.

When the Romans arrived, they found the city gates locked against them. Partisans of Hyrcanus, who controlled the upper city, opened the gates, but the supporters of Aristobulus fortified themselves on the temple hill. The bridge between the upper city and the temple area was destroyed, and for a period of three months the defenders of the temple held out against the Romans. When Pompey finally breached the northern fortifications, the forces of Aristobulus were butchered. A Jewish psalmist expressed his reaction to these events a decade or so later in a mournful lament:

> When the sinner waxed proud, with a battering-ram he cast down fortified walls,
> And thou didst not restrain him.

Alien nations ascended Thine altar,
   They trampled it proudly with their sandals;
Because the sons of Jerusalem had defiled the holy things of the Lord,
   Had profaned with iniquities the offerings of God. . . .
For the nations reproached Jerusalem, trampling it down;
   Her beauty was dragged down from the throne of glory.
She girded on sackcloth instead of comely raiment,
   A rope was about her head instead of a crown.
She put off the glorious diadem which God had set upon her,
   In dishonor was her beauty cast upon the ground. (*Ps. Sol.* 2:1–3, 20–22.)

The fall of the temple inaugurated an era of Roman rule in Judea which lasted, with few interruptions, for almost seven hundred years. The Jewish community was placed under Roman proconsular rule. Hyrcanus II remained high priest, but he was stripped of his royal title. The Hasmonean kingdom was greatly reduced in size, covering only a limited area in Judea, Galilee, Idumea, and a small strip of land in the Jordan Valley. All non-Jewish cities conquered by the Hasmoneans were now lost. In 61 B.C. Aristobulus was forced to march in the victor's triumphal procession in Rome. Numerous Jews were enslaved and brought to Rome, becoming the nucleus of the large Jewish community in the capital after their release.

The period between the taking of Jerusalem by Pompey and the establishment of the Herodian dynasty in 37 B.C. was turbulent. Repeatedly the princes of the dispossessed line of Aristobulus sought to wrench Jerusalem from the firm grip of the Romans and their vassals, Hyrcanus II and his Arabic vizier, Antipater of Idumea. Already reduced to mourning by Pompey's conquest, Jerusalem was still more humiliated in 54 B.C. when the Roman proconsul of Syria, Marcus Licinius Crassus, plundered the temple treasures.

In 49 B.C. civil war broke out in Rome. Its effect was to remove Pompey from the Judean scene, although the province remained under Roman control. Pompey's forces were defeated in Egypt by the armies of Julius Caesar. Pompey himself was slain and his body left for some time decapitated and unburied on the shore. In this turn of events the pious in Israel saw the hand of God:

"Delay not, O God, to recompense them on their heads,
   To turn the pride of the dragon into dishonor."
And I had not long to wait before God showed me the insolent one
   Slain on the mountains of Egypt,

> Esteemed of less account than the least, on land or sea;
> His body, born hither and thither on the billows with much insolence,
> With none to bury him, because He had rejected him with dishonor (*Ps. Sol.*
> 2:29–31).

Hyrcanus and Antipater had wisely thrown their support on the side of Julius Caesar; they were duly rewarded the following year. Against the claims of Antigonus, the last surviving Hasmonean claimant to the throne, Caesar reappointed Hyrcanus hereditary high priest and ethnarch of the Jews, while Antipater was made a Roman citizen and governor of Judea.

It is in this period that the name of Herod first enters the historical record.[11] The son of Antipater, Herod was only twenty-five years old at this time, but he proved himself a man of energy and initiative as prefect of Galilee, and then as military governor of Palestine. In the turmoil following the assassination of Julius Caesar, it was Herod who frustrated the attempt of Antigonus to conquer Palestine and regain his throne. Not until the Persian attack on Palestine in 40 B.C. did Herod confront a situation with which he was unable to cope. Placing his family in the stronghold of Masada, he fled to Rome to seek the aid of Mark Antony.

For three years (40–37 B.C.) Judea had two kings. Antigonus ruled as king and high priest, supported by the Persian army, while through the offices of Mark Antony and Octavian, Herod had been appointed king by the Roman senate in the year 40. Not until 37, however, was the senatorial appointment recognized in Judea. It was necessary for Herod first to quell rebellions in Galilee and then to defeat the Persian armies. Jerusalem itself withstood a siege lasting several months. When Herod finally took possession of the city, his entry was marked by wild plundering on the part of his Roman allies and the execution of practically all of the old Hasmonean aristocracy. Antigonus was executed by order of Mark Antony. From that time until the New Testament opens, the will of Herod the Idumean king determined the destiny of the ancient province of Judea.

Herod had received his throne through Roman appointment, and for five generations the Herodian family pursued a consistent policy of fidelity to Rome. Pompey, Julius Caesar, Mark Antony, and Octavian, all of whom were at one time supreme in the East, found in the Herods able and efficient supporters. When the Republic was replaced by the Empire, and Octavian became emperor, it was the same. In days of adversity as well as prosperity, the shrewd Herods were on the side of Rome. How certainly they could be relied upon was shown after the Battle of Actium, when Octavian defeated Mark Antony for control of the East. Herod, who had loyally supported Antony, boldly avowed his friendship for the fallen warrior but offered to serve Octavian as faithfully as he had his rival. He was immediately accepted as a trustworthy ally upon whose shrewdness and political astuteness one could depend (Josephus, *Antiquities* XV, §§ 183–201; *War* I, §§ 386–97).

Though from Rome's point of view he was a ruler of ability and energy, Herod never succeeded in gaining the respect and affection of the Jews. Alluding to his Idumean origin, they described him contemptuously as "half-Jew." It was to the Romans that he was Herod the Great, for he carried forward in his corner of the empire the great plans of Octavian, the Augustus Caesar of Luke 2:1. The Romans saw Herod as a capable ruler, public-spirited in his liberality, a patron of the arts and literature, whose strong hand kept his dominions at peace. To the Jews he was little more than an Arab usurper with purely secular ambitions and goals, whose record was one of savage murders prompted by insane jealousy and suspicion. He had not hesitated to slay even his own sons who had fallen under the weight of suspicion of conspiring for his throne. So well was this fact known that Augustus had coined the Greek pun "It is better to be Herod's swine (*hun*) than his son (*huion*)"—presumably because as a Jewish king Herod was not supposed to eat pork, but his family was not exempt from his wrath (Macrobius, *Saturnalia* II. iv. 11). This atmosphere of suspicion is presumed by the opening chapters of the Gospel of Matthew with its account of Herod's plot to kill the child Jesus, whom he feared as a potential rival to the throne from the line of David (Matt. 2:16–18).[12]

So ruthless were his crimes and so hated was he by the people that Herod knew there would be great rejoicing at his death. His final decree, therefore, was that an entire town should be put to the sword that there might be weeping in Judea when he died. This reckless and cruel order was not carried out. Herod's death was the signal not for weeping but for uprisings, swift suppression by Rome, and after a breath's pause, continued Herodian rule supported by the legions of Rome.

8. THE PERIOD OF UNCERTAINTY

During the period covered by the New Testament, the political status of Judea changed several times. Of the two rulers associated with Jesus at his birth and his death, one is king of Judea, the other a Roman procurator. Within less than one generation, responsibility for Judea had passed from Herodian to Roman hands. Yet the Apostle James was put to death in Jerusalem in the early forties by a Herodian, Herod Agrippa I, King of Judea (Acts 12:1–2). Less than half a generation later Paul stood before the Roman procurators Felix and Festus, prefects of Judea through whom he made his appeal to Caesar in Rome. The political fortunes of Judea in the first century swing like a pendulum between the two alternatives of Herodian rule and Roman procuratorial administration.

The intention of Herod the Great was declared clearly in a will deposited in Rome, subject to the approval of Caesar. His son Archelaus was to receive the royal title as king of Judea. Two other sons, Herod Antipas and Herod Philip, he designated tetrarchs respectively of Galilee and Perea, and of the northern districts of Trachonitus, Batanea, and Gaulinitis.[13] Herod's death was the signal for revolt among the Judeans and for anxiety among his heirs.

As the three sons made their individual ways to Rome, so did a delegation from Jerusalem which recited Herod's crimes before Augustus and begged for self-government under Roman supervision. While the emperor deliberated, tension mounted in Judea. Once the iron hand of Herod was removed, the highest Jewish authorities were powerless to halt or control popular unrest. There were many sources of resentment: the repressive measures of Herod, the presence of a Roman legion in Jerusalem, the extinction of the last representatives of the Hasmonean dynasty, and the puppet status of the high priests, freely appointed or deposed for political expediency. Those who taught the people, the Pharisees, were divided in their attitude toward foreign rule. To listen to one school, Roman intervention was a punishment imposed by God, to be borne patiently in penitence for sin; others spoke of the yoke of a "wicked kingdom," to be broken and cast off when the time was appropriate. Zealotic factions urged immediate armed resistance in the spirit of Judas and his brothers who had broken the Seleucid yoke. Such divergent points of view remind us of the different ways in which people had reacted to the measures of Antiochus Epiphanes in the days of the Maccabees (see above, pp. 44–50).

The catalyst in this ferment was the Roman procurator, Sabinus, who abused his authority. Angry crowds, their numbers swollen by pilgrims in Jerusalem to celebrate the ancient harvest festival, the Feast of Weeks (or Pentecost), publicly attacked him. Almost simultaneously the flames of revolt broke out in Idumea, Galilee, Jericho, and Perea. Popular excitement was fanned by the remembrance of the God of the Maccabees and

by the expectation of the Days of the Messiah. Only the prompt intervention of the governor of Syria, P. Quintilius Varus, accompanied by
two Roman legions, quelled the riots, bringing death or enslavement to
thousands of Jews. A generation later the hopes and frustrations associated
with this period of uncertainty could be recalled: "Before these days
Theudas arose, giving himself out to be somebody, and a number of men,
about four hundred, joined him; but he was slain and all who followed
him were dispersed and came to nothing."[14] Augustus finally approved
Herod's will, with the provision that Archelaus would rule as ethnarch
until he proved himself worthy of the royal title.

Herod's realm was thus divided into three parts, each of which had its
own history. Of the three, Judea and Galilee are of special interest to the
student of the New Testament.

A. ARCHELAUS

Supported militarily by Varus, Archelaus reigned as ethnarch for ten
years. His rule was recklessly despotic (cf. Matt. 2:22). He arbitrarily
removed high priests from office. Extensive building operations imposed
a heavy burden of taxation upon the people. The divorce of his wife to
permit his marriage to the widow of a half-brother offended Jewish sensitivity. Police measures against the populace were harsh and oppressive.
In A.D. 6 a delegation from Jerusalem and Samaria charged the ethnarch
with misgovernment before Augustus, and Archelaus was exiled to Gaul.
Judea was annexed to the Roman province of Syria, and a Roman procurator was dispatched to administer Judean affairs.

The years 6–41 saw the administration of six Roman procurators. Because of the ministry of Jesus of Nazareth in Galilee, the best known of
the six is Pontius Pilate, prefect of Galilee from A.D. 26 to 36 (see below,
p. 123, n.47). The official residence of the procurators was the coastal town
of Caesarea, which Herod the Great had transformed into a miniature
replica of Rome. The procurator had to be in Jerusalem only on festival
occasions, when the city's population swelled to a quarter of a million
people. Passover, Pentecost, and Tabernacles commemorated the saving
acts of God in the Old Testament; feelings ran high and were always
capable of eruption. From a Roman point of view the situation was dangerous. Any spark of revolt had to be quickly extinguished. Luke mentions
certain "Galileans whose blood Pilate had mingled with their sacrifices"
(Luke 13:1), perhaps with reference to Zealots who looked to each feast
time as the possible moment for God's decisive intervention on behalf
of Israel.

B. HEROD ANTIPAS

Herod Antipas figures prominently in the Gospels, both in connection with John the Baptist (cf. Mark 6:14 ff. and parallels) and Jesus (cf. Luke 23:6–12). Antipas was more successful than Archelaus in maintaining his tenure of office. Although Galilee and Perea were divided by territories controlled by Samaria and Decapolis, he governed them for more than forty years (4 B.C.–A.D. 39). Like his father he was proud and shrewd—Jesus referred to him as "that fox" (Luke 13:32). But he tended to be more relaxed and indolent than Herod. To defend himself he rebuilt and fortified key cities. To secure himself from attack by the fierce Nabatean tribesmen from Arabia whose lands bordered on Perea, he married the daughter of their king, Aretas IV. His most important building project was a magnificent capital, named in honor of the emperor Tiberius. Antipas chose for the site of the city an ancient cemetery, disregarding Jewish ceremonial law about contact with the dead. The tetrarch had little interest in such matters.

Like Archelaus, Antipas incurred resentment and trouble when he divorced his wife to marry Herodias, the wife of a half-brother. The denunciation of this marriage by the wilderness prophet, John the Baptist, could be silenced (Mark 6:14–28), but about six years later the rejection of his daughter was avenged by Aretas in a series of incisive Nabatean attacks and the utter devastation of the tetrarch's troops. In these events many of the people saw the hand of God punishing Antipas for the execution of John.[15]

The fate of Antipas was sealed when Gaius Caligula came to the imperial throne in A.D. 37. One of his early acts was the release of Herod Agrippa from imprisonment in Rome. The emperor gave him not merely the northern tetrarchy of Philip, who had died three years earlier, but the title of king as well. Although Herodias was the sister of Agrippa, she was displeased in this turn of events and jealous for the dignity of her husband. She gave him no rest until he reluctantly promised to appear before the emperor to request the royal title. Antipas knew that he did not enjoy the favor of the new emperor as he had that of Tiberius. When he appeared before Caligula, a letter from Agrippa was delivered to the emperor accusing Antipas of plotting with the enemies of Rome. The same kind of intrigue that had characterized the administration of Herod the Great now came back to haunt his heirs. Antipas was exiled to southern Gaul and his tetrarchy was added to the domains of Agrippa—an appropriate reward for shrewd service to Rome. Two years later the emperor Claudius added Judea to Agrippa's realm. Thus for three and a half years (A.D. 41–44) Herod Agrippa I ruled the kingdom of his grandfather, Herod the Great, except for the region of Ituria.

C. HEROD AGRIPPA I   ACTS 25:

To the Jewish people Agrippa appeared different from the rest of the Herodian family. His descent could be traced not merely to Herod the Great, but to Hasmonean origins through Mariamne, his grandmother. Unlike the other members of the family, Agrippa ingratiated himself with his subjects by a scrupulous observance of the law.[16] His first public acts after arriving in Palestine in A.D. 38 were deeds of piety. Caligula had presented him with a golden chain to replace the iron one he had worn during imprisonment; this he presented to the temple. Other generous donations followed. By the time Cladius extended Agrippa's kingdom to include the province of Judea he had won the devotion of the Jews.

Agrippa's great plan was the construction of a Third Wall to protect the weak north side of Jerusalem. Skillful use was made of a bend in the course of the Kidron Valley, with the result that his builders were able to strengthen the protecting walls significantly. Had the walls been completed according to the original design, the city would have been virtually invulnerable to conquest in antiquity. The Roman government intervened, however, and prohibited the continuation of the project. When Agrippa died suddenly in A.D. 44, Claudius reorganized his kingdom into a Roman province. Thus the reign of Herod Agrippa I was merely a brief interlude between two periods of direct Roman control of Judea.

D. PRELUDE TO DESTRUCTION

The second period of procuratorial rule (A.D. 44–66) was one of continuous unrest. The Jews refused to be reconciled to Roman rule. The wisest administrators failed to understand the religious scruples of the people. The worst of them helped precipitate a war which was disastrous for Judaism. It was as if three of the four horsemen of the Book of Revelation were galloping across the land: war, famine, and death (Rev. 6:3–8). Tumult, deep discontent, and the frustration of high hopes provided the somber prelude to ultimate destruction.

The situation was ripe for the appearance of a messianic figure. Josephus refers to several pretenders who appeared at various times during this period, promising to those who followed them miraculous signs that would validate their claims.[17] To judge by what was promised—the dividing of the waters of the Jordan at a word of command, or the collapse of the walls of Jerusalem, or the unearthing of the vessels of the first temple—these false prophets presented themselves as messianic leaders patterned after Moses or Joshua. A succession of false messiahs appeared and gathered followers, but the movements which took their impetus from them were dissipated with their capture and death. Thus a prophet named Theudas attracted a large crowd when he promised to lead his people out into the wilderness, crossing the Jordan as if on dry land; but Procurator Cuspius Fadus had him promptly executed.[18] During the administration of M. Antonius Felix (A.D. 52–60) a Jewish prophet from Egypt gathered a multitude in the wilderness, promising to lead them to the Mount of Olives to witness the fall of the walls of Jerusalem at his word. Roman soldiers decimated the credulous mob which followed him, but the Egyptian escaped.[19] Reference was made to this incident when a Roman tribune questioned Paul concerning his identity: "Are you not the Egyptian, then, who recently stirred up a revolt and led the four thousand men of the assassins out into the wilderness?" (Acts 21:38). The allusion to "the assassins," or *sicarii* (so called because of the knives [*sica*] these men hid in the folds of the robes), indicates that the messianic movement had attracted the most fanatical and homicidal of the Zealots. If the number "four thousand" is not an exaggeration, it indicates that such popular movements were not inconsequential.[20] The retreat to the wilderness is significant because of the widely held expectation that the messiah would lead his people to triumph from the Judean desert.[21] Roman reprisals against such movements tended to unite not merely nationalists and religious enthusiasts but the masses of the people into a single party pledged to fight Rome through the guerrilla tactics of terrorism, plunder, and assassination.

The fifth in this second series of procurators was Porcius Festus (A.D. 60–62), an honest and able administrator. Unfortunately, the situation had deteriorated to the point that it was beyond cure. In spite of Festus' efforts to pacify the country, assassins and religious fanatics were as active as ever. Rioting between Jews and Gentiles in Caesarea expressed locally the bitter hostilities which could erupt elsewhere at any time. Nero decided this quarrel in favor of the Gentiles, whom he designated masters of the city. Seething resentment over this verdict was one of the major causes of the impending war. When Festus died in office, anarchy broke out in Jerusalem until the arrival of his successor, Lucceius Albinus (62–64).

During the disturbances the high priest Ananus had several of his enemies stoned, including the head of the Jerusalem church, James, the Lord's brother.

The new procurator made no attempt to restore order. His behavior was erratic. He arrested indiscriminately both those who were favorable to the Romans, and their enemies, the assassins, but released anyone who paid the required bribe. When Albinus was recalled to Rome, he proceeded to execute convicted criminals but freed all other prisoners irrespective of the crime for which they were accused.

Albinus had robbed individuals; his successor, Gessius Florus (64–66) plundered whole towns. Upon payment of a bribe, brigands were allowed to act unhindered. Under Florus, who epitomized evil and violence, the situation became so unbearable, Josephus reports, that the Jewish nation preferred to be destroyed with one stroke rather than endure decimation by degrees. Accordingly, from A.D. 66 to 70 it heroically fought a war that could only end in tragic defeat. Four years prior to the open rebellion a farmer named Joshua, the son of Ananus, appeared in Jerusalem during the celebration of the Feast of Tabernacles and cried out ominously: "A voice from the east, a voice from the west, a voice from the four winds, a voice against Jerusalem and the holy house, a voice against the bridegrooms and the brides, a voice against this whole people!" (Josephus, *War* VI, § 301).

No prophecy was ever fulfilled more tragically!

9. THE MISPLACEMENT OF HOPE

In the autumn of 66 a guerrilla band of Zealots led by a certain Menaḥem seized Herod the Great's old fortress of Masada on the desolate shores of the Dead Sea, massacring the Roman garrison. Within Jerusalem the war party led by Eleazar ben Ananias, the son of a former high priest, gained control of the city. Eleazar immediately stopped the temple sacrifices instituted to honor the emperor. These two acts of open rebellion ignited the First Jewish Revolt against Rome.

The course of events has been recorded in detail by Josephus in his *History of the Jewish War*. It is less important to know the changing fortunes of war, however, than to understand the hopes of the Jewish people who joined the insurgents. It is necessary to appreciate properly the messianic overtones of the revolt and the intensity of excitement which messianism stirred at crucial periods in the conflict.

In Book VI of *War* Josephus seeks to summarize the several causes of the disastrous rebellion, among which is one that he underscores:

But what more than all else incited them to war was an ambiguous oracle, likewise found in their sacred Scriptures, to the effect that at that time one from their country would become ruler of the world. This they understood to mean someone of their own race, and many of their wise men went astray in the interpretation of it. The oracle, however, in reality signified the sovereignty of Vespasian, who was proclaimed emperor on Jewish soil (§§ 312–13).

Reference to this prophecy is also found, with slight variation, in Tacitus (*Histories,* v.13) and Suetonius (*Vespasian,* 4), who agree in stressing its significance as a cause of the revolt. The prophetic passage to which reference is made may be Daniel 2:44: "And in the days of those kings the God of heaven will set up a kingdom which shall never be destroyed, nor shall its sovereignty be left to another people. It shall break in pieces all these kingdoms and bring them to an end, and it shall stand for ever." To judge by Josephus' statement, the prophecy was interpreted to refer to a single individual who would become sovereign of the world. The establishing of a kingdom implies the anointing of a king, and to the Jewish people on the eve of the rebellion this king could only be the Messiah. Scraps of evidence found in Josephus and the rabbinic material suggest that distinctly messianic hopes had been projected on at least two of the insurgent leaders, Menaḥem ben Hezekiah and Simon bar Giora.

All such hopes were misplaced. This had been seen as early as A.D. 68, when the head of the vanishing peace party within Jerusalem, Rabbi Joḥanan ben Zakkai, left the city and secured Roman permission to establish an academy in Jamnia, within the coastal plain of Sharon.[22] The choice of Jamnia proved to be a wise one. The town itself had remained loyal to the Romans, and Vespasian had already begun to populate it with deserters from the Jewish ranks. It was an important commercial center, with a port of its own, and was situated in the midst of the most fertile and desirable land in Palestine. It was to this district that many refugees from Jerusalem inevitably turned after the city was destroyed. Joḥanan saw that this region was capable of being the future center of Judea and Judaism. He obtained a vineyard which would serve as a place of assembly for scholars and their pupils. When Jerusalem was in flames everything had been prepared for Jamnia to become the center from which the reconstruction of Judaism could take place.[23]

Although Titus ordered Jerusalem to be destroyed, the destruction of a city built of stone could not be complete. It survived as an appendix to the camp of the Tenth Roman Legion, which had been left behind to police the area. Jerusalem thus became a small garrison town. Although the Christians returned from Pella, and seven Jewish synagogues existed on Mount Zion, its glory had passed. Jerusalem was no longer the center for either Judaism or Christianity. The aftermath of misplaced hope was costly defeat and humiliation.

Fifty years later (A.D. 132–135) a second attempt was made to remove Jerusalem and Judea from Roman control. Known as the Bar Kokhba Revolt, because Rabbi Akiba had recognized Simeon bar Kosiba as *Bar Kokhba* (The Son of a Star, i.e., the messianic "star out of Jacob" of Num. 24:17), it was as abortive as the First Revolt. For two whole years the Jewish army warded off the superior military resources and forces of the Romans. A new coin sequence bore the inscription Year One of the Liberty of Israel. The sacrifices were resumed, and it is even possible that some kind of temple building was constructed. But this dramatic resistance to Rome came to an end in A.D. 135—on the ninth of *Ab,* the same date as the burning of the temple in 70, if rabbinic tradition is to be believed. By this time a reaction to militant messianism had set in which is graphically expressed by a retort to Akiba who had claimed Simeon to be the Messiah: "Akiba, grass will grow out of your jaw, and the Messiah will not have come!" (*j. Ta'anith* IV. 7, 68a; *Lamentations Rabbah* II.2, § 4). Such a reaction was the inevitable result of sharp disappointment in misplaced hopes. Messianism had proved pernicious and destructive. The messianic hope was not abandoned, but it could no longer be presumed that a time of national crisis meant its fulfillment was imminent.

In connection with the events of the first and second century it was not uncommon to ask, What is the name of the Messiah? The answers of different groups within Judaism were many: his name is Menaḥem ben Hezekiah, or Simon bar Giora, or Theudas, or Simeon bar Kokhba, or a host of others. All of these answers proved false; the hopes placed in these men were uniformly disappointed. To the question, What is Messiah's name? the writers of the New Testament had a common answer: His name is Jesus, "for he will save his people from their sins" (Matt. 1:21). They argued that to seek redemption through any other person was folly, "for there is no other name under heaven given among men by which we must be saved" (Acts 4:12). They performed deeds of healing through faith in that name (cf. Acts 3:16). When it became necessary to do so, they willingly suffered reproach for that name, finding in the designation "Christian" a badge of honor through which to glorify God (1 Peter 4:14–16). Each of the documents of the New Testament bears in its own way on the claim that Jesus is the Messiah. It is to these books that we turn to allow the New Testament to speak.

NOTES

1. Ezra, Nehemiah, 2 Chronicles, Esther, Daniel, Haggai, Zechariah, Malachi.

2. See J. MacDonald, *The Theology of the Samaritans* (1964); L. A. Mayer, *Bibliography of the Samaritans* (1964).

3. On Alexander see W. W. Tarn, *Alexander the Great* (1948), 2 vols. Cf. P. Jouguet, *Macedonian Imperialism and the Hellenization of the East* (1928).

4. See W. H. S. Jones, "Hellenistic Science and Mathematics," *Cambridge Ancient History,* Vol. VIII (1959), pp. 284–311. Henceforth *C.A.H.*

5. See E. Bevan, "Syria and the Jews," *C.A.H.,* Vol. VIII (1930), pp. 495–533; M. Rostovtzeff, "Ptolemaic Egypt," *C.A.H.,* Vol. VII (1954), pp. 109–54; *idem,* "Syria and the East," pp. 155–96.

6. This designation comes from Onias, a name borne by the major high-priestly family of the Ptolemaic period.

7. See E. Bickerman, *The Maccabees* (1947); P. Barry, "Antiochus IV Epiphanes," *Journal of Biblical Literature,* 29 (1910), pp. 126–38.

8. These allies of Judas were known as the Hasidim (i.e., "the pious"). See 1 Macc. 2:43 f.; 7:12 ff.; 2 Macc. 14:6.

9. See 1 Sam. 13:8–14; 2 Chron. 26:16–18; 1 Kings 13:1–4; cf. Num. 16: 39 f.; 18:6 f.

10. See W. S. Anderson, *Pompey and His Friends, and the Literature of the First Century B.C.* (1963).

11. See A. H. M. Jones, *The Herods of Judea* (1938); S. Perowne, *The Life and Times of Herod the Great* (1956).

12. A Jewish document, roughly contemporary with the lifetime of Jesus, parallels this account in describing Herod as one who "shall slay the old and the young, and he shall not spare" (*Assumpt. Moses* 6:4).

13. See S. Perowne, *The Later Herods* (1958).

14. Acts 5:36. This Theudas is not to be confused with a prophet by the same name who appeared much later. See below, p. 58, and n. 18.

15. Josephus, *Antiquities,* XVIII, §§ 116, 119. See further A. W. Verrall, "Herod Antipas," *Journal of Theological Studies,* 10 (1909), pp. 322–53.

16. *Antiquities,* XVIII, § 6; XIX, §§ 5–8.

17. See, e.g., *Antiquities,* XX, §§ 97–99, 160–72, 185–88; *War,* II, §§ 258–63, 433–48; VI, §§ 281–87; VII, §§ 252–74, 437–42.

18. *Antiquities,* XX, §§ 97–99; cf. Exod. 14:21–22; Josh. 3:1–17. See the suggestive essay by W. K. L. Clarke, "A Prophet like unto Me," in *New Testament Problems* (1929), pp. 39–47.

19. *Antiquities,* XX, §§ 169–72; *War,* II, §§ 261–62; cf. Josh 6:1–20.

20. Josephus (*War,* II, § 261) actually speaks of 30,000 followers. This discrepancy with Acts may be due to a misreading of the numeral symbol: $\Delta =$ 4,000; $\Lambda = 30,000$.

21. The expectation was grounded in the deliverance provided for Israel in the wilderness following the Exodus, and the prophetic call for Israel to return to its wilderness existence. See especially U. Mauser, *Christ in the Wilderness* (1963), pp. 54–61.

22. *b. Gittin* 56a, b; *Echa Rabbati* I. 5; *Aboth de Rabbi Nathan* IV. For the danger involved in the decision to leave the city see Josephus, *War,* IV, §§ 377–88.

23. On Jamnia see W. M. Christie, "The Jamnia Period in Jewish History," *Journal of Theological Studies,* 26 (1925), pp. 347–64; W. D. Davies, "Jamnia," in *The Setting of the Sermon on the Mount* (1964), pp. 256–315.

SELECTED READING

Avi-Yonah, M., *The Holy Land From the Persian to the Arab Conquests (536 B.C. to A.D. 640): A Historical Geography.* Grand Rapids: Baker, 1965.

Barrett, C. K., *The New Testament Background; Selected Documents.* New York: Macmillan, 1957.

Cornfeld, G. ed., *Daniel to Paul: Jews in Conflict with Graeco-Roman Civilization.* New York: Macmillan, 1962.

Cross, F. M., *The Ancient Library of Qumran and Modern Biblical Studies,* rev. ed. Garden City, N.Y.: Anchor Books, 1961.

Dupont-Sommer, A., *The Essene Writings from Qumran.* Cleveland: Meridian, 1962.

Grant, M., *The World of Rome.* New York: New American Library, 1961.

Lieberman, S., *Greek in Jewish Palestine.* New York: Jewish Publication Society, 1950.

Milik, J. T., *Ten Years of Discovery in the Wilderness of Judaea.* Naperville: Allenson, 1959.

Perowne, S., *The Later Herods.* London: Hodder and Stoughton, 1958.

—— *The Life and Times of Herod the Great.* London: Hodder and Stoughton, 1956.

Pfeiffer, R. H., *History of New Testament Times with an Introduction to the Apocrypha.* New York: Harper, 1949.

Schubert, K., *The Dead Sea Community.* New York: Harper, 1959.

Tarn, W. W., *Alexander the Great.* Vol. I: *Narrative.* Cambridge: University Press, 1948.

—— *Hellenistic Civilization.* London: E. Arnold, 1927.

IV

✤

PREFACE TO THE GOSPELS

THAT there is a uniqueness to the message of the New Testament even the least initiated in biblical studies would agree. But it is not so well known that the apostolic message necessitated a new form. The coming of Jesus Christ released among his followers a freedom and power of communication that rendered many existing literary forms obsolete.[1] Among the modes which either came into being or received new significance from the Christian movement are the Gospel, the Epistle, the "Acts" and the Apocalypse. The most distinctive of these four is the Gospel.

1. THE LITERARY FORM

The Gospel form was not a literary accident. However spontaneous in origin, the Gospels owe their style as well as their substance to the appearance of Jesus of Nazareth. As witness documents, they were expressions of faith written to foster faith (cf. John 20:31). They were not propaganda tracts for those who had never heard the Christian message, but documents created for the church so that those who had heard might gain a fuller understanding of the truth.

Though they record many events of the "life of Jesus," the four Gospels are in no sense biographies. What kind of biography is it that tells us nothing of Jesus' home life or of how he spent his youth, nothing of his personality traits or physical appearance, nothing of his inner thoughts and feelings? The Gospels supply none of this information. Although they arrange the events of Jesus' life in a coherent sequence, their prime interest is not chronological, nor do they make any claim to completeness. Following a principle of selectivity, they pass over large areas of Jesus' life to concentrate on a few of his discourses, healings, and exorcisms, and preeminently the last week of his life.

The substance of the Gospels' witness is based not on the purely individual research of four authors but on the church's common proclamation (or *kerygma*) of the words and deeds of Jesus. From the beginning, this tradition formed the core both of the missionary preaching and of the instruction of converts in the Christian community. Its content was well defined and familiar to the leaders of the congregations. Paul refers in strictest terms to that which he had "received" (1 Cor. 11:23; 15:1–3) as authoritative, not only in the church but over the church and over the Apostle himself (cf. Gal. 1:8).

The preface of Luke's Gospel indicates that this document was also based upon elements handed down from "those who from the beginning were eye witnesses and ministers of the word" (Luke 1:1–4). Since Luke draws extensively upon Mark, it is likely that he includes the Marcan narrative among these earlier witnesses.[2]

Such a concept of the Gospels as tradition must be tested in the light of the documents themselves. The literary dependence of both Matthew and Luke upon Mark has become largely a matter of common agreement among scholars. Verbal agreements and agreements of order among the three synoptics are so close that some kind of direct literary relationship is indicated. In the "triple tradition" (i.e., areas where all three share common material) Matthew and Luke generally agree with each other only insofar as they agree with Mark. Mark is a "middle term" between them. In the double tradition (i.e., material shared by Matthew and Luke only), however, there are also remarkable verbal similarities, consisting mostly of words of Jesus. Since we have no evidence of a direct literary relationship between Matthew and Luke, a "sayings" source "Q" (for the German word *Quelle,* source) is generally posited. Thus synoptic literary criticism has led most scholars to the so-called Two-Document Theory (Mark and Q being the two basic sources).[3]

That this purely literary solution leaves many questions unanswered becomes clear when we see that the synoptic Gospels do not take the form of an unbroken narrative. Apart from the Passion accounts, and to a lesser extent some of the sections descriptive of Jesus' ministry, much of the Gospels is composed of brief pericopes—self-contained accounts linked together often by rather slender threads.[4] These separate units have certain peculiarities. According to Mark 2:15–17:

> And as he sat at table in his house, many tax collectors and sinners were sitting with Jesus and his disciples; for there were many who followed him. And the scribes of the Pharisees, when they saw that he was eating with sin-

ners and tax collectors, said to his disciples, "Why does he eat with tax collectors and sinners?" And when Jesus heard it, he said to them, "Those who are well have no need of a physician, but those who are sick; I came not to call the righteous, but sinners."

Here is a most important incident; yet the whole acount is exceedingly brief, culminating in Jesus' statement, "I came not to call the righteous, but sinners." No elaboration is made upon the utterance, nor is any connection established between this pericope and the next (2:18–22). They both stand as independent, self-contained units (cf. also Mark 2:1–12, 13–14, 23–27; 3:1–6).

On the other hand, in the account of Jesus' teaching in Mark 4 or the report of the healing of a man with an unclean spirit in Mark 5, brevity appears not to have been a consideration. The narrative of the death of John the Baptist (Mark 6:17–29) is recounted in such detail as to include even some biographical data surrounding King Herod and his illicit union with his brother's wife. Does such variation represent only the author's whim? Has he sharply curtailed the telling of certain incidents, only in a fit of expansiveness to enlarge upon others? Or does he possess some of his information in very detailed form and other reports of Jesus' life or teachings only in small and isolated fragments?

2. FORM CRITICISM AND THE SYNOPTIC GOSPELS

In the early decades of this century, some German scholars began to look closely at questions such as these.[5] They became convinced that the differences in the form of Jesus' words and deeds in the Gospels were the consequence of the way in which the Gospel tradition had been put to use in the early church. From their examination of the Gospels they concluded that, apart from the Passion narrative, the substance of the Gospels can be divided into two categories: the words of Jesus and the narrative materials.

A. THE WORDS OF JESUS

Except for some of the parables, Jesus' words appear as brief, self-contained units, independent of any extended historical framework. Some of them characteristically occur within specific situations in which Jesus is involved, as when the scribes challenged Jesus's actions in forgiving sins (Mark 2:1–12), eating with sinners (Mark 2:15–17), or healing on the Sabbath (Mark 3:1–6). The conclusion to such an encounter is always a *pronouncement* by Jesus clarifying his authority ("the Son of man is Lord even of the Sabbath"), or his mission ("I came not to call the righteous but sinners"), or the will of God ("whoever does not receive the Kingdom of God like a child shall not enter in").

Other sayings less closely related to a narrative setting are grouped in blocks, as in Mark 4:21–25:

(a) And he said to them, "Is a lamp brought in to be put under a bushel, or under a bed, and not on a stand?

(b) For there is nothing hid, except to be made manifest, nor is anything secret, except to come to light.

(c) If any man has ears to hear, let him hear." And he said to them, "Take heed what you hear;

(d) the measure you give will be the measure you get, and still more will be given you.

(e) For to him who has will more be given; and from him who has not, even what he has will be taken away."[6]

These sayings have no direct connection with the preceding parable of the sower, or with the parable of the seed that follows, or even necessarily with one another. They are simply representative sayings of Jesus placed together because of some common features of vocabulary or theme.[7]

It is instructive to study these same sayings as they occur in Matthew and Luke. Matthew contains all but one of them but locates them in quite different contexts. The first and fourth sayings appear independently in the Sermon on the Mount (Matt. 5:15; 7:2). The second is included in the mission instructions that Jesus gives to his disciples (10:26). The last comprises part of the explanation as to why Jesus teaches in parables (13:12).

Luke follows Mark in using the material in a block (Luke 8:16–18) but like Matthew also employs the sayings individually in a variety of contexts (cf. 11:33; 12:2; 6:38; 19:26).

B. NARRATIVE MATERIALS

The bulk of the narratives have to do with the miraculous activities of Jesus: his exorcisms, healings, and demonstrations of power. Although Jesus's sayings are recorded briefly and with few details, the accounts of his deeds, especially the miracles, tend to be characterized by a fullness of presentation. They frequently include biographical background on individuals being healed, the circumstance under which the cure was effected, and the reaction of observers. Although some of these pericopes include statements of Jesus, this is not their chief characteristic; the act itself occupies the center of the stage.

From these observations the form critics concluded that during the period in which the Gospel had existed in oral form, the material had been shaped and formulated by the early witnesses and proclaimers of the word. The form given to units of material reflected the different ways in which the tradition had been used. The problem was to establish the precise relation between each form and its particular use in the church, thus fixing the life situation (*Sitz im Leben*) within which the various oral and literary forms developed.

According to form critical reconstructions, as it expanded the church was confronted with a diversity of needs and interests. These concerns were *missionary* (presenting Jesus' life in such a way as to win new converts), *catechetical* (instructing the converts in their new faith), *apologetic* (answering the Jewish and pagan detractors of the faith), and *disciplinary* (protecting the church's life and belief against dangers from within). Such interests varied as the church moved into new environments. The materials required to instruct Christians in Palestine could be quite different from those necessary for the same purpose in Antioch, Ephesus, Corinth, or Rome. Cultural differences required adaptation. Diversity of need influenced not only what was remembered (and therefore taught), but also how it was remembered. Thus the form as well as the content of the gospel materials in the Hellenistic churches could differ considerably from what was adopted in the church at Jerusalem. Each church faced the problem of how to translate the gospel message into language that would be understood in a particular cultural environment, without distortion of the essential truth received from Jesus and the apostles.

The form critics were prepared to take one further step. Having recognized the oral forms and assigned to them a particular life situation, they now sought to establish the relative historical credibility of the individual accounts. It was at this point that the early exponents of form criticism became unnecessarily radical in their conclusions. They made the fatal error of shifting the role of the Christian community from shaper and preserver of the gospel tradition to the position of its creator. This assumption blinded them to several crucial facts:

1. The gospel arose in a Jewish milieu where tradition was sacred and established procedures existed by which it was maintained.

2. From the beginning the apostles had a proprietary interest in this tradition and a zealous concern to preserve and protect it.

3. There had never been a concept of the church without ministry. Through the original apostles, as well as the prophets and teachers who followed, this ministry was a ministry of the word. The word of God,

therefore, in the form of gospel tradition, was never subservient to the community. It existed distinct from the church and had authority over it.

4. Even before Paul's labors, the tradition had come to possess a certain fixity.

5. The gospel materials were reduced to writing within the lifetime of first-generation believers.

6. Rather extensive communication among individual churches throughout the Empire, including even Jerusalem, was a distinguishing feature of primitive Christianity.

In spite of these considerations, and as an inevitable consequence of assigning an essentially creative role to the church, the form critics found it increasingly difficult to accept the historical reliability of the gospel tradition, either in its totality or in its individual parts. Beyond the fact that Jesus lived and taught they found little agreement and even less certainty. As a result, form criticism stood for a time largely self-discredited in the eyes of more sober investigators of Christian origins.[8]

Further reflection showed that the initial error of the approach was not so much in its methodology (although lack of precision had been very damaging) as in its critical presuppositions. Form criticism had too quickly posited extremely late dates for the Gospels. It had been virtually hypnotized by Hellenistic parallels to the New Testament and overlooked parallels from Judaism that were at least as relevant. What was more serious, it had allowed its skeptical theological and philosophical assumptions to overwhelm its scientific objectivity. Nevertheless, the form critics did bring to the text the right questions. They recognized that each individual pericope in the Gospels had its own history and life situation. It was established beyond reasonable doubt that prior to their literary composition the Gospels had passed through a significant "prehistory" in oral form in the life of the church.

The effect of these conclusions has been to revolutionize synoptic studies. Despite all that is erroneous in the form-critical approach, and despite the many false detours into which it has led, W. D. Davies is quite right in saying that "all serious students of the New Testament today are to some extent Form Critics."[9] No longer can the synoptic materials be understood simply as literary productions; the student of the New Testament must recognize in them a living word already operative in the community of Christian faith, a word that bears in its form and structure the marks of its advent into history. Besides being a record of history, it is itself history and thus a historic word in the fullest sense of the term.

Several positive gains can be derived from a recognition of the value of form criticism:

1. It helps immeasurably in the appreciation of the distinctive style and structure of synoptic tradition. The form of the written Gospels essentially mirrors that of the oral tradition which preceded them. Before the Gospels had come into being, the forms by which the materials were preserved had already achieved a certain fixity. Although the Gospel writer would have some freedom to select and arrange his traditions in accordance with a particular literary and theological purpose, his tendency was to remain faithful to that which he had received. Such conservatism indicates that precisely in these forms the tradition had already achieved a unique authority.

2. It is neither possible nor necessary to demand a complete harmonization of the chronologies of the different Gospels. Though some accounts were probably handed down in fixed historical or geographical settings (e.g., Jesus' ministries at Capernaum, Jericho, or Samaria), most of the pericopes were arranged according to very different principles. The concern of the authors was more mnemonic than chronological: like any preacher or teacher they wanted something that would be easily remembered.

Consequently the Gospel narratives are grouped according to a variety of patterns. Sometimes it is according to content or circumstance (Sabbath day teachings, controversies with scribes, a typical day in Capernaum, sayings by the sea). In other cases numerical interests are at work (e.g., Matthew records five great discourses of Jesus, seven parables of the Kingdom, ten miracles in sequence). A more subtle aid to memory involved the use of catchwords—key terms by which otherwise unrelated events could be linked together. In Mark 9:42, for example, a word of Jesus against causing the little ones *to sin* is followed in verses 43–48 by warnings against allowing one's hand or foot or eye to cause one *to sin*. The sayings have been joined by the verbal catchword, "to sin." Then verses 48 and 49 are similarly connected by the catchword "fire," and verses 49 and 50 by "salt." Chronological and even topical considerations have here given way to the interests of teaching and memorization.

3. Form criticism helps explain some otherwise perplexing variations in parallel accounts of the same incident. A detail omitted by one evangelist may be included by another because it carries for him a certain relevance with respect to the situation out of which he writes.[10] Although not every difference can be explained in this way, more attention is now given to such factors.

4. In the genius of each individual pericope is to be located the genius of the Gospels as a whole. Each incident or saying in the life of Jesus as it is taught or proclaimed in the tradition has the possibility of bearing a valid witness to Jesus apart from and independent of any other event.[11] That is precisely the nature of each Gospel as a whole and of each unit within the Gospel tradition—to bear witness to Jesus of Nazareth, the Lord of the church. It is this element which distinguishes the Gospels from all other literature. Their concern is not simply to record but to set forth the living testimony of Jesus present in the church. In telling who Jesus was, as well as what he said and did, the Gospels disclose also who Jesus *is*—who he is in the Roman church of Mark, what he says to Matthew's Jewish community of Antioch, what he is doing in the Hellenistic church of Luke. It is ultimately the Risen Jesus who bears testimony to himself, the man of Nazareth. In the Gospels we hear what he says through the Spirit to the church. It is this witness-bearing function— witness to Jesus and witness from Jesus—which explains the incontestable loyalty with which the authors adhere to the word of Jesus, even though they sometimes exercise remarkable freedom in presenting that word.

NOTES

1. Cf. Ernst Fuchs, *Studies of the Historical Jesus* (1964), pp. 66, 68: "The New Testament developed in the literary Gospels a completely new stylistic genre, which should not be labelled 'minor literature.' . . . The early church is itself a language phenomenon. It is precisely for this reason that it has created for itself a memorial in the new stylistic form of the Gospel." See A. Wilder, *The Language of the Gospel* (1964).

2. For Mark's link with the Apostle Peter, see the testimony of the second-century bishop Papias in Eusebius, *Hist. Eccl.* III, xxxix, 15.

3. For more detail and much fuller development (even into a *four*-document theory), see B. H. Streeter, *The Four Gospels* (1925), pp. 150–360.

4. The arrangement is often topical rather than chronological. In Mark 2:1–3:6, for example, five accounts of conflict between Jesus and the scribes or Pharisees have been brought together.

5. Among the form-critical works that have been translated into English, see especially Martin Dibelius, *From Tradition to Gospel* (1919; Eng. trans. 1934), and Rudolf Bultmann, *The History of the Synoptic Tradition* (1931; Eng. trans. 1963).

6. For other such blocks of sayings, see Mark 8:34–9:1; 9:41–50.

7. In this example note how (a) and (b) have to do with light, (c) with hearing, and (d) and (e) with reward.

8. See, e.g., the critique of this approach by C. S. C. Williams in A. H. McNeile, *An Introduction to the Study of the New Testament,* 2d rev. ed. (Oxford, 1953), pp. 46–58. In one pungent expression Williams says, "Form-critics write as though the original eye-witnesses were all caught up to heaven at the Ascension and the Christian Church were put to live on a desert island" (p. 53).

9. *Invitation to the New Testament* (1966), p. 97.

10. Matthew, for example, recalls *two* blind men healed by Jesus on one occasion (20:30) while Mark and Luke mention only one. This detail is possibly to be connected with the principle enunciated in Matthew 18:16 that "every word may be confirmed by the evidence of two or three witnesses" (cf. Deut. 19:15).

11. Martin Kähler made this point seventy years ago, in *The So-called Historical Jesus and the Historic, Biblical Christ* (1896; Eng. trans. 1964), p. 81.

SELECTED READING

Bultmann, R., *The History of the Synoptic Tradition.* Oxford: Blackwell, 1963.

Dibelius, M., *From Tradition to Gospel,* 2d ed. New York: Scribner, 1935.

Riesenfeld, H., *The Gospel Tradition and its Beginnings. A Study in the Limits of 'Formgeschichte.'* London: A. R. Mowbray, 1957.

Stonehouse, N. B., *Origins of the Synoptic Gospels: Some Basic Questions.* Grand Rapids: Eerdmans, 1963.

Streeter, B. H., *The Four Gospels: A Study in Origins.* London: Macmillan, 1953.

Taylor, V., *The Formation of the Gospel Tradition,* 2d ed. London: Macmillan, 1945.

V

✳

THE STORY OF JESUS

WHEREAS form criticism addresses itself to the individual Gospels and the small units of tradition from which they are built, life-of-Jesus research centers upon the single theme that is common to them all—Jesus of Nazareth, his baptism, his proclamation and acts in Galilee, his journey to Jerusalem, his death and resurrection. This is the *kerygma* which furnishes the basic structure around which all of the other traditions cluster in the Gospels.

Four points should be noted in connection with this common Gospel outline.

1. Although the outline antedates all of our written Gospels, it is most clearly reproduced in Mark. Precisely for this reason Matthew and Luke made Mark the basis for their Gospels. Even a hasty reading of the sermons of Peter and Paul recorded in the Book of Acts reveals their close correspondence with the pattern of the Markan account (note especially Acts 10:37 ff.; but cf. also 2:22 ff.; 13:23 ff.).

2. The main emphasis of this outline was upon Jesus' deeds (cf. Acts 2:22), his proclamation (10:36), and his death and resurrection (3:13 ff.; 4:10 f.; 5:30 f.; 10:39). His extensive teaching ministry was not mentioned in the sermons of Acts and was little emphasized in Mark's Gospel. It belonged not to the basic *kerygma*, but to the more formal instruction given to converts and to members of the church. Most of Jesus' sayings were gathered separately, and not until the writing of Matthew and Luke was the large body of this material (i.e., the Q source) incorporated into the Gospel narrative.

3. In the kerygmatic account of Jesus' ministry, his birth and early life are simply passed over. Though Matthew and Luke partially fill in this lacuna, even they are more concerned to interpret the total event of Jesus' coming, especially against the backdrop of the Old Testament Scriptures. Only in that context is Jesus' miraculous birth narrated and only then does the advent of the Messiah as God's own Son find its ultimate expression.

Even in the infancy records of Matthew and Luke, the omission of biographical detail is striking and can hardly be accidental. Never do the Gospel writers locate the meaning of Jesus in his human development or his religious precocity. It is not his descent "according to the flesh" that they wish to emphasize but his designation as God's Son by the Holy Spirit (cf. Rom. 1:3–4). For this reason the church's earliest witness to Jesus began not with his birth but with his baptism.

4. The gospel begins not with Jesus himself but with John the Baptist. This is the unanimous witness of the four Gospel writers, and is confirmed also from the Book of Acts (cf. 1:22; 10:37; 13:24). Why John's ministry and baptism had this importance is not always made clear. It seems to belong to that which is assumed. In order to clarify this starting point of the history of Jesus, we turn first to John and his baptism.

1. THE PROPHETIC FORERUNNER

A. A Prophet in Israel

In retrospect, a Christian observer would have to say that John's appearance in the wilderness was the most important event in Israel's life in more than three hundred years. The absence of a prophet during this entire period had been interpreted to mean that the prophetic task was accomplished. The next prophet would in fact be "the Prophet," an eschatological figure whose appearance would signal the events of the "last days" (Deut. 18:15–19; 1 Macc. 4:42–46; 14:41). That the populace actually understood John the Baptist in these terms is strongly supported by the sources available from the period. The Jewish historian Josephus, for example, bears testimony to John's reception among the people:

> But to some of the Jews the destruction of Herod's army seemed to be divine vengeance, and certainly a very just vengeance, for his treatment of John, surnamed the Baptist. For Herod had put him to death, though he was a good man and had exhorted the Jews to lead righteous lives, to practice justice towards their fellows and piety towards God, and so doing to join in baptism. . . . When others, too, joined the crowds about him, because they were aroused to the highest degree by his sermons, Herod became alarmed. Eloquence that had so great an effect on mankind might lead to some form of sedition, for it looked as if they would be guided by John in everything that they did. (*Antiquities,* XVIII, § 118 f.).

The New Testament evangelists are no less decisive. Each writer knows that it is the Baptist's appearance in the wilderness that inaugurates the Kingdom proclamation. It is John's call to repentance that lays the basis for the Christian understanding of sin and its cure. It is his baptism that furnishes the sign and seal under which the Christian proclamation is received.

Not only the Gospels but the sources behind them witness to John's greatness. Certain of these sources appear to come from the inner circle of John's followers: for example, the narratives of his unusual birth, and the hymns celebrating it,[1] the account of the circumstances of his wilderness call, the record of his meteorlike appearance as the prophet of repentance who confronted Israel and brought her to the banks of the Jordan. The almost messianic aura with which these accounts surround Jesus' forerunner suggests that their ultimate source may well have been John's own disciples.

John's life before his call remains unknown to us. Since his parents were aged even at his birth (Luke 1:5–7), it is likely that others had to assume the responsibility for his upbringing. It has been suggested that he was reared by Essenes in the Qumran community near the Dead Sea.[2] It is conceivable that this was "the wilderness" where John "grew and became strong in spirit . . . till the day of his manifestation to Israel" (Luke 1:80). Even if this should be the case, however, a careful comparison of the Qumran Covenanters with John the Baptist reveals differences so extensive as to make this possibility unimportant. Far from acknowledging a priestly community, John apparently rejected his priestly heritage and retreated to the wilderness—alone—there to realize his destiny. That John should have turned expectantly to the wilderness ought not to surprise us. The same factors that had led the Essenes to withdraw from the mainstream of Judaism were at work again—a purchased priesthood, a temple embellished by profane hands, a holy city filled with pagans. With many others among the pious in Israel, John saw the wilderness as the path to renewal.[3] It was in the wilderness, in the fifteenth year of Tiberius Caesar, that the "word of God came to John the son of Zechariah" (Luke 3:1 ff.). The prophetic ministry that resulted was one that stirred all Israel with its radical demand for repentance, its alarm of impending judgment, and its witness to a greater person yet to come.

John's opening proclamation conveys a profound sense of the catastrophic. He heralds a judgment that like a desert fire forces even the viper to flee, a cyclonic wind of the Spirit that will drive the chaff utterly away, a purging holocaust that will consume every unproductive and unrighteous tree. Now is Israel's decisive moment, her appointed time. That for which she was called and to which every prophet gave testimony is now at hand. Israel must repent, for God's Kingdom is dawning.

Those who heard John's preaching would not have failed to recognize this familiar prophetic appeal. But to his preaching John added something wholly novel—baptism in the Jordan River. There have been speculations that John's baptism was derived from the Jewish practice of baptizing proselytes[4] or from the regular ablutions of Jewish worship or from the rites of initiation practiced at Qumran.[5] No clear line of dependence can be shown in support of any of these theories. Baptism appears rather as a unique activity of this prophet, a prophetic sign so striking that John was henceforth known simply as "the Baptizer."

The summons to be baptized in the Jordan meant that Israel must come once more to the wilderness. As the people of God long ago had been separated from Egypt by a pilgrimage through the water of the Red Sea, so Israel is exhorted again to experience separation; the nation is called to a second Exodus in preparation for a new covenant with God. Mere membership in the old community of faith was insufficient for entrance into the Kingdom of God. Anticipating the protests of some of his hearers, John cried out: "do not presume to say to yourselves, 'We have Abraham as our father'; for I tell you, God is able from these stones to raise up children to Abraham" (Matt. 3:9; cf. Luke 3:8).

B. THE PROPHETIC ANNOUNCEMENT

The second stage of John's proclamation seems to have come less from his own initative than from questions raised by those who came to him. Luke especially makes this clear (3:15 f.); it was "as John was finishing his course" (Acts 13:25) that he began to speak of an individual messianic figure still to come:

> I baptize you with water; but he who is mightier than I is coming, the thong of whose sandals I am not worthy to untie; he will baptize you with the Holy Spirit and with fire. His winnowing fork is in his hand, to clear his threshing floor, and to gather the wheat into his granary, but the chaff he will burn with unquenchable fire (Luke 3:16–17; cf. Matt. 3:11 f.; Mark 1:7 f.).

In referring to this new Baptizer, John avoided traditional messianic terms: he echoes the expectation of a returning Elijah[6]; the designation "coming one" suggests Psalm 118:26 with its ascription of praise to "him who comes in the name of the Lord."* The announcement is framed in accordance with Israel's expectation either of the eschatological coming of God himself or of his chosen representative, the Messiah. The precise identity of the coming one remained hidden even from John until he witnessed the descent of the Spirit at the baptism of Jesus (John 1:31 ff.). Only then could his testimony become explicit (John 1:34, 36).

From the moment of Jesus' baptism, John's importance began to wane. His statement that Jesus "must increase, but I must decrease" (John 3:30) aptly describes both the Baptist's intention and the actual subsequent history. It was Jesus and his followers, not John, who represented the "wave of the future." Jesus testified of his great predecessor that "the law and the prophets were until John; since then the good news of the kingdom of God is preached" (Luke 16:16).

Just as the Old Testament does not lose its significance by being fulfilled in Jesus, so John the Baptist continues to address the Christian church long after his historical career has run its course. The summons to confession and forgiveness and the call to bring forth fruit worthy of repentance is one that the new community of faith never outgrows. It is an appeal that recurs in the New Testament and in later Christian literature under a variety of forms. To this degree, individual and corporate life in Christ is shaped by the one who came "in the way of righteousness" (Matt. 21:32) and who baptized Jesus in the waters of the Jordan in order "to fulfill all righteousness" (Matt. 3:15).

2. THE BAPTISM OF JESUS

When Jesus was approximately thirty years of age he came to the wilderness to be baptized. We are never told why this event should mark the beginning of his ministry. No reference is made to a prophetic calling like that given to John, Isaiah, or Jeremiah. When the day arrives, Jesus simply goes out to the wilderness and identifies himself with sinners in the waters of cleansing.

For one who would himself later baptize others in the Holy Spirit, such an action was wholly unexpected—it became, in fact, a stone of stumbling to many in the Christian church. Only from the perspective of subsequent events would the true meaning of Jesus' submission to the Baptizer be grasped even partially. That so much misunderstanding should be risked can only mean that Jesus' response to John's summons had momentous implications for him personally, for his relationship with John, and for later Christian thought and practice. Though the New Testament nowhere systematically interprets Jesus' baptism, an examination of the Gospel accounts provides some insight into its significance.

A. THE BAPTISM AS CONSECRATION

In its simplest terms, Jesus' baptism can be understood as an act of obedience, a direct response to the will of God, by which he is set apart for a task. John's own resistance to Jesus' baptism and the puzzled attitude of the later church is well expressed in the question, "I need to be baptized by you, and do you come to me?" Jesus' answer is, "Let it be so now; for thus it is fitting for us to fulfil all righteousness" (Matt. 3:14–15). Jesus' answer does not deny the unusualness of his action or the right of John to be perplexed. Neither does he disallow that he is the greater and John the lesser. All that is affirmed is the absolute necessity for John and Jesus to obey God. Something else is at stake here that John is not expected to understand. It is sufficient for him to know that what is done is the righteous and perfect will of God. Jesus' absolute obedience to God as his Father stands over against all human calculations or expectations and becomes an important factor in understanding not only Jesus' baptism but many of his subsequent actions. An early hymn to Christ shows how firmly the confessing church had laid hold of this insight into the career of him,

> "who, though he was in the form of God, did not count equality with God a thing to be grasped, but emptied himself, taking the form of a servant, being born in the likeness of men. And being found in human form he humbled himself and became obedient unto death, even death on a cross" (Phil. 2:6–8).

Though such passages do not refer directly to the baptism of Jesus, this event sets the pattern for the ministry that follows.

In numbering himself with those who responded to John, Jesus assumes the role of the whole people of Israel. For that reason obedience and humility are to him signs not of defeat but of victory. At this point Israel had failed in its mission. The nation was neither repentant for its sins nor submissive to God's judgment upon its unrighteousness. The people never allowed God's chastisement upon them to accomplish its task and bring forth the peaceable fruits of righteousness. Jesus in the waters of Jordan has returned to the wilderness to become the one true Israelite. Standing there undefiled, he takes upon himself God's judgment against Israel so that Israel might go forth to a new Exodus from the slavery of sin and death.

⌇ B. THE BAPTISM AS ANOINTING

It would be wrong to assume that Jesus' part in this drama was entirely passive. According to Luke, it was in answer to Jesus' prayer that heaven opened and the Holy Spirit came down as a dove (3:21 f.). The occasion is reminiscent of the first Exodus when, after the Israelites had cleansed themselves, God came down upon Mount Sinai in the sight of all the people (Exod. 19:11). As Israel's eschatology centered in a hope for a second Exodus, the prayer for God to "come down" once more in grace became a familiar one. "Bow thy heavens, O Lord, and come down! Touch the mountains that they smoke!" (Ps. 144:5). The hope that God would "rend the heavens and come down" (Isa. 64:1) was associated with a prayer for the renewed activity of the Spirit of God: "Then he remembered the days of old, of Moses his servant. Where is he who brought up out of the sea the shepherds of his flock? Where is he who put in the midst of them his holy Spirit . . . ?" (Isa. 63:11). It is against this background that we are to understand the synoptic account of Jesus' baptism. God has kept his promises. He has torn the heavens and given the Holy Spirit to his chosen servant.

C. THE BAPTISM AS DIVINE APPROVAL

In the baptismal waters, Jesus heard God say to him, "Thou art my beloved Son; with thee I am well pleased" (Mark 1:11). This formulation of the heavenly voice represents a combination of two Old Testament passages. The phrase "Thou art my Son" (Psalm 2:7) expresses the dignity that belongs to the Messiah. The remainder of the address, "with thee I am well pleased," is couched in the language of the Servant Songs of Isaiah (Isa. 42:1). If the Psalm reference guarantees to the Messiah his ultimate elevation, the allusion to Isaiah stamps Jesus' mission as that of a servant. It is not a king, elevated and ruling, who appears in the role of John's "coming one," but the lowly and mysterious suffering servant of Isaiah. Accordingly what is suggested by Jesus' act of baptism is confirmed by divine revelation. From this beginning Jesus knew that his lot would be both difficult and perilous. For him to become God's servant, "despised and rejected of men; a man of sorrows and acquainted with grief . . . wounded for our transgressions, bruised for our iniquities" (Isa. 53:3, 5), involved an ominous threat to his very existence. It is no coincidence that when he later spoke of his own death, he characterized it precisely as a second baptism (Luke 12:50; cf. Mark 10:38–45). This helps us to understand why in each of the synoptic Gospels the baptism of Jesus is directly followed by his first confrontation with the forces of evil.

3. THE TEMPTATION IN THE WILDERNESS

Endowed with the Holy Spirit, Jesus is now thrust by the Spirit into the wilderness. Like Israel in the years of desert wandering, Jesus is subjected to the experience of testing. He is brought face to face not only with the perils of nature—hunger and wild beasts—but with the prince of evil himself.

Since Jesus was alone in the wilderness, he must himself have been the source of the disciples' knowledge of this incident. The emphasis, however, does not fall upon Jesus' private feelings. The purpose of the narrative is to convey to the church necessary knowledge about the Son of God and his mission. Against the temptation to use the power of God to "make these stones bread" in order to relieve his hunger, and possibly even the physical sufferings of the entire world, Jesus answers simply from Deuteronomy, "Man shall not live by bread alone, but by every word that proceeds from the mouth of God" (Deut. 8:3; Matt. 4:4). When urged to prove his divine sonship by casting himself down from the pinnacle of the temple, he again quotes Scripture: "You shall not tempt the Lord your God" (6:16; Luke 4:2). On being offered all the thrones of earth to seize and subdue, Jesus refuses to abandon his call from God by bowing down to Satan: "You shall worship the Lord your God, and him only shall you serve" (6:13; Luke 4:8).

The struggle here portrayed cannot be confined to a single incident. Temptation occurs whenever anything threatens to divert Jesus from his mission as servant of God. Satan appears not once but many times: in John the Baptist, protesting that he should not baptize Jesus; in the disciples, wanting to call fire down upon their enemies, and later, to take up the sword for the sake of the kingdom; in the scribes and Pharisees, trying to trap Jesus in his words; in the multitudes, whose hunger and sicknesses made an incessant demand upon him; in the demonic forces responsible for hunger and sickness; in Peter, attempting to spare Jesus the cross; in his enemies, defying him to come down from the cross— behind these forces stands always the same tempter and the same temptation. Literal though it may be, the temptation in the wilderness is also symbolic. This brief encounter with Satan epitomizes the continual character of Jesus' ministry from its beginning in the waters of Jordan to its completion at Calvary.

4. JESUS THE PROCLAIMER

The arrest of John the Baptist was a crucial event in the life of Jesus. It became the signal for him to renew John's proclamation but with a striking difference. What John had announced as a prophet before the event, Jesus proclaims as one who himself initiates the event. What had been for John a hope becomes in Jesus' word a present reality. Matthew attributes to John and Jesus exactly the same message, "Repent, for the kingdom of heaven is at hand" (3:2; 4:17), but on Jesus' lips these words have a new ring—they actually bestow the grace of which they speak. This is why for Jesus repentance does not require mourning or fasting as it does for John (Mark 2:18 ff.). Such a practice would in these circumstances be inappropriate, for this is God's hour of fulfillment. It is like a wedding, with Jesus as the bridegroom (2:19–20). God has begun to act on behalf of his people Israel. The long-awaited messianic age is dawning. For this reason Jesus assures his followers: "Blessed are the eyes which see what you see! For I tell you that many prophets and kings desired to see what you see, and did not see it, and to hear what you hear, and did not hear it" (Luke 10:23–24; cf. Matt. 13:16 f.).

Jesus' proclamation manifests an authority and certitude that distinguishes his word from all others (Mark 1:22, 27). In the very act of declaring God's forgiveness, he heals the sick and forgives their sins (Mark 2:10 ff.); in announcing the recovery of sight to the blind, he restores to men their ability to see (Mark 10:46–52). Whatever he teaches about God he exemplifies in his own person. It is on behalf of God himself that Jesus welcomes the outcasts, blesses the poor, judges the unrighteous, restores the sinner, or quiets the storm. All that God requires, Jesus now commands. He does not invite men to become disciples; he summons them. He does not speculate on the meaning of the law; he restates and intensifies the law (Matt. 5:17–20). More than this, he *is* the law (5:21 f., 27 f.). Nothing remains outside his jurisdiction—neither the lowest tax collector nor the sacred precincts of the temple.

Inevitably, such a proclamation requires from men a decision about the proclaimer himself. The message and the messenger are inseparably bound together. His "gracious words" (Luke 4:22) actually *bring* the Kingdom to his hearers. In Jesus' baptism, the Spirit of God has anointed him "to preach good news to the poor . . . to proclaim release to the captives and recovering of sight to the blind . . . to proclaim the acceptable year of the Lord" (Luke 4:18–19). Thus God himself draws near to man in the words that Jesus speaks. To speak of Jesus as proclaimer is to speak of God's Kingdom as a present reality. When John the Baptist in prison sends messengers to Jesus to ask whether he is really the coming one, the answer is: "Go and tell John what you hear and see: the blind receive their sight and the lame walk, lepers are cleansed and the deaf hear, and the dead are raised up, and the poor have good news preached to them. And blessed is he who takes no offense at me" (Matt. 11:4–6).

To those who do take offense at him and refuse his summons to the Kingdom, his word becomes a sign of judgment: "The men of Nineveh will arise at the judgment with this generation and condemn it; for they repented at the preaching of Jonah, and behold, something greater than Jonah is here" (Matt. 12:41).

A. The Proclamation

The centrality of the Kingdom in the synoptic Gospels is at least partially measured by the frequency with which the term occurs: fifteen times in Mark, thirty-nine in Luke, and forty-six in Matthew.[7] Yet Jesus never defines what he means by the Kingdom, nor do any of his hearers ask for an explanation. The reason for this is that every Jew already had a clear idea of what this Kingdom meant to him. It was the heart of his life and the object of his hopes. It provided the touchstone for all his piety and religious observances. The Kingdom of God was not subject to the confusions and uncertainties of the changing political order. It was not a realm, or an administrative system like that of the Romans, but simply and solely God's rule over his people Israel. Though the Lord had reigned over his creation from the very beginning, he began to rule over a nation chosen by grace when he made his covenant with Abraham. He had confirmed his promises by delivering the Israelites from the land of Egypt into a land of their own, revealing to them his laws, and raising up for them a priesthood, a temple, and a line of kings. Even though these symbols of his presence sometimes yielded to the shocks and bruises of history, one thing remained sure. Israel's future, like her past, belonged to God. He alone was King. Despite the nation's persistent disobedience and periodic rebellions, God's firm purpose was to prepare Israel for that day when he would exercise his rule directly and totally over the whole world.

The question which divided Israel in Jesus' times, therefore, was not whether God ruled, but when and how his rule would be realized upon the earth. Would his decisive intervention in human affairs come through political developments involving Greece or Rome or Persia, or would it be a purely supernatural event? Could it be hastened by individuals "taking upon themselves the yoke of the kingdom of heaven" in prayer and good works?[8] What would be the role of Israel as a nation? Would God raise up a messianic king of David's line to avenge past wrongs and restore Jewish political fortunes to their former eminence?

Thus Jesus' gospel of the Kingdom spoke not to the fringe of Israel's belief but to its very heart. Even though the idea of the rule of God was an old and familiar one, Jesus' utterance introduced at least three new emphases:

1. There is a shift in the chronology of the Kingdom. Jesus proclaimed its advent to be "at hand." In one respect this word differs not at all from that of the Baptist. Both John and Jesus were prophets of the long-expected age of consummation. The difference was that Jesus' word actually brought to pass the decisive event of which it spoke. Though for Jesus the Kingdom of God on earth remains a future Kingdom, its power is already at work in the present, impinging upon man's actual situation. The Kingdom "exercises its force"* (Matt. 11:12); it has "come upon" men (12:28; cf. Luke 11:20), and is "in their midst"* (Luke 17:20). It can no longer be thought of in future terms alone, for the future belongs only to those who in the present moment welcome its redemptive power.

2. There is a shift in the Kingdom's sphere of penetration. Jesus agrees with John the Baptist and the Old Testament prophets that judgment belongs to the final manifestation of God's rule, but for Jesus this judgment has already begun. His purpose is not only to proclaim God's reign but to effect its penetration in the world, even into the very strongholds of evil. Jesus has bound Satan, the "strong man," entered his house, and robbed him of his goods (Mark 3:27). Those who are demon-possessed are set free (Mark 5:1 ff.); those bound by Satan's afflictions are released (Luke 8:2; 11:14; 13:16); those held by the power of sin are forgiven (Mark 2:9–12; Luke 7:48, 49). When his disciples report their success in such tasks as these, Jesus can say, "I saw Satan fall like lightning from heaven." Whenever Jesus subdues the demonic "by the finger of God," the Kingdom of God has made its presence felt (Luke 11:20; cf. Matt. 12:28). Wherever he acts to effect God's reign, a skirmish with the powers of evil has been waged and won.

3. There is a new understanding of the Kingdom as it affects Israel. There were in Israel those who dreamed of a political rebirth by which their nation would overthrow Rome and become the dominant world power. Jesus himself anticipated a renewed world in which his twelve disciples would one day judge Israel's twelve tribes (Matt. 19:28), but nowhere do his words encourage any materialistic hopes or feelings of nationalism. He never presents himself as an earthly messiah who will lead Israel's armies against its foes to restore on the earth the ancient Davidic line. When the crowds who see his mighty deeds attempt to force the issue by making him king, Jesus withdraws into seclusion (John 6:15). To the

end he maintains that his Kingdom does not arise out of this world or come by human efforts (John 18:36). Nevertheless, the very term "kingdom" had strong political implications that inevitably raised the suspicions of the Roman authorities. However openly Jesus spoke of the Kingdom of God, he could indicate his own relationship to it only in the most guarded tones. His purposes were not political but redemptive in nature; they were not national but universal in scope.

B. CALL TO DECISION

The Jewish background of the Kingdom idea indicates that the purpose of Jesus' proclamation was not to provide new information but to call men to decision. No longer can the hearer afford to equivocate with his life; he cannot "serve two masters" (Matt. 6:24), nor can he postpone taking a stand with relation to the will of God. Because the time for God to judge the world has come, each individual must decide whether or not he is prepared to accept God's verdict upon his life. Such a decision is not to be made carelessly. Like a man planning to build a tower, he who stands before the summons of God must weigh all the implications of his choice (Luke 14:28–30). He must be as prudent as a king confronted by hostile forces who carefully considers the size of his army and, if he is outnumbered, sues for peace while the enemy is still far away so as to avoid the impending disaster (14:31–32). Similarly, if the hearer of the Kingdom proclamation decides to seek God's mercy, he must act now, before judgment comes nearer. If he repents in this decisive moment, God is more than ready to forgive and receive him with joy (15:7, 10).

Such repentance does not, however, take place without far-reaching consequences. The person who chooses this way must recognize that God's presence in a man's life imposes radical demands upon him. Without hesitation he must forsake everything that interferes with the total obedience to which God has called him. Therefore Jesus declares:

> If your right eye causes you to sin, pluck it out and throw it away; it is better that you lose one of your members than that your whole body be thrown into hell. And if your right hand causes you to sin, cut it off and throw it away; it is better that you lose one of your members than that your whole body go into hell (Matt. 5:29–30).

In the face of God's summons no excuses are accepted and no postponements are granted (Luke 14:16–24). Not even the legitimate concerns of family responsibility are permitted to delay the response. For some, the urgency of the hour did not permit even a funeral for one's father or a farewell to one's parents (Luke 9:59–62). To those who thought that their obligation to relatives took precedence over the summons to the Kingdom, Jesus said: "If any one comes to me and does not hate his own father and mother and wife and children and brothers and sisters, yes, and even his own life, he cannot be my disciple" (Luke 14:26). To gain the whole world only to lose one's very life is a poor bargain indeed (Mark 8:36 f.).

Ultimately Jesus speaks of decision for the Kingdom in positive terms. The Kingdom is not for him an agony or stringent burden imposed upon man but the end of all his searching. In speaking against anxiety over material things, Jesus urged his disciples to "seek first his kingdom and his righteousness, and all these things shall be yours as well" (Matt. 6:33). When a man discovers the infinite worth of God's redemptive rule, no sacrifice is too great to make in order that he might receive it. He is willing to become as a little child in his humility toward God and his unquestioning obedience (Mark 10:15). When he sits down at God's banquet table with the outcasts of the earth, the poor, the maimed, and the blind (cf. Luke 14:12–14, 21–24), he considers himself fortunate to have been included with them, knowing that his own attendance is only by the mercy of God. When he has done what God commanded, he acknowledges that he is no more than an unworthy servant (Luke 17:10).

It is at this point that the gospel of the Kingdom which Jesus announced and the gospel of Christ proclaimed in the early church find their closest correlation. In both instances man is addressed by the love and grace of God. He is called to submit to the rule of God and to receive from his King a new life. His hope comes to rest wholly in God's provision for his forgiveness. In the age of the Christian gospel it is important to remember that before Jesus became the one proclaimed, he was the proclaimer. Behind the church's message *about* Jesus can be heard the message *of* Jesus himself, always summoning men to the same decision that became necessary the very first time he said, "the time is fulfilled, and the kingdom of God is at hand; repent and believe in the gospel."

5. THE MIGHTY WORKS OF JESUS

There is nothing more certain in Jesus' ministry than that he accomplished many miraculous feats. This is the unanimous witness of the Gospel writers and their sources, as well as of the summaries of Jesus' ministry recorded in the Book of Acts (e.g., 2:22; 10:38). It is even attested by those least sympathetic to Jesus' activities, the Jewish authorities quoted in the Talmud.[9] The importance of miracles in Jesus' ministry can be seen from the amount of space devoted to them in the Gospels. In Mark, 47 percent of the first ten chapters and 31 percent of the total presentation has to do directly or indirectly with this subject.

One can hardly discuss miracles as if they originated with Jesus. Already in the Old Testament they furnish the basis for God's revelation.[10] To speak of miracle in the biblical context is to speak of God and of his self-disclosing acts. This is what gives meaning to the miraculous and lays the basis for the following definition: A miracle in the Bible consists of a direct act of God (as distinct from something grounded in natural causation) whereby he causes his power over nature and human history to become overtly manifest so that man through grace and by faith might know of God's holiness and love as they find expression in his redemptive purpose. It is this redemptive character of biblical miracles that gives them their importance. The supreme miracle of the Old Testament is God's deliverance of Israel out of Egypt. The centrality of this event does not arise simply out of its "bigness" but from the fact that it marks the climax of God's redemptive activity in the Old Testament. Here God draws near in a special way, for a unique reason, and with momentous results. In their deliverance from the waters of the Red Sea, the Israelites learned the meaning of their past as children of Abraham and found out that their future as well belonged to God.

This Red Sea miracle was no isolated expression of God's redemptive activity but was accompanied by a large number of concomitant signs to support and attest it. These other miracles form an integral part of the total drama that unfolds. They exhibit the dynamics of God's saving act both in its initial stages (e.g., the appearance to Moses in the burning bush and the ten plagues against Egypt) and in its accomplishment (e.g., the miraculous events in the wilderness). As signs, they point beyond themselves to the Person who brought them to pass. Before the Exodus, God tells Israel:

> I am the Lord, and I will bring you out from under the burdens of the Egyptians, and I will deliver you from their bondage, and I will redeem you with an outstretched arm and with great acts of judgment . . . and you shall know that I am the Lord your God, who has brought you out from under the burdens of the Egyptians (Exod. 6:6–7).

In all such incidents, the revelation of God in his miraculous deeds is dependent on whether or not Israel will believe. Belief remains always the choice and obligation of those who experience the mighty works. Miracles in themselves cannot create knowledge of God; only for those who are willing to see and hear can they become occasions for genuine faith: "How long will this people despise me? And how long will they not believe in me, in spite of all the signs which I have wrought among them?" (Num. 14:11; cf. Deut. 29:2 ff.).

It is against this Old Testament background that we must view the miracles of Jesus. By the time he appeared to proclaim the dawn of the Kingdom, Israel had come to realize that her deliverance from Egypt was not merely an act of fulfillment but the renewing of a promise. Her Exodus experience had been a foretaste of that day when God would come down and complete his redemptive purposes. If the Exodus of the past was accompanied by marvelous works, how much more would this be true of the greater Exodus in the future. It was inevitable, therefore, that Jesus' mission should include not only his proclamation of the word of the Kingdom but the accomplishment of certain extraordinary acts by which the presence of God's reign was both attested and effected.

Several crucial utterances of Jesus make it clear that his miracles are ordered events belonging to the Kingdom of God: he not only connects his exorcism of demons with the inbreaking rule of God (Matt. 12:28; Luke 11:20) but characterizes all his miraculous cures in terms derived from Isaiah's picture of the messianic age (Matt. 11:5; cf. Isa. 35:5 f.). These "mighty works" (Greek: *dynameis*) are literally the extensions of the power of God into the world, like his "strong right arm" that led Israel out of slavery in Egypt. Through them and the messenger who performs them God effects his reign among men and in the fullness of time establishes his authority on earth. They are not primarily evidences of Jesus' humanitarian concerns or even expression of his personal triumph. They are genuine messianic acts that point to the messianic Kingdom and beyond the Kingdom to God the King.

It is proper to ask: What do the miracles teach about the Kingdom? In this regard it is significant that, as far as we know, Jesus did not perform a single punitive miracle.[11] This is extraordinary in view of the miracles of judgment against Egypt that preceded the Exodus. In spite of the personal desires of his disciples (Luke 9:54), Jesus acts always *for* man, never *against* him. The soldiers who come to arrest him are not burned up by fire, the people who mock him are not eaten by bears, and the man who betrays him is not swallowed up by the earth. The Kingdom of God is not represented by such acts. Its coming in Jesus means blessing and not cursing, mercy and not wrath. Though judgment is still impending for those who reject the message, all the preliminary manifestations of God's reign are tokens of his love. They are not directed against man but against his enemies: Satan, the spiritual foe, is defeated, physical illness is overcome, and the storms of man's environment are subdued. Thus the miracles of Jesus characterize the Kingdom of God as essentially good news.[12] They depend not on man's righteousness but wholly on the mercy of God. All the multitude who gather to him are fed, and all the sick who come to him are healed. No one is turned away because he is found "unworthy," and no one qualifies because he is "good." However weak and erring their faith, God's mercy avails for all who reach out to Jesus in their need.

Beyond their function as signs of the Kingdom's presence, the miracles also bear testimony to Jesus personally. God's reign is not present in history as a general principle but concretely in Jesus himself. Only he can accomplish its deeds, and its deeds in turn accredit him alone. Though his disciples share in his mighty works, they do so only at his express command and on his authority. His acts, like his words, confront the beholders with the very presence of God. They demand a decision not only about the realities portrayed but also concerning the person in whom they are portrayed. Though the purpose of Jesus' miracles in the synoptic accounts is not specifically to create faith in him, this is the implication of his actions for the disciples. Though not intended as evidences for his divinity, the miracles convey a sense of "otherness" and "uniqueness" which the disciples can associate with God alone.

The reason for this is that several characteristics of Jesus' activity set him apart from all others, past or present, who performed similar deeds. On the one hand, his miracles are seen as immediate consequences of the power of God. They are never ascribed to Jesus' "greater faith," or "more earnest prayers," or "deeper spiritual understanding." They originate solely within the divine purposes; they are manifestations of God's rule in man's history. On the other hand, they do in some sense arise out of Jesus' own will and initiative. His emphatic use of the first person pronoun in this regard is noteworthy:

"But if it is by the finger of God that *I* cast out demons. . . ."

"You dumb and deaf spirit, *I* command you, come out of him. . . ."

"Take heart, it is *I;* have no fear. . . ."

Such uses correspond to his authority in teaching ("But *I* say unto you . . .") and remind us that Jesus often effects the will of God simply by his word

(Matt. 8:8, 16). It is not surprising that the crowds who observed him declared: "We never saw anything like this!" (Mark 2:12). These twin factors in the miracles—the sovereignty of God and the authoritative will and word of Jesus—meant that in these mighty works men were confronted with God himself. Peter's outcry on the catch of fishes, "Depart from me, for I am a sinful man, O Lord" (Luke 5:8), reflects what must have been a common feeling in the presence of Jesus' works.

But if Jesus' acts had this character, why then did not all believe and follow him? Why did even the disciples find faith so difficult? The answer is that for Jesus' contemporaries the miracles proved both too little and too much. They proved too much in the sense that his enemies were unable to ignore him. If he could have been dismissed as a local healer or traveling exorcist, the religious authorities would never have bothered to oppose him. But the facts of the situation did not permit so easy a solution. His remarkable feats demanded some further explanation, and his opponents were constantly under pressure to find an answer. The miracles proved too little in one important respect: whereas Jesus' activity on behalf of others was virtually unlimited, his work on behalf of himself was almost non-existent. Never had a servant of God appeared so weak and helpless to defend himself. To the embarrassment of his followers, Jesus never sought God's power against human opposition. When it became obvious that he who could have accomplished so much was willing to do so little, either for the political ambitions of his friends or even in his own defense, the larger number turned away from him (see John 6:15, 30, 66).

This underlines the most important fact about Jesus' miracles: They do not compel belief or violate the free decision of man either for or against Jesus. They are for those who have eyes to see and ears to hear and a heart to believe what the miracles reveal. In the synoptic narratives Jesus refuses to grant spectacular cosmic signs to impress or overwhelm the curious (Matt. 12:38 f.; 16:4). It is John's Gospel that contributes the insight that the miracles themselves are the "signs" (*sēmeia*) by which the various aspects of the work of God are made known. But even in John this revelatory quality of the miracles is not self-evident to the beholder. Even the disciples do not fully understand until after Jesus has been "glorified" in his death and resurrection.[13] But where faith exists, each miracle becomes an event of revelation. To the Gospel writers the end is known even from the beginning. The cross and resurrection have given meaning to the miracles as signs, even as the signs point the way to the cross and resurrection. For all four Evangelists, the mighty works of Jesus illumine to a major degree the redemptive event that he brings to pass.

6. DISCIPLESHIP

The proclamation of Jesus and his miracles elicited a remarkable early response to his ministry in Galilee. Very quickly his fame drew throngs of people from distant points to hear him. At times the sheer weight of their numbers posed a serious threat to his activities (cf. Mark 3:9, 20; Luke 12:1). These hearers were not all of the same order. They grouped around Jesus in concentric circles. At the far edge stood those labeled in the text as the "crowds" (e.g., Mark 2:13; 4:1; Matt. 4:25 f.). They heard his word gladly—particularly at the outset—brought their sick for healing, and in some instances literally trailed Jesus for several days from place to place (e.g., Mark 8:2). Others became adherents of the message that Jesus proclaimed. In response to his call they followed not merely *after* Jesus as the crowd did but *with* him. They became his "disciples."

Although disciples or pupils were a common enough phenomenon in the Judaism of Jesus' day (cf. Mark 2:18), the discipleship which Jesus invokes demanded a new kind of involvement. The disciples of the Pharisees would apprentice themselves to a rabbi to be instructed in the law so that they in turn might become rabbis and teachers of the people. Discipleship for the followers of Jesus involved a call to a life situation with totally new requirements. Believing the word of the Kingdom, they were now to order their lives according to its demand. In them God's reign was to be realized. They were to live as revolutionaries of the will of God. His law in their lives was no longer to be confined to the routine legal prescriptions and prohibitions common to Judaism. What was required instead was a total response to the complete truth of God.

Secondly, they were summoned to become "fishers of men" (cf. Mark 1:17). The Kingdom meant for them not separation from man's predicament or withdrawal to a desert place, but involvement and mission. As men go to the sea to catch fish, so they were to go to the world and catch men. Their responsibility for the mass of humanity that surrounded them could be compared to that of a shepherd for wandering sheep or of harvesters for ripened fields of grain. They were to proclaim to men the presence of the Kingdom by word and deed (see Matt. 9:36–38).

A third stipulation was that Jesus' disciples abandon all else to be "with him" (Mark 3:14; cf. Matt. 12:30). This requirement makes clear what "following Jesus" really means. Disciples are those who have entered into such a close relationship to Jesus that they literally share his life situation, even at the cost of severe personal deprivation. As Jesus warns one prospective adherent, "Foxes have holes, and birds of the air have nests; but the Son of man has nowhere to lay his head" (Matt. 8:20). Discipleship of this order requires one to renounce all that he possesses; to forsake every human bond that might constrain him, and every form of security. Once made, the decision permits no options: "No one who puts his hand to the plow and looks back is fit for the kingdom of God" (Luke 9:62).

Great as the demands of discipleship are, its rewards are of equal magnitude. To the disciple is given the privilege of knowing the mysteries of God, including not only the particular revelation of the Kingdom (cf. Matt. 13:11) but also the knowledge of God as Father which is reserved for "the Son and any one to whom the Son chooses to reveal him" (Matt. 11:25–27). In contrast with the people at large, and even with the spiritual leaders under the old covenant, the disciples are allowed to see and hear what the Father is making known (Matt. 13:16 f.; cf. 13:10–15). Theirs is an access to the Father enjoyed only by his children. They may ask, therefore, for his "good gifts," confident that their requests will be granted (Matt. 7:7–11; Luke 11:5–13). If they seek his Kingdom, it shall be theirs, and their material needs shall be met as well (Luke 12:31–32; Matt. 6:33).

Although Jesus' disciples are never totaled, their number was not small. Luke refers to them on occasion as a "great crowd" (6:17; 19:37). Among those included are the "twelve" (Mark 3:14–19); a group of seventy who perform a special mission for Jesus (Luke 10:1 ff.); and such individuals as Joseph of Arimathea (Mark 15:43 and parallels), Zacchaeus (Luke 19:2), Nathanael (John 1:45 ff.), Nicodemus (John 3:1 ff., 19:39), and Cleopas (Luke 24:18). The five hundred brethren to whom Jesus appeared after the resurrection (1 Cor. 15:6) probably belong to this number, as well as the one hundred and twenty persons in Jerusalem who gathered before Pentecost (Acts 1:15). Also counted among Jesus' followers was a large group of women who, after the resurrection, are clearly numbered with the company of believers (cf. Luke 8:2; Mark 15:40 f.; Acts 1:14 f.). Since their service during Jesus' lifetime is confined to ministering to him and his disciples and does not involve a direct part in the mission, they are nowhere designated as "disciples."

Early in his Galilean ministry Jesus made a crucial decision regarding those who gathered around him. After a whole night spent in prayer (Luke 6:12 f.), he chose twelve men to become virtually his constant companions. At the beginning they served as his envoys (hence their title, apostles, or "sent ones"). Under his authority they made a circuit of the

Galilean cities, preparing the way for him by healing the sick, casting out demons, and announcing the Kingdom of God (Mark 6:7–13; Matt. 10:1–4). After this they accompanied him on all his journeys, including the final one to Jerusalem.

The choice of the Twelve marks a further disclosure of the meaning of Jesus' mission. The number, apparently, is meant to correspond to the twelve tribes of Israel. Through Jesus' proclamation, Israel is to be reborn as a new people of God now being gathered (cf. Matt. 16:18). The disciples, with the Twelve at the center, constitute the visible expression of this new reality. This new Israel does not exist over against the old, but for it. Renewal is God's intention for all the "lost sheep of the house of Israel" (Matt. 10:6). His promise to the Twelve is that: "in the new world, when the Son of man shall sit on his glorious throne, you who have followed me will also sit on twelve thrones, judging the twelve tribes of Israel" (Matt. 19:28; cf. Luke 22:30).[14]

Beyond this symbolic function, it is difficult (and unwise) to isolate the ministry of the Twelve from that of the rest of the disciples in any rigid fashion. Jesus does not distinguish a number of alternate levels at which men can respond to his call. As the gospel is essentially one word, so discipleship has only one dimension. The demand upon the newest disciple differs not at all from that required of those who stand closest to Jesus. Therefore, the Gospel writers are not overly concerned to indicate whether Jesus is speaking to the inner three (Peter, James, and John), to the Twelve, to the seventy, to all the disciples, or to the later church. What he says to any he says to all (Mark 13:37). Because all equally bear the name of "disciple," this is the prevailing term in the Gospel record.[15]

It is, however, possible to identify at least two characteristics of the Twelve which help us to summarize their activities.

1. The Gospels often present them as acting on behalf of the wider circle of Jesus' followers. Both their individual responses to Jesus' call and their implementation of the mission seem to be regarded as in some sense typical. They consistently serve as a focal point for the larger group. In their personalities and social backgrounds as well they probably represent a cross section of the new community of faith. They are not learned or religious men, but simple fishermen or tax collectors, men of Galilean peasant stock. They illustrate in their lives the principle that Jesus "came not to call the righteous, but sinners" (Mark 2:17).

2. Their proximity to Jesus places them in a better position to receive

instruction from him and to become interpreters of his words and deeds. This is particularly true from the time of Peter's confession until Jesus' resurrection. In this capacity they become apostles in an official or semi-official sense. In the earliest church at Jerusalem they are authoritative teachers and witnesses of the resurrection (Acts 1:22; 2:42). They do not, however, function as an "institution"; the apostolate is not self-perpetuating. In fact little mention of them is made outside of the Gospels and Acts. Organizationally, the primitive church revolves around the leadership of James and the elders at Jerusalem, while the mission functions largely through the efforts of Peter and Paul. Once the twelve disciples had borne witness to Jesus' redemptive deed and passed on the word with which Jesus had instructed them, their function as the Twelve ceased. From then on their task was no different from that of the other disciples. They served as guardians of the tradition as well as missionaries and teachers, but this task, like the others, was shared by all who had been with Jesus from the beginning (cf. John 15:27; Luke 1:2).

7. THE TEACHING OF JESUS

If Jesus' ministry to the crowds who listened to him was one of proclaiming the Kingdom, his ministry to disciples was one of teaching. When we think of this phase of his activity, the Sermon on the Mount comes first to mind, especially such portions of it as the Beatitudes and the Lord's Prayer. Jesus' teaching, however, encompasses a far greater range of material than this, including a large number of parables, innumerable short maxims, and several important interviews and controversies. Almost all of Jesus' activity in fact seems to have been related to his teaching. At the Capernaum synagogue, when he casts an unclean spirit from a man, the onlookers exclaim, "What is this? A new *teaching*!" (Mark 1:27). The authority with which he worked miracles and proclaimed the rule of God was matched by the manner of his instruction. "And they were astonished at his teaching, for he taught them as one who had authority, and not as the scribes" (Mark 1:22; cf. Matt. 7:28). However different his method from that of the Jewish rabbis, Jesus continued to the end of his career to be known as "the Teacher." Although he was known not to have been formally trained in the Pharisaic schools (cf. John 7:15; Mark 6:2), even his enemies addressed him at times with this honored title ordinarily reserved for scholars learned in the law (Mark 12:14, 19, 32).

The element in Jesus' teaching that stands out above the rest for its decisive influence on subsequent generations both inside and outside of the Christian church is his ethical instruction. Despite the brevity of Jesus' words in this area, their impact is so compelling and their appeal so universal that even to the present day scarcely a writer approaches the subject of personal or social ethics without taking account of them. Whatever opposition is expressed toward the Christian faith, and even toward the teaching of Jesus, his statements relating to moral behavior are resisted only by the most radical. Typical of many testimonies of non-Christians is the verdict of the Jewish scholar Joseph Klausner:

> The main strength of Jesus lay in his ethical teaching. If we omitted the miracles and a few mystical sayings which tend to deify the Son of Man, and preserved only the moral precepts and parables, the Gospels would count as one of the most wonderful collections of ethical teaching in the world."[16]

This statement does not mean that Klausner in any way embraces Jesus' "ethical system." On the contrary, having examined it, he finds it so idealistic as to be impractical: "It is not an ethical code for the nation and the social order of today. . . ."[17]

The fact is, of course, that Jesus never intended to promulgate an "ethical code" in the sense in which Dr. Klausner speaks of it.[18] He had no intention of annulling the law of Moses or replacing it with a new moral formulation. Jesus' quarrel was not with law.[19] He did not reject the legal codes of the state (cf. Mark 12:14 f.) or of the temple (Matt. 17:24 f.) or of Moses (Matt. 5:17 f.; 23:2 f.). In many different ways he acknowledged their necessary function. He did not oppose all efforts to relate God's law to the needs of society. Even Moses had done this in allowing divorce to the Israelites ("For your hardness of heart he wrote you this commandment," Mark 10:5).

What he did oppose was the identification of "social ethics" (i.e., the rules governing behavior in the Jewish commonwealth) with the obedience which every true Israelite owed to the revealed will of God. He denounced those who were willing to adopt the mildest of demands made upon a sinful society and make them the final expression of their own conformity to the law. He steadfastly resisted the codification and limitation of the moral law to those "safe" areas worked out by the scribal lawyers. The intent of the Jewish legalists was to "hedge" or protect the law of God by insuring its observance in every situation of life, and to preserve the individual Israelite even against accidental violations of its prescripts. But each attempt to fence the law with more "posts" resulted only in the appearance of more "gaps." Although the law was amplified into 248 commands of things to be done and 365 things prohibited, along with count-less applications and exceptions,[20] there were always more cases not covered by the law than were covered. These gaps became an important element in Jewish casuistry: they allowed the possibility of so treating an individual situation as to remove it entirely from the law's jurisdiction[21] while at the same time leaving room for extra merit to be gained by performing ad-ditional works not required by the law. This naturally led to a system without adequate safeguards against self-righteousness.

Equally oppressive to Jesus in the scribal approach to the law was the confusion of ritual act with moral response to God. Jesus did not oppose ritual as such. He sent the cleansed leper to the temple to offer the pre-scribed sacrifice and be declared ritually clean (Mark 1:44). In his own conduct he appears generally to have observed the rules governing ritual behavior. But to equate ritual compliance with that total obedience to God that can originate only in the heart was for Jesus unthinkable. He had no patience with those who would limit man's moral responsibility only to what was authorized by the ritual code. To forbid healing of the sick on the Sabbath (cf. Mark 3:2–5), or forgiveness of prostitutes and dis-honest tax collectors because they were unclean (cf. Luke 5:29–32; 7:36–50), was to Jesus a clear evidence that the meaning of God's law has been totally misunderstood. Although he did not come to annul the food laws, he knew that not what goes into a man but what comes out of his mouth and heart is what defiles him. Hence Mark could say that by his teaching Jesus "declared all foods clean" (7:19; cf. Acts 10:15).

What Jesus offered as more fundamental to ethics than the legal practices of the Jews can be formulated under two headings: the requirement of a new kind of righteousness exceeding that of the scribes and Pharisees (Matt. 5:20), and the commandment of love.

A. THE NEW RIGHTEOUSNESS[22]

The standard of righteousness that Jesus raises before man is not simply an intensified version of the law. Ultimately the standard is God himself. "You, therefore, must be perfect," he says, "as your heavenly Father is perfect" (Matt. 5:48). What does this mean?

1. It means that righteousness cannot be confined to a stipulated, limited response. Against such reductionism he sets forth his "antitheses," among which are the following:

You have heard that it was said to the men of old, "You shall not kill; and whoever kills shall be liable to judgment." But I say to you that every one who is angry with his brother shall be liable to judgment (Matt. 5:21–22).

You have heard that it was said, "You shall not commit adultery." But I say to you that every one who looks at a woman lustfully has already committed adultery with her in his heart (5:27–28).

2. It means that righteousness is not merely something external, but comes from within the life (Matt. 12:35). Righteous behavior is only possible as the consequence of an inward change. A person must examine his deeds by examining first the source from which they flow. His motivation must not be a desire to be seen and praised by men but solely to glorify God (Matt. 5:16; 6:1–6, 16–18).

3. Nevertheless, righteousness is not purely "internal" in the sense that it can be measured by one's emotions. It must be judged according to the specific deeds it produces. Men, like trees, are known by their "fruits" (Matt. 7:16–20).

4. The new righteousness that Jesus announces claims the whole man. Deeds, words, thoughts—all equally fall under the demand of God. There are no actions, no casual remarks or passing notions, that "don't matter." All of life stands under God's scrutiny: "I tell you, on the day of judgment men will render account for every careless word they utter; for by your words you will be justified, and by your words you will be condemned" (Matt. 12:36–37). What better index is there of a man's true character than his thoughtless word, his unguarded response, or the action for which he has had no opportunity to prepare? At such moments he forgets his pretensions and inadvertently exposes his real self.

5. The righteousness of which Jesus speaks is not merely passive or negative. It is not the cessation of activity but an attitude that seizes the initiative in implementing God's commands. Jesus blesses the "peace makers," not the "peace keepers." The young man who has kept the law from his youth finds that Jesus still requires him to "go, sell what you have, and give to the poor, and you will have treasure in heaven; and come, follow me" (Mark 10:21).

By the same token the most severe denunciations are reserved for those who could have acted but in the name of righteousness did nothing. The unprofitable servant in one of the parables was the one who received a thousand dollars from his master but buried it for safekeeping (Matt 25:18). Because he was unwilling to risk anything, he lost everything even his soul (25:30). In the parable of the good Samaritan (Luke 10:29–37), the priest and Levite were condemned because of what they failed to do. Confronted with an opportunity to act in righteousness, they were unmoved by human need and unmotivated by their own understanding of the law. By doing nothing, they condemned themselves. In God's King-dom no one is pronounced righteous simply by default. Jesus is not satisfied with anything less than the active expending of one's very life.

B. THE COMMANDMENT OF LOVE

If righteousness is to be gauged by the nature of God himself (Matt. 5:48), then it cannot be separated from love. Asked by a lawyer, "Teacher, which is the great commandment in the law?" Jesus answers:

> "You shall love the Lord your God with all your heart, and with all your soul, and with all your mind. This is the great and first commandment. And a second is like it, You shall love your neighbor as yourself. On these two commandments depend all the law and the prophets" (Matt. 22:35–40).

Here Jesus has simply combined two Old Testament precepts (Deut. 6:5 and Lev. 19:18). Love is not for him an independent concept or abstract principle that forms the basis of a new ethical system. It is man's obedient response to God's act and God's demand. Love of God is simply the first requirement of obedience to God, while love for one's neighbor appears as the concrete realization of this obedience in any number of personal life situations.

This does not imply that the two aspects of the love commandment can be identified with one another or even regarded as being of equal ultimacy. Without question, love for God is primary.[23] It precedes and determines an individual's relation to his neighbor. No one who loves his neighbor can say that in that very act, with nothing else necessary, he truly loves God. To do so would be to substitute his relation to his neighbor for his relation to God, and thus in the end to deny God. Rather, he loves God even as the one who is entirely apart from his neighbor. Then, precisely because he does love God, he will love his neighbor as well.

The reverse, however, is also true. A man must not love his neighbor merely as a means by which to love God. His service to the neighbor can never be just for the sake of the Kingdom. This would be to regard his neighbor as a faceless object instead of a fellow human being, a handy vehicle through which to love someone infinitely higher and greater. In the end this person would not be loving his neighbor but denying him.

Jesus' teaching is simple and clear, guarding against both of these aberrations. Man is required to love God *and* to love his neighbor. He is, moreover, to love his neighbor with the same abandonment of self that he practices toward God. Jesus said, "love your neighbor *as yourself*." He who knows what it means to love God will also know what it means to love one's neighbor. He who replaces his self-love with love of neighbor will know to what lengths he must be prepared to go in putting his love to work. Instead of rules, Jesus provides concrete illustrations of what love entails.

Foremost in this respect he points to the practice of forgiveness. He taught his disciples to pray: "Forgive us our debts, as we also have forgiven our debtors," adding the comment: "If you forgive men their trespasses, your heavenly Father also will forgive you; but if you do not forgive men their trespasses, neither will your Father forgive your trespasses" (Matt. 6:12, 14–15). His previous injunction, "Love your enemies and pray for those who persecute you" (Matt. 5:44), clearly presupposes this same unlimited willingness to forgive even those who hate and injure the servants of God. Because it belongs to the love commandment, forgiveness in Jesus' teaching is radically conceived. It sets no boundaries and makes no computations. When Peter asks, "Lord, how often shall my brother sin against me, and I forgive him? As many as seven times?" Jesus replies, "I do not say to you seven times, but seventy times seven" (Matt. 18:21–22; cf. vss. 23–35).

Another related aspect of love is the willingness to refrain from entering into judgment against one's brother (cf. Matt. 7:1–5), and to give preference to one's brother over oneself in situations of potential rivalry (cf. Mark 10:43 f.).

Perhaps the most important illustration of love in action comes in Jesus' parable of the good Samaritan. Here he shows that one's neighbor is that person, whoever he may be, who stands in need of help. Moreover, the love that is owed to the neighbor is radical in its extent and eminently practical in its expression. The Samaritan not only offers to the wounded man personal services by administering first aid but lays at his disposal all of his own resources ("he set him on his own beast and brought him to an inn, and took care of him," Luke 10:34). Finally, he assumes complete responsibility for the man's future (instructing the innkeeper, "Take care of him; and whatever more you spend, I will repay you when I come back," v. 35). There is no sentimentality or emotion, but the doing of what needs to be done. To the one who asks what love of neighbor means, Jesus says: "Go and do likewise" (v. 37).[24]

It is here that the difference between love (*agapē*) as Jesus defined it and love (*erōs*) as it was known in the Hellenistic world, becomes clear *Erōs*, however noble the context in which it appears, is a love which de mands; *agapē* is a love which bestows. It is no accident, therefore, that *erōs* is never used by the New Testament writers. It would never occur to them to confuse two such irreconcilable ideas.[25]

c. The Authority for Jesus' Teaching

Because the range and intensity of Jesus' teaching is unparalleled in Judaism, the question of its source and authority inevitably arises. The question was in fact first addressed to Jesus himself. Clearly, the difference between Jesus and other Jewish teachers is not that his knowledge was drawn from a source different from theirs. He stands in complete agreement with them that the written Old Testament law is the infallible norm for all teaching (Matt. 5:17 f.).[26]

Yet there is a crucial difference between the ways in which Jesus and the scribes conceive of the law's nature and authority. For the rabbis, the law exists as an independent creation of God, supreme and unchanging. For Jesus, on the other hand, the law is always preeminently the law *of God.* Its authority resides not in some independent virtue it possesses, but in the fact that it is God who requires it. That which defines the law and controls its application to human life is the knowledge of God which it provides. Jesus' teaching is therefore based not upon the legal precepts of the Old Testament but upon its *theology* (doctrine of God) in the strict sense.

Jesus does not find in the Scriptures a teaching about God basically contrary to that represented by the scribes and Pharisees. He does, however, heighten the teaching and radically extend its application. From the biblical truth that God is Creator ("bestowing sun and rain upon the just and the unjust alike," Matt. 5:45), Jesus deduces a principle governing the disciples' behavior toward evil men. Similarly, he draws upon the Old Testament's underlying assumption that God providentially cares for the universe and relates it radically to God's tender concern for human needs:

> "Therefore I tell you, do not be anxious about your life, what you shall eat or what you shall drink, nor about your body, what you shall put on. Is not life more than food, and the body more than clothing? Look at the birds of the air: they neither sow nor reap nor gather into barns, and yet your heavenly Father feeds them. Are you not of more value than they?" (Matt. 6:25–26).

Behind these examples of Jesus' sharpening of traditional concepts is his characteristic identification of God as Father. The importance of this title can be seen from its frequency in the Gospels (66 occurrences in the synoptics—45 of these in Matthew alone—and 118 in John). So central is this term in New Testament thought that apart from it Christianity scarcely can be understood. James Moffatt has said that "a religion may call God by several names, but there are titles for God without which it would not be itself, and for Christianity the supreme title is that of 'Father.' "[27]

Jesus was not the first to introduce this way of thinking about God. The idea of the deity as Father and man as his son is found in many religions and occurs in ancient Hellenistic thought. But to Jesus, man is no offspring of the gods. Jesus knows of no divine kinship "in which all men share, who, as reasonable beings in a reasonably governed universe, call God their Father."[28] Here, as elsewhere, Jesus' thought is wholly oriented toward the Old Testament, where God is the Father of Israel by his own sovereign choice and action. By God's election Israel becomes his "first-born son" (Exod. 4:22; cf. Deut. 32:6). This relationship is not the natural consequence of Israel's existence but the supernatural result of God's act. Always in view is the great miracle by which he loved his "son" and called Israel out of Egypt (Hos. 11:1). As a concerned Father, the Lord had sustained his child through the trials in the wilderness (Deut. 1:31), disciplining him that he might learn to keep the commandments (8:5). Though the son rebelled against him, God continued to hope for his return (Isa. 1:2, 18 f.). When he came in repentance, his Father would receive him gladly (Jer. 31:9).

This strand of Old Testament faith underlies Jesus' teaching on God as Father. God is not a heartless judge or unyielding tyrant but one who brings to his adopted sons infinitely more affection and concern than even the best of human fathers show toward their natural offspring. He cannot regard his children in statistical terms: if ninety-nine are safe and one is in danger he reaches out to the weak or straying one in unremitting love until he finds him (see Luke 15:11–32). He knows every circumstance and every need of his children. He provides for their material necessities (Matt. 6:25–34). He strengthens them in persecution and grants them power of utterance when they stand trial before magistrates (Mark 13:11; Luke 13:11 f.).

This Father-son relationship establishes for Jesus' disciples a directness of approach to God unmatched in Judaism and unparalleled (except for Moses and the patriarchs[29]) even in the Old Testament. Later Judaism, with its emphasis on the holiness and transcendence of God, tended to remove him from man's world. Intermediaries (angels, the law, and the temple priesthood) took his place in the common life of Jewish piety.

Jesus' teaching placed God and the worshiper once more on intimate terms. Nowhere is this more evident than in Jesus' instruction of his disciples on prayer. Whereas the devout Jew was expected to address God as "Lord God of Abraham, God of Isaac, God of Jacob! God Most High, Creator of heaven and earth! Our Shield and the Shield of our Fathers,"[30] Jesus tells his followers simply to pray "Father" or "Our Father who art in heaven." Directness and simplicity are to characterize their requests. God's response does not depend on any deserving posture they may assume but solely on the mercy and love of a Father for his own children (cf. Matt. 7:7–11; Luke 18:13 f.).

Although Jesus speaks of God to his disciples as "your Father" and also as "my Father," and alludes in his own prayer life to several of the petitions of the prayer which he taught his followers,[31] he nowhere actually joins with them in addressing God as "our Father." To Mary Magdalene he speaks of "my Father and your Father . . . my God and your God" (John 20:17). This suggests that Jesus understood his own sonship to be of a different order from that of the disciples. They are *adopted* sons who come into a filial relationship through repentance, while Jesus is the *natural* child, the "only" Son who uniquely manifests the Father's character.[32] It is in fact the Father who declares Jesus to be the Son (Mark 1:11; 9:7, and parallels; Matt. 11:27; 16:18).

The sonship of Jesus, moreover, is not something which he achieves through his mission; rather, it is itself the very basis of the mission. It is as the Son that Jesus proclaims the Kingdom. When he speaks of God as his Father, he is not only revealing a truth about God; he is also unveiling a mystery about himself (cf. Matt. 11:25–27). Throughout most of his ministry he hides his sonship beneath the ambiguous term "Son of man."[33] Only from the time of Peter's confession do the disciples even begin to comprehend the full import of Jesus' sonship.[34] Then, as the Gospel accounts draw to a close, the facts become clear: Jesus has been able to teach his disciples as "sons of your Father who is in heaven" (Matt. 5:45)[35] because he is God's Son in a unique sense. They become God's sons through the "miracle" of the mission that Jesus has undertaken in their behalf.

These conclusions underscore the point that it is the disciples alone who are in a position to receive and act upon Jesus' instruction. For them the teaching is but a natural corollary to the proclamation. Its purpose is to provide them with a graphic image of the kind of life to be lived by those who on earth acknowledge the authority of the Kingdom of Heaven. As T. W. Manson expresses it:

The moral standard set up by Jesus is therefore to be conceived as given to the New Israel—the community of his followers—as the Old Law was given to the Chosen People to be the charter of their existence as a people of God. Entrance into the kingdom or discipleship—they come to much the same thing—involves acceptance of the way of life which Jesus teaches and exemplifies. In the result the moral teaching of Jesus appears not as an independent ethic—either "interim" or any other sort—but as an integral part of his conception of the Kingdom of God. It is the way of the Kingdom, the way in which God's will may be done on earth as it is done in heaven, the way in which the subjects of the Heavenly King may show their loyalty to him through obedience to his will.[36]

The moral requirements of Jesus are therefore not meant to be imposed upon society. Apart from that radical change in man's nature and will which comes only through the gospel of the Kingdom, such demands are meaningless. Jesus himself does not approach sinners armed with a set of ethical precepts, but wherever God's forgiveness has become operative Jesus intends his word of command to be imposed radically.

It is not that the disciple is to think he can fulfill this word as if he were already in heaven. This would be self-deception. But he is to be one whose very life articulates the petition, "Thy will be done, on earth as it is in heaven" (Matt. 6:10). Even though such a demand may mean for him suffering or death—as it did for Jesus (Mark 14:36)—if he obeys this word and follows the Son of God he will find that he has taken to himself an easy yoke and a light burden (Matt. 11:25–30).

8. THE CRISIS

Jesus' question to his disciples on the way to Caesarea Philippi, "Who do you say that I am?" points up crisis in his ministry. Whereas previously he had avoided all questions about his identity, he now assumes the initiative in raising this very issue. A turning point has apparently been reached. Jesus now sets about preparing his disciples for the eventualities of a new situation (Mark 8:27–31 and parallels).

The geographic aspect of this crisis is that Jesus is about to conclude his ministry in Galilee and undertake a mission to Judea and Jerusalem (Mark 10:1). His messianic calling allowed no other possibility. How could one sent to the lost sheep of Israel exclude Judea from the sphere of his concern? The testimony of John's Gospel is that prior to his final visit Jesus worshiped in Jerusalem at several of the Jewish feasts. If he did not carry out a full-orbed ministry there, he performed some miracles and at least engaged in a number of significant controversies with Jerusalem authorities (John 2–3, 5, 7–8, 9–10). According to Luke he had preached "in the synagogues of Judea" (4:42). It was therefore no mere display of rhetoric when he cried out: "O Jerusalem, Jerusalem, killing the prophets and stoning those who are sent to you! How often would I have gathered your children together as a hen gathers her brood under her wings, and you would not!" (Matt. 23:37; Luke 13:34).

Beyond this, there was a widespread conviction in Israel that the time of the Messiah's appearing would be the Passover feast and the place would be Jerusalem, "the city of the great King."[37] Even Jesus' disciples, when they drew near to Jerusalem, "supposed that the kingdom of God was to appear immediately" (Luke 19:11). To Jesus as well, Jerusalem had overtones of crisis and finality. He sees its impending destruction as the major sign of the end of the age (Matt. 24:15: Luke 21:20–24). After his resurrection he identifies Jerusalem as the place where the Holy Spirit will be poured out and accordingly instructs his disciples to wait there for the promised gift (Luke 24:49; Acts 1:4). Most important, however, for Jesus' decision to make Jerusalem the new stage of his activities is that it is for him a place of *death*. Not at all intimidated by the cruelest traps that Herod can lay for him in Galilee, he sends word to the king:

> Go and tell that fox, "Behold, I cast out demons and perform cures today and tomorrow, and the third day I finish my course. Nevertheless I must go on my way today and tomorrow and the day following; *for it cannot be that a prophet should perish away from Jerusalem*" (Luke 13:32–33).

Jesus' last trip to the holy city, then, is not simply to add another stop to his itinerary as he goes around proclaiming the Kingdom. He goes to Jerusalem specifically to *die*.

The firmness of his resolve and the intensity of his concentration frightens the disciples (Mark 10:32) and offends the Samaritans, through whose territory he journeys (Luke 9:53). Because his death is to be a redemptive event that will mean life for many, Jesus' concern is to prepare his disciples to accept it as God's saving act. Apart from some understanding by those for whom it is accomplished, the redemptive event would in the end prove meaningless.

This is why Jesus spends so much time on the journey instructing the disciples, especially in certain parables that speak most profoundly of man's need and God's provision (e.g., Luke 15, 16; Matt. 18:23–35; 20:1–16).

In the disciples' hands are the "keys of the kingdom" (Matt. 16:19). Before they can accept what is to happen and then effectively continue the work of Jesus, two basic changes must take place in their thinking.

1. They must be willing to surrender their preconceptions and traditional beliefs about the Messiah and the Kingdom, allowing God to carry out his redemptive purposes in his own way. A suffering Messiah is alien to them; they do not understand how the life of the Kingdom can be realized through the death of the King.

2. They must learn that discipleship is more than simply acquiescence or passive submission before God's act. It means following Jesus to the very end. To accept the fact of a suffering Messiah is one thing; to share in his sufferings is quite another. It is no accident that immediately after Peter's confession, Jesus adds some pointed instructions on total commitment and possible martyrdom (Mark 8:34 ff.). The disciples are not to be mere spectators in the events to come but participants as well.

It is with these considerations in view that Jesus asks his disciples, "Who do you say that I am?" Their temptation is to classify him within one of the traditional categories of Jewish expectation, or as a reembodiment of some figure already known—Elijah or one of the prophets or even John the Baptist (Mark 8:28; cf. 6:14 f.). Resisting this temptation, Peter answers, "You are the Christ" (Mark 8:29), adding, according to Matthew, "the Son of the living God" (16:16). To a degree, Peter is still speaking from the standpoint of his own expectations. "The Christ" is the Messiah, the anointed king of David's line who is to come and restore Israel's fortunes. But in another sense Peter has transcended his inherited presuppositions. He knows Jesus does not fit the traditional mold of messiahship and in his confession witnesses to a uniqueness beyond that which he can rationally explain. It is ultimately *against* his built-in prejudices that he acknowledges Jesus to be the Father's supreme and final revelation to man.

For this reason, Jesus' word of commendation to Peter recorded in Matthew is entirely appropriate: "Blessed are you, Simon Bar-Jona! For flesh and blood has not revealed this to you, but my Father who is in heaven" (16:17). This does not mean that from this moment Peter had abandoned all of his former ideas. His misguided response to Jesus' announcement of impending death (Matt. 16:22) and his absurd proposal of dwellings for Jesus, Moses, and Elijah on the mountain of transfiguration (17:4) furnish ample proof of his limitations. Nevertheless he had by God's grace perceived something which the disciples had not seen before. Though there was much that could not be known until Jesus had been raised from the dead, this breakthrough was of sufficient scope that Jesus could now move directly toward Jerusalem. For the first time he began to speak openly of the events that would take place there.

9. JESUS' PASSION SAYINGS

Peter had confessed Jesus as the Christ; Jesus responded in terms of "Son of man." Peter had thought of messianic glory; Jesus' answer referred to suffering (Mark 8:31 and parallels).[38] Although Mark indicates that Jesus announced these things "plainly" (8:32), little of what he said was really understood by the disciples. When he spoke of his resurrection, they questioned what he meant (Mark 9:10). Scripture and tradition told them Moses and Elijah had been caught up alive into heaven.[39] Why should their Christ have to die and then rise? When the prediction was repeated, Mark notes that they "did not understand the saying, and they were afraid to ask him" (9:32; cf. Luke 9:45).

Why then did Jesus begin here to speak of his passion? It was surely not his intention to provide the disciples with a sort of chronological checklist by which simply to mark off key happenings as they occurred. Such a procedure would make of them analysts or detached observers of Jesus' passion instead of those who grow in faith and understanding through its accomplishment.

Essentially, Jesus' words regarding his impending death and resurrection are prophetic utterances. Their intent, like that of most Old Testament prophecies, is not to record history in advance but to provide certainty that the history, when it happens, indeed represents what God has planned and carried out. The full import of prophecy cannot be grasped until after the event.

The fact that Jesus spoke of his passion in prophetic utterance does not, however, mean that his teaching was inherently vague or unspecific. When the disciples looked back upon his sayings, they were amazed at the openness with which he had spoken and the remarkable manner in which his words were fulfilled. So definite, in fact, are the utterances as they appear in the narrative that it seems difficult to account for the disciples' behavior during the passion. Why, if Jesus spoke in such plain language concerning his betrayal, death, and resurrection, were his followers so poorly prepared for what happened? Why did Jesus' death come as such a surprise to them? Why were they not content to wait out the three-day interval for his reappearance? And when in fact he did arise, why were they so overwhelmed to find the tomb empty that their first thought was that the body had been stolen? (John 20:2; cf. Luke 24:3 f.).

Answers to these questions hinge upon several factors:

1. The synoptic passion sayings are by necessity recorded in an extremely abbreviated form. Inevitably such a reduction tends to produce an oversimplified picture of the events. The items retained were naturally the ones that expressed most clearly and simply the gospel of Jesus' death and resurrection as the church proclaimed it.

2. The Gospel writers have the advantage of knowing the precise events to which every prediction of Jesus referred. Thus their record of these sayings takes on the form in which the disciples came to know the reality of the fulfillment. When the Gospels were written, there was no longer any uncertainty regarding the order of the events or their causal connections. Since their concern was that their readers also perceive the full truth of Jesus' utterances, they could hardly be expected to transcribe the prophecies with less clarity than is embodied in their own postresurrection understanding.

3. On the other hand, the disciples who actually heard Jesus' words had no adequate frame of reference in which to receive Jesus' passion sayings. Nothing in their expectation of a glorious Kingdom of God prepared them for the betrayal, mocking and scourging, murder, and burial of the Messiah, much less a miraculous reappearance after three days. Even though Jesus' proclamation of the Kingdom had brought a new dimension to their thinking and revolutionized many aspects of their spiritual perception, the net effect of all this had not been to diminish their high hopes. On the contrary, it intensified them. The greater their faith in Jesus as God's Messiah, the more certain they were that by a mighty display of power he would vanquish their foes and establish the reign of God in the world.

Accordingly, when Jesus began to speak to them of his passion, their ears were not attuned to hear him as a later Christian would hear. Some of his statements they did not comprehend at all. Others they managed to accommodate to their own expectations. The result was that what happened in Jerusalem turned out to be the exact opposite of their expectation. To understand this it is necessary to examine separately three items within, or related to, the passion utterances.

A. THE SIGN AT JERUSALEM

There was one implication involved in the passion sayings that the disciples must have received with great joy and anticipation: the prospect that they would follow Jesus to Jerusalem (see Luke 9:51 ff.). For them such a journey could only mean that the time had come for Jesus to produce a mighty sign which would inaugurate the Kingdom.

Some time earlier, when the Pharisees had continually pressed for a special demonstration of his authority, he had replied that no sign would be granted except that of the prophet Jonah (Matt. 12:38–40; 16:1–4). The evangelist Matthew knew that he spoke of his resurrection (12:40), and even the disciples understood that he was denying to the Pharisees a spectacular cosmic sign on their terms. Nevertheless, they may well have assumed that in due time an unmistakable sign would be given that would authenticate Jesus' mission once and for all. Furthermore, it was remembered that Jesus had promised to build (or rebuild) the temple. This, also, one of the Gospel writers connects with the resurrection (John 2:19, 21); but Jesus' enemies took his statement very literally (Mark 14:58), and it is not impossible that the disciples did so as well.[40] Finally, Jesus added to his first passion prediction a statement that there were some disciples "standing here who will not taste death before they see the kingdom of God come with power" (Mark 9:1). Such words as these must have engendered in Jesus' followers an overriding optimism. This, coupled with traditional Jewish beliefs, led them to approach Jerusalem fully expecting to witness the Kingdom's final manifestation (Luke 19:11).

The first events that transpired in the holy city only served to heighten this expectation. As Jesus entered Jerusalem riding upon an ass, a great company of worshipers at the Passover feast welcomed him with jubilation, waving palm branches and crying, "Hosanna! Blessed is he who comes in the name of the Lord!" (Mark 11:9 and parallels). Spontaneously the disciples joined the demonstration (Luke 19:37 ff.), filled with joy because now for the first time Jesus seemed willing to accept the acclaim they were all too ready to give.

Soon after his arrival in the city, Jesus entered the temple precincts with violence, overturning the tables of the money changers and driving out those who sold pigeons for sacrifice at high rates to the poor. To the disciples it must have seemed that the one who would rebuild the temple in all its splendor was beginning his purge of the existing structure and hierarchical system. The great sign was under way, and soon all their hopes would come to fruition.

The sad fact was that the disciples had misread the signs and failed to heed the passion predictions. Jesus' rejection and death therefore struck them with a numbing shock. It was a catastrophe that they were unable to assimilate into their thinking. When it was over, they could only say, wistfully, "We had hoped that he was the one to redeem Israel" (Luke 24:21).

B. THE RAISING OF JESUS

A persistent theme in the passion sayings is that he will "on the third day be raised" (Matt. 16:21; Luke 9:22). Jesus was of course speaking of his resurrection, but the disciples seem not to have understood this. Those who took the saying seriously may have related it simply to a coming vindication and exaltation. Of God's people, the prophet Hosea had written: "After two days he will revive us; *on the third day he will raise us up,* that we may live before him" (Hos. 6:2).

But when Jesus speaks of rising *from the dead,* it is beyond the disciples' comprehension. Mark tells us that they "kept the matter to themselves, questioning what the rising from the dead meant" (9:10). Some perhaps took it as a figure of speech,[41] but ensuing events make it extremely doubtful that any of them took the statement literally.

C. HIS SUFFERING AND DEATH

The most characteristic feature of the passion prophecies is the reference to Jesus' rejection, betrayal, and death. Very early in his ministry he had hinted at this theme (cf. Mark 2:20), but now it receives a more extended treatment. It has its place within the great passion utterances (i.e., Mark 8:31; 9:31; 10:33) and elsewhere (see, e.g., Mark 9:12; 10:38; 10:45; 14:17–21, 27). It becomes the subject of a major parable (Mark 12:1–11) and the focus of speech and action at the Last Supper and in the garden of Gethsemane.

Two elements of this teaching may have particularly impressed themselves upon the disciples. (1) They could hardly have missed the conspicuous way in which Jesus connected his afflictions with the purposes of God. Suffering for him was not a detour from his messianic task but the specific requirement of it. It was a divine necessity, the inevitable fulfillment of the Scriptures (see, e.g., Mark 9:12; 14:21, 49). (2) The betrayal and death that Jesus faced was to take place on behalf of others. He would "give his life as a ransom for many" (Mark 10:45) and by his blood established with the disciples a covenant (14:24).

Though the disciples must have heard Jesus teach these things regarding his death, they were severely limited in understanding. They had no ready-made categories by which to accept a suffering messiah. Even though such categories existed in the Old Testament, the disciples inherited patterns of interpretation which dissociated suffering from the person of the Messiah. The language in which Jesus alluded to his death was drawn substantially from the Servant Songs of Isaiah 40–55, especially chapter 53. Jesus' word was that he, the Son of man, must "suffer" and be "rejected," "treated with contempt," "mocked," "spit upon," "scourged," and "killed." Isaiah 53 describes the Servant as "despised and rejected by men," "one from whom men hide their faces," "stricken, smitten by God, and afflicted," "wounded," "bruised," "oppressed," and "afflicted," who "poured out his soul to death." Jesus came "to give his life as a ransom for many" (Mark 10:45), "for many" to pour out his blood (14:24). Correspondingly, the Servant "was wounded for our transgressions, he was bruised for our iniquities; upon him was the chastisement that made us whole. . . . and the Lord has laid on him the iniquity of us all . . . yet he bore the sin *of many,* and made intercession for the transgressors" (Isa. 53:5–6, 12).

The disciples may have observed such correspondences as these. But what did they mean? As far as we can determine, no Jewish interpreter had identified the Servant in his experience of suffering as a messianic figure. Therefore, the passion sayings remained an enigma.

Another notable feature of Jesus' teaching on his death was his distinctive use of the title Son of man. Previously he had applied this designation to himself with reference to his authority (cf. Mark 2:10, 28), but now it became a part of the vocabulary of his impending ordeal. He spoke to the disciples as if they should grasp the import of this title in this kind of context. "How is it written of the Son of man, that he should suffer many things and be treated with contempt?" he asked (Mark 9:12). But this is precisely what they did not know. Did Jesus mean that the Son of man was the same as the Servant? Or was it that in Daniel 7:13 the "one like a son of man" represented the "saints of the Most High" who suffer great afflictions (Dan. 7:21, 25) before they finally receive the Kingdom (7:14, 22, 27)?

Even with all of these difficult theological and interpretive questions in their minds, the biggest stumbling block for Jesus' disciples was his statement that he must die. Peter went so far as to remonstrate publicly on this subject with his Teacher ("God forbid, Lord! This shall never happen to you," Matt. 16:22). Jesus, however, not only persisted in his grim prophecy but connected his death with a betrayal by one of his own disciples! (Mark 14:18). Once again, though they heard his solemn warning, they were psychologically unable to receive it at face value. Each disciple was sure that *he* would never betray Jesus and was unprepared to accept the fact that any of his fellows could do so. If they did not betray him, then certainly he would not die but would live to accomplish the sign of which he had spoken. Nothing that he said could change this fixed impression. So confident were the disciples of their basic assumptions that when they drew near to Jerusalem they actually began to quarrel among themselves as to who should have the places of honor when Jesus entered into his glory (Mark 10:35 ff.). Events were soon to prove them desperately and totally mistaken.

10. THE MISSION TO JERUSALEM

As Jesus traveled from Galilee to Jerusalem, he continued to heal the sick (Mark 9:17–29) and to summon disciples to the Kingdom (10:17–27). If his mind was set on Jerusalem and the hour of his affliction, it was not at the expense of his ministry to the people. In Jerusalem as elsewhere he would seek to gather the lost sheep of Israel.

A. THE ENTRY

Events which held one meaning for the disciples often bore quite another for Jesus. To initiate his final mission he adopted a dramatic plan. Drawing upon a prophecy of Zechariah, he borrowed an ass and, surrounded by his followers and a crowd of curious admirers, rode into Jerusalem. The purpose of his action was to call attention to the prophet's words:

> Tell the daughter of Zion,
> Behold, your king is coming to you,
> humble and mounted on an ass,
> and on a colt, the foal of an ass (Matt. 21:5; cf. Zech, 9:9).[42]

Those in Jerusalem who witnessed or heard of the entry could not help but be reassured and at the same time frightened by it. Those who feared that Jesus' coming would ignite a general uproar in Jerusalem had their anxieties calmed. In spite of Jesus' great popularity and the ambitions of those who accompanied him, he entered Jerusalem in the humblest fashion. No swords glimmered in the sun; no spears reached to the sky. He came as a king of peace "in the name of the Lord" (Mark 11:9). Any who might have expected help from him and his followers to throw off the Roman oppression were doomed to disappointment.

Nevertheless Jesus' procession into the city was threatening to some. It was apparent that he had not come to Jerusalem as a simple itinerant preacher of Galilee. Rather, he came as God's anointed, God's final word to Jerusalem that this was the day of her visitation (Luke 19:44). Like Galilee before her, Jerusalem had now to make her decision. It was the eleventh hour (Matt. 20:9). The king had prepared his marriage feast and the invitations were going out (22:1–10). If the city rejected Jesus' summons, its holy place would be forsaken and utterly destroyed (Matt. 23:28; Luke 19:43 f.).

B. THE CLEANSING OF THE TEMPLE

The second of Jesus' public acts in Jerusalem was as dramatic as the first. In expelling the bankers from the temple courtyard, he reestablished this area as a place for prayer and teaching. These very precincts became the arena for his continuing public ministry. The popular acclaim that had surrounded his entry into the city followed him here as well (Matt. 21:14–16).

If his activity meant mercy for the poor and humble of Jerusalem, it meant judgment for the religious authorities. His effective curse upon a barren fig tree (Mark 11:12–14, 20–21) symbolized the doom of the chief priests and elders of the Jews. They also, as barren ones, were soon to wither away to the very roots of their authority. Stunned by Jesus' boldness, they immediately moved to challenge him (Mark 11:28 f.). Only his popularity with the throngs who gathered in the temple to hear him (Luke 10:19) protected him from arrest. Though the authorities tried to intimidate him and force him from the temple confines, Jesus remained resolute in his occupancy of his Father's house.

C. THE FINAL TEACHING MINISTRY

It is Luke who summarizes most succinctly the daily schedule that Jesus observed during the last week of his life: "And every day he was teaching in the temple, but at night he went out and lodged on the mount called Olivet. And early in the morning all the people came to him in the temple to hear him" (21:37–38).

The extent of the teaching ministry in the temple can be seen from the range of subjects treated. In addition to such familiar themes as the Kingdom, the law, prayer, and faith, special questions were raised on obedience to Caesar, the future resurrection of the dead, and current messianic beliefs. The purpose of much of this interrogation was to trap Jesus into making unwise statements. The Pharisees wanted to elicit comments from him that would antagonize the Roman government (e.g., Mark 12:13–17). The

Sadducees hoped to embarrass him before the multitudes so as to separate him from this support (e.g., Mark 12:18–27). Only then would they feel free to seek his life. Though Jesus was never ensnared by these questions, the pressure from the authorities eventually brought about his arrest and trial. Just as he had predicted, one of his own disciples, Judas Iscariot, betrayed him to his enemies, but not before he had brought his teaching ministry to its conclusion.

D. JESUS AND THE FUTURE

Since each of the synoptic Gospels preserves an eschatological discourse near the end of Jesus' ministry (Mark 13; Matt. 24–25; Luke 21), it can be assumed that at this time he carried on his most extended discussion of the events associated with the end of the age.[43] Like other collections of teaching, this material owes its shape in some measure to the uses to which it was put in the early church. In places we can see how Christians profited from what Jesus said and how they applied it to specific situations—trials before magistrates (Mark 13:9–13), and even the fall of Jerusalem itself in A.D. 70 (Mark says, "let the reader understand," 13:14). Yet in this particular discourse, such tendencies were subject to definite limitations by the very nature of the material.

Even more obviously than in the case of the passion sayings, we are dealing here with prophetic declarations. This time, however, they focus not upon the immediate future but upon the events to come to pass after the completion of Jesus' redemptive mission in Jerusalem. Not only for the disciples who heard but for the post-resurrection church as well, they were at least in part unfulfilled sayings. Even the Gospel writers did not presume to know their final significance. Though they recognized within them allusions to persecutions and to Jerusalem's collapse, they saw much else that transcended known history. They could therefore understand these particular utterances of Jesus only as prophecy. History and eschatology—contemporary events and final events—were so intertwined in the discourse that none—hearers or writers or readers—were equipped to draw a map of the future. They could only stand in openness and faith before a future that belonged to God alone. Jesus cautioned: "But of that day or that hour no one knows, not even the angels in heaven, nor the Son, but only the Father" (Mark 13:32).

Several items within the eschatological discourse deserve special attention. It is noteworthy that in this framework, no less than in the passion predictions, Jesus speaks of himself as the Son of man, now unmistakably depicted in the colors characteristic of the Book of Daniel: "And then they will see the Son of man coming in clouds with great power and glory" (Mark 13:26; cf. Dan. 7:13). This coming is indistinguishable from the final revealing of the Messiah, or "Christ": "And then if any one says to you, 'Look, here is the Christ!' or 'Look, there he is!' do not believe it" (Mark 13:21).

This "advent" (*parousia*, Matt. 24:3, 27) involves both blessing and judgment. For "the elect" (Mark 13:20, 27) it is the end of their great affliction, as they are gathered together into the Son of man's presence. For the world it terminates a series of wars and famines ("the beginning of the sufferings," Mark 13:8) and ushers in the final manifestations of God's wrath: a darkened sun and moon, and stars falling from the sky. The end of the matter is that those who have denied the Son of man will be sent away to eternal punishment (Matt. 25:41), while the righteous inherit eternal life and a Kingdom prepared for them before the world began (Matt. 25:34).

The real purpose of this glimpse into the future that Jesus grants his disciples is not to satisfy their curiosity but to exhort them to watchfulness. This does not mean that they must spend their time scanning the heavens, but that they must conduct their lives continually in view of the Christ's return and their own accountability to him. The Kingdom does not come "with observation"* (Luke 17:21), but its rewards come to those who are faithful and prepared. Essentially the same response is required of the disciples whether the event in question is Jesus' passion or his glorious return. Having commanded them, "*Watch* . . . , for you know neither the day nor the hour" (Matt. 25:13), he was soon to add, "*Watch* and pray that you may not enter into temptation" (26:41).

E. The Last Supper

Conscious that events were now hastening to an end, Jesus prepared to eat a last meal with his disciples. It was to be their celebration of the ancient Passover rite. Although there is some question regarding the actual time when Jesus and his disciples shared this supper,[44] there is no question as to Jesus' intention. Knowing that he would soon surrender his body to death and his blood as a covenant for many, he inaugurated for his disciples a new observance in the context of the Passover celebration. As Israel had been bound to the ancient redemptive event through the Passover, and by its observance reconstituted as the people of God, so Jesus by this last meal bound his followers to his death and provided for their establishment as the new Israel.

At the appropriate time, therefore, Jesus took bread, offered thanks, and distributed it to the disciples with the words: "Take; this is my body" (Mark 14:22). Although much of the significance of his action escaped them, the disciples sensed at least the awful solemnity of the occasion and perhaps also the fact that Jesus was informing them of the redemptive event to come. They may have understood that by sharing this bread with them he was somehow allowing or inviting them to share in that event.

Again, Jesus gave thanks over a cup of wine passed so that all might drink. This wine he called his "blood of the covenant" (Mark 14:24). The ancient covenants had been ratified by the blood of animals, but Jesus assured his disciples a place in the Kingdom by *his own* blood, to be poured out in his death.

In spite of the fact that they all shared in these symbolic elements, there was a terrifying sense in which Jesus was all alone. It was *his* body of which all partook. It was not the blood of many that was to be shed but his blood alone, the one in place of the many. It soon became clear that no one else was able to drink his cup of agony or submit to his baptism of fire (cf. Mark 10:38 ff.; Luke 12:49 f.). As Jesus and his disciples went out from the meal he told them: "You will all fall away; for it is written, 'I will strike the shepherd, and the sheep will be scattered' " (Mark 14:27).

Nowhere was the truth of this prediction more graphically demonstrated than in the incident which followed. According to his custom, Jesus removed to the Mount of Olives to spend the night (Luke 22:39; cf. 21:37). This time, however, he took his disciples with him. As they had shared his bread and cup, he invited them also to share his nightly prayer vigil. Taking his three closest companions, Peter, James, and John, somewhat apart from the group in an olive orchard called Gethsemane, he agonized in prayer to his Father that the cup of wrath that was to be his portion might pass from him—"yet not what I will, but what thou wilt" (Mark 14:36). Three times he repeated the petition; three times also he asked the disciples to watch with him in his hour of trial (Matt. 26:38, 40 f.). But they were unable to rise to the crisis. The discipline of steadfast prayer proved too much for them, and they soon fell asleep. Those who were to become the very pillars of the church had failed their Lord in a moment of truth.[45] The biblical writers could not forget this scandal, nor were they willing to suppress it. With an urgency heightened by this past defeat, they repeated Jesus' words: "Watch . . . lest he come suddenly and find you asleep. And what I say to you I say to all: Watch" (Mark 13:35–37).

F. ARREST AND TRIAL

Ironically it was in the very midst of this internal crisis involving Jesus, his Father, and his disciples that the outward conflict between Jesus and the temple authorities also came to a head. Judas, the betrayer, led to the garden a heavily armed group of chief priests and temple guards. Jesus was arrested and taken that very evening before an examining council (Mark 14:43–53) so that formal charges might be lodged against him.[46] This was no easy assignment, because their real grievances against Jesus were not matters of illegality according to either Jewish or Roman law. It would not have served their purpose to convict him on some minor charge, for it was his death which they desired. When attempts to find satisfactory witnesses failed (Mark 14:55–59), as a last resort they sought to condemn Jesus by his own words. Though he had bested them in the past in questions about messianic belief (cf. Mark 12:35 ff.), they now put to Jesus the direct question whether he was the Messiah (Mark 14:61). Almost any answer would put him in a difficult position. That he was the Messiah, truly conceived, he could not deny, but the high priest's understanding of what "the Christ, the Son of the Blessed," meant was a different matter. Jesus chose another alternative. Without denying his messiahship, he seized the opportunity to express it in his own terms: "I am; and you will see the Son of man sitting at the right hand of Power, and coming with the clouds of heaven" (Mark 14:62). The answer proved totally unexpected to the high priest. Jesus had spoken in these terms to his disciples but not to his opponents. His unequivocal identification of himself with the Son of man of Daniel's prophecy was sheer blasphemy to the examining council. Daniel 7:13 ff. describes a heavenly figure who appears in the very presence of God, the Ancient of Days. More than Davidic messiahship is involved here. "Son of man" in this framework is not an expression for mere humanity but for a glory that belongs to God alone: "And to him was given dominion and glory and kingdoms, that all peoples, nations, and languages should serve him" (Dan. 7:14). All debate over proper grounds of accusation against Jesus was now academic. From his own lips had come blasphemy far beyond any that the high priest had hoped to elicit (Mark 14:63–64). Jesus had virtually made himself God by claiming divine glory and divine prerogatives. All that remained now was to find charges by which he could be successfully accused to the Romans.

The charges finally advanced were that Jesus opposed paying taxes to Rome, that he constantly stirred up the people, and that he claimed to be king of Israel (Luke 23:2). The next morning, when these accusations were brought before Pontius Pilate, the Roman governor, their absurdity was obvious. Pilate quickly ascertained from his interview with Jesus that Jewish dogma and tradition was at stake, not the cause of Caesar (John 18:33–38). Whatever kingship Jesus envisioned, Pilate was satisfied that it was "not of this world" (18:36). It was apparent that the Jewish authorities were attempting to use the power of Rome for their own purposes (Mark 15:10).

Pilate's first word to them, therefore, was that they should carry out their petty counsel on their own (John 18:31). The chief priests, however, were ready to take no such risk, since they were not on firm legal ground in undertaking to administer capital punishment (18:31–32). Instead they simply repeated their charges that Jesus was a Galilean revolutionary. Having no stomach for what the Jews desired, Pilate tried unsuccessfully to refer the whole matter to the Galilean jurisdiction of Herod (Luke 23:6–12). Failing this, he sought to satisfy a now bloodthirsty mob by having Jesus beaten and released (23:16). His last expedient was to fall back on the Roman custom of releasing a prisoner from among the Jews at Passover time as an expression of Roman forbearance (Mark 15:6 ff.). He left it to the crowd to choose who would be released: Barabbas, a radical insurrectionist feared even by the Jews, or Jesus. To his surprise the crowd, at the incitement of the chief priests, called for the release of Barabbas. Pilate, not wishing to prolong an awkward situation, finally yielded.[47]

G. THE CRUCIFIXION

The bestiality of a crucifixion is beyond description. As a death penalty it was reserved principally for non-Roman criminals, especially runaway slaves and insurrectionists. Its purpose was to serve as a grim warning to others who might be tempted to follow the path of violent resistance. Crucifixion normally began with the severest of beatings and ended only after a prolonged and intense period of agony on the cross. Jesus' death followed this pattern. He was beaten so badly that he was unable even to carry his own cross. At the place of execution he was stripped of his garments, fastened to the cross, and lifted up for the final experience of humiliation and torment. Even his clothes were no longer considered his possessions but were callously divided among four soldiers (John 19:23–24). His tormentors appeared for the last time, railing at him and daring him to save himself (Mark 15:29–32). Finally, however, they grew tired of the sport and left Jesus to endure his final afflictions—alone. Standing near in these last hours were Mary, his mother, some other faithful women, and one disciple whom he particularly loved (John 19:26). The rest had scattered like sheep, just as he had predicted—but they would return.

In the hearing of those who were present he spoke what the Christian church has come to call the seven words from the cross. Luke records that Jesus prayed for the forgiveness of his murderers (23:34) and promised eternal life to one of the criminals hanging next to him (23:43). As he breathed his last, Jesus uttered a prayer based on Psalm 31:5 and often used by devout Jews before going to sleep each night: "Father, into thy hands I commit my Spirit!" (Luke 23:46).[48] John preserves a saying by which Jesus committed his mother into the care of the disciple whom he loved: "Woman, behold your son!" (19:26–27), as well as the brief exclamations "I thirst" (19:28) and "It is accomplished"* (19:30). Mark and Matthew indicate that on the cross Jesus quoted from Psalm 22, the great Davidic Psalm of suffering. They cite only the beginning of the Psalm: "My God, my God, why hast thou forsaken me?" The fact that they record this outcry also in the Aramaic language that Jesus used indicates that it was stamped indelibly on the disciples' memories. Nevertheless, there is some possibility that Jesus may have quoted the whole Psalm. If so, then those who thought he cried for water may have heard that part of the Psalm which runs: "my strength is dried up like a potsherd, and my tongue cleaves to my jaws" (Ps. 22:15). Those who thought he was calling to Elijah for help to come and take him down (Mark 15:35–36) may have heard not only the "Eli" of his initial cry (Matt. 27:46) but the prayers to the Lord for help in verses 19–21 of the Psalm. By this cry of ultimate anguish Jesus not only gave vent to the very real separation from his Father that was now his lot but also indicated to all who had ears to hear that David's utterance was now being fulfilled in the things that were happening to him. Whether Jesus cited the whole Psalm or only the first line is, in the end, not too important. For those who know the Psalm the effect is equally overwhelming. Among its words are:

My God, my God, why hast thou forsaken me?
  Why art thou so far from helping me, from the words of my groaning?
O my God, I cry by day, but thou dost not answer;
  and by night, but find no rest (1–2).

But I am a worm, and no man;
  scorned by men, and despised by the people.
All who see me mock at me,

they make mouths at me, they wag their heads;
"He committed his cause to the Lord; let him deliver him,
let him rescue him, for he delights in him!" (6–8).

I am poured out like water,
    and all my bones are out of joint;
my heart is like wax,
    it is melted within my breast;
my strength is dried up like a potsherd,
    and my tongue cleaves to my jaws;
    thou dost lay me in the dust of death.
Yea, dogs are round about me;
    a company of evildoers encircle me;
    they have pierced my hands and feet—
I can count all my bones—
    they stare and gloat over me;
they divide my garments among them,
and for my raiment they cast lots.
But thou, O Lord, be not far off!
    O thou my help, hasten to my aid! (14–19).

I will tell of thy name to my brethren;
    in the midst of the congregation I will praise thee:[49]
You who fear the Lord, praise him!
    all you sons of Jacob, glorify him,
    and stand in awe of him, all you sons of Israel! (22–23).

The italicized expressions indicate that not only in what Jesus was heard to say but in what his enemies did to him at his crucifixion this Psalm's details come to fulfillment: in the rejection and the mocking and the scourging, in the nails that affixed him to the cross, and in the casting of lots for his clothing. The fact that Jesus' very last recorded utterances (Luke 23:46; John 19:30) are words of trust and victory coincides with the fact that Psalm 22 also ends on a triumphant note.

When the soldiers came to break Jesus' legs in order to hasten his death, they found him already dead. As a criminal his body would normally have been disposed of without special attention, but Joseph of Arimathea, a man of some standing in Jerusalem, asked permission to give Jesus a burial. When this was granted, he received the body from the cross, wrapped it in a linen shroud, and placed it in his privately owned tomb. A rock was rolled in place to protect the body, and Matthew notes that soldiers were assigned to guard the sepulcher (27:62–66).

H. THE RESURRECTION

It is exceptionally difficult to reconstruct the sequence of events surrounding Jesus' resurrection. Matters are complicated by the fact that the action proceeds on such a wide front. Many different individuals were involved, and many incidents took place independently of one another and perhaps simultaneously. Each Gospel writer appears to have had access to a considerable amount of information. Probably none of the writers included all that he knew of the event. Characteristically, each selected those incidents which best furthered the overall purpose of his particular Gospel. The inevitable reduction and compression that takes place in such circumstances means that the detailed chronology is beyond what we can reconstruct with any certainty. Nevertheless the main outline of what happened is clear.

On the morning after the Sabbath some of the women went to the tomb to finish the preparation of Jesus' body for permanent burial. When they arrived they found the tomb empty. This they immediately reported to the disciples, recounting also that while still at the tomb they had seen an angel and received the heavenly message that Jesus was risen (Matt. 28:1–8). The disciples discounted this story (Luke 24:11), apparently concluding with Mary Magdalene that the body had been stolen. She too had been at the tomb, at least long enough to see that the stone had been removed, and had lamented, "They have taken the Lord out of the tomb, and we do not know where they have laid him" (John 20:2).

It was within such a context of unbelief that both the disciples and the women met the risen Jesus. The order of the resurrection appearances is extremely problematical. Paul, drawing upon an independent tradition, gives us our most complete account (1 Cor. 15:5 ff.). He lists appearances to Peter, to the Twelve, to more than five hundred brethren, to James, and to "all the apostles," as well as his own distinctive encounter on the way to Damascus. The Gospels also mention appearances to Mary Magdalene and to two disciples on the Emmaus road.

What is important in each of these accounts is that the disciples' belief in the resurrection rested on the empirical experience of meeting the risen Jesus. These were not usually individual encounters but took place in the company of others. Nor were they confined to one occasion, or one place. They extended over a period of forty days (Acts 1:3), and must have encompassed several different kinds of circumstances—table fellowship, for example (Luke 24:30–31), and fishing (John 21:1–14). Though

Jesus had said: "After I am raised up, I will go before you to Galilee" (Mark 14:28), appearances both in Galilee (Matt. 28:16–20; John 21:1–14) and in Jerusalem (Luke 24; John 20) are recorded.

At first the disciples were baffled by this new turn of affairs. Until they understood the Scriptures they were unable to assimilate this unexpected development into their thinking. Gradually, however, in company with Jesus, they began to recognize what Sonship and Messiahship involved for this unique person who was their Teacher and Lord.

NOTES

1. See A. S. Geyser, "The Youth of John the Baptist," *Novum Testamentum,* 1 (1956), pp. 70–75.

2. See W. H. Brownlee, "John the Baptist in the New Light of Ancient Scrolls," *Interpretation,* 9 (1955), pp. 71–90. Of the Essenes, Josephus says, "Marriage they disdain, but they adopt other men's children, while yet pliable and docile, and regard them as their kin and mould them in accordance with their principles" (*War* II, § 120).

3. See especially U. Mauser, *Christ in the Wilderness* (1963).

4. For discussion of this position see T. W. Manson, "John the Baptist," *Bulletin of the John Rylands Library,* 36 (1954), pp. 401 f.; C. Kraeling, *John the Baptist* (1951), p. 204; and T. M. Taylor, "The Beginnings of Jewish Proselyte Baptism," *New Testament Studies,* 2 (1956), pp. 193–98.

5. Cf. John A. T. Robinson, "The Baptism of John and the Qumran Community," *Harvard Theological Review,* 50 (1957), pp. 175–91. For the opposite point of view, see H. H. Rowley, "The Baptism of John and the Qumran Sect," *New Testament Essays,* A. J. Higgins, ed. (1959), pp. 218–29.

6. See Mal. 3:1 ff.; 4:5 f., and cf. J. A. T. Robinson, "Elijah, John and Jesus," *Twelve New Testament Studies,* (1962), pp. 28–52.

7. The preferred expression in Matthew is "Kingdom of heaven," while in Mark and Luke it is "Kingdom of God." Matthew reflects Jewish Christian piety, with its avoidance of the name of God. The two phrases are entirely synonymous.

8. See especially *Mishna Berakhoth* II, 2, and the midrash commentary *Sifré Deuteronomy,* Ha'azinu, § 323, f. 138b, cited in C. G. Montefiore and H. Loewe, *A Rabbinic Anthology* (Meridian Books, 1963), pp. 3, 200.

9. For a treatment of Jewish opinions of Jesus' miracles, see H. van der Loos, *The Miracles of Jesus* (1965), pp. 156–75.

10. Alan Richardson, *The Miracle Stories of the Gospels* (1941), p. 4: "Without the Sign of the Red Sea there would have been no Yahweh-religion, no Israel and no Old Testament."

11. The cursing of the fig tree (Mark 11:13 f., 20 ff.) is a symbolic act directed not against man but for man. Though its symbolism may have to do with impending judgment upon Israel, its purpose for Jesus' disciples is to inculcate faith in God and confident prayer (11:22–25).

12. It may be significant that John the Baptist, whose proclamation emphasized more the aspect of judgment in the Kingdom, performed no miracles (see John 10:41), nor is his Kingdom declaration ever called a "gospel."

13. Similarly, in the synoptics the one legitimate sign is that of Jonah: his three days in the great fish typify the three days of Jesus' resurrection (Matt. 12:39 f.).

14. Note in Acts 1:15–26 the importance laid upon the fact that the number of the apostles must be exactly twelve.

15. The Twelve are referred to as such less than thirty times. "Disciple" (*mathētēs*) occurs more than two hundred and forty times with reference to Jesus' followers.

16. *Jesus of Nazareth* (1929), pp. 381.

17. *Ibid.*, p. 414.

18. For an incisive evaluation of Klausner's approach to the "ethics of Jesus," see T. W. Manson in *The Teachings of Jesus* (1931), pp. 285 f.

19. G. Bornkamm, *Jesus of Nazareth* (1960), pp. 99 f., states: ". . . we must not, of course, forget for one moment that Jesus does not intend to abolish the scriptures and the law, and to replace them by his own message. They are and remain the proclamation of God's will."

20. Read for example the regulations concerning Sabbath observance in the Talmudic tractate *Shabbath*.

21. See for example *'Erubin,* the next tractate after *Shabbath,* which teaches all the ways by which the strict Sabbath observance can, by legal fiction, be avoided.

22. On this subject see H. Branscomb, *The Teachings of Jesus* (1931), pp. 163–77, to whom much is owed in this section.

23. Cf. Bornkamm, *op. cit.,* p. 110.

24. Cf. *loc. cit.*

25. See the work of A. Nygren, *Agape and Eros,* Vol. I (1932), Vol. II (1939).

26. See R. Bultmann, *Jesus and the Word* (1958, reprint of 1934 edition), pp. 61–64.

27. *The Theology of the Gospels* (1912), p. 99.

28. Bornkamm, *op. cit.,* pp. 124 f.

29. See, e.g., Gen. 18:22–33; Exod. 32:31 f.; 33:7–23.

30. See R. Bultmann, *Theology of the New Testament,* Vol. I (1951), pp. 23 f. Cf. *The Standard Prayer Book,* trans. by S. Singer (1922), pp. 53 f.

31. E.g., "Father" (Matt. 11:25; Mark 14:36); "not what I will but what

thou wilt" (Mark 14:36); and "remove this cup from me" (14:36).

32. Though the term "only" or "unique" ("only-begotten" in the KJV) does not occur in the synoptics but exclusively in John (1:14, 18; 3:16, 18), it corresponds in meaning to the term "beloved" in the voice of God at Jesus' baptism and transfiguration (Mark 1:11; 9:7, and parallels).

33. On the ambiguity of this title see E. Schweizer, "The Son of Man," *Journal of Biblical Literature,* 79 (1960), pp. 119–29; and for general background, see O. Cullmann, *The Christology of the New Testament* (1963, first published 1957), pp. 137–92. On the equivalency of "the Son" and "Son of man" in John's Gospel, see below, p. 403.

34. Manson, *op. cit.,* p. 98.

35. Cf. Matt. 13:38, "sons of the kingdom"; 13:38, "in the kingdom of their Father"; 17:26, "the sons are free."

36. *Op. cit.,* p. 295.

37. Matt. 5:35. On these expectations, cf. E. Stauffer, *Jesus and His Story* (1960), p. 83.

38. The three major passion predictions are found in Mark 8:31; 9:31, and 10:33 f., with parallels in Matthew and Luke. The common elements in these are: rejection and being "delivered up," death, and resurrection "after three days."

39. Mark 9:4 ff. Cf. 2 Kings 2:11, Deut. 34:6, and such late Jewish documents as the *Assumption of Moses* (first century).

40. This is especially plausible in view of the possibility that the messianic "son of David" seems to have been expected to build the temple (2 Sam. 7:13; Zech. 6:13).

41. For a use of the metaphor of the raising of a dead body to express spiritual renewal of a people, see Ezek. 37:1–14.

42. John quotes the same text with a note that the disciples understood the significance of what had happened only later, "when Jesus was glorified" (12:15–16).

43. On this discourse see G. R. Beasley Murray, *Jesus and the Future* (1954).

44. The synoptics definitely refer to the meal as a Passover (Mark 14:12; Luke 22:15), while in John the eating of the Passover appears to be still future even after Jesus' arrest (18:28). John in fact seems to correlate the day and hour of Jesus' death with the actual slaying of the Passover lamb (19:14), which took place in the afternoon before the meal (i.e., "between the evenings," Exod. 12:6; *Mishna Pesaḥim* V, 3). It is possible that the discrepancy can be explained on the basis of different calendars (i.e., that the Last Supper was a Passover meal by a sectarian calendar, not by the official Jerusalem calendar). On the whole matter, see A. Jaubert, *The Date of the Last Supper* (1965).

45. This is of course illustrated even more radically in the case of Peter, who actually denied Jesus three times.

46. On matters relating to Jesus' trial, see A. N. Sherwin-White, "The Trial of Christ in the Synoptic Gospels," in *Roman Society and Roman Law in the New Testament* (1963), pp. 24–47.

47. Pilate's vacillation and his final capitulation to the Jewish priests seems strangely out of character with what is known of him from extrabiblical sources (Josephus and Philo). He was a notorious anti-Semite, "naturally inflexible, a blend of self-will and relentlessness," said Herod Agrippa I, according to Philo (*Embassy to Gaius,* 38). His weakness in the case of Jesus probably stems from fear for his own position. The emperor Tiberius had begun to take strong measures against repressive anti-Semitism, and Pilate may have feared lest he antagonize the Jews once too often. The outright threat against Pilate, recorded in John 19:12, "If you release this man, you are not Caesar's friend," may have been decisive.

48. For reference to Jewish custom, see the Babylonian Talmud, *Berakhoth 5a.*

49. It is of some interest that the author of the Epistle to the Hebrews attributes these last two clauses within the Psalm specifically to Jesus (2:12).

SELECTED READING

Bornkamm, G., *Jesus of Nazareth.* New York: Harper & Row, 1961.

Bultmann, R., *Jesus and the Word.* New York: Scribner's, 1958 (1st ed., 1934).

Cullmann, O., *The Christology of the New Testament.* Philadelphia: Westminster, 1963.

Dodd, C. H., *The Parables of the Kingdom,* rev. ed. New York: Scribner's, 1965.

Ladd, G. E., *Jesus and the Kingdom.* New York: Harper & Row, 1964.

Manson, T. W., *Ethics and the Gospels.* New York: Scribner's, 1961.

———— "Materials for a Life of Jesus" in *Studies in the Gospels and Epistles,* M. Black, ed. Philadelphia: Westminster, 1962. Pp. 3–145.

———— *The Teaching of Jesus.* Cambridge: University Press, 1935.

Peter, J. F., *Finding the Historical Jesus.* New York: Harper & Row, 1966.

Ridderbos, H., *The Coming of the Kingdom.* Philadelphia: Presbyterian and Reformed, 1962.

Schnackenburg, R., *God's Rule and Kingdom.* New York: Herder and Herder, 1963.

Stauffer, E., *Jesus and His Story.* New York: A. A. Knopf, 1960.

Taylor, V., *The Life and Ministry of Jesus.* New York: Abingdon, 1955.

Van der Loos, H., *The Miracles of Jesus.* Leiden: Brill, 1965.

VI

THE JERUSALEM CHURCH

WERE it not for his resurrection, Jesus of Nazareth might have appeared as no more than a line in Josephus' *Antiquities of the Jews*—if mentioned at all. The witness of the Gospels is unequivocal that following the crucifixion, Jesus' disciples were scattered, their hopes quenched by the course of events. What halted the dissolution of the messianic movement that had centered in Jesus was the resurrection. In Acts, Luke traces the emergence of the Jerusalem church directly to the resurrection and the events associated with it.

1. THE WITNESSING COMMUNITY

The appointment of his disciples by the risen Christ to be witnesses to his resurrection clarifies an early concern to complete the apostolate. Following the ascension, Peter spoke of the necessity of filling the vacancy created by the death of Judas: "So one of the men who have accompanied us during all the time that the Lord Jesus went in and out among us, beginning from the baptism of John until the day when he was taken up from us—one of these men must become with us a witness to his resurrection" (Acts 1:21–22). The reference to the lordship of Jesus and to the necessity of completing a twelvefold witness provides an insight into the self-consciousness of the group. They are the true Israel, a witnessing community called into existence by God in a day of a new Exodus, when the nations would be gathered from east and west, from north and south, even as Isaiah had recorded:

> Bring forth the people who are blind, yet have eyes,
> who are deaf, yet have ears!
> Let all the nations gather together,
> and let the peoples assemble.

Who among them can declare this,
and show us the former things?
Let them bring their witnesses to justify them,
and let them hear and say, It is true.
"You are my witnesses," says the Lord,
"and my servant whom I have chosen,
that you may know and believe me
and understand that I am He" (43:8–10).

In current Jewish thinking, resurrection and judgment belonged together (e.g., Dan. 12:2–3). The risen Lord provided evidence that the resurrection had begun; his word of appointment, "You shall be my witnesses" (Acts 1:8), marked the fulfillment of Isaiah's oracle of judgment. It was, therefore, necessary to appoint one to take Judas' place in order that the community might be prepared for the judgment. During the paschal feast Jesus had pledged that his disciples would "sit on thrones judging the twelve tribes of Israel" (Luke 22:30). The election of Matthias provided that no throne would be unoccupied.

Both the occurrence of the resurrection and the fulfillment of Scripture were signs that Israel had entered upon a new and final phase in the divine program of redemption. It was a rabbinic dictum that the prophets spoke with reference to "the last days," the period marked by the presence of the Messiah and the fulfillment of the prophetic promises.[1] The apostolic fellowship, conscious of having entered into this period, expressed its whole being in terms of the fulfillment of Scripture. The twin emphases on resurrection and fulfillment appear repeatedly in the witness borne to Israel, a witness summarized in the pointed appeal, "Save yourselves from this crooked generation" (Acts 2:40).[2]

The ascension brought an end to the series of resurrection appearances and prepared for the event of Pentecost when the Holy Spirit was bestowed upon the church. Early rabbinic tradition reflected upon the absence of the Holy Spirit from contemporary Judaism. When Rabbi Eliezer (ca. A.D. 80–120) asked, "Why is the Holy Spirit so little in evidence among Israel?" the response was a citation of Isaiah 59:2, "Your iniquities have separated between you and your God."[3] A frequently repeated account tells of a voice heard from heaven as Pharisaic teachers gathered together: "One man here is worthy of the Holy Spirit, but his generation is not worthy. Therefore, the Holy Spirit shall not be given."[4] In both instances a single point is made: the reception of the Holy Spirit is a communal affair and depends upon a "worthy" generation. Called into existence by the risen Lord, the Jerusalem church received the gift of the Holy Spirit. Their worthiness as a community consisted solely in radical commitment to God's Servant, Jesus. They had entered upon the worthy age, which they designated by the old prophetic phrase, "the last days." This phrase occurs in Peter's explanation for the Spirit's presence within the fellowship:

> This is what was spoken by the prophet Joel:
> "And *in the last days* it shall be, God declares,
> that I will pour out my Spirit upon all flesh. . . .
> *In those days* I will pour out my spirit; and they
> shall prophesy" (Acts 2:16–18).

The post-resurrection situation and the presence of the Spirit made the church a fellowship of believers conscious of living in the last days.

The principal sources for reconstructing the character and life of the Aramaic-speaking Jerusalem church are Acts 1–12, 15, and 21; Galatians 2, and perhaps the Epistles of James and Jude. To judge primarily from Acts, there were in the early church points both of continuity and discontinuity with contemporary Judaism.

2. CONTINUITY WITH JUDAISM

A. ATTENDANCE AT THE TEMPLE

Luke reports that the company of believers continued to meet and worship in the temple.[5] A debated question is whether members of the community also participated in the temple sacrifices. There is in Acts 21 evidence that at least on one occasion the leadership of the Jerusalem church did subscribe to sacrificial practices. Upon the urging of James and the elders, Paul paid the expenses of four men who had taken a Nazirite vow. Paul joined in the purificatory rites with them, and specific reference is made to an offering on behalf of the four (Acts 21:26).[6]

B. ADOPTION OF THE SYNAGOGUE PATTERN

That Christians in Jerusalem organized themselves for worship on the synagogue pattern is evident from the appointment of elders and the adoption of the service of prayer. The provision of a daily dole for widows and the needy reflects current synagogue practice (Acts 2:42; 6:1). It is possible that the Epistle of James reflects the prevailing Jerusalem situation; in James 2:2 reference is made to a wealthy man coming "into your *assembly*." The term translated "assembly" is literally "synagogue," not the more usual word "church." The use of "synagogue" to describe the gathering may reflect an early situation in which Jewish Christians continued to assemble in halls of worship frequented prior to their conversion.

3. DISCONTINUITY WITH JUDAISM

A. JESUS AS LORD AND CHRIST

There were at least two essential points of discontinuity which set the Jerusalem church apart as distinctive from current Judaism. The first is the affirmation that Jesus is the Messiah whom God has raised from the dead. Voiced repeatedly in the mission proclamation of the church, this declaration is couched in language reminiscent of John the Baptist, requiring of Israel repentance and baptism. There is something new in the demand, however. Those who joined the Christian movement have to repent and be baptized *in Jesus' name*. The requirement is striking, for there is no indication that Jesus and his disciples had continued the baptismal rite of John during the Galilean ministry. Its adoption in the early church may be related to the presence of the Holy Spirit within the community, for John had baptized with water in anticipation of the bestowal of the Spirit. Baptism in Jesus' name gave visibility to the confession that Jesus was both Lord and Christ (Acts 2:36) and served to separate the new Israel from its past.

Those who were baptized "devoted themselves to the apostles' teaching and fellowship, to the breaking of bread and the prayers" (Acts 2:42). Christians gathered privately by household groups in which they "broke bread," sharing meal fellowship "with glad and generous hearts" (2:46). It is possible that this reference has in view no more than participation in the daily meal. The allusion to joy and gladness of heart would reflect the fact that the Risen Lord had made himself known to his disciples in the breaking of bread (Luke 24:28–35); or the breaking of bread may refer to the Eucharist, the church's reenactment of the Lord's Supper. In either case, we can still hear echoes of the prayers uttered by the early Christians at their gatherings.

The Apostle Paul twice designates all prayer by the cry "Abba," the Aramaic word for Father (Gal. 4:6; Rom. 8:15). Jesus had cried "Abba" in the Garden of Gethsemane (Mark 14:36), and had taught his disciples to pray in this manner in the Lord's Prayer.[7] This prayer may have been often on the lips of Christians gathered to break bread. Other prayers have been handed down in the language of a primitive eucharistic liturgy found in the *Didache,* a manual for church leaders, written in the first half of the second century:

And concerning the Eucharist, hold Eucharist thus: First concerning the Cup, "We give thanks to thee, our Father, for the Holy Vine of David thy Servant, which thou didst make known to us through Jesus thy Servant; to thee be glory for ever." And concerning the broken bread, "We give thee thanks, our Father, for the life and knowledge which thou didst make known to us through Jesus thy Servant. To thee be glory for ever!" (9:1–3).

This liturgy is unusual in speaking of the cup before the bread. Some prayers in early Christian worship were undoubtedly uttered spontaneously and are lost to us. The oldest liturgical prayer that has been preserved, both transliterated from the Aramaic and translated into Greek,[8] is the invocation *marana tha*, "Our Lord, come!" From *Didache* 10:6 it is known that this prayer furnished the climax to the eucharistic feast. For many phrases of the eucharistic prayers preserved in the *Didache* there are word-for-word parallels in early Jewish prayers. The cry *marana tha*, however, is uniquely Christian. It embodies a distinctive affirmation of the Lordship of Jesus, invoking his presence at the feast and anticipating the day when the church would break bread in the Kingdom of God (Luke 14:15).

B. POSSESSION OF THE HOLY SPIRIT

A second essential point of discontinuity which distinguished the Jerusalem church from contemporary Judaism was the possession of the Holy Spirit. The significance of this fact can scarcely be overemphasized. The bestowal of the Spirit at Pentecost was demonstrated initially through prophetic speech (Acts 2:4–12) and later through wonders and signs accomplished by the apostles (2:43). The intimate association which the Twelve had shared with Jesus was now sustained in the larger fellowship of the Jerusalem church through the Holy Spirit. Luke expresses the quality of life which characterized the church by stating that believers continued in the apostolic "fellowship" (*koinōnia*, Acts 2:42).[9]

What it meant for the community to experience life in the Holy Spirit is set forth in Acts 4:32 ff. There, in a summary statement, we read of the singleness of heart and mind within the company, the power of the apostolic witness, the gracious favor of God upon the group, and the generosity of the company in its willingness to provide for the needy in their midst. All of these factors demonstrated the presence of the Spirit within the church.

4. THE MISSIONARY PROCLAMATION

The essential witness and affirmations of the community were set forth in the proclamation (*kerygma*) and instruction (*didachē*) of the apostles.

The core of the *kerygma,* so far as this can be reconstructed from Acts, consisted of four elements: (1) the assertion that God had fulfilled the prophetic promises, thus introducing "the last days"; (2) the confession that Jesus of Nazareth is God's exalted Servant who has been vindicated through the resurrection; (3) a demand for repentance, together with the promise of the forgiveness of sins; (4) the affirmation that personal witness confirms the proclamation. Each of these elements is significant:

1. The community understood its total existence in terms of the fulfillment of Scripture. Convinced that God was the Lord of history who had revealed his sovereign purpose in the Scriptures, the apostles found anticipations of their own experience, as well as the ground of their confidence, in the biblical text. The fulfillment of the prophetic word in the public ministry, death, and resurrection of Jesus demonstrated that he was the Messiah appointed for Israel: "What God foretold by the mouth of all the prophets, that his Christ should suffer, he thus fulfilled. . . . And all the prophets who have spoken, from Samuel and those who came afterwards, also proclaimed these days" (Acts 3:18, 24). In stressing the fulfillment of Scripture, the leaders of the church emphasized the continuity of the Christian movement with Israel's history of revelation and redemption and their self-awareness of being heirs to the ancient promises. Accordingly, the *kerygma*—and the *didachē* based upon it—was grounded in an authoritative word of revelation.

2. The focus upon "Jesus of Nazareth, a man attested to you by God" (Acts 2:22) as the mediator of salvation, tied the proclamation to history. In the early preaching Jesus was designated Lord and Messiah (2:36), servant of God (3:13, 26), the holy and righteous One, and the author of life (3:14 f.), showing clearly that the historical facts concerning Jesus had been accorded a theological interpretation. The several designations reveal the church struggling to express itself adequately as each embodies one or more aspects of Jesus' person and work. None of them does justice to the fullness of what the church knew of Jesus, but together they portray a divinely appointed Savior, put to death in accordance with God's predetermined counsel but raised from the dead by God, who exalted him as Lord and Christ. The confession that Jesus is Lord especially articulated the primitive Christian confidence in the God who had acted for men's salvation through Jesus of Nazareth.

3. The preaching of repentance and faith solicited a total response to the *kerygma.* Though the terminology is familiar from John the Baptist and from Jesus in his Kingdom proclamation, the emphasis is new. It

falls not on what God is about to do but on what he has already done in raising up his Servant Jesus.

4. The insistence that the apostolic company were witnesses to God's act (cf. Acts 2:32; 3:15) adds the weight of personal challenge to the demand and serves to link the message with history only recently past. The mission proclamation, as understood by the community, concerned the one decisive event in all of human history—God's redemption of man through Jesus Christ.

5. GOD'S HOLY SERVANT JESUS

Perhaps the understanding of Jesus most distinctive to the Jerusalem church is expressed in the phrase "servant of God." In the Old Testament such outstanding men as Moses, Joshua, David, and Daniel were called "servant of God" by virtue of the dignity and honor of their relationship to the Lord Yahweh. The expression is thoroughly Semitic, and its continued use can be traced through portions of the Jewish liturgy which date to the period of the second temple. In Acts, "servant of God" is found three times in a primitive prayer and twice in a sermon attributed to Peter in very early Jerusalem material.[10] These are the only occurrences of the designation in the New Testament. It is found occasionally in documents of the late first and second centuries, primarily in liturgical contexts.[11] Though very ancient in the church, it was soon abandoned, apart from the conservative language of liturgy in which such primitive expressions tended to lie embedded from earliest times.

Within the Jewish-Christian context of the Jerusalem church, a servant Christology emphasized Jesus' dignity. It provided an exact parallel to the Old Testament concept of the servant of the Lord as a designation of honor. Jewish documents from the same general period and later apply the title servant to the Messiah, precisely in contexts which speak of his exaltation and glory, as does Acts 3.[12] But with the rapid growth of the Greek-speaking element of the church, the term apparently came to be considered less adequate, conveying the notion of subordination rather than dignity. Gradually it ceased to be used. Only within the context of the Aramaic-speaking Jerusalem church did "servant of God" continue to be viewed as a meaningful expression of faith. The term affirmed Jesus' messianic authority and implied that the judgment of the Jewish leaders who condemned him had been wrong and had been reversed by God.[13] He was the righteous and greater successor of those distinguished men of the Old Testament whom God had graciously called his "servant." Its meaning in a Jewish milieu was thoroughly consonant with its application by the primitive church to Jesus.

That it was the Palestinian Christians who first adopted the designation is indirectly attested by the disappearance of "servant of God" as a description of the Messiah in the later documents of Palestinian Judaism, apparently in reaction to the early description of Jesus as Servant. Epiphanius reports that the servant title continued to be used by Jewish Christians to the end of the first century. Commenting on the Aramaic-speaking sect known as the Ebionites, this fourth-century church father writes that they proclaimed "one God and Jesus the Messiah as his servant"* (*Panarion* XXIX. 3).

6. CONFLICT AND SUFFERING

Conscious as it was of being the new people of God gathered through the Messiah and in possession of the Holy Spirit, the Jerusalem church inevitably faced conflict. Luke reports the arrest of Peter and John by Jerusalem authorities who warned them not to continue proclaiming the resurrection (Acts 4:1-21). When the warning was not heeded, the apostles were arrested and scourged (5:17-40). Disturbances created by Stephen in synagogue disputes resulted in the expulsion of a large segment of the church from Jerusalem (8:1; 11:19). In the early forties Herod Agrippa I imprisoned some members of the church and executed James the son of Zebedee (12:1-5).

When Peter left Jerusalem, the leadership of the church passed to James, the Lord's brother. He it was who presided at the Jerusalem Council when the question concerning requirements for Gentile admission to the church was raised by the church of Antioch (Acts 15:13-21). In the course of his speech James gave voice to the self-consciousness of the Jerusalem church, and to its basis in the Old Testament. Pointing out that God had spoken in the Scripture about a mission to the Gentiles, he cited Amos 9:11 f. According to the citation God would first rebuild the fallen dwelling of David (i.e., Israel), and when that has been done the way would be opened for Gentiles to seek the Lord (Acts 15:15-18). The fallen dwelling of David was nothing other than the Jerusalem church itself. In God's plan the salvation of Israel was to be the decisive event, for it would make possible the redemption of the Gentiles. James believed that God's intention was that Israel should be saved, precisely through the church, the new Israel now called into being. Such a viewpoint was incompatible with Judaism's view of the election of Israel. Eventually James suffered violent death by stoning, instigated by the Jewish priesthood during a period of confusion when Judea was awaiting the arrival of a new procurator (see below, pp. 326–328).

With the outbreak of hostilities between zealotic factions within Judaism and Rome, the Christians of Jerusalem fled to Pella in Transjordan, gradually returning to the city after its fall and occupation by the tenth Roman legion.[14] Though a succession of bishops continued, and though Jerusalem was honored as the mother church of an expanding mission, it lost the position of ecclesiastical leadership that once had distinguished it. The center of gravity for the Christian movement shifted to such centers as Antioch, Ephesus, and Rome. Theirs were the churches that would shape the doctrine and infuse new life into the mission which had begun in Jerusalem and finally penetrated "to the ends of the earth" (Acts 1:8), the heart of imperial Rome.

NOTES

1. *b. Sanhedrin* 99a, "All the prophets prophesied only in respect of the Days of the Messiah."

2. See, for these two emphases, Acts 2:29–36, 38–40; 3:13–15, 17–26.

3. *Sifré Deuteronomy* on 18:12, § 173.

4. *Tosephta Soṭah* XIII. 3 (pp. 318 f.); *j. Soṭah* IX. 24b; *b. Soṭah* 48b; *b. Sanhedrin* 11a.

5. Luke 24:53; Acts 2:46 f.; 3:1; 5:12, 42.

6. Cf. Num. 6:14 f.; *Mishnah Nazir* VI. 6 ff.

7. See esp. Luke 11:2, where the Old Syriac version retains the primitive Aramaic form, Abba.

8. The Aramaic prayer occurs transliterated in 1 Cor. 16:22 and *Didache* 10:6; it is found translated into Greek (and thence into English) in Rev. 22:20.

9. Cf. 2 Cor. 13:13, "the fellowship brought about by the Holy Spirit."*

10. Acts 4:24–30, "our father David, thy servant . . . thy holy servant Jesus . . . thy holy servant Jesus"; 3:13, 26, "the God of Abraham . . . glorified his servant Jesus. . . . God, having raised up his servant . . ."

11. *I Clement* 59:2, 3, 4; *Didache* 9:2, 3; *Epistle of Barnabas* 6:1; 9:2; *Martyrdom of Polycarp* 14:1, 3; 20:2; *Epistle of Diognetus* 8:9, 11; 9:1.

12. E.g., *IV Ezra* 7:29; 13:32, 37, 52; 14:9; II Baruch 70:9; *Targum to Isaiah* 52:13; 53:12.

13. This is the dominant theme of the Petrine speeches: Acts 2:22–24, 36; 3:13–15; 4:10; 5:30, 31; 10:36–40.

14. Eusebius, *Hist. Eccl.* III, xi–xii; IV, v.

SELECTED READING

Barrett, C. K., *Luke the Historian in Recent Study*. London: Epworth, 1961.

Filson, F. V., *Three Crucial Decades: Studies in the Book of Acts*. Richmond: John Knox, 1963.

Join-Lambert, M., *Jerusalem*. New York: Putnam's, 1958.

Longenecker, R., "Christianity in Jerusalem," in *Paul: Apostle of Liberty*. New York: Harper and Row, 1964. Pp. 271–88.

Munck, J., "Jewish Christianity according to the Acts of the Apostles," in *Paul and the Salvation of Mankind*. Richmond: John Knox, 1959. Pp. 210–46.

Schlatter, A., *The Church in the New Testament Period*. London: S.P.C.K., 1955.

VII

✳

STEPHEN AND THE MISSION
OF THE HELLENISTS

THE transition from the predominantly Aramaic-speaking church, with its center in Jerusalem, to the church of the Gentiles throughout the Empire found preparation in a significant body of Hellenistic Jews who became Christians. Whether it is correct to speak of this group as constituting "the Hellenist church" is a debated point. What is certain is that Luke, who alone describes their existence and mission, found in this group the middle term between Jerusalem and the later church, which was predominantly Gentile in character.

1. "STEPHEN, FULL OF GRACE AND POWER"

When a need arose for more careful supervision of the business affairs of the primitive church seven men were appointed to this task. Each of the seven had a Greek name, and one was a proselyte (Acts 6:1–5); they were Hellenists, members of the international Jewish community resident in Jerusalem, who had become Christians. The common adoption of the Septuagint and of the Greek language for the liturgy served to distinguish their synagogues from those in which Hebrew and Aramaic were in use. It is probable that these seven men had provided leadership for their respective communities prior to their conversion, earning the distinction of a "good reputation." Their activities were by no means limited to business affairs. The Seven stood in much the same relationship to the Hellenists that the Twelve did to the Aramaic-speaking wing of the church. They performed "wonders and signs," entered into synagogue debate, and proclaimed the gospel with power (Acts 6:7–10).

The access which these leaders possessed to the foreign community at

Jerusalem resulted in violent theological conflict between Christian Hellenists and non-Christian Hellenistic Jews from various regions. When formal charges of blasphemy are lodged against Stephen, one of the Seven, he is arrested and brought before the high court, the Sanhedrin. The charges relate to the temple and to Mosaic customs, presumably the ceremonial law (6:9–15).

Stephen's speech before the Sanhedrin is the longest in the Book of Acts. Its great significance is that it affords an insight into the thinking of the Hellenist leadership. The fact that after Stephen's execution large numbers of the community were forced to flee from Jerusalem indicates that Stephen was not merely expressing his own opinion; his viewpoint was that of a significant and influential group. The speech consists of a strong apologetic for the gospel, with a radical reinterpretation of Israel's sacred history.[1]

Three main themes are developed, each of which seems to have been central to the theological understanding of the Hellenists:

1. Stephen insists that from its inception God's redemptive acts had in view a goal toward which all of the divine promises pointed. The goal had been reaffirmed in the life and death of the Righteous One, whom God had sent to his people. In developing this theme Stephen emphasizes the motif of pilgrimage and promise. God called Abraham to an almost continual pilgrimage, sustained by the promise that one day he would possess the land (7:2–5). Implied in this call to the patriarch was the call of Israel to be the pilgrim people of God. But the Israelites resisted pilgrimage and displayed a constant failure to recognize the reiteration of the promise of God. They not only slew the prophets who proclaimed the advent of the Righteous One, but when he came they betrayed and murdered him (7:52).

2. The history of the Jewish people is marked by constant rebellion and resistance to the purposes of God and the deliverers appointed by him. Stephen develops the motif of rejection by men but vindication by God, exemplified in the lives of Joseph (7:9 f.) and Moses (7:27 f., 35 f., 39), but coming to sharpest expression in the crucifixion and resurrection of Jesus. The opposition encountered by Moses is so emphasized that one might easily miss the point that Stephen says almost nothing about Moses as Israel's lawgiver. Through the technique of conspicuous underplay of this element, Moses becomes an example of consistent obedience to God, a prophet who proclaims to all Israel the coming of another prophet like himself whom "God will raise up . . . as he raised me up" (7:37). By

contrast, Israel is seen as the people who have continually despised God, oppressing all of his witnesses—Joseph, Moses, the prophets, and finally the second Moses, the Righteous One who was betrayed and murdered, Jesus of Nazareth. Implied in Stephen's vision of the Son of man standing at the right hand of God (7:55 f.) is the affirmation that the God who vindicated Joseph and Moses has now vindicated Jesus, who stands exalted in the divine presence.

3. God has never confined his call, his revelation, or his blessing to one place; it is wrong to think that a single place, the temple, is now the locus of the divine presence. Stephen notes the call and activity of God in Mesopotamia (7:2), Haran (7:4), Canaan (7:4–7), Egypt (7:22 ff.), and the wilderness (7:30–34); but there appears to be no emphasis upon the holy land of Israel itself. Abraham was merely a transient wanderer in the land (7:4 f.). Only near the end of his historical survey does Stephen speak of the entrance of Israel into the land, and then it is to witness Solomon's attempt to confine God to a permanent house. Yet even Solomon recognized that "the Most High does not dwell in houses made with hands" (7:48). For Stephen, the most meaningful time in Israel's experience was the pilgrimage in the wilderness, typified by the mobility and transitory nature of the tabernacle (7:44–50).

So radical was this interpretation of Israel's past that it enraged the court. Stephen was stoned to death, but his martyrdom laid the basis for a postscript to the history he had so eloquently recited: God would now continue to make himself known far beyond the limits of the temple and the holy land.

2. THE HELLENIST MOVEMENT AND THE YOUNGER CHURCHES

The violent conflict between Stephen and the international Jewish community in Jerusalem resulted in legal action against the Hellenist wing of the church (Acts 8:1). The fact that the apostles remained in Jerusalem at a time when many Christians had to be quickly evacuated from the city suggests that the Judean members of the church were not implicated. The purpose of the Sanhedrin's action—to drive the Hellenists out of the city —was achieved. From this point onward they are never mentioned as constituting a significant segment of Jerusalem Christianity.

Nevertheless, the evacuation resulted in the opening of new areas to the gospel proclaimed by the Hellenists, and several younger churches were brought into being. Philip, another of the Seven, visited Samaria, a stronghold of Hellenistic culture, and then the coastal towns of Palestine before finally establishing his residence in Caesarea (8:5, 40; 21:8). His experience in Samaria with the magician Simon was an incident which could have occurred in almost any great city of the Roman Empire possessing a cosmopolitan, syncretistic population. Philip's conversation with an Ethiopian, who may have been a proselyte to Judaism, illustrated the biblical orientation of the mission (8:35).

Other Hellenists followed routes leading to the large population centers to the northwest, along the Phoenician coast and on into Cyprus (11:19). New assemblies were established in the seaport republics of Ptolemais (21:7), Tyre (21:3 f.), and Sidon (27:3), and in the great Syrian metropolis of Antioch, which was destined to become the new center of Christian Hellenism. It was at Antioch that the dispersed disciples first addressed themselves to Gentiles as well as to other Hellenistic Jews (11:19-20).

A mission to the Gentiles was not a Christian innovation. In this matter, as in many others, Christianity built upon a foundation provided by diaspora Judaism. The word "diaspora" is the technical term for the settlement of Jews outside of Palestine. It must be remembered that the Hellenists had been part of the diaspora. As a result of wars, enslavement, deportation, and voluntary emigration, communities of Jews were established in nearly every major city of Asia, North Africa, and Europe during the Hellenistic-Roman period. It has been estimated that in the first century four to four and a half million Jews were to be found within the Roman Empire.[2] The diaspora constituted the greater part of this number. With the synagogue at its center, Jewish communal life evidenced impressive solidarity even in a Hellenistic setting. Dispersed Jews demonstrated tenacity in the observance of their convictions and were seldom absorbed into the life of the syncretistic peoples of the Mediterranean world.

Against Hellenistic religious and philosophical currents a vigorous apologetic developed. Isolated phrases from older Greek literature were cited to prove that in moments of insight even the Greeks had paid homage to the Jewish doctrine of one God. Early Jewish apologists argued that Greek thought owed much to Moses. Anti-Semitic propaganda was not allowed to circulate unchallenged; Jewish origins, customs, and attitudes were presented in as favorable a light as possible. In general, those elements of Jewish life and thought were stressed which would be acceptable to the enlightened critics of the time.[3] Though Alexandria was the center of this intellectual thrust, the Jewish Scriptures were almost everywhere available in Greek and were expounded each Sabbath in the synagogue. From the first there were curious Gentiles to be found among the congregation, and many of these listeners soon became genuinely attracted to Judaism.

In this way the proselyte movement was born. Gentiles embraced the God of Abraham, Isaac, and Jacob, and renounced their former way of life. While the demand for circumcision prevented many men from becoming full converts, a significant number of Gentiles became loosely attached to the synagogues and began to follow the beliefs and observances of Judaism. These were the so-called God-fearers.[4] From a Jewish perspective, this was the intended result of God's promise to Abraham:

> Go from your country and your kindred and your father's house to the land that I will show you. And I will make of you a great nation, and I will bless you, and make your name great, so that you will be a blessing. I will bless those who bless you, and him who curses you I will curse; and by you all the families of the earth shall bless themselves (Gen. 12:1-3).

Even before Christianity began its mission, the hope that blessing for the nations would be channeled through the children of Abraham was kept alive in Judaism. From the second century, in a Jewish document reflecting upon the fall of Jerusalem, comes a startling statement of God's purpose: "I will scatter this people among the Gentiles, that they may do good to the Gentiles" (*II Baruch* 1:7). Within the context of the proselyte movement to "do good to the Gentiles" was to introduce them to the God of Israel.

The synagogue was as crucial in the Christian mission as it was in the extension of Judaism. Itinerant preachers used the synagogue to gain a hearing for the new faith. According to the Book of Acts, the initial response to the proclamation of life in Christ came from Gentiles living on the fringe of the Jewish community and already committed to the basic tenets of biblical revelation. The Christian mission was able to step into a vital tradition of outreach created and cultivated by diaspora Judaism. When driven from the synagogue the Christians turned to marketplace evangelism or to the use of a lecture hall. But wherever the synagogue was found, there were the traditional language and thought forms, shaped in the interaction of Judaism and Hellenism, which prepared the way for the followers of Christ.

In turning to the Gentiles the Christian Hellenists appear to have been motivated by two major tenets in their theology: (1) The call of God is the call to be a pilgrim, and (2) God does not confine his revelation or presence to any one place. What God ultimately intended was that his word must go to the Gentiles as well as to the Jews.[5]

In cosmopolitan Antioch the way was open for significant developments in the understanding and expression of the primitive messianic faith. The church at Antioch became sufficiently distinguished from traditional and Hellenistic forms of Judaism to be dubbed with a new name by citizens of the city: "in Antioch the disciples were for the first time called Christians" (Acts 11:26). In time a calculated program of missionary expansion was undertaken by Barnabas and Saul, independent of Jerusalem, with Antioch as the base. As an independent venture, it was virtually certain to come into conflict with conservative elements in the Jerusalem church. The success of the mission depended upon a translation and restatement of the Palestinian messianic faith in terms which would be intelligible and meaningful to the mixed populations of Hellenistic and Roman cities where an understanding of biblical categories could not be assumed.

The key to the difference between the Jerusalem church and the Hellenists lies in their contrasting views of the temple. The Jerusalem apostles had remained in that city, apparently waiting for the coming of the Messiah to Jerusalem, the center of the earth from a Jewish point of view. The fact that some elements in the church had continued to attend the temple may even have been due to an expectation that the prophetic word of Malachi 3:1–2 would be fulfilled:

> Behold, I send my messenger to prepare the way before me, and the Lord whom you seek will suddenly come to his temple; the messenger of the covenant in whom you delight, behold, he is coming, says the Lord of hosts. But who can endure the day of his coming, and who can stand when he appears?

There is no awareness in Jewish Christianity that this passage may have been fulfilled when Jesus cleansed the temple.

The Hellenists, on the other hand, proclaimed to all the world the exalted Lord Jesus Christ, the transcendent Son of man, now reigning at God's right hand. This is the point of Stephen's vision just prior to his death.[6] For the Hellenists the glory of the Son of man transcends the glory of the temple. The consequence of Stephen's death was an exodus from the religious community in Jerusalem, with its hopes centering in the temple, to proclaim to the world the Lord of Glory now reigning in heaven. The existence of the people of God was no longer a matter of literal continuity with Israel's past, but of faith in God's act through Jesus Christ. The nation to whom the divine promises had been given was Israel; but those who would participate in their realization would be a people called into being by an act of sovereign grace who responded to that call in faith and obedience. Increasingly they were Gentiles. Thus the Hellenists, with their theological understanding of mission, prepared the way for Gentile dominance in the church.

In historical perspective the function of the Hellenists was to serve as a middle term between Jewish and Gentile Christianity. The Hellenists were Jews, with a broad cultural appreciation for the Greek world. They had embraced the gospel within the context of the Jerusalem mission conducted by the apostles. In typically Jewish fashion they based their theology upon a biblical presentation of Christ. Following the expulsion from Jerusalem, the leaders of the emerging younger churches maintained their contacts with the church there, providing financial aid in periods of famine and poverty. On the crucial matter of Gentile admission to the church, the Hellenists submitted to the judgment of Jerusalem as expressed by James and the elders (Acts 15:13-29). It was the church in Antioch which had requested that judgment and which first received the decree when it was adopted. All of these relationships gave the Hellenists firm contacts with Jerusalem Christianity. Their contacts with the later church, made up almost entirely of Gentile elements, were equally meaningful. The use of the Greek language and the Septuagint, together with a cultural heritage in Hellenism, equipped the Hellenists for the Gentile mission. The theological conviction that God does not limit his revelation and redemption to one place nurtured an intellectual and spiritual climate in which a mission to Gentiles could materialize. From the ranks of the Hellenists were recruited the key missionaries to spearhead the Gentile mission, including Saul of Tarsus.

Being forced to reaffirm in new categories the Palestinian messianic faith for the cosmopolitan Hellenistic cities, where one would encounter both raw and sophisticated forms of paganism, the Hellenists gave shape to much of the material that ultimately became the New Testament. Christianity in its canonical form is less the achievement of Galileans than of these cultivated representatives of international Jewry who became its principal sponsors. The adoption of Greek as the language of the documents which would constitute the new Scripture; the emergence of great church centers in Caesarea, Antioch, Alexandria, Ephesus, and Rome; the nurture and development of the mission theology which informs the New

Testament—these were the lasting achievements of the Hellenists. Theologically the road from Jerusalem to Ephesus, Corinth, or Rome runs through Antioch, the formative center of Christian Hellenism.

NOTES

1. Reviewing the history of the nation from the call of Abraham to the building of Solomon's temple, Stephen addresses himself to three topics:

   1. The patriarchal period (Acts 7:2–16);
   2. Moses and the law (7:17–43);
   3. The tabernacle and the temple (7:44–50).

The initial section introduces the central themes of the speech; the second deals with the charge of blasphemy against Moses; the third with the charge of blasphemy against God and the temple. The thrust of Stephen's address is that it is not he and the Hellenistic Christians who were blasphemous violators of the law, but unregenerate Israel, who in all stages of its history had refused to obey the commandments of God, rejecting both the living oracles delivered by Moses and the deliverers raised up by God.

2. A. Harnack, *The Mission and Expansion of Christianity in the First Three Centuries* (1908), Vol. I, p. 10.

3. On Jewish apologetics see S. Liebermann, *Greek in Jewish Palestine* (1942), pp. 81 ff. Prime examples of such propaganda literature include the *Letter of Aristeas,* the Wisdom of Solomon, and the writings of Philo of Alexandria.

4. See Acts 10:1, 22, 35; 13:16, 26, 43, 50; 16:14; 17:4, 17; 18:7.

5. The means by which this understanding was impressed upon the leadership of the Jerusalem church is set forth at length in Acts 10 in the narrative of the conversion of Cornelius and his household in Caesarea, and is repeated extensively in Acts 11. Cf. also James' viewpoint in Acts 15:14–21, discussed above, p. 131.

6. For several suggestions concerning the significance of Jesus' posture see C. K. Barrett, "Stephen and the Son of Man," in *Apophoreta: Festschrift für Ernst Haenchen* (1964), pp. 32–38.

SELECTED READING

Barrett, C. K., "Stephen and the Son of Man," in *Apophoreta: Festschrift für Ernst Haenchen.* Berlin: A. Toppelmann, 1964. Pp. 32–38.

Downey, G., *A History of Antioch in Syria from Seleucus to the Arab Conquest*. Princeton: University Press, 1961.

Haddad, G., *Aspects of Social Life in Antioch in the Hellenistic-Roman Period*. New York: Hafner, 1949.

Manson, W., "Stephen and the World Mission of Christianity," in *The Epistle to the Hebrews*. London: Hodder & Stoughton, 1951. Pp. 25–46.

Metzger, B. M., "Antioch-on-the-Orontes," *Biblical Archaeologist*, 11 (1948), pp. 69–88.

Simon, M., *St. Stephen and the Hellenists in the Primitive Church*. London: Longmans, Green & Co., 1958.

VIII

PAUL AND THE CHURCH OF THE GENTILES

BY THE end of the first century the church was almost wholly Gentile in character. Isolated pockets of Jewish Christianity continued to exist in Palestine and Syria, but the main currents of Christian life and thought were little influenced by them.

The emergence of the church of the Gentiles posed thorny problems for the leaders of the primitive Christian community. What requirements would be imposed upon Gentiles before they would be admitted to the church? What relationships could exist between Jewish and Gentile congregations and between Jews and Gentiles within the same congregation? In an assembly composed of Gentile believers what would assure continuity with the revelation of God received by Jewish Christianity? More than any other individual, one man wrestled with such questions as these —Saul of Tarsus, known more familiarly as Paul.

1. THE MAN PAUL

The most important bearer of the gospel to the Gentiles was the missionary-apostle Paul. By the time of his death every major church center in Asia and Europe had either been established through his labors or had had some contact with his mission. He made the letter an important vehicle for pastoral supervision and care. Thirteen of the twenty-seven "books" of the New Testament are actually letters Paul addressed to churches and individuals.

An insight into Paul's background and work is afforded by distinguishing three periods in his life. The period of his youth extends to the time when, on a journey to Damascus, he encountered the risen Lord and became a Christian. The data which bear upon this period are meager, and insufficient to determine its duration. The commonly received opinion that Paul was born and grew up in Tarsus, only later coming to Jerusalem to study with Gamaliel, is challenged by the one text which provides specific information about the years of his youth, Acts 22:3. Paraphrased, the text reads: "I am a Jew, born at Tarsus in Cilicia, but my parental home, where I received my early upbringing, was in this city [Jerusalem]; and under Gamaliel, a person well known to you, I received a strict training as a Pharisee, so that I was a zealot for God's cause as you all are today."[1] Thus, while Paul was born in Tarsus, his home nurture and the first molding of his intellectual and spiritual character took place in Jerusalem. Consequently, Paul was not a typical Jew of the diaspora but, as he says, "an Aramaic-speaking Jew born to Aramaic-speaking parents,"* whose one delight was to pursue the righteousness found in the law (Phil. 3:4–6). His outstanding quality was zeal, demonstrated by mastery of rabbinic tradition and violent persecution of the church. Paul's frequent references to zeal may indicate that during this period he patterned his life after the patriarch Phineas, whose zeal for God in violently suppressing idolatry in Israel had won divine approval.[2]

Paul's experience on the Damascus road (Acts 9:1–9; 22:3–21; 26:9–20) resulted in his conversion and introduced the second period of his life, his first years as a Christian. Luke's description of this event as essentially a resurrection appearance is confirmed by the apostle's own references to having seen the risen Lord (1 Cor. 9:1; 15:8). For him this encounter was no less overwhelming than the great theophanies, or visible manifestations of God, in the Old Testament. It was the turning point of Paul's life. Henceforth the zealot for God would be the bondslave of Jesus Christ.[3] The cruel pursuer of Christians would come to pursue the "prize of the upward call of God in Christ Jesus" (Phil. 3:14).

Little is known about the years of this second period spent in the region surrounding Damascus and in the vicinity of Tarsus in Cilicia and Syrian Antioch. Mention is made of a brief visit to Jerusalem after a three-year sojourn in Arabia[4] and Damascus, and then of a significant return visit after fourteen years of labor in Cilicia and Syria (Gal. 1:17–2:1). While the absence of specific data makes this portion of time appear as a mere incident in Paul's biography, its long duration gives it a place of no little significance in the development of his thought. It was precisely during these years, spent in Tarsus, Cilicia, and Antioch, that ample opportunity was provided for contact with Hellenistic culture. It seems highly probable that Paul's knowledge of Hellenism was acquired consciously during this second period in his life, and that from the beginning he viewed Hellenism in the perspective of God's revelation in Christ.

To the third period of Paul's life belong the great missionary journeys throughout Western Asia and Greece, and ultimately his arrival at Rome. This is the time from which his letters come; this is the time referred to almost exclusively in the Book of Acts. The apostle's historical and theological importance may be traced directly to the extensive labors of this final segment of his life, covering about eighteen years. Due to the limitations imposed by our sources, when we speak about the man Paul it is inevitably the Paul of the third period who is in view.

To paint the portrait of Paul with a few deft strokes is an impossible task. He emerges from the sources as a complex, intense individual who resists reduction to a stereotyped image. It is rather in the reconstruction of Paul's involvements in the life situation of the churches that those qualities of personality and emotion will emerge which distinguish him from those among whom and with whom he labored.

2. THE APOSTLE TO THE GENTILES

If Paul sometimes called himself a "bondslave of Jesus Christ," he more often preferred the word "apostle," qualified by a rich variety of terms.[5] His awareness of his place within the purpose of God finds its most pointed expression in his understanding of himself as an "apostle of Jesus Christ." As used by Paul, "apostle" means an authoritative representative of Christ, chosen by God to participate significantly in the vital task of proclaiming the gospel. When Paul designates himself a "called apostle" he means that God has called him to a task of utmost import—to be the ambassador of Christ through whom the powers of the new age have already been released. To be an apostle is to be caught up in the crisis of God's redemptive purpose which will culminate in a new order of existence.

Paul's divine call was to a very specific task. He was set apart to minister to the Gentiles: "he who had set me apart before I was born, and had called me through his grace, was pleased to reveal his Son to me, in order that I might preach him among the Gentiles" (Gal. 1:15–16; cf. Acts 9:15 f.; 22:14 f., 21). The language is reminiscent of the call of the prophet Jeremiah in its twofold stress on consecration to a task prior to birth and appointment to the Gentiles (Jer. 1:5).

In addition to the two primary elements of the necessity of mission to the Gentiles, and the formulation of the call in prophetic categories, Paul's understanding of his task includes a third aspect. He defines his call in priestly terms, as indicated by the italicized words in the following quotation:

> But on some points I have written to you very boldly by way of reminder, because of the grace given me by God to be *a minister of Christ Jesus to the Gentiles in the priestly service of the gospel of God, so that the offering of the Gentiles may be acceptable, sanctified by the Holy Spirit* (Rom. 15:15–16).

Paul pursues his mission conscious of the grace bestowed upon himself and of the responsibility this entailed. His posture is that of a priest before God; his offering consists of the Gentiles. Having completed his mission in the East, he now turns to the West. To be the apostle to the Gentiles implied a sense of urgency, compelling him to press on to new centers where men could be confronted with the claims of Christ.

To Paul, preaching is of primary importance. He writes often of the necessity laid upon him to proclaim Christ. When he reflects on his mission he emphasizes preaching. More important, he speaks of the fulfillment of prophecy. This is evident in Romans 15, where he underscores his ambition to proclaim the gospel where other evangelists have not preached by citing Isaiah 52:15, "They shall see who have never been told of him, and they shall understand who have never heard of him." (Rom. 15:21). Similarly in Romans 10 he speaks of proclamation in the framework of his own mission activity and finds in his personal experience the fufillment of texts closely associated with the Servant of the Lord (Isa. 52:7; 53:1, cited in Rom. 10:14–17). This observation fits into a larger pattern of the utmost importance when it is noted that other texts concerned with the Servant's distinctive ministry are, in the Acts narrative, also associated with Paul's mission (Isa. 49:6 cited in Acts 13:46 f.; Isa. 42:7, 16; 61:1, alluded to in Acts 26:17 f.). This evidence suggests that Paul viewed his own apostolic ministry among the Gentiles as a fulfillment of the prophetic word concerning the Servant of the Lord.

This conclusion is at first sight startling, for it is clear from early Christian preaching that Jesus is the Servant of the Lord of whom Isaiah spoke (see above, p. 109). In Isaiah 42:6–7 God addresses his Servant:

> I am the Lord, I have called you in righteousness,
>   I have taken you by the hand and kept you;
> I have given you as a covenant to the people,
>   a light to the nations [Gentiles],

> to open the eyes that are blind,
> to bring out the prisoners from the dungeon,
> from the prison those who sit in darkness.

The evangelist Matthew cites the larger context of this passage in connection with Jesus' ministry of healing (Matt. 12:17–21), but there is a distinctive note in the text which is not exhausted by Jesus' mission in "Galilee of the Gentiles." The Servant's mission is both to Israel *and* to the nations. He is given by God to be "a covenant to the people" Israel, and "a light to the Gentiles." Jesus had limited his mission to "the lost sheep of the house of Israel" (Matt. 15:24), and his journeys did not exceed the limits of Palestine. But after the resurrection, the commission to go to the Gentiles was made explicit (28:18–20). The evidence falls into place when it is recognized that Jesus *is* the Servant of the Lord who proclaims the good news of redemption to the Gentiles *through* his apostles. He does so especially through Paul. That Paul understood this is clear from an extended passage in his letter to the Romans:

> For I tell you that Christ became a servant to the circumcised to show God's truthfulness, in order to confirm the promises given to the patriarchs, and in order that the Gentiles might glorify God for his mercy. As it is written,
> "Therefore I will praise thee among the Gentiles,
> and sing to thy name";
> and again it is said,
> "Rejoice, O Gentiles, with his people";
> and again,
> "Praise the Lord, all Gentiles,
> and let all the peoples praise him";
> and further Isaiah says,
> "The root of Jesse shall come,
> he who rises to rule the Gentiles;
> in him shall the Gentiles hope."
> May the God of hope fill you with all joy and peace in believing, so that by the power of the Holy Spirit you may abound in hope (15:8–13).

Paul's confidence that prophecy has been fulfilled in his preaching to the Gentiles reflects an awareness that he has been called to continue the ministry of the Servant among the Gentiles. Recognition of this fact explains a prominent feature found in Paul's letters: the stress on suffering as an integral part of apostleship (e.g., 1 Cor. 4:9 ff.; 2 Cor. 4:7 ff.). This emphasis is intelligible when the sufferings of the Servant are recalled (Isa. 53:2 ff.). Identification with the Servant's mission entails suffering.

Paul's apostleship did not go unchallenged in Galatia or at Corinth. It was in response to challenge that the sharpest affirmations of his appointment occur: "Paul an apostle—not from men nor through man, but through Jesus Christ and God the Father, who raised him from the dead" (Gal. 1:1). With evident satisfaction he recalls the circumstances in which the leadership of the Jerusalem church clearly recognized that the gospel for the Gentiles had been entrusted to him in a peculiar sense (2:6–10). From beginning to end Paul knows himself as the apostle to the Gentiles. Yet his pastoral concern and passionate eagerness to reach men for Christ transcended formal distinctions between Jews and Gentiles. His heart was burdened for Israel as well. While he labored primarily among the Gentiles, his missionary pattern was invariably "to the Jew first," and then to the Greeks. His ultimate confidence was in the immeasurable generosity of God's purpose for men.[6]

3. TASK THEOLOGIAN

Paul should be regarded as a "task theologian," that is, one who worked out his theological insights within the frame of reference provided by his task as apostle to the Gentiles. Just as the prophets faced concrete situations in the life of Israel and their writings are accounts of their involvements with the people, so Paul addressed himself to specific mission situations in the life of the church. He was essentially a missionary, not a theologian, in spite of the depth of his theological thought. It was in the context of human relationships, of conflict and anguish, of deep concern for the truth of the gospel and the freedom to which it called men, that Paul found the stimuli for theological reflection. The intensity of Paul's thought and its incisive theological character reflect his particular gifts, his educational background, and the degree to which his mind was keenly disciplined. But in designating Paul a task theologian, the emphasis is intended to fall on the initial term "task." It was this which was primary for him.

It was Paul's task to provide the rationale for the place of the Jews and the Gentiles in the redemptive plan of God, and to insist that the time for the inclusion of the Gentiles was *now*. Each of Paul's epistles bears upon this task in its own way, and must be assessed for its distinctive contribution to his thought. But it was the life situation of particular churches facing concrete problems in the relationship of Jews and Gentiles that prompted Paul's letters. To Paul belongs a unique function, *to initiate* the final stage in the redemptive timetable, the period of the Gentile church (Rom. 9–11), and *to disclose* God's eternal plan which had previously remained hidden, that through the gospel Gentiles have full participation in the life and fellowship provided by Christ Jesus (Eph. 3:1–13).

Though Paul was not the only person who involved himself in the Gentile mission, he was more than merely one among many. Because he radically obeyed the call of God to be the apostle to the Gentiles, it is Paul who furnishes the framework in which the mission to the Gentiles was advanced.

NOTES

1. For this paraphrase and the evidence to support it see W. C. van Unnik, *Tarsus or Jerusalem, The City of Paul's Youth* (1962).

2. Cf. Num. 25:10–13; Ps. 106:31; Sir. 45:23–24; 1 Macc. 2:26, 54, and the interpretation of W. Farmer, "The Patriarch Phineas," *Anglican Theological Review,* 34 (1952), pp. 26–30.

3. Rom. 1:1, Phil. 1:1; cf. Titus 1:1. On Paul's conversion see especially D. M. Stanley, "Paul's Conversion in Acts: Why the Three Accounts?" *Catholic Biblical Quarterly,* 15 (1953), pp. 315–18; and J. Munck, *Paul and the Salvation of Mankind* (1959), pp. 11–35. The relevant Pauline texts include Gal. 1:11–16; 1 Cor. 9:1; 15:8; Phil. 3:7–14.

4. The precise area designated by "Arabia" is uncertain.

5. Cf. Rom. 1:1–6; 1 Cor. 1:1; 2 Cor. 1:1; Gal. 1:1; Eph. 1:1; Col. 1:1; 1 Tim. 1:1; 2 Tim. 1:1; Titus 1:1.

6. Cf. Eph. 3:8; 1 Cor. 9:19–23; Rom. 11:33–36.

SELECTED READING

Knox, W. L., *St. Paul and the Church of the Gentiles.* Cambridge: University Press, 1939.

Metzger, H., *St. Paul's Journeys in the Greek Orient.* London: S.C.M., 1955.

Munck, J., "The Apostle to the Gentiles," in *Paul and the Salvation of Mankind.* Richmond: John Knox, 1959. Pp. 36–68.

Nock, A. D., *Early Gentile Christianity and Its Hellenistic Background.* New York: Harper Torchbooks, 1964.

———— *St. Paul.* London: Thornton Butterworth, 1938.

Van Unnik, W. C., *Tarsus or Jerusalem, The City of Paul's Youth.* London: Epworth, 1962.

IX

✤

FIRST AND SECOND THESSALONIANS— THE DYNAMICS OF THE GENTILE MISSION

THE dynamics of the Gentile mission to an urban center and the problems which emerged with the founding of a church are illustrated by the two letters to the Thessalonians. The first letter affords a glimpse into certain dimensions of the Hellenistic society which the Christian mission sought to penetrate. It indicates the meaning of commitment to Jesus Christ for men among whom idolatry had been commonplace and to whom immorality had been a way of life. The second letter exposes the anxieties raised by the eschatological note in the gospel. It addresses itself to a misunderstanding that had created a crisis within the congregation. Together these documents—our earliest Pauline correspondence—mark the emergence of the letter form as an invaluable aid to the Gentile mission.

1. THE MISSION TO THESSALONICA

When Paul, Silas, and Timothy left Philippi they traveled west along the Egnatian Way, an overland military highway extending some 530 miles from Dyrrhachium on the Adriatic coast across Macedonia to Neopolis and eastward. To judge from Acts (17:1) they were detained neither by Amphipolis, the capital of the district, nor by Apollonia.[1] Their goal was Thessalonica, the most important and populous center in Macedonia at that time.[2] Surrounded by a rich and well-watered plain and situated on the inmost bay of the Thermaic Gulf, Thessalonica was the chief seaport of Macedonia, and after A.D. 44 a naval station for the imperial fleet. Its fine harbor facilities served powerful commercial and trading interests.

As early as 148 B.C., when Macedonia became a Roman province, this city had assumed importance as the administrative seat of the provincial government. Military garrisons were from time to time stationed there. In the closing days of the Roman Republic, as a reward for supporting Octavian and Antony against the assassins of Caesar in the decisive battle of Philippi (42 B.C.), Thessalonica had been declared a free city.[3] This status is reflected in the New Testament references to the popular assembly for the transaction of public business (Acts 17:5) and to the civil magistrates elected by the people, the Greek politarchs (17:6, 8).[4] The city was strongly loyal to Rome and the emperor. Its population included many nationalities and diverse, highly developed religious groups.[5] The presence of an established Jewish community with a synagogue was especially attractive to Paul (17:1).

The apostle arrived in Thessalonica in the year 49[6] and remained there for at least three weeks (17:2). During this time he supported himself and his companions through skilled labor and through gifts received from the Christians in Philippi (cf. Phil. 4:16). He made the synagogue the focus of his mission, explaining from the Scripture that it was necessary for the Messiah to suffer and rise from the dead, and that Jesus is the Messiah (Acts 17:2-3). This phase of the mission met with only moderate success: a few members of the synagogue, several Gentiles who lived on the fringe of the Jewish community, and some women from the better families in the city joined Paul and Silas (17:4). The real thrust of the mission took place in the market, and in the streets and lanes of Thessalonica where the missionaries persuaded a considerable number of Gentiles unreached by the synagogue to abandon idolatry and to confess the lordship of Jesus.

> *Your faith in God* has gone forth everywhere, so that we need not say anything. For they themselves report concerning us what a welcome we had among you, and how *you turned to God from idols, to serve a living and true God, and to wait for his Son from heaven, whom he raised from the dead, Jesus who delivers us from the wrath to come* (1 Thess. 1:8-10).

The italicized words echo the preaching which had undergirded the mission to Thessalonica. Paul had urged "faith in God." The futility of serving dead idols was exposed in the proclamation of the "living and true God," a standard element both in Jewish and Christian polemic against idolatry.[7] The heart of Paul's message, however, was distinctly Christian —the presentation of Jesus as Son of God and Savior. Jesus had been demonstrated to be the Son of God with power through the resurrection

from the dead.[8] Pagan society, with its idolatry and immorality, calls forth
the wrath of God[9]; Jesus alone is the Savior who rescues men from this
coming wrath. Though now in heaven, he will come in sovereign triumph.
When he comes, only the blameless will be exempt from his judgment.[10]

The words that Paul chooses to shape his message exhibit his alertness
to the conventions of the society in which he labors. In speaking of Jesus'
coming (*parousia*) as an awesome event, he employs terms known from
inscriptions at Thessalonica and elsewhere. During official visits of a ruling
monarch to a Hellenistic city, a public ceremony based on long sanctioned
custom would take place. The populace would go outside the city walls to
meet the ruler and form a triumphal procession escorting him back into
the city. The great fourth-century preacher John Chrysostom, commenting
on 1 Thessalonians 4:17, enables us to sense the majesty of Paul's description of Jesus' *parousia*:

> When a king made his entrance into a city, certain ones among the dignitaries,
> the chief officials and those who were in the good graces of the sovereign
> would go forth from the city in order to meet him, while the guilty and
> the criminals are kept within the city where they await the sentence which the
> king will pronounce. In the same manner, when the Lord will come, the
> first group will go forth to meet him with assurance in the midst of the air,
> while the guilty and those who are conscious of having committed many sins
> will await below their judge.[11]

Throughout the first letter there is also evidence of the exhortation and
instruction which Paul gave to those who came to faith. The believers were
charged "to lead a life worthy of God, who calls you into his own kingdom
and glory" (2:12). They were taught to expect trial and affliction for the
sake of the gospel (3:3–4; cf. Acts 14:22). Practical instruction extended
to such important areas as personal morality and holiness (1 Thess. 4:1–8),
love for one another (4:9), social conduct (4:11) and work (4:11–12;
cf. 2 Thess. 3:10). Distinctly eschatological teaching was also presented
(1 Thess. 5:1; cf. 2 Thess. 2:5), not as an end in itself but to encourage
the new converts to persevere in the faith.

Shortly after Paul's synagogue ministry in Thessalonica, certain Jewish
leaders instigated a serious disturbance by enlisting a crowd of the rabble.
Jason, whose house appears to have been the center of the mission, was
dragged before the public assembly along with several other Christians.
The charge was ominous: "they are all acting against the decrees of Caesar,[12]
saying that there is another king, Jesus" (Acts 17:5–8). While the civic
authorities did not take seriously this accusation of treason, it was impera-

tive that there be no unnecessary disturbance in the city if it was to retain its free status. Jason was made to provide security that there would be no further disturbances; Paul and Silas left the city by night (17:10). Nevertheless, the church had been established sufficiently to permit the appointment of elders to labor in the work of the Lord (cf. 1 Thess. 5:12-13).

2. THE REPORT FROM THESSALONICA

Paul moved on to Berea, Athens, and finally Corinth (Acts 17:10–18:1). Although the mission to Thessalonica had been initially successful, he remained anxious about his converts. When it became impossible to satisfy a strong desire to return to Thessalonica ("Satan hindered us," 1 Thess. 2:18), the apostle while yet in Athens dispatched Timothy (3:1–3), who afterward rejoined Paul in Corinth. His report greatly encouraged the apostle, but there was also sobering news.

The disruptions and persecution which had plagued Paul's labors continued to afflict the young church. The Thessalonians had suffered derision and harassment from their "own countrymen" (2:14). By way of encouragement Paul reminds his readers that they had received the word of God "in much affliction, with joy inspired by the Holy Spirit" (1:6). The shameful treatment of the missionaries at Philippi as well as the opposition encountered at Thessalonica was well known to them (2:1–2). Opposition was no more than what they could expect: "when we were with you, we told you beforehand that we were to suffer affliction; just as it has come to pass, and as you know" (3:4).

Potentially far more destructive were rumors impugning Paul's integrity and that of his gospel. It was asserted that Paul's religious appeal was grounded in error. The gospel was not a divine reality but a human delusion. The apostle was being compared to roving charlatans who were a part of the scenery of any great Hellenistic city, exploiting superstition and making themselves a burden to the people.[13] Such men were impostors who moved from town to town, working solely for their own advantage, with no real concern for those who flocked to them. That this was true of Paul, it was suggested, was blatantly clear from the fact that he had departed by night and had not returned. Moreover, he would not return. It was insinuated further that Paul's enthusiastic gospel of the Spirit had led to impurity and excesses.

Paul's answer was forthright. As to his message, Paul reminds the Thessalonians that "our gospel came to you not only in word, but also in power and in the Holy Spirit and with full conviction" (1:5). It is not "the word of men but . . . the word of God, which is at work in you believers" (2:13).

Regarding his motive, Paul responds in candidness, "You know what kind of men we proved to be among you for your sake" (1:5). The believers could remember how he had worked night and day at his own trade to support his company in order not to be a burden upon any of the impoverished people of the city (2:9). Was Paul's failure to return a proof that he cared nothing for his converts? When he had been separated from them ("in person not in heart") even for a short time, he had eagerly desired to return and see them face to face, "because we wanted to come to you—I, Paul, again and again—but Satan hindered us" (2:17–18; cf. 3:6, 9–11).

On the question of his behavior Paul's answer is plain: "You are witnesses, and God also, how holy and righteous and blameless was our behavior to you believers" (2:10). In love and tenderness Paul had played the role of a nurse caring for her children (2:7). But on the matter of purity Paul had acted as a father with his children, charging each one to lead a life worthy of God, who had called them into his own Kingdom (2:11–12). Paul's final prayer for the believers in this section of the letter is that God may establish their hearts "unblamable in holiness" (3:13).

3. THE WEAK, THE FAINTHEARTED, AND THE IDLE

Paul's desire to return to Thessalonica reflected a concern to supply something lacking in the faith of the believers (1 Thess. 3:10). Even under the most favorable circumstances spiritual difficulties would have arisen in a nascent church composed of converts from paganism. In light of the actually existing situation at Thessalonica they were inevitable. The final two chapters of Paul's first letter are devoted to the nurture of the congregation in specific areas of shortcoming and uncertainty. What he has written is prompted by the temptations of "the weak," the discouragements of "the fainthearted," and the unbrotherly conduct of "the idle" (5:14).

By "the weak" Paul means those who are weak with respect to some aspect of faith. To judge from 1 Thessalonians 4:3–8 moral weakness was the particular problem of this group. In Hellenistic society sexual immorality was a matter of relative unimportance; in Hellenistic religion fertility rites were an accepted form of consecration to a deity in certain of the mysteries and cults. The weak needed to perceive more thoroughly that consecration to the living God was both religious and moral. Paul recalls the instructions he had given to the new converts:

> For you know what instructions we gave you through the Lord Jesus. For this is the will of God, your sanctification: that you abstain from immorality; that each one of you know how to take a wife for himself in holiness and honor, not in the passion of lust like heathen who do not know God; that no man transgress, and wrong his brother in this matter, because the Lord is an avenger in all these things, as we solemnly forewarned you. For God has not called us for uncleanness, but in holiness. Therefore whoever disregards this, disregards not man but God, who gives his Holy Spirit to you (4:2–8).

"The fainthearted" were fearful on two distinct but related matters. Even though only a few months had elapsed since Paul left Thessalonica, some from the fellowship had died. Death was an awesome reality in the ancient world. Grim inscriptions along the roads reminded travelers that it was the common experience of all men. The anxiety of the fainthearted concerning those who had died may be explained in one or more ways. It is possible, for example, that Paul had proclaimed the death and resurrection of Jesus (cf. 1:10) but had neglected to instruct the Thessalonians that they would participate in the resurrection. Moreover, certain of Jesus' words, if known, were open to the interpretation that true faith in Christ precludes all possibility of death.[14] What then did the presence of death in the midst of the church mean? Again, Paul had spoken much about the glorious event of Jesus' coming with all his saints, the *parousia*. Did the death of Christians exclude them from sharing in the triumphant climax to history? Such questions as these, along with natural concern for departed friends, may have caused deep grief.

The encouragement furnished by Paul's response can be appreciated when his words are contrasted with a letter of consolation dating from the second century, found among the Oxyrhynchus papyri.[15]

> Irene to Taonnophris and Philo good comfort.
> I am as sorry and weep over the departed one as I wept for Didymas. And all things whatsoever were fitting, I have done, and all mine, Epaphroditus and Thermuthion and Philion and Apollonius and Plantas. But, nevertheless, against such things one can do nothing. *Therefore comfort one another.* Fare ye well" (Oxyrhynchus Papyrus No. 115).

The letter of consolation both opens and closes with the note of comfort. But its most striking feature is a frank recognition that no real basis for comfort has been provided. After the expression of sincere sympathy, after the grief and tears, after the appropriate memorials, the fact of utter help-lessness remains: "nevertheless, against such things one can do nothing." The concluding advice to "comfort one another" is a statement of resig-nation in the face of invincible death.

How different is the encouragement Paul offers to the fainthearted in Thessalonica:

> But we would not have you ignorant, brethren, concerning those who are asleep, that you may not grieve as others do who have no hope. For since we believe that Jesus died and rose again, even so, through Jesus, God will bring with him those who have fallen asleep. For this we declare to you by the word of the Lord, that we who are alive, who are left until the coming of the Lord, shall not precede those who have fallen asleep. For the Lord himself will descend from heaven. . . . And the dead in Christ will rise first; then we who are alive, who are left, shall be caught up together with them in the clouds to meet the Lord in the air; and so we shall always be with the Lord. *Therefore comfort one another* with these words (1 Thess. 4:13–18).

The reason they are not to "grieve as others who have no hope" is that God who raised Jesus from the dead will also raise those believers who have "fallen asleep." For them, death is no ultimate catastrophe; not even Jesus, the Lord of life, had been spared the experience of death. But he rose again. Because of his resurrection, "sleep" is no longer just a euphe-mism for the finality of the grave. It is a description of a rest which is fol-lowed by an awakening.

The second concern of the fainthearted was their unpreparedness for the "day of the Lord," when God comes to judge all men and to unleash his wrath.[16] Paul had instructed them that the day of the Lord would come with an unexpected suddenness, "like a thief in the night," catching the wicked unaware (5:2–3). Without a blameless life men could not enter into eternal fellowship with the Lord (cf. 3:13; 5:22 f.). Who was sufficient for such things? The fainthearted were fearful for their own salvation.

As early as the first chapter Paul had anticipated his words of encourage-ment when he wrote, "for we know, brethren beloved by God, that he has chosen you" (vs. 4). In chapter 5 he takes up their concern in earnest, perhaps in response to a specific request for further information concern-ing "the times and the seasons" (vs. 1). Paul assures his readers that they have no need for additional instruction. While it is true that the Lord comes suddenly and there is no escape for the sons of darkness (5:2–3), he quickly adds: "But you are not in darkness, brethren, for that day to surprise you like a thief. For you are all sons of light and sons of the day; we are not of the night or of darkness" (5:4–5). What is needed is not further enlightenment concerning the day of the Lord but a fresh determination to demonstrate the vigilance and sobriety characteristic of the day (5:6–8). To dispel unnecessary fears once for all Paul reassures his readers through a strong affirmation: "For God has not destined us for wrath, but to obtain salvation through our Lord Jesus Christ, who died for us so that whether we wake or sleep we might live with him" (5:9–10). This clarifies an earlier reference to "Jesus who delivers us from the wrath to come" (1:10). The day of the Lord is a day of wrath, but not for God's redeemed people. It is for the benefit of "the fainthearted" in the church that Paul tells the Thessalonians to "encourage one another and build one another up, just as you are doing" (5:11).

Finally there was in the church a group that Paul designates as "the idle." These were men whose refusal to work had disrupted the life of the Christian community and incurred the disrespect of outsiders. When he was with them Paul had laid down a rule. "If any one will not work, let him not eat" (2 Thess. 3:10). In disregard of this explicit instruction some of the congregation were not only idle but apparently had sought to be supported by the other brethren. When support was refused on the ground of the apostolic dictum, the idle had made their plea on the basis of "love of the brethren." This would seem to be the background presupposed by Paul's words in 1 Thessalonians 4:9–12:

> But concerning love of the brethren you have no need to have any one write to you, for you yourselves have been taught by God to love one another; and indeed you do love all the brethren throughout Macedonia. But we exhort you, brethren, to do so more and more, to aspire to live quietly, to mind your own affairs, *and to work with your hands, as we charged you;* so that you may command the respect of outsiders, and be dependent on nobody.

4. CRISIS AT THESSALONICA

Only a tentative reconstruction can be offered of the events between the reception of Paul's first letter to the church and the composition of the second. The external situation at Thessalonica appears little changed. Persecution has continued (2 Thess. 1:4; cf. 2:17; 3:3 ff.). Paul, Silas, and

Timothy are still together, apparently in Corinth (1:1), where opposition to the gospel also persists (1:7; 3:1–2). The scanty evidence suggests that the second letter was addressed to Thessalonica in A.D. 50, perhaps no more than two months after the first.

Its immediate occasion was the emergence of a new crisis in the congregation. Some of the brethren were convinced that Paul had said the day of the Lord was actually present (2:2). This not only furnished a new argument for the idle but rekindled the fears of the fainthearted. If the day of the Lord had come, no time remained to acquire the holiness and the faith, hope, and love on which Paul had insisted in his first letter (cf. I Thess. 3:13; 5:8). The wrath reserved for unbelievers would certainly overtake the Christians as well! When the elders saw that the crisis was more than they could cope with effectively, they sent word to Paul by the first of their number who had occasion to journey to Corinth (cf. 2 Thess. 3:11, "For we hear that . . .").

Second Thessalonians was written in response to this urgent request for help. It is devoted almost entirely to encouraging the same fainthearted Christians previously addressed (1:3–3:5) and readmonishing the idle (3:6–16). There is a vivid reference to the final judgment (1:6–10), a brief sketch of the events which precede the consummation (2:3–8) and a characterization of the appearance of the Lawless One, whose coming counterfeits the *parousia* of the Lord (2:9–12). But precisely in these passages Paul emerges as a pastor who offers these descriptions not for their own sake but for practical encouragement of his converts. Thus nothing is said about the events surrounding the manifestation of the Lawless One (2:9–12) until Paul has spoken of his destruction (2:8). The intention is not to introduce new truths but to remind the Thessalonians of the oral instruction the apostle had given while still in their midst (2:5). A theology of history and judgment is implied in the letter, but it is subordinated to a distinctly pastoral concern. Accordingly it is mistaken to turn to Second Thessalonians for a blueprint by which to read the "signs of the times" and to plot the course of the unveiling of the Anti-Christ. While much that Paul wrote in chapter 2—for example, the identity of the power or person who restrains the Lawless One (2:6 f.)—remains obscure to the modern reader, the affirmation that all things take place by God's sovereign will is transparent. This, together with its corollary that God had destined believers to life and fellowship with himself (1:5–7, 11–12; 2:1, 13–17; 3:1–5), was the message that the fainthearted needed to hear.

The remainder of the letter addresses itself to the persistent problem of idleness. *"Now we command you,* brethren, in the name of our Lord Jesus Christ, that you keep away from any brother who is living in idleness and not in accord with the tradition that you received from us" (3:6). These words and those which follow (3:7–16) are addressed primarily to the majority rather than to the idle who are placed under the discipline of separation. Yet Paul cautions the church to exercise love in their discipline, not looking upon a Christian who refuses to work "as an enemy" but warning him "as a brother" (3:15).

What is particularly significant in this second letter is the role assigned to "tradition" both in the discussion of the day of the Lord and in the treatment of the idle. In the first instance the Thessalonians are urged not to be unsettled in their convictions because of some prophetic utterance or even a letter purporting to be from an apostle (2:1–2); the tradition of teaching delivered to the church remains normative for the testing of doctrine (2:5; cf. 1 Thess. 5:21). At the conclusion of chapter 2 Paul writes: "So then, brethren, stand firm and hold to the *traditions* which you were taught by us, *either by word of mouth or by letter"* (2:15). Similarly, the offense of the idle in the congregation is twofold: not only were they living in idleness, but their conduct indicated a rejection of "the tradition that you received from us" (3:6). That the second letter is itself a repository of the tradition Paul makes clear when he says: "If any one refuses to obey *what we say in this letter,* note that man, and have nothing to do with him, that he may be ashamed" (3:14).

The statements on the tradition in Second Thessalonians reveal the high sense of authority Paul possessed. From the time of his earliest letters Paul was acutely conscious of the theological importance of tradition, both oral and written. This importance is assumed in all of his subsequent letters. What must be appreciated is that Paul's recognition of the crucial role of tradition resulted from his response to the dynamics of the Gentile mission. Tradition is not an end in itself. Paul was a task theologian, and tradition was one tool he used in the performance of the task to which God had called him.

NOTES

1. See P. E. Davies, "The Macedonian Scene of Paul's Journeys," *Biblical Archaeologist,* 26 (1963), pp. 91–106.

2. Strabo, *Geography*, Vol. VII, p. 323. See further P. E. Davies, *ibid.*, pp. 105–6; W. A. MacDonald, "Archaeology and St. Paul's Journeys in Greek Lands," *Biblical Archaeologist*, 3 (1940), pp. 18–24.

3. Pliny, *Natural History*, IV. 10, 36.

4. The technical title "politarch" is not found in any extant Greek literature, but no less than seventeen inscriptions, five from Thessalonica, attest its existence in Macedonian cities. See E. D. Burton, "The Politarchs," *American Journal of Theology*, 2 (1898), pp. 598–632.

5. See C. Edson, "Cults of Thessalonica" (Macedonica III), *Harvard Theological Review*, 41 (1948), pp. 153–75.

6. For a reconstruction of the chronological data see T. W. Manson, *Studies in the Gospels and Epistles* (1962), pp. 260–66.

7. Cf. Acts 14:15–17; 17:24–29, and see B. Gärtner, *The Areopagus Speech and Natural Revelation* (1955), pp. 203–28, "The Polemic Against Idolatry."

8. Paul's formulations elsewhere reinforce this conclusion: see Acts 17:30–31; Rom. 1:4.

9. Cf. Rom. 1:18–32; Eph. 4:17–18; 5:6.

10. 1 Thess. 2:19; 3:13; 4:16–17; 5:8–10, 23.

11. *In Thess.*, Homily VIII. For this and other references see E. Peterson in the *Theological Dictionary of the New Testament*, G. Kittel, ed., Vol. I (1964), p. 380.

12. It is interesting to speculate on what decrees are meant. The Caesar in question is Claudius, who that very year (A.D. 49) issued a decree expelling the Jews from Rome because of disorders originating, apparently, in the Jewish-Christian mission (see below, p. 312). Had knowledge of this fact come to the attention of the synagogue leaders in Thessalonica?

13. In view are men like Simon Magus (Acts 8:9) and Elymas the sorcerer (13:8). For an account of how such a charlatan operated, see A. D. Nock, *Conversion* (1933), pp. 93–97, on a certain Alexander; for the relevant text in translation see *Hellenistic Religions*, F. C. Grant, ed. (1953), pp. 95–98.

14. E.g., John 11:25–26, "I am the resurrection and the life; he who believes in me, though he die, yet shall he live, and *whoever lives and believes in me shall never die.*" Cf. John 8:51 ff.

15. See A. Deissmann, *Light From the Ancient East*, 5th ed. (1927), pp. 176–78.

16. For the Old Testament use of "the day of the Lord" see L. Köhler, *Old Testament Theology* (1957), pp. 218–27, "Salvation by Judgment."

SELECTED READING

Davies, P. E., "The Macedonian Scene of Paul's Journeys," *Biblical Archaeologist*, 26 (1963), pp. 91–106.

Edson, C., "Cults of Thessalonica," *Harvard Theological Review,* 41 (1948), pp. 153–204.

Faw, C. E., "On the Writing of First Thessalonians," *Journal of Biblical Literature,* 71 (1952), pp. 217–25.

Frame, J. E., *The Epistles of St. Paul to the Thessalonians.* New York: Scribner's, 1912.

Manson, T. W., "The Letters to the Thessalonians," in *Studies in the Gospels and Epistles,* M. Black, ed. Philadelphia: Westminster, 1962. Pp. 259–78.

Morris, L., *The Epistles to the Thessalonians.* Grand Rapids: Eerdmans, 1959.

THE AEGEAN REGION
Locating places mentioned in Paul's letters

0   MILES   150

THRACIA

MACEDONIA

Philippi

Thessalonica Amphipolis   Neapolis

Berea

EPIRUS

Samothrace

Nicopolis

Troas

AEGEAN

ASIA

Athens

Corinth

Ephesus

ACHAIA

Miletus

AEGEAN SEA

CRETE

MEDITERRANEAN SEA

X

✳

FIRST CORINTHIANS—
THE EROSION OF THE CHURCH

THE object of Paul's prodigious labors in Macedonia and Achaia was to plant the church on Greek soil. In response to a night vision, the Apostle and his party had entered Macedonia with the gospel (Acts 16:9–19). A nucleus of believers was gathered at Philippi, Thessalonica, and Berea, but in each instance Paul was forced to withdraw from the city by concerted opposition. Turning southward into Greece, he reached Athens and delivered his witness before the most important governmental body in the city, the Areopagus (17:16–34). Yet his stay was brief. Not until he arrived at Corinth was the pattern of penetration, opposition, and withdrawal altered. Here Paul met Aquila and Priscilla and took up residence with them. Like himself, they were newcomers to the metropolis—and tentmakers (18:1–3). At first the apostle concentrated his efforts on the Jewish synagogue, and not without success, for Crispus, the ruler of the synagogue, and his household came to faith (18:8). However, in the face of sustained opposition Paul, encouraged by a vision, turned to the Gentiles (18:9–10). Assisted by Silas and Timothy, he labored in Corinth for eighteen months until a congregation was firmly established. After Paul's departure from the city, Apollos strengthened the believers (18:27–28).

In spite of able pastoral leadership, the church's position was precarious in a pagan center known for the extravagance of its pleasures and vice. On every side, believers were subjected to influences which, if unresisted, could only erode the lines of distinction between the gospel and popular Hellenistic wisdom. It is probable that Paul began his mission in Corinth sometime in A.D. 50. Five years later there was considerable evidence that his converts had at critical points adjusted their thinking to the intellectual and social climate of their environment. The result was an erosion of the church sufficiently serious to call forth First Corinthians. The letter was written from Ephesus in response to a report from leaders of the church who requested Paul's counsel on several perplexing problems.

1. THE CHURCH OF GOD AT CORINTH

From Paul's point of view, Corinth was admirably suited as a center for the Christian mission. The city dominated the narrow neck of land which joined the southern part of the Greek peninsula to the mainland. It was served by two harbors, Cenchreae on the east side of the Isthmus and Lechaeum on the west. Because of hazardous weather at the tip of the peninsula, nearly all trade from the east and the west moved overland from sea to sea through Corinth. Larger ships unloaded passengers and cargo at one port, knowing that a ship would be waiting at the other to continue the voyage. Smaller ships were hauled four miles overland on the *Diolkos,* a boat railroad consisting of wooden rollers over which ships were pulled by manpower.[1] Through Corinth passed travelers and commerce from every part of the civilized world.[2] This was of great importance to Paul; since the postal system in the Roman Empire was restricted to official business, private letters had to be entrusted to individuals traveling from one center to another. In the absence of general postal service, it was advantageous to be located within a thriving commercial and shipping center from which transportation and communication was available to any point in the Empire. In Corinth, Paul was able to remain in continual contact with his churches by letter and personal messenger. The two letters to Thessalonica, and on a later occasion one to Rome, were dispatched during his stay in the city.

While Corinth could boast a long and illustrious past in which it had contributed much to the development of Greek art and culture, the actual city to which Paul came was less than one hundred years old. Disaster had overtaken Corinth in 146 B.C. when it sought to resist the intervention of Rome in Greek affairs. After the fall of the city, the Roman general Mummius ordered the execution of its male population and the sale of its women and children as slaves. The city had been reduced to ruins for a century when Julius Caesar determined to plant a Roman colony on the site. By 44 B.C., the rebuilding was sufficiently advanced to permit re-population. The new city experienced phenomenal growth and prosperity under Augustus and his successors. It was made the capital of the province of Achaia and the administrative seat for southern Greece. Its reputation as a vibrant metropolis, crowded with foreign visitors from all the Mediterranean lands in search of wealth or pleasure, was deserved. When Paul entered the city in A.D. 50, the reconstruction of Corinth along Roman lines was still in progress.[3] A relatively new city might be expected to be more receptive to the proclamation of a novel religious message than a center such as Athens, whose cultural history had been unbroken for several hundred years.

A primary consideration in the choice of Corinth for extended residence may have been the biennial celebration of the Isthmian Games.[4] After the Olympic contests held once every four years, the games held at Isthmia, less than ten miles from Corinth, and the ancient sanctuary of Poseidon, were the most splendid and best attended of the national festivals of Greece. Preparation for the games took several months and attracted to Corinth a multitude of delegates, athletes, merchants, and visitors. The crowds of people that thronged to the games would permit the apostle and his associates to reach men who could then carry the gospel message farther. The games were held in the spring of A.D. 51 while Paul was at Corinth. An extended passage in First Corinthians, in which the apostle depicts himself as an athlete training for the footrace and the boxing match, suggests that he may even have been present:

> Do you not know that in a race all the runners compete, but only one receives the prize? So run that you may obtain it. Every athlete exercises self-control in all things. They do it to receive *a perishable wreath,* but we an imperishable. Well, I do not run aimlessly, I do not box as one beating the air; but I pommel my body and subdue it, lest after preaching to others I myself should be disqualified (9:24–27).

Paul's description of the winner's crown as "a perishable wreath" is of special interest, for the crown bestowed differed with the site of the games. The Olympic wreath was made of wild olive, the Pythian of laurel, the Nemean of green wild celery. At Isthmia there were two types of crowns, one of pine and the other of *withered* celery. Paul's allusion to "a perishable wreath" may refer to a crown of celery which was already withered when conferred.[5]

While Corinth was ideally situated to provide a base for Paul's mission, certain aspects of its situation were wholly undesirable. The metropolis had mushroomed until it was the fourth largest in the Empire. Its international reputation as an "open" city in which every form of vice was permitted attracted an unstable, transient population. The Greek language received nouns, verbs, adjectives, and adverbs coined from the root "Corinth" to express the life of luxury and licentiousness. The city boasted the only amphitheater in Greece as well as numerous theaters, baths, taverns, and shops. In Corinth, the melting pot of Achaia, one could see the Empire in miniature. Its only aristocracy was one of wealth, while its sole tradition was the pursuit of profit and pleasure. The Corinthian ideal is caught in the declaration of one of its young men: "I am living as becomes a man of breeding. I have a mistress who is very fair. I have never wronged any man. I drink Chian wine, and in all other respects I contrive to satisfy myself, since my private resources are sufficient for these purposes."[6]

A confusing variety of Oriental and Hellenistic cults had taken root in the new city and were represented by temples, shrines, and altars. None was more famous than the temple of Aphrodite, goddess of love. This sanctuary was situated on top of the Acrocorinth, a plateau towering eighteen hundred feet above the city; the temple boasted a small army of wardens, officials, and servants, including one thousand priestesses involved in cult prostitution.[7]

Life in the city was not easy for the resident. Paul addressed the Christians as "the church of God . . . those set apart for holiness in Christ Jesus, called to be holy"* (1:2). Yet it is evident from First Corinthians that some believers continued to share the festive occasions in pagan temples (8:10; 10:7–22) and that the level of morality within the church was in some instances indistinguishable from the temple morality of Corinth at large (5:1–13). This was the extent to which the church had been eroded by its environment. To speak of the church of God *at Corinth* is to express the heart of the problem. Although Paul could describe the church as "God's garden"* (3:9), the jungle was the metaphor more appropriate to Corinth.

The reader of First Corinthians is confronted with a perplexing variety of congregational problems. Boastful groups bickered about the relative merits of their teachers and falsely prided themselves upon their wisdom. Men who violated all social customs and offended even pagan moral standards existed alongside rigorists who proposed "spiritual marriages," where pledged affection, not physically consummated, was considered the proper arrangement for a Christian husband and wife. Ecstatically gifted women clamored for freedom, disturbing the worship service by shouting across the room to their husbands and seeking to abandon the customary hair covering. There was an almost magical approach to baptism, while the

Lord's Supper had been reduced to the status of a debauched feast. Officious individuals, swelled with a sense of their own importance and knowledge, had wounded the consciences of some of the brethren. An unbridled religious enthusiasm tended to convert spiritual privilege into social license. While some members of the church held firmly to the traditions Paul had established, others denied the future resurrection of believers. Such was the baffling diversity of life and expression that marked the church of God at Corinth.

2. CROSS AND WISDOM

Disunity and bickering is the concern of the first major section of Paul's letter (1:10–4:21). Having concluded the introductory greeting with an acknowledgement of the faithfulness of God who had called the Corinthians to fellowship (koinōnia, 1:9), the apostle turns immediately to the problem of dissension in the community. The antagonism among church members was manifesting itself in slogans centering on the relative merits of their favorite teachers. Groups had banded together, rallied by the cry, "I belong to Paul"—or Apollos, or Cephas, or the Lord himself (1:11–13). Of the teachers named, it is probable that only Paul and Apollos had actually been in Corinth; they alone are mentioned repeatedly throughout the section (3:4–7, 22; 4:6). The Corinthians knew of Cephas (i.e., Peter) and Christ only through the instruction they had received from their former pastors. Whenever Paul speaks of Apollos, he describes his ministry favorably (cf. 16:12), and there is no hint in the text that the several cliques were factions which could be distinguished from each other theologically.[8] Paul's argument is directed not against the message proclaimed by Apollos or Cephas but against the whole church caught up in a cult of personality. In the affirmation "I belong to Paul," it is the arrogance in the word "I" that the apostle finds so objectionable. Invidious comparisons incited jealousy and strife; they tended to obscure the essential relationship of the entire church to Christ and to reduce the Christian revelation to the level of pagan wisdom (1:13, 17; 3:3–5).

Useful background for understanding Paul's argument is provided by some acquaintance with a group of itinerant and highly successful teachers and rhetoricians known as Sophists.[9] The term does not denote any single philosophical school but a particular style of teaching, which by Paul's day was restricted largely to rhetoric. The Sophists were wisdom teachers and popular debaters who traveled from place to place, winning disciples through their eloquence as orators and their proposals for easy success in life. Paul's depreciation of "the wise man," "the debater of this age," and "the wisdom of this world" (1:20–21), as well as his use of certain technical terms familiar to the vocabulary of the Sophists, suggests that pretensions to wisdom at Corinth were shaped, perhaps unconsciously, by Sophists who made their way to the Isthmus.

Paul's description of those whom God had called is intelligible in this light. He reminds the Corinthian believers that few of them were men of wisdom (*sophoi*) or powerful or well born; on the contrary, they were uneducated, powerless, and unesteemed (1:26–28). Hellenistic society believed that the gods could grant one's desires for wisdom, influence, and social prestige if they chose to do so.[10] The Sophists claimed that adherence to their wisdom put the fulfillment of such dreams within the reach of every man. The Corinthians had apparently cast Paul and Apollos, Cephas and Christ, in the role of Sophists. They had confused the gospel with Hellenistic wisdom, the Christian teachers with professional Sophists, and themselves with the wise of the world.[11] In sharp contrast, Paul asserts that the gospel is foolishness (1:18–25), that the Christian teachers are servants and stewards of God, accountable to him (3:3–8; 4:1–5), and that the Corinthians are immature and without wisdom (2:6–3:3).

That God has no respect for human standards of wisdom is demonstrated by the cross of Christ. The proclamation of Christ crucified is the heart of Paul's gospel (1:17 f.; 2:2; 15:3). Opposed to all of man's pretensions, the cross scandalizes both Jews and Greeks, but to men of faith it exhibits both the power and the wisdom of God (1:18–25). The world, in its wisdom, labels God's act in Christ foolishness, but the foolishness of God is wiser than men (cf. 3:18–21).

In support of his argument, Paul appeals both to the Corinthians themselves and to his preaching of the cross. The members of the congregation are an indication that God has placed no premium on wisdom or on any other standard of worldly success. Few of them have any grounds for boasting. Consequently, if a man wishes to boast, let him boast in the Lord (1:26–30; cf. 4:6–7). Paul's proclamation of a crucified Savior has not been characterized by eloquence or wisdom. Unlike the Sophist, the apostle has refused to cast his message in persuasive or clever speech but has relied wholly upon the demonstration of the power of God (1:17; 2:1–5).

3. HOLINESS AND FREEDOM

The note of freedom was prominent in the gospel Paul preached. Christ set men free from the fears and powers that tyrannized life in the Hellenistic world: "where the Spirit of the Lord is, there is freedom" (2 Cor. 3:17). Through Christ men were called to responsible freedom in the realm of personal relationships. At Corinth, however, freedom had degenerated into license, encouraged by the slogan "All things are lawful" (1 Cor. 6:12). Not only was there immorality within the congregation, but on one occasion it took the form of incest—offensive even by pagan standards. The church, which should have been reduced to grief, was quite proud of the whole affair, boasting arrogantly of the freedom they possessed in Christ (5:1–6). In the strongest terms Paul reminds the believers that they have been called to personal and corporate holiness.

While the apostle concerns himself with various aspects of sexual ethics in chapters five through seven, he has anticipated his argument from the beginning. Already in the address of the letter he characterized the church of God at Corinth by the phrases "those set apart for *holiness* in Christ Jesus, called to be *holy*"* (1:2). When responding to the Corinthian claim to wisdom, Paul held forth Christ Jesus "whom God made our wisdom, our righteousness and *holiness* and redemption"* (1:30). Describing the Christians as "God's building" (3:9), Paul specifies that he has in mind not just any structure but the temple of God: "Do you not know that you are God's temple and that God's Spirit dwells in you? If any one destroys God's temple, God will destroy him. For God's temple is *holy,* and that temple you are" (3:16–17). The fact that Paul reintroduces the image of the temple when treating the problem of immorality (6:19–20) indicates that the stress on holiness in the first section of the letter is deliberate and purposeful, preparing for Paul's judgment and admonition in this section.

In the case of a man who had been living immorally with his stepmother, which the ancient world regarded as incest, Paul's sternness is mitigated only by the concern that the offender may be saved from wrath on the day of judgment (5:5). He has already pronounced judgment upon the man and commands the church in solemn assembly "to deliver this man to Satan for the destruction of the flesh" (5:3–5). The formula is ominous in tone. The discipline of separation was imposed upon any individual who claimed to be a Christian but who was guilty of offenses ranging from immorality and idolatry to greed and drunkenness (5:9–11).

By definition, church discipline involves a judgment upon "those inside the church" (5:9–13). Its exercise anticipated the consummation, when God will judge the world and angels through his people (6:2–3). Yet at Corinth, grievances between members of the church were settled in pagan courts of civil law. The incongruity between these facts is set forth by

Paul in stinging fashion. Mocking the Corinthian boast of wisdom, Paul asks, "Can it be that there is no man among you wise enough to decide between members of the brotherhood, but brother goes to law against brother, and that before unbelievers?" (6:5–6).

Paul's final word to those abusing their freedom is addressed to men who had argued that just as the stomach and food are intended for each other, so it was appropriate to satisfy the sexual appetites of the body. Three times Paul picks up the slogans with which they had justified relationship with a prostitute (6:15–18), and in each instance he qualifies their cliché by a statement restoring a Christian perspective (6:12–13):

The Immoralists	*Paul*
"All things are lawful for me	but not all things are helpful."
"All things are lawful for me	but I will not be enslaved by anything."
"Food is meat for the stomach and the stomach for food	—and God will destroy both one and the other. The body is not meant for immorality, but for the Lord, and the Lord for the body."

The response to the freedom conferred in Christ is a life of holiness (6:15–20).

At this point, Paul begins to answer questions which had been posed for him in a letter from the church. Its outline can be sketched from Paul's formula of response, "now concerning . . ." (7:1, 25; 8:1; 12:1; 16:1). The Corinthians had written asking specific guidance of a variety of practical issues including marriage, the eating of meat which may have been offered to idols, the exercise of spiritual gifts, and the collection for the relief of the poor in Jerusalem.

Their first questions bore on marriage, separation, divorce, celibacy, and asceticism (7:1–40)—personal relationships not unrelated to those upon which Paul had already touched. Declaring that any physical union constitutes a marriage, Paul had cited the classic statement from the Old Testament, "the two shall become one"* (Gen. 2:24; 1 Cor. 6:16). The transition to the discussion of marriage requested by the church was therefore a smooth one. The new element is the Corinthian concept of a "spiritual marriage." From the assumption that celibacy was a higher state than marriage, pledged affection was never consummated (cf. 7:2–5,

36–38). Paul concedes that normally a consummated marriage is advisable, and he permits only a temporary renunciation of conjugal rights. But it is clear that the most diverse attitudes coexisted at Corinth: pride in incest, habitual immorality, the consideration of separation as a condition more consistent with Christian existence, and the pursuit of celibacy. These apparently opposite tendencies may actually reflect a single point of view—a contempt of the body. If the body is of inferior value, one man may conclude that it is irrelevant whether one subdues it, while another views the bodily appetites as the cravings of a lower nature which must be rigorously denied. Both points of view are erroneous. Paul affirms the right to marry and places no restraint upon husband and wife (7:28, 35). His one concern is to secure "undivided devotion to the Lord" (7:35). If at Corinth there was a widespread contempt for the body, Paul's insistence that the physical body was meant for the Lord as a temple sacred to him assumes great significance. It will have a distinct bearing on the question of bodily resurrection (ch. 15). For the apostle, a proper view of the physical body held the key to both holiness and freedom.

4. LOVE AND KNOWLEDGE

The second problem posed in the letter from Corinth was the divided attitude within the church toward eating meat which had been offered to idols. The question was complex, for it concerned not merely attendance at a pagan temple banquet (8:10; 10:14–22) but the eating of meat sold in the marketplace and consumed at home (10:25). Paul's response (8:1–11:1) stresses the limitation imposed on personal liberty by love for God and the brethren. The writers of the letter had urged their knowledge regarding the unreality of the gods represented by idols and their confession of the one God which rendered harmless the eating of meat offered in sacrifice (8:1–6). The apostle's acknowledgement of the measure of truth in their position is tempered by the necessity to be concerned with the less mature brethren. He argues that it is better to relinquish personal rights than to wound the conscience of a brother, thus sinning against Christ (8:7–13).

Throughout his response Paul echoes phrases used in their letter. His correspondents had written, "all of us possess *knowledge*" (8:1, 4). The possession of knowledge was identical with the denial of the existence of reality beyond an idolatrous object and adherence to the one true God. "Knowledge," as used by the Corinthians, meant specifically *the knowledge of God*, in contrast to their former veneration of idols (cf. 6:9–11;

12:2). The content of their knowledge is further defined by a confession consisting of two parallel strophes, each containing three lines (8:6)*:

I	II
"There is one God, the Father,	"There is one Lord Jesus Christ,
from whom are all things	through whom are all things
and for whom we exist."	and through whom we exist."

According to this confession, the unique principle from which all things come and to which they return is the one God, who is known to the Christians as Father. Jesus Christ is the mediator through whom God has created all things and through whom the Corinthians turned to God. Possession of this knowledge, they claimed, conferred the liberty to eat meat which had been offered in votive sacrifice without qualms of conscience or fear (cf. 8:9; 10:23). Their position was grounded in knowledge; they had written only because of a divided opinion within the congregation regarding their attendance at pagan temples.

Paul asserts the primacy of sacrificial love over both knowledge and liberty (8:1, 9). The principle that he articulates has relevance not merely to the issues raised in the immediate context but to the exercise of spiritual gifts as well (chs. 12–14). He writes, " 'Knowledge' puffs up, but love builds up," and anticipating the conclusion to the hymn in praise of Christian love (13:12) he adds: "If any one imagines that he knows something, he does not yet know as he ought to know. But if one loves God, one is known by him" (8:1–3). What Paul has done is to redefine true knowledge as *being known by God,* having shifted the emphasis from the knowledge which men possess to that possessed by God.[12] Love for God, not the knowledge of God, is the sign that a man really possesses knowledge. The true knowledge received from God manifests itself in love for both God and men.

The importance of this point is clarified when Paul qualifies the generalized claim of the writers: "However, *not all* possess this knowledge" (8:7). There were men in the congregation who, though accustomed to temple meals, still ate the food as a *real* offering to a *real* god, defiling their consciences. Their consciences were weak with respect to faith and to character, for they continued to eat at pagan banquet tables, encouraged by "the strong" in spite of the fact that their consciences judged them and destroyed them (8:8–11). The actual food consumed was unimportant, but the effect upon men for whom Christ had died was vitally important.

Love for Christ and for these men dictated the voluntary renunciation of personal liberty (8:13).

When the Corinthians wrote to Paul, they had seen the issue of conflict in the congregation only in terms of *knowledge* and *conscience*. Paul placed it within the sharper perspective of *liberty* and *love*. The question to be asked of any act is not: Is it permitted? but: Is it beneficial? Does it contribute to the advantage of another man? The Christian seeks to glorify God by pursuing the advantage of the many, in order that they may experience salvation. In doing this, no advantage accrues to him, for he is merely emulating Jesus Christ (10:31–11:1).

The pattern of quotation and rebuff Paul has followed earlier in the letter (6:12–13; 8:1–4; 10:23) recurs in a new section on church worship (11:2–34). The Corinthians appear to have written that they remember Paul in everything and maintain the traditions even as he delivered them to the church (cf. 11:2), for the section opens with an ironical commendation for their preservation of the tradition. The apostle then lists two specific areas in the life of the church in which the tradition he had delivered was being violated. The first involved the women of the congregation who refused to wear the head mantle which signified their subordination in the plan of God (11:2–16).[13] The details of what was involved are not clear, and Paul's argument is not transparent. But his final word is crystal clear in its intention: "If any one is disposed to be contentious, we recognize no other practice, nor do the churches of God" (11:16). The tradition is authoritative and must be observed.

Abuses at the Lord's Supper also involved a disregard of the tradition Paul had committed to the church (11:17–34). In Corinth and elsewhere, the Eucharist was observed within the context of a common meal. The conduct of believers at the meal, however, was indistinguishable from that of pagans gathered in one of the popular clubs of the day.[14] Their gluttony, crudeness, and drunkenness rendered impossible the discernment of the Lord's body (11:17–22, 27–29). The result had been judgment upon the congregation in the form of sickness and death (11:30). It is distinctly possible that the Corinthians had developed a hypersacramental and magical conception of baptism and the Eucharist. This would explain Paul's apparent depreciation of baptism at the opening of his letter (1:13–17) and the Corinthian dismay that those who had eaten the sacramental meal could experience sickness and death. Paul's reference to the Israelites, who had been baptized into Moses and had eaten spiritual food and drink but perished (10:1–5), and his interpretation of the judgment of God which had been administered at Corinth in connection with the Eucharist (11:27–32), stand opposed to all magical conceptions of the rites of the church. Baptism confers only the possibility and necessity of obedience to the Lord. The Eucharist demands an attitude of love and responsibility toward fellow Christians. Worthy participation presupposes a self-judgment that looks back to the judgment of God acknowledged in baptism and anticipates the consummation when the world will be judged by the Lord (11:26, 28–32).[15]

The theme of worship is sustained in chapters 12 through 14, which treat the question of spiritual gifts and, more specifically, what may have been a relatively new phenomenon within the church, ecstatic speech. The detailed instruction Paul gives to the church in chapter 14 suggests that there was no existing tradition to which he could appeal on the matter of tongues. But the principle of love and edification, first expressed in connection with the eating of meat (8:1), was directly relevant to the situation at Corinth. Paul imposes three rules upon those endowed with charismatic gifts: (1) the gift must promote the unity of the congregation (ch. 12); (2) it must be informed by selfless love (ch. 13); (3) it must contribute to the edification of the church (ch. 14).

5. PNEUMATIC ENTHUSIASM

Before concluding with various final instructions (ch. 16), Paul writes at length of the resurrection of believers. His argument builds upon the tradition he shared in common with the Jerusalem apostles concerning the death and resurrection of Jesus (15:3–11). Paul's treatment of the resurrection of believers and the nature of the resurrection body was prompted by a denial at Corinth of the resurrection of the dead (15:12). There is no hint in chapter 15 that anyone within the church at Corinth denied Jesus' resurrection; it was the future resurrection of believers that was discounted. In this light, it is instructive to compare another denial of a future resurrection to which Paul gives attention:

> 1 Corinthians 15:12: How can some of you say that *there is no resurrection of the dead?*

> 2 Timothy 2:17–18: Among them are Hymenaeus and Philetus, who have swerved from the truth by holding that *the resurrection is past already.*

In the latter passage, the two heretical teachers seem to have taught that by virtue of the resurrection of Jesus the Christian community had been projected into the future age and that the qualities of resurrection life were already in force.[16] While too much can be read into a fragmentary reference, such teaching points to a view of Christian existence characterized by (1) a general unconcern with the future, since resurrection life has been achieved; (2) a perspective on human relationships, the keynote of which is *freedom*; (3) a distinctive Christology stressing the presence and *reign of Christ* rather than his coming.

If a similar point of view existed at Corinth, many of the problems within the congregation and the distinctive emphases of Paul's letter are explained. If Jesus' resurrection exhausted the event, and was not merely its initial stage, there could be no further resurrection of the dead. It is precisely against the thesis that the resurrection has been accomplished in its totality that Paul's argument in chapter 15 is directed. On the authority of a revealed word, he asserts that Christians will participate in a yet future resurrection which is related to the resurrection of Jesus, just as the full harvest is related to the firstfruits which furnish the pledge and guarantee of that harvest (15:20–28). Paul counters the false declaration by emphatically distinguishing between the present and the future existence of believers: "flesh and blood cannot inherit the kingdom of God" (15:50).

Were the Corinthians encouraged to think of a post-resurrection existence because they possessed the Holy Spirit? It is distinctly possible. Richly endowed by the Spirit, they seemed to have already attained the goal of salvation. If this was true, future apocalyptic expectations could be reinterpreted as the spiritual possession of the individual believer in the present. Christian existence, affirmed in baptism and nurtured through the Lord's Supper, became distinctly *pneumatic* (from *pneuma* = Spirit). Under these conditions, the task of the church in the world was to demonstrate the freedom characteristic of the angels. The result was *pneumatic enthusiasm*, a self-centered, otherworldly variety of religious experience stemming from a peculiar theology of grace.[17]

In restoring order, Paul appeals to the tradition observed in the churches (11:16; 14:33–34), argues from the well-known Hellenistic simile of the body (12:14–27), and imposes his apostolic authority (14:34–36). He does not hesitate to shame his readers by emphasizing their immaturity and urging common sense (13:11; 14:19–20, 32–33). A sharp rebuke is given to the disorderly women: "What! Did the word of God originate with you, or are you the only ones it has reached?" (14:36). Pneumatic enthusiasm encouraged precisely such a point of view.

The diversity and severity of congregational problems at Corinth is perplexing. At numerous points the church had been eroded by its environment. But all of the situations encountered can reasonably be assumed to have arisen as expressions of pneumatic freedom supported by an over-realized eschatology. This is the value of the proposal that pneumatic enthusiasm provides the frame of reference in terms of which First Corinthians should be read.

NOTES

1. N. M. Verdelis, "How the Ancient Greeks Transported Ships Over the Isthmus of Corinth," *Illustrated London News*, No. 231 (1957), pp. 649–51.

2. See O. Broneer, "Corinth: Center of St. Paul's Missionary Work in Greece," *Biblical Archaeologist*, 14 (1951), pp. 78–96; J. A. Callaway, "Corinth," *Review and Expositor*, 57 (1960), pp. 381–88. For a wealth of detail from the second century, see Pausanias, *Description of Greece*, Book II, "Corinth" (Loeb ed.), Vol. I, pp. 246–57.

3. O. Broneer, *ibid.*, pp. 80–82.

4. See especially O. Broneer, "The Apostle Paul and the Isthmian Games," *Biblical Archaeologist*, 25 (1962), pp. 1–31, reprinted in the *Biblical Archaeologist Reader*, Vol. II (1964), pp. 393–420.

5. *Ibid.*, pp. 16–17.

6. Athenaesus, *The Deipnosophists*, IV. 167e (Loeb ed.), Vol. II, p. 261.

7. Strabo, *Geography*, VIII. 6.20.

8. See J. Munck, "The Church without Faction: Studies in I Corinthians 1–4." in *Paul and the Salvation of Mankind* (1959), pp. 135–67.

9. The primary source is Philostratus and Eunapius, *The Lives of the Sophists* (Loeb ed., trans. by W. C. Wright, 1922). Cf. Munck, *op. cit.*, pp. 153 f., 158 f., 162–64.

10. A. D. Nock, *St. Paul* (1937), pp. 174 f., with quotations from the Greek magical papyri.

11. Munck, *op. cit.*, pp. 152–66.

12. Cf. Gal. 4:9 for the same shift. R. Bultmann, *Gnosis* (Bible Key Words, Series II, 1958), pp. 42 f., points out that for Paul true knowledge "is not something achieved by man, but has its roots in God's knowledge of man. . . ."

13. Cf. O. Motta, "The Question of the Unveiled Women (I Cor. 11:2–16)," *Expository Times*, 44 (1932–33), pp. 139–41.

14. On pagan clubs and their rites, common meals, and idol sacrifices, see W. M. Ramsey, "Historical Commentary on the Epistles to the Corinthians" in *Expositor*, 6th series, 1–3 (Jan., 1900–June, 1901).

15. See C. F. D. Moule, "The Judgment Theme in the Sacraments," in *The Background of the New Testament and its Eschatology,* W. D. Davies and D. Daube, eds., 1954, pp. 464–81.

16. Cf. W. L. Lane, "I Tim. IV. 1–3: An Early Instance of Over-Realized Eschatology?" *New Testament Studies,* 11 (1964), pp. 164–67.

17. Cf. R. A. Knox, *Enthusiasm: A Chapter in the History of Religion* (1950), p. 3: "Our traditional doctrine is that grace perfects nature, elevates it to a higher pitch. . . . The assumption of the enthusiast is bolder and simpler: for him, grace has destroyed nature and replaced it."

SELECTED READING

Broneer, O., "The Apostle Paul and the Isthmian Games," *Biblical Archeologist,* 25 (1962), pp. 1–31, reprinted in the *Biblical Archaeologist Reader,* Vol. II (Garden City: Doubleday, 1964), pp. 393–420.

———, "Corinth: Center of St. Paul's Missionary Work in Greece," *Biblical Archaeologist,* 14 (1951), pp. 78–96.

Callaway, J. A., "Corinth," *Review and Expositor,* 57 (1960), pp. 381–88.

Dean, J. T., *St. Paul and Corinth.* London: Lutterworth, 1947.

Ehrhardt, A., "Social Problems in the Early Church," in *The Framework of the New Testament Stories.* Cambridge: Harvard University Press, 1964. Pp. 275–312.

Héring, J., *The First Epistle of St. Paul to the Corinthians.* London: Epworth, 1962.

Munck, J., "The Church without Factions: Studies in I Corinthians 1–4," in *Paul and the Salvation of Mankind.* Richmond: John Knox Press, 1959. Pp. 135–67.

XI

✳

SECOND CORINTHIANS AND GALATIANS— CHALLENGES TO PAUL'S APOSTLESHIP

PAUL'S letters bear witness to the remarkable authority he assumed over the churches, even those congregations where he was personally unknown. His authority rested upon his call from God to be an apostle of Jesus Christ, an ambassador whose word was weighted with the dignity of the Lord he represented. The question that dominates Second Corinthians is that of Paul's apostolic credentials. While many details remain shrouded in obscurity, this letter also provides evidence for the presence of a non-Pauline Jewish-Christian mission to Gentile centers.

Among the churches of southern Galatia, Paul had to defend his gospel as well as his authority. Although Galatians has traditionally been treated as a classic statement on justification by faith, more than two fifths of the letter is a defense of Paul's apostleship. Together these two documents present Paul as a man of warmth and deep feeling who experienced sometimes comfort, sometimes grief and anger, in the defense of his ministry and in the discipline of churches as well as individuals.

1. STRAINED RELATIONSHIPS WITH CORINTH

As a document, Second Corinthians both delights and provokes us.[1] It alone alludes to the deadly peril Paul endured in Asia, the severity of which caused him to despair for his life (1:8–10); it provides the only extensive catalogues of his apostolic sufferings (4:8–10; 6:4–10; 11:23–33; 12:10) and the only reference to his visionary experience of being caught up to the "third heaven" (12:2–4); it is our sole basis for determining Paul's relationship to the church at Corinth subsequent to the writing of First Corinthians. These matters were so well known both to Paul and to

178

the Corinthians that allusions were sufficient to recall the course of events. In seeking to understand what was involved the modern interpreter is at many points reduced to inference and shrewd guesswork.

The reconstruction of the apostle's visits to the Corinthians remains one of the most thorny of Pauline problems. Twice in 2 Corinthians he states that he is ready to come to Corinth *a third time* (12:14; 13:1), while much of the letter is intelligible only in terms of *a second, painful visit* that he has already made to the Isthmus. Paul first came to Corinth in A.D. 50–51, on the second missionary journey, when he labored in the city for eighteen months (Acts 18:1–8). Throughout the course of his extended stay in Ephesus, on the third journey (Acts 19–20), the Corinthians maintained contact with him by emissary and by letter. Paul had dispatched a brief letter to them, which has not been preserved, urging them not to associate with immoral men (1 Cor. 5:9–11). His words were misunderstood, and when the Corinthians wrote to elaborate their position and to pose a number of questions on which they sought counsel, the apostle penned First Corinthians (see above, pp. 170 ff.).

Recognizing that the situation required specification, Paul sent Timothy overland through Macedonia to represent him at Corinth (1 Cor. 4:16 f.; 16:10 f.). Timothy was well known to the Corinthians, having labored with Paul and Silas when the church was being established (Acts 18:5; 2 Cor. 1:9).[2]

Sustained concern appears to have motivated Paul's own sudden decision to go to Corinth. The Book of Acts sheds no light on this second visit. All that can be said for certain is that the visit was brief in duration and painful in character. Paul writes, in retrospect, "I made up my mind not to make you *another painful visit*" (2 Cor. 2:1).

When Paul arrived in Corinth shortly after the church had received First Corinthians, he recognized that his letter had not accomplished its purpose. Those who had scoffed arrogantly at the apostle's warning that he was coming soon (1 Cor. 4:18–21) had not repented of their sin; in flagrant violation of the apostolic word of admonition, disorder continued to rend the church. Reluctant to place the church under a ban, Paul had administered a severe rebuke to the entire congregation. He warned that if he came again to the Isthmus and found the same practices countenanced, he would not spare them (cf. 2 Cor. 12:20–13:3, 9–10). Paul then withdrew, allowing the church time to put its house in order.

Paul's reluctance to exercise his authority "for tearing down" (2 Cor. 13:10) may have been interpreted by some in the congregation as a sign of weakness. From this time the sentiment began to gain currency at Corinth that "his letters are weighty and strong, but his bodily presence is weak, and his speeech of no account" (10:10).

Meanwhile Timothy had arrived in Corinth only to be insulted and abused (cf. 2:5; 7:12). Although the abuse had been heaped upon Timothy, in its intention it had been directed toward the apostle. When Paul, therefore, learned what had happened he wrote a letter so severe that it later grieved him even to think of what he had written to the church (cf. 2:2–11; 7:8–13). This letter is also lost,[3] but it apparently addressed an ultimatum to the congregation either to punish the one who inflicted the injury and demonstrate an acceptable repentance or to reap the wrath of God.

Paul sent this painful letter to Corinth through Titus, with the understanding that his lieutenant would meet him in Troas at the earliest possible time. When his associate was delayed, the apostle was so disquieted he could not remain in Troas (2:12–13). He hastened to Macedonia, where he was met by Titus with the news that the Corinthians had responded to the letter with godly sorrow and had punished the offender in accordance to the judgment of the majority (7:5–7). Titus' report was the immediate occasion of Second Corinthians. This communication exposes the alternating depths of anguish and affection, grief and joy, affliction and comfort, which the apostle experienced in his relationships with the Corinthian church.

2. THE TRUE AND FALSE APOSTLE

It is evident that Paul did not conform to the image of an apostle as conceived by the believers in Greece.

1. The Corinthians complained that they could not understand Paul. For one thing, he boasted too much of his authority. Yet he was unskilled in speaking. Moreover, there were occasions when he acted as if he were emotionally unbalanced. Without dodging the issues, Paul frankly acknowledges a degree of truth in the complaint, but he hastens to clarify his motives and intentions (1:13 f.; 5:13; 10:8, 10). If he is unskilled in speaking, he will send to Corinth "the brother who is famous among all the churches for his preaching of the gospel" (8:18). At the same time, Paul insists that his refusal to persuade men of the truth of the gospel by eloquence rests upon the conviction that God has commissioned him to speak, and on God's power he may confidently rely (2:17; 4:2, 13–14; 5:11).

2. Paul's change of plans for an extended stay at Corinth (1 Cor.

16:5–6) provided the grounds for the charge that he was vacillating and that he made his plans like a worldly man (2 Cor. 1:15–17). Paul's answer is a forthright affirmation of his integrity:

> As surely as God is faithful, our word to you has not been Yes and No. ... But it is God who establishes us with you in Christ, and has commissioned us; he has put his seal upon us and given us his Spirit in our hearts as a guarantee.
>
> But I call God to witness against me—it was to spare you that I refrained from coming to Corinth (1:18, 21–23; cf. also 4:2; 10:2–6).

The marks of the apostle's ministry are "truthful speech and the power of God" (6:7).

3. The Corinthians complained that Paul caused them pain (2:2); specifically, he frightened them with letters (10:9). Paul could hear behind the formulated charge a cry of genuine anguish. He had himself shared that anguish: "For I wrote you out of much affliction and anguish of heart and with many tears, not to cause you pain but to let you know the abundant love that I have for you" (2:4). The letter which had caused so deep an expression of grief within the congregation was actually written to spare the church a further painful visit (1:23–2:3). While the apostle momentarily regretted having written so severely, in the perspective of the godly repentance which his words had induced, he saw that pain was a goad to righteousness in the hands of the Lord (7:8–13). The truth was that Paul had found no rest until he had learned of the conciliation achieved through his letter and the admonition of Titus (7:5–7).

4. A recurring charge that Paul praised himself received a variety of responses. Paul denied that any self-commendation was intended (3:1–3; 5:11 f.). His purpose had not been to call attention to himself but to proclaim "Jesus Christ as Lord, with ourselves as your servants for Jesus' sake" (4:5). If Paul did speak of commending himself, it was specifically as a servant of God:

> We put no obstacle in any one's way, so that no fault may be found with our ministry, *but as servants of God we commend ourselves in every way:* through great endurance, in afflictions, hardships, calamities, beatings, imprisonments, tumults, labors, watching, hunger; by purity, knowledge, forbearance, kindness, the Holy Spirit, genuine love, truthful speech and the power of God . . . (6:3–7).

Moreover, his intention had always been that the Corinthians would remove from him any cause to boast. His desire had been that they should be his letters of recommendation (3:1–3).

5. The lament that the apostle severely restricted the believers is intelligible when we remember the unusually low level of morality at Corinth (see above, pp. 165 f.). The gospel was a call to personal holiness in the service of God, and therefore entailed the restriction of unbridled license. When Paul demands the separation between righteousness and iniquity (6:14–15), he returns to the image he had earlier developed of the church as a temple:

> For we are the temple of the living God; as God said,
> *"I will live in them and move among them,*
> *and I will be their God,*
> *and they shall be my people."*
> Therefore come out from them,
> and be separate from them, says the Lord,
> and touch nothing unclean;
> then *I will welcome you,*
> and *I will be a father to you,*
> *and you shall be my sons and daughters,*
> says the Lord Almighty (6:16–18; cf. 1 Cor. 3:16; 6:18–20).

The call for a life of separation unto the Lord is solidly based upon the foundation of the "new covenant" which God had established with the Corinthians. The substance of the citation is made up of Old Testament passages centering in the covenant (see, e.g., Exod. 25:8; 29:45; Lev. 26:12; 2 Sam. 7:14; Ezek. 20:34; 37:27; Jer. 31:31 ff.); Paul uses them to show that covenant privilege implies a corresponding obligation to live worthy of the Lord who graciously binds himself to his people. The italicized words constitute *the promises* of the covenant which find their affirmation in Jesus Christ (cf. 2 Cor. 1:19–20). Personal purity does not represent "restriction," but a joyful response to God: *"Since we have these promises,* beloved, let us cleanse ourselves from every defilement of body and spirit, and *make holiness perfect in the fear of God"* (7:1). This is why the apostle has no hesitation in denying the charge made against him: "You are not restricted by us, but you are restricted in your own affections" (6:12).

It is possible that Paul's zeal for the collection (cf. 1 Cor. 16:1–4) was viewed as a further instance of restriction. From the Corinthian point of view, he had been arrogant in demanding what could only be labeled "an exaction" (2 Cor. 9:5) and "a burden" (cf. 8:13). Sensitive to this reaction, the Apostle speaks at length about the collection (chs. 8–9).

He holds before the church not merely the example of the Macedonian churches (8:1–5) but a boast he had made in Macedonia about the readiness of the Achaians with their gift (9:1–5). Paul's skill in handling objections raised to his proposals is nowhere more apparent than here. He delicately compliments the church ("as you excel in everything . . . see that you excel in this gracious work also," 8:7), refuses to command ("I say this not as a command, but to prove . . . that your love also is genuine," 8:8), cites the example of the Lord ("though he was rich, yet for your sake he became poor," 8:9), and offers his counsel ("in this matter I give my advice," 8:10). Trusted associates are dispatched to assist the church to fulfill its promise of the gift, "so that it may be ready not as an exaction but as a willing gift" (9:5). The ultimate incentive held before the congregation is the opportunity to glorify God by an act of obedience in acknowledgment of the gospel of Christ (9:13). In his interaction with the complaint of the church, Paul has moved from an argument based on equity and ability (8:10–15) to a plateau where one may reflect on the magnitude of what God has done: "Thanks be to God for his inexpressible gift!" (9:15).

6. The Corinthians complained that Paul did not love them because he had refused to accept even partial support from the church during the entire period of his labor among them; yet he had permitted Christian brethren from Macedonia to send him gifts on more than one occasion (11:7–11; 12:13). Long before approaching this objection directly, Paul exposed its fallacy. Even the earlier severe letter had as its true purpose "to let you know the abundant love that I have for you" (2:4). The apostle magnifies his ministry of reconciliation (5:16–6:2) precisely because he longs to see its ultimate fruit in the relationship between the Corinthians and himself. With keen emotion he confesses his deep affection for the church and pleads for their love: "Our mouth is open to you, Corinthians; our heart is wide. You are not restricted by us, but you are restricted in your own affections. In return—I speak as to children—widen your hearts also. . . . Open your hearts to us" (6:11–13; 7:2). In refusing support from the Corinthians, Paul's one desire was not to burden the church. He chose deliberately to abase himself so that they might be exalted. "And why? Because I do not love you? God knows I do!" (11:7–11). With biting irony, Paul challenges the Corinthians to provide real evidence that they had been neglected in his affections: "For in what were you less favored than the rest of the churches, except that I myself did not burden you? Forgive me this wrong!" (12:13).

7. Finally, the Corinthians were scandalized by Paul's "weakness" (10:1; cf. ch. 10:10). The quality of humility which the apostle had demonstrated was not highly esteemed in the Greek world. What the Corinthians had failed to see was that Paul's "weaknesses" were actually the conditions of his ministry (12:7–10) and that this ministry had found its first embodiment in Christ. Twice he calls attention to the relationship between the Lord and weakness: at one crucial point in the letter Paul grounds his plea on "the meekness and gentleness of Christ" (10:1); near the end he calls attention to the paradox of Christ who "was crucified in weakness, but lives by the power of God" (13:3–4). This element of paradox provided the key to Paul's behavior. Though he admitted to being "weak *in him* [Christ]," he quickly adds, "but in dealing with you we shall live with him by the power of God" (13:4).

Agitating this whole situation were also certain itinerant Jewish leaders who had recently come to the city; Paul labels them contemptuously the "superlative apostles" (11:5; 12:11). Their demeanor and posture could not have been more diametrically in contrast with Paul's. Though they were not the instigators of the opposition between Paul and the Corinthians, they served to bring strained relationships to a climax. Whereas Paul had been attacked and ridiculed, they were welcomed enthusiastically by many in the church. We know nothing of their origin; they could have come from any city in the Empire. They may have brought as their credentials precisely the kind of letters of recommendation that Paul lacked (cf. 3:1). What distinguished them from Paul were their open boasts that they were apostles and their unembarrassed demand for financial support (11:7–15; 12:13–18). The critical point about them which called forth Paul's torrent of heated language was that they were exploiters of the church, "false apostles, deceitful workmen, disguising themselves as apostles of Christ" (11:13). Using them as a foil, Paul draws a self-portrait of the true apostle, scarred from affliction and weakness, always carrying in his body the death of his Lord (4:10). Unable to boast of honor and power, he is like his Lord, a suffering and dying figure who knows triumph only in the midst of infirmity and defeat (2:14–16; 4:7–12; 6:4–10; 11:23–29). The blindness of the Corinthians at this point has served only to cause mutual embarrassment. "I have been a fool! You forced me to it, for I ought to have been commended by you. For I am not at all inferior to these superlative apostles, even though I am nothing. *The signs of a true apostle were performed among you* in all patience, with signs and wonders and mighty works" (12:11–12). The Corinthians failed to detect the tension between inward glory and outward failure that distinguishes the apostle as a man laden "with gifts from his Lord and with suffering in the world."[4] Second Corinthians patiently rehearses once more "the signs of a true apostle" which render visible a Lord crucified in weakness but alive by the power of God. The apostle is an ambassador for Jesus Christ, entrusted with the ministry of reconciliation (5:18–21). Though his own existence is characterized by death, the life which flows from his ministry authenticates his service for his Lord (4:10–12).

3. CHALLENGE FROM THE JUDAIZERS

In writing to the Corinthians, Paul poses the hypothetical possibility of someone's coming and preaching "another Jesus than the one we preached" and of the church accepting "a different gospel from the one you accepted" (2 Cor. 11:4). This language recurs in the letter to the Galatians as a description of stark reality that threatens to strangle life in Christ. Like Second Corinthians, Galatians sheds valuable light on Paul's life and ministry. Challenged to demonstrate the integrity of his call and defend his right to shape the faith of the churches, Paul responds with a fiery defense of his gospel and apostleship.

The letter circulated among a number of centers named comprehensively "the churches of Galatia" (Gal. 1:2; cf. 3:1; 1 Cor. 16:1). "Galatia" is an ambiguous title for a broad swath of land extending from the Mediterranean northward to the Black Sea. Politically, it was the official designation for a Roman province organized in 25 B.C. in the southern portion of this territory. Ethnographically, the name was applied to the more remote northern region, whose indigenous people were Gallic in ancestry. Paul's apparently consistent practice of using geographical terms officially recognized by the Roman government strongly favors the hypothesis that "Galatia" is a provincial designation. Elsewhere, when Paul groups churches together he adopts Roman provincial titles: "The churches of *Asia*" (1 Cor. 16:19); "the churches of God . . . in *Judea*" (1 Thess. 2:14); "the churches of *Macedonia*" (1 Cor. 16:19; 2 Cor. 8:1; 9:2). A reference to "the churches of *Galatia*" (1 Cor. 16:1) as having a part in the collection for the needy Christians in Jerusalem is of particular interest. Whenever Paul speaks of this project in his letters he uses provincial names (2 Cor. 8:1; 9:2, 4; Rom. 15:26), pitting the churches of one province against those of another in a wholesome rivalry. Paul and Barnabas had evangelized this area on the first missionary journey, founding churches at Derbe, Lystra, Iconium, and Pisidian Antioch (Acts 13–14). If it was

Paul's intention to address these church centers, there was no general term he could have chosen except "Galatia."[5]

Some time after the establishment of these predominantly Gentile churches (Gal. 4:8–9),[6] a serious attempt was made to draw the Galatians away from the gospel which Paul had proclaimed to them (1:6–9). Teachers arrived who subsumed the gospel under the larger category of Judaism. Evidently appealing to the Old Testament promises to Abraham and his seed, these "Judaizers" taught that salvation depended upon the covenant of circumcision which God had concluded with Abraham as well as upon faith in Jesus Christ.[7] In order to become a Christian, a Gentile had to first become a full proselyte to Judaism, submitting to circumcision and showing himself zealous for the law. While the teachers had stopped short of imposing the whole law upon the Galatians, they had persuaded them to adopt the calendar of Jewish feasts and fasts (3:7, 9, 14; 4:10, 21–31; 5:1–12).

Paul immediately sensed the implications of this synthesis, which he labeled an attempt to pervert the gospel of Christ (1:7). Unless checked, it would require eventually that all Gentile Christians live under the law and express their faith within the religious and cultural confines of Judaism. The theological issue revolved on the axis of legal righteousness as against righteousness through faith.

In addition, the Judaizers had launched a personal attack on Paul himself. In an attempt to discredit his gospel, they challenged his authority as an apostle. True apostleship, they claimed, required a direct commission from Christ, yet Paul had no independent knowledge of Christianity beyond what he had learned in Jerusalem from the Twelve. Moreover, he preached the gospel in a distorted form. He desired to please men by dispensing a gospel which had been accommodated to Gentile tastes at crucial points.

The first two chapters of Galatians provides primary evidence for this serious challenge to Paul's apostleship. His thundering reply rises in indignation and alarm at a moment when the churches of Galatia were on the verge of succumbing to the arguments of the Judaizers. The letter thus addresses an intensely concrete mission situation in which both the doctrinal and the personal issues are coming to a head. In sharpest terms Paul sketches the contrast between apostleship and the pleasing of men (chs. 1–2), between the gospel and the law (chs. 3–4), and between freedom and bondage (chs. 5–6).

At the very beginning of the epistle the apostle alerts the Galatians that there is to be no dodging of the basic conflict: "Paul an apostle—not from men nor through man, but through Jesus Christ. . . . For I would have you know, brethren, that the gospel which was preached by me *is not man's gospel*. For I did not receive it *from man,* nor was I taught it, but it came *through a revelation of Jesus Christ*" (1:1, 11–12). The falseness of the charge that Paul had learned the gospel from the Jerusalem Twelve becomes evident in the rehearsal of the circumstances of his conversion (1:13–2:14). "I did not confer with flesh and blood, nor did I go up to Jerusalem to those who were apostles before me, but I went away into Arabia; and again I returned to Damascus" (1:16–17). Not until three years later did he confer with Cephas (Peter) and with James, the leader of the Jerusalem church (1:18 f.). It was only after fourteen years that he and Barnabas returned to Jerusalem to confer with "the pillars" of that church (2:1–10). These conferences, Paul protests, added nothing to his gospel. On the contrary, it was clearly recognized that the same God who had laid hold of Peter for a mission directed to Jews was working through Paul to bring Gentiles to a knowledge of Christ. The "pillar apostles" had in fact then extended to Paul and Barnabas the right hand of fellowship in recognition of the divine call. It was in fact basic agreement on the essentials of the gospel which gave meaning to Paul's contention with Peter at Antioch (2:11–16).[8] Paul and the Jerusalem Twelve preached the same gospel (cf. 1 Cor. 15:1–11); it was the Judaizers who urged *another* gospel of alien character.

Moreover, the fact that the apostle is opposed and persecuted indicates that he is not in the business of pleasing men (Gal. 1:10; 5:11–12, 26; 6:12, 17). It is his preaching of the cross, not circumcision, which brings the lash of the whip (5:11). Not Paul but the Judaizers are selfishly accommodating the gospel: "It is those who want to make a good showing in the flesh that would compel you to be circumcised, and only in order that they may not be persecuted for the cross of Christ" (6:12). In contrast to Second Corinthians, with its extensive lists of the sufferings which identify the true apostle, Paul here contents himself with a single, eloquent declaration: "Henceforth let no man trouble me; for I bear on my body the marks of Jesus" (6:17).

In the second section, the apostle turns to the larger questions of law and gospel (chs. 3–4). Throughout these middle chapters, appeal is made to the Galatians' experience (cf. 3:1–5; 4:8–11). Before the arrival of the Judaizers the divine message had borne rich fruit in their midst. By responding in faith to the truth of this gospel, they showed their true credentials as sons of Abraham. The argument was important because the Judaizers had made much of the promises granted to the patriarch and his descendants. The Galatians had been urged to submit to circumcision, as Abraham had done, in order to become his children. Paul reminded them that Abraham's faith and his reception of God's promises had preceded the covenant of circumcision as well as the giving of the law at Sinai (3:6–29; 4:21–31).

Such an argument shows that Paul took seriously the scriptures of the Old Covenant. He appeals to them repeatedly. What he opposed was not the law but Judaistic attempts at self-justification through observance of the law. He insisted that the law's function was to expose the nature and universality of transgression: all men were in sin's bondage and guilty before God. The categorical rule was "Cursed be every one who does not abide by all things written in the book of the law, and do them" (Deut. 27:26; Gal. 3:10). Failure to obey the law involved all men in this curse. Because man is a slave to sin, only God can put him in the right. Justification is provided through Christ, who submitted to the law's curse: "Cursed be every one who hangs on a tree" (Deut. 21:23; Gal. 3:13). Salvation, therefore, is never *achieved* through performance of the works of the law; it is *received* as God's gift of life provided through Christ crucified.

The final section of the letter (chs. 5–6) develops the contrast between bondage and freedom. Paul anticipates this discussion in 4:21–31 with his allegory of Abraham's two sons. This imagery in turn sets the stage for a clarion call to freedom in 5:1: "For freedom Christ has set us free; stand fast therefore, and do not submit again to a yoke of slavery."

The demand for Gentile circumcision entailed consequences the Judaizers had never spelled out. By his death Christ had rescued men from those powers that enslaved them and separated them from God (1:4; 3:13; 4:4–11). The Holy Spirit within their hearts authenticated their sonship with the prayer, "Abba, Father" (4:6–7). Possessing such freedom of utterance and access to God, how could they now return to bondage under the law? Acceptance of the terms specified by the Judaizers involved perils so serious that Paul's solemn language is virtually unparalleled:

Now I, Paul, say to you that if you receive circumcision, Christ will be of no advantage to you. I testify again to every man who receives circumcision that he is bound to keep the whole law. You are severed from Christ, you who would be justified by the law; you have fallen away from grace (5:2–4).

This must not be construed as a condemnation of Jewish Christians who were in any case already circumcised, as was Paul himself. To such men Paul had addressed himself in another context: if God's call came to a man while he was a Jew, "let him not seek to remove the marks of circumcision"; if the call came while he was a Gentile, "let him not seek circumcision" (1 Cor. 7:17–20). Paul did not condemn the practice of the Jewish-Christian community in Jerusalem. What he condemned was the declaration that such rites were necessary for salvation in the Gentile churches. Imposed as law, they would in effect repudiate the sufficiency of Christ's death, break the vital bond of faith in him, and leave man helpless as before in slavery to sin and death.

As a triumphant alternative Paul offers the righteousness of Christ bestowed freely on those who exercise faith:

> For through the work of the Holy Spirit, as a result of faith, we Christians eagerly wait for the justification which we may confidently expect. For when a man is related to Jesus Christ, neither his state as circumcised nor uncircumcised makes any difference. What makes a difference is Christian faith active in love* (5:5–6).

True freedom finds expression in loving service of others. Such service not only fulfills the whole law (5:14) but exhibits those spiritual qualities of life against which there is no law (5:22–23). The Holy Spirit thus provides for the adjustment and control of the Christian's life which permits the application of church discipline with gentleness (6:1–5) and a zeal for well-doing on behalf of all men (6:7–10).

The bitterness of the conflict and the extreme peril to which his churches had been exposed left the apostle exhausted. Brushing the last vestiges of the quarrel from himself, he found his peace in the knowledge of his own close relationship to the crucified One: "Far be it from me to glory except in the cross of our Lord Jesus Christ, by which the world has been crucified to me, and I to the world" (6:14). Over against the distinguishing marks of circumcision championed by the Judaizers, Paul could point to "the marks of Jesus" (6:17), the scars incurred through the flogging and stoning that he joyfully endured for the sake of his Lord. These were for Paul not only the insignia of the true minister of God but tokens of the "new creation" (6:15). Crucified to the old world by his sufferings, he embraced the new with confidence that "if any one is in Christ, he is a new creation; the old has passed away, behold, the new has come" (2 Cor. 5:17).

NOTES

1. The unity of Second Corinthians is here assumed. J. H. Kennedy, *The Second and Third Epistles to the Corinthians* (1900), argued that chapters 1–9 and chapters 10–13 of 2 Corinthians were incomplete parts surviving from two distinct letters which had been mistakenly joined together at an early date. The argument has been repeated and refined by many later writers, most recently by G. Bornkamm, "The History of the Origin of the So-called Second Letter to the Corinthians," in *The Authorship and Integrity of the New Testament,* K. Aland, D. Guthrie, *et al.* (1965), pp. 73–81. The defense of the integrity of Second Corinthians has assumed as many different forms as the attack upon its unity. See J. Munck, *Paul and the Salvation of Mankind* (1959), pp. 168–171; P. Hughes, *Paul's Second Epistle to the Corinthians* (1962), pp. xxi–xxxv; A. M. G. Stephenson, "A Defense of the Integrity of 2 Corinthians," *The Authorship and Integrity of the New Testament, op. cit.,* pp. 82–97.

2. It is possible that Timothy is the brother referred to in 2 Cor. 8:22: "we are sending *our brother* whom we have often tested and found earnest in many matters, but who is now more earnest than ever because of his great confidence in you," since in 1:1 he is described as "Timothy *our brother.*" For a summary of conjectures see Hughes, *op. cit.,* pp. 312–16.

3. For the alternative proposal that the letter written with tears is First Corinthians, see Stephenson, *op. cit.,* pp. 85–97; Hughes, *op. cit.,* pp. xxviii–xxx, 54–65, 275–78. A chief objection to this proposal is the description of the effects the letter produced upon the congregation, together with its relevance to the apostle personally.

4. Munck, *op. cit.,* p. 186; the contrast between the true and the false apostle is carefully developed on pp. 175–87.

5. The question of destination is fully treated by W. M. Ramsay, *A Historical Commentary on St. Paul's Epistle to the Galatians* (1900), pp. 1–234, and E. D. Burton, *A Critical and Exegetical Commentary on the Epistle to the Galatians* (1921), pp. xvii–xliv.

6. It is probable that Galatians was written before Romans on the third missionary journey, perhaps from Ephesus (see Burton, *op. cit.,* pp. xliv–xlix). Romans presents calmly and deliberately the material which in Galatians is shaped by the heat of controversy.

7. Presumably, the Judaizers are Jewish Christians from the strict Judaic wing of the Jerusalem church who earlier had made a strong plea for circumcision as a requirement for Gentile admission to the church (Acts 15:1). An alternate suggestion has been developed recently by Munck, *op. cit.,* pp. 87–134. He argues that the Judaizers were actually Galatians, who as Gentiles had no knowl-

edge of Jewish Christianity or of the Jerusalem Twelve other than what they had gleaned from Paul himself.

8. See J. Gresham Machen, *The Origin of Paul's Religion* (1947), pp. 104–113, 119–30.

SELECTED READING

Barrett, C. K., "Paul and the 'Pillar Apostles,' " in *Studia Paulina in honorem J. de Zwaan.* Haarlem: E. F. Bohn, 1953. Pp. 1–19.

Burton, E. D., *The Epistle to the Galatians.* New York: Scribner's, 1920.

Hughes, P., *Paul's Second Epistle to the Corinthians.* Grand Rapids: Eerdmans, 1962.

Knox, D. B., "The Date of the Epistle to the Galatians," *Evangelical Quarterly,* 12 (1941), pp. 262–68.

Lindsey, P. P., "Paul and the Corinthian Church," *Journal of Biblical Literature,* 68 (1949), pp. 341–50.

Machen, J. G., *The Origin of Paul's Religion.* Grand Rapids: Eerdmans, 1947. Pp. 71–113.

Manson, T. W., "The Problem of the Epistle to the Galatians" and "The Corinthian Correspondence (1) and (2)," in *Studies in the Gospels and Epistles,* M. Black, ed. Philadelphia: Westminster, 1962. Pp. 168–89, 191–224.

Munck, J., "The Judaizing Gentile Christians: Studies in Galatians" and "The True and the False Apostle: Studies in II Corinthians," in *Paul and the Salvation of Mankind.* Richmond: John Knox, 1959. Pp. 87–134, 168–95.

Ridderbos, H. N., *The Epistle to the Galatians.* Grand Rapids: Eerdmans, 1954.

XII

✳

ROMANS—JEWS AND GENTILES
IN ONE CHURCH

ROMANS has always had a special attraction for systematic theologians, who have produced some of the most distinguished commentaries on the epistle. Their work has fostered the widespread opinion that Romans is essentially a theological treatise in which Paul sets forth his system of Christian doctrine.

It is true that Romans is laden with theological insights. But to the degree that the missionary character of the letter is obscured, it is false to hold that Romans is primarily a theological document. It is necessary to reiterate that Paul was always a task theologian who expressed theological truth precisely in the concrete context provided by his mission to the Gentiles.

1. A MISSION DOCUMENT

Paul is writing to a congregation he had never visited. This is indicated by the specific statement that he had often wished to come to Rome but had thus far been prevented from doing so (Rom. 1:13). There is no way of knowing how the church came to be established on the Tiber. Residents from Rome were present in Jerusalem on the day of Pentecost (Acts 2:10), and Italians stationed militarily in Caesarea had come to faith quite early (10:1–11:18). Moreover, the relative ease of travel during the Imperial Age made it possible for any number of Christians to reach the capital, there to furnish the nucleus for a gathering of believers. It seems clear that when the emperor Claudius expelled the Jews from Rome in 49 (see below, p. 312) there was already an active Christian movement within the Jewish quarter of the city, and that Aquila and Priscilla had participated in it (cf. 18:1–2). There is no evidence that the founding of the church was the work of any apostolic figure. By the time Paul penned this letter the congregation was largely Gentile in character; since Paul knew himself to be the apostle to the Gentiles he assumed that it belonged within his sphere of missionary endeavor. He writes: "I have often intended to come to you . . . in order that I may reap some harvest *among you as well as among the rest of the Gentiles*" (Rom. 1:13). Having completed his mission in the east, Paul turned westward with a single ambition—to preach the gospel in centers where Christ has not already been named, "lest I build on another man's foundation" (15:20).

If this is true, why then does Paul wish to reach Rome, where the church is well established? The apostle's answer reiterates that he had been prevented from coming to Rome:

> This is the reason why I have so often been hindered from coming to you. But now, since I no longer have any room for work in these regions, and since I have longed for many years to come to you, *I hope to see you in passing as I go to Spain, and to be sped on my journey there by you*, once I have enjoyed your company for a little (15:22–24).

The hindrance of which Paul speaks both at the opening and close of his letter (1:13; 15:22) was the necessity to fulfill his mission to the Gentiles in the east. His work having been completed there, he may now come to Rome. But the italicized words indicate that Paul has no intention of remaining in Rome. He will merely pass through, for his face is set resolutely toward the Iberian peninsula where Christ is yet unknown. The encouragement that he may receive from Rome—which is only hinted at in 1:1–12—is here made explicit. The capital must serve as the base for further mission. The apostle urges the Christians there to thrust him forward to Spain. It is for this reason that Paul writes. His letter is essentially a missionary manifesto. The parallel references at the opening and close of the body of the letter mark Romans in its entirety as a mission document.

2. THE RIGHTEOUSNESS OF GOD

Paul's thought is thoroughly God-centered. When he writes about salvation he speaks of the righteousness *of God*. Explaining his eagerness to preach the gospel at Rome, he states:

> For I am not ashamed of the gospel: it is the power of God for *salvation* to every one who has *faith, to the Jew first* and also *to the Greek*. For in it the *righteousness of God* is revealed through faith for faith; as it is written, "*He who through faith is righteous* shall live." For *the wrath of God* is revealed from heaven against all ungodliness and wickedness of men who by their wickedness suppress the truth (1:16–18).

This passage is pivotal for all that follows. Not only does it begin the body of the letter, but the words italicized above introduce the key themes Paul treats—salvation through faith, God's provision for Jew and Gentile, the justification of believers and wrath upon the ungodly. Throughout the epistle these themes are interwoven, for each is a corollary of the righteousness of God.

The context in which Paul introduces the concept of the righteousness of God is the most striking feature of his exposition. Every passage in which Paul speaks of righteousness occurs within a larger context discussing the relationship of Jews and Gentiles in the one church of Christ.[1] In each instance they illustrate the thoroughly missionary character of Romans. Paul's teaching on justification by faith is best understood as the answer to a persistent question: How is it possible for the Jew and the Gentile to stand on the same level of advantage before God?[2]

Briefly, Paul's answer is a demonstration that all men stand on the same level of *dis*advantage. They have rebelled against God and stand condemned before him (1:18–3:20). Both Jew and Gentile have earned wages paid in the coin of a realm whose prince is death (6:23). Both stand in the same necessity to be put in the right through God's reconciling action in Christ.

As a biblical theologian Paul knew that God's righteousness stemmed from his holiness. In and through the gospel he finds revealed the righteousness of God and the wrath of God (1:17–18). The note of wrath is by no means unique to Paul; it is grounded in the Old Testament teaching.[3] Wrath is God's judging righteousness, as distinguished from his saving righteousness. Paul saw that, consistent with God's character as just and holy, the revelation of God's righteousness entails the revelation of his wrath. For Paul salvation is *from* wrath as well as *unto* God.[4]

In a few pregnant verses Paul brings together the several strands of thought he has been developing:

> While we were *yet helpless,* at the right time *Christ died for the ungodly.*
> . . . But God commends his own love to us in that while we were *yet sinners*

Christ died for us. Since, therefore, we are *now justified* by his blood, much more shall we be saved by him from *the wrath of God.* For if while we were *enemies* we were *reconciled to God* by the death of his Son, much more, now that we are reconciled, shall we be *saved by his life.* Not only so, but we also rejoice in God through our Lord Jesus Christ, through whom we have *received our reconciliation** (5:6, 8–11).

The italicized words catch the keynotes in Paul's gospel. God displayed his righteousness, his holiness, and his love in turning away wrath through his Son. When Paul speaks of the righteousness of God he has in mind the particular historical manifestation in the life and death of Jesus. God justifies the man who has faith in Jesus as the focus of reconciliation.[5]

The emphasis upon faith is crucial to Paul. Declaring that the law and the prophets bear witness to the new display of God's righteousness (3:21), Paul derives biblical support for his teaching especially from two texts. First in appearance is the word from the prophets: "He who *through faith is righteous* shall live" (cf. Hab. 2:4). The second text is taken from the law: "Abraham *believed God,* and it was *reckoned* to him as *righteousness*" (cf. Gen. 15:6). The point seized by Paul in both texts is that the righteousness of God is appropriated *through faith.* If this was so under the Old Covenant, it is no less true within the frame of reference provided by the New.

3. THE LAW OF GOD

From the time of Ezra, Judaism had expressed its self-consciousness in terms of possessing the law of God. A common Pharisaic conviction, repeated throughout rabbinic literature, is that God would have abandoned Israel to the fate of other nations long forgotten in the dust of history had it not been for the law. In the midst of the harshest realities of war and oppression the law is proof that God has not forsaken his people.[6] Possession of the law was one of the great advantages of Judaism: "Then what advantage has the Jew? Or what is the value of circumcision? Much in every way. To begin with, the Jews are entrusted with the oracles of God [i.e., the law]" (3:1–2). It was inevitable then that in pursuing the question how the Jew and the Gentile could stand on the same level of advantage before God, Paul would have to touch upon the law of God.

The apostle insists that the relative advantage of the Jew in possessing the law has been neutralized. It has in fact become an absolute deficiency because of failure to obey the law (2:13). A Jew cannot claim any special benefit from his circumcision unless he lives up to that law to which circumcision is a witness (2:25–29). In this turn of events Paul finds the fulfillment of Isaiah 52:5, "The name of God is blasphemed among the Gentiles because of you" (2:24). As in the matter of God's righteousness, the social context of Paul's discussion of the law is the relationship of Jews and Gentiles in one church.

In a church fast becoming predominantly Gentile in character there were other questions concerning the Mosaic law. What was the function of the law—why was it given? Was the law an instrument of sin? What was Christ's relationship to the law? Paul explores these questions for his readers over the course of several chapters, but most fully in chapter 7, which could be entitled "An Apology for the Law."

The pivotal verses for understanding Paul's presentation are verse 5, which introduces the theme of 7:7–25, and verse 6, which anticipates the argument of chapter eight.

> 7:5—*While we were living in the flesh,* our sinful passions, aroused by the law, were at work in our members to bear fruit for *death* (cf. 7:7–25).

> 7:6—*But now* we are *discharged from the law,* dead to that which held us captive, so that we serve not under the old written code but in *the new life of the Spirit.*

In the first passage human life is characterized as *flesh,* a term which here describes the *whole man* who faces his Creator as sinner.[7] Paul is saying that sin is a power which seizes the whole man and reduces him to captivity and ultimately to death: "I am fleshly, the purchased slave of sin"* (7:14). While the law was the revealed will of God, holy and good, it was powerless to deliver the life which it promised, for it was weakened by man *as flesh.* Apart from God's intervention man is reduced to a cry of intense anguish: "Wretched man that I am! Who will deliver me from this body of death?" (7:24).

The second passage could be paraphrased, "But now that Christ has come we are discharged from the law, dead to sin which held us captive, so that we serve God . . . in the new life which is created by the Holy Spirit." It indicates that God has acted, judging sin and vanquishing its power through Christ. Paul summarizes his argument in one pithy statement:

> For God has done what the law, weakened by the flesh, could not do: sending his own Son in the likeness of sinful flesh and for sin, he condemned sin in the flesh, in order that the just requirement of the law might be ful-

filled in us, who walk not according to the flesh but according to the Spirit (8:3–4).

The Holy Spirit, given by God to all who believe in Christ, becomes the dynamic for fulfilling "the just requirement of the law." The meaning of walking according to the Spirit is clarified throughout chapter eight. But what is most striking is that Paul clearly has in mind a congregation in which there are Jews as well as Gentiles. Speaking of the spirit of sonship which God bestows upon all who are led by his Spirit, Paul writes: "When we cry, 'Abba! Father!' it is the Spirit himself bearing witness with our spirit that we are the children of God" (8:15–16). The Jewish Christian uses the intimate Aramaic designation for father, Abba, when addressing God. The Gentile acknowledges his sonship with the cry of Father. The law of God, which might have separated Jew and Gentile, is replaced by the Spirit of God who unites them in common worship.[8] The context remains the relationship of Jews and Gentiles in the one church of Christ.

4. THE VERACITY OF GOD

In Romans 8:28 ff. Paul asserts in the strongest terms that those whom God calls may trust him in everything. His peroration rings with confident joy: nothing "will be able to separate us from the love of God in Christ Jesus our Lord" (8:39). Yet earlier in the chapter the privileges of sonship and of being counted as heirs are bestowed upon the church of Jews and Gentiles (8:16–17), although they had belonged originally to Israel.[9] But increasingly the church was becoming Gentile; the privileges were becoming *Gentile* prerogatives. Thus the question had to be raised: Is God reliable? Can he be trusted with regard to his intention and purpose for Israel? The answer is provided in Romans 9–11. Centrally in view is God's purpose and plan, which is set forth with great care (cf. 9:6; 11:33–36). Because Paul focuses attention on God and his acts within the larger context of the history of salvation, chapters 9 through 11 are crucial to an understanding of Romans.

The substance of these chapters concerns primarily the destiny of the people of Israel. This theme is by no means new; the antithesis of Jew and Gentile can be traced in all of the previous chapters. At no point, however, has it been treated fully. Moreover, Paul had earlier raised the question concerning the advantage of being a Jew, to which the answer was, "First of all, the Jews are entrusted with the word of God"* (3:1–2).

"First of all" anticipates something more, but the thought is left incomplete until chapter 9, where the advantages of Israel are fully listed (9:4–5; 11:28–29). Thus in spite of the sharp change in mood and tone between 8:39 and 9:1 the definite continuity of chapter 9 with all that has preceded must not be neglected.

In this new section Paul states that the failure of Israel to respond to grace is not a frustration of God's eternal plan and purpose. Rather it is in complete agreement with divine principles applied throughout the history of the covenant people.

At no other point in his letters does Paul cite the Old Testament text as much as he does here. In order to prove the veracity of God, Paul has to demonstrate that the present situation corresponds to the word of prophecy.[10] Accordingly, Scripture is cited as both a witness for and an accuser against Israel, and to establish God's faithfulness in realizing his eternal plan. This sovereign purpose of God is a saving purpose. His absolute will is directed toward the salvation of his people, whether Jew or Gentile. The present developments are not chance happenings but stand within God's purpose as delineated in Old Testament prophecy. When Paul refers to the element of surprise ("this mystery," 11:25), he does not mean the salvation of the Gentiles, for this had been prophesied in the Scripture. The surprise is that *now* is the time when God is gathering the Gentiles, even though the prophecies which spoke of a glorified Jerusalem to which the Gentiles bring their gifts remained unfulfilled.

Central to Paul's thinking throughout the whole of this argument is the biblical concept of the remnant. It is clear from the Old Testament that Israel was never what we would regard as an ideal people of God. She is described as stubborn,[11] answering God's grace with ungratefulness, his loyalty with disloyalty, his goodness with evil. Israel merited and experienced God's judgment repeatedly throughout her history. Nevertheless, a part of Israel was preserved and saved from the time of the wilderness wanderings (Joshua and Caleb) to Paul's day (Rom. 11:1). In this perspective Israel's history is the history of the remnant, and of the remnant of the remnant.

The very existence of a remnant indicates that God's judgment on Israel was not total. Accordingly, the remnant is a sign both of divine wrath and of divine grace. Inasmuch as divine grace prevails, the remnant becomes a unique witness for salvation. That God leaves a remnant is a witness to his grace and a comforting reality.[12] More important, the remnant that experiences salvation is henceforth considered the nucleus of a new people of God, or *all Israel*. The object of salvation is never the preservation of the remnant for its own sake, but the creation of a new people.

Chapter 9 depicts God's act in establishing the remnant through calling and hardening, while chapter 10 illustrates the human response in acceptance or rejection of saving faith. In chapter 11 the comforting note breaks through:

> I ask, then, has God rejected his people? By no means! I myself am an Israelite. . . . God has not rejected his people whom he foreknew (vss. 1–2; cf. Ps. 94:14).

> So too at the present time there is a remnant, chosen by grace (vs. 5).

> What then? Israel failed to obtain what it sought. The elect obtained it, but the rest were hardened (vs. 7).

> . . . and so all Israel will be saved (vs. 26).

In this light the continuity of 8:39 and 9:1 ff. becomes clearer. Paul concludes chapter 8 with the joyful assertion that nothing "will be able to separate us from the love of God in Christ Jesus our Lord" (vs. 39). The extended section which follows (chs. 9–11) prove that this is true even with reference to Israel. The remnant principle, so well known from the Old Testament, continues to be exercised under the New Covenant. Now it has been extended to the Gentiles as well. To use Paul's image, the Gentile branches, being from a wild olive tree, "were grafted in *among them*"* and participate "*with them*"* in the root and fatness of the olive tree (cf. 11:17–24). In the New Covenant, Jews and Gentiles are called simultaneously according to God's sovereign purpose "in order to make known the riches of his glory for the vessels of mercy, which he has prepared beforehand for glory, even us whom he has called, not from the Jews only but also from the Gentiles" (9:23–24).

The calling of God, however, must not be conceived as an act occurring independently of the message of divine grace and justification (10:8–17). God's call remains his free act, but historically he confronts man concretely in Jesus Christ, calling an individual to the obedience of faith. In this light chapters 9 to 11 constitute a hymn of praise and comfort. Although a hardening has come upon a part of Israel (11:25), another part will always hear and respond to God's call until unbelief is finally overcome and "all Israel will be saved" (11:26).

In the chapters immediately following, Paul addresses himself to a number of practical duties which fall to the lot of believers. These concern their relationship to one another within the fellowship of faith and their conduct in the exercise of social and political responsibilities (chs. 12–14). His primary concern is to urge them to dedicate themselves without reservation to the God who shows his faithfulness and generosity to Jews and Gentiles alike. What Paul has to say at this point to the church in Rome draws its strength from the fact that these admonitions immediately follow chapters nine through eleven. This becomes clear when 12:1 is paraphrased: "I appeal to you, brethren, on the ground of the veracity of God. . . ."

Whether Paul is discussing the righteousness of God, the law, or the veracity of God, it is striking that in the letter to the Romans the context is constantly the relationship of Jews and Gentiles in the one church. It cannot be doubted that Paul's argument is theologically significant. But neither can one fail to see that the apostle to the Gentiles remains a teacher with a pastoral concern for the hearts of men. With all of its profound depth, Romans remains a thoroughly missionary document, informing the church of this day as it did the church in Rome.

NOTES

1. See Rom. 1:17; 2:13; 3:4, 21–26, 28; 4:2 f., 9; 5:1, 9, 12–19; 8:30–33; 9:30; 10:3 f., 6, 10.

2. The context-in-life of Jewish-Gentile relationships is highly significant but has frequently been neglected by interpreters. It is present only in Romans, Galatians, and Ephesians. Its essential absence from Paul's other epistles may account for the fact that Paul speaks of justification by faith only in Romans and Galatians (where the context is polemical), apart from a brief allusion in Titus 3:5. See further W. D. Davies, *Paul and Rabbinic Judaism,* 2d ed. (1955), pp. 221–23.

3. See R. V. G. Tasker, *The Biblical Doctrine of the Wrath of God* (1952).

4. Cf. Rom. 3:24 f.; 5:12–21, on which see L. Morris, *The Apostolic Preaching of the Cross,* 2d ed. (1960), pp. 125–85, and R. Nicole, "C. H. Dodd and the Doctrine of Propitiation," *Westminster Theological Journal,* 17 (1955), pp. 117–57.

5. The terms which describe the inbreaking of salvation appropriately stress God's sovereign initiative: God's righteousness is *revealed* (1:17); it is *displayed* (3:25–26).

6. Cf. the early rabbinic comment on Lev. 26:44: "And what has been left to them that it might be said they were not abhorred or spurned? Indeed, all

the goodly gifts which were given to them were taken away from them. And if it had not been for the book of the Law which was left to them they would not have been different from the nations of the whole world" (*Sifra* VIII. 10 [Weiss, ed., p. 112c]).

7. See especially W. Kümmel, *Man in the New Testament* (1963), pp. 49–61.

8. Cf. 10:4, "Christ is the end of the law, that every one who has faith may be justified," on which see J. Murray, *The Epistle to the Romans,* II (1965), pp. 49–51.

9. Cf. Exod. 4:22; Deut. 1:31; Isa. 43:6; Jer. 31:9; and especially Rom. 9:4, "They are Israelites, and to them belong the sonship . . . and the promises."

10. The following word statistics are enlightening: in 11:1–6, where Paul proves that there is yet a remnant according to God's promise, 39 out of 105 words occur as quotation of the Old Testament (i.e., 37 percent). In 11:7–10, where it is shown that Israel's failure was also within God's plan, 45 out of 71 words are Scripture (63 percent). Paul's argument rests on the revealed plan of God demonstrating that the present situation is precisely what God had indicated it would be.

11. Cf. Exod. 32:9; 33:3, 5; Isa. 43:24, *et al.*

12. Cf. Pss. 124; 126; Mic. 3:12; Zech. 8:12; Mal. 3:20.

SELECTED READING

Barrett, C. K., *The Epistle to the Romans.* New York: Harper, 1957.

Blaiklock, E. M., *Rome in the New Testament.* London: Inter-Varsity Fellowship, 1959.

Cerfaux, L., *The Church in the Theology of St. Paul.* New York: Herder & Herder, 1959. Pp. 17–66, 72–79.

Manson, T. W., "St. Paul's Letter to the Romans—and Others," in *Studies in the Gospels and Epistles,* M. Black, ed. Philadelphia: Westminster, 1962. Pp. 225–41.

———— "The Significance of Christ as Saviour," in *On Paul and John.* London: S.C.M., 1963. Pp. 29–65.

Morris, L., *The Apostolic Preaching of the Cross,* 2d ed. London: Tyndale, 1960.

Munck, J., "The Manifesto of Faith: Comments on Romans" and "Israel and the Gentiles," in *Paul and the Salvation of Mankind.* Richmond: John Knox, 1959. Pp. 196–209, 247–81.

Murray, J., *The Epistle to the Romans,* 2 vols. Grand Rapids: Eerdmans, 1963–1965.

XIII

⁂

PHILIPPIANS AND PHILEMON—
THE INVOLVEMENT OF
THE APOSTLE

THE degree to which Paul involved himself in the life of his churches must be measured not only by controversy—as in Second Corinthians and Galatians—but by two delicate expressions from his pen. Philippians is an acknowledgment of a gift Paul had received while in custody, and provides the apostle an opportunity to address again a church he had established perhaps a decade earlier. Philemon is a masterpiece of intercession on behalf of an escaped slave from Colossae. These letters expose a sensitive and deep involvement with persons as well as churches, infusing warmth into the New Testament portrait of Paul, the apostle and the man.

1. THE MISSION TO PHILIPPI

Following the Jerusalem Council, which secured the measure of freedom required by the Gentile mission, Paul and Barnabas appear to have divided between them the territories covered on the first missionary journey. Barnabas and Mark sailed for Cyprus. Paul and Silas went overland through Syria and Cilicia into Galatia, where (at Lystra) Timothy was added to the party (Acts 15:36–16:3). Paul's original intention had been to penetrate the Roman province of Asia, but at two decisive points he was checked: (1) "forbidden by the Holy Spirit to speak the word in Asia," the Apostle turned northward to Pisidian Antioch, crossed the Sultan Dagh mountain range, and continued north until he approached the borders of Bithynia, a senatorial province in northwest Asia Minor lying along the southern shore of the Black Sea (Acts 16:6); (2) when the party determined to enter Bithynia, taking the road north to Nicomedia, "the Spirit of Jesus did not allow them" (Acts 16:7). Accordingly they turned west toward Troas, a Roman colony and the regular port of call on journeys between Asia and Macedonia. Here, in a night vision, Paul saw a man pleading, "Come over to Macedonia and help us." Luke, who joined Paul at Troas,[1] recalls the eagerness with which the missionaries responded to this latest indication of the will of God: "immediately we sought to go on into Macedonia, concluding that God had called us to preach the gospel to them" (Acts 16:9–10). The course from Galatia to Philippi was thus marked out by divine vision, opening and closing doors of opportunity to the travelers. The four sailed directly to Samothrace and from there to Neapolis, the port city of Philippi where the Via Egnatia, the great overland highway from Dyrrachium, reached the sea. Eight miles inland from Neapolis they entered Philippi, "a chief city of the district of Macedonia, and a Roman colony"* (Acts 16:12).[2]

Philippi owed its importance to its geographical position. Macedonia is a mountainous province, and the city of Philippi extended from the summit of a mountain down the south side but overlooked a fertile plain, the alluvial basin of the Strymon River. The plain was separated from the sea by an elevated ridge which was impassable except for a natural depression east of the city. Consequently all travelers to the eastern provinces had to pass through Philippi to gain access to the sea.

In 42 B.C. the struggle for control of the Roman world was climaxed on the plain of Philippi. There the combined armies of Marc Antony and Octavian overtook and defeated the republican forces of Brutus and Cassius, the assassins of Julius Caesar. Recognizing Philippi's strategic location, Octavian commemorated his victory by reorganizing the existing community as a military colony. This entailed the settlement within the city of a large number of veterans, all Roman citizens, and the conferral of a Roman form of constitutional government. Under the provisions of the *jus Italicum,* the legal position of the colonists with respect to the ownership and transfer of property, payment and exemption from certain taxes, and local administration and law became the same as if they were on Italian soil. The official language of the colony was Latin, as in Rome; its coinage was Roman; its two chief magistrates were appointed in Rome and were exempt from interference by the provincial governor. In every respect a colony was intended to be a piece of Rome transplanted abroad. In 31 B.C. still more colonists were sent to Philippi following Octavian's victory at Actium. On this occasion the city received its full title, *Colonia Iulia Augusta Philippensis.*[3]

The city's proud status as a Roman colony furnishes the background to the account of Paul's mission in Philippi (Acts 16:12–40). The duration of the mission is unknown. Luke speaks of a stay within the city for several days preceding a Sabbath and then of residence for an unspecified time in the house of Lydia (Acts 16:12–15). Apart from the reference to Lydia and her household, who early came to faith, all of Luke's interest is concentrated on a single incident which precipitated the arrest, public beating, and expulsion of Paul and Silas. In the absence of a Jewish community in Philippi the apostle necessarily directed his message to Gentiles who were resident aliens in the city and toward enfranchised citizens. Typical of the first category was Lydia, a woman from Thyatira in Asia who had come under the influence of the synagogue, presumably in her native city where there was a prominent Jewish settlement. She had established residence in Philippi as a seller of dyed cloth and of the purple dye for which the Lydians were famous as early as the Homeric period (cf. *Iliad* IV. 141 f.). Together with her household she customarily observed the Jewish Sabbath, gathering for prayer "outside the gate" (Acts 16:13), in keeping with the Roman regulation that foreign cults must be practiced beyond the limits of the city gates. She and her household responded to Paul's presentation of the gospel and submitted to baptism, furnishing the nucleus for the church which appears to have gathered in her house (cf. Acts 16:40).

Paul's activity among resident citizens is known to us only because of the manner in which an official accusation against him was formulated. The charge was prompted by an incident involving a slave girl possessed by a spirit of divination.[4] When the spirit was expelled and the girl was no longer able to enrich her owners through her mantic speech, they seized Paul and Silas and dragged them before the municipal magistrates whose seat was in the marketplace. The formal indictment was that "these men who are Jews disturb our city and introduce customs which it is not allowed to us Romans to adopt and practice"* (Acts 16:20–21). The statement contains two distinct, though connected, charges: (1) Paul and Silas are accused of instigating riots and (2) of introducing an alien religion. The second charge is of particular interest, for it asserts a principle which, to judge from extant records, had not been invoked since the second century B.C. While officially the Roman citizen was not permitted to practice any alien cult that was not sanctioned by the State, in common practice he might do so providing his cult did not violate the laws and customs of Roman life. In effect this meant that any foreign cult was permitted which did not involve political or social crimes. The investigation and suppression of foreign cults was generally relaxed in the late Republican and early Imperial age. In the few cases in which the extravagances of a particular sect provoked a temporary ban upon its activities, it was the criminal activities of the sect—not the general principle of excluding alien cults—which occasioned intervention. What is remarkable about the second charge against Paul and Silas is the assertion of the ancient principle of incompatibility against an alien sect: "they introduce customs which we being Romans may not adopt."* The appeal for the magistrates to intervene is grounded not on the depravity of the practices which Paul urged but on their alien (un-Roman) character.[5]

Apart from its legal background, the indictment is important for indicating that Paul had not confined his mission to the riverside or to private gatherings within Lydia's house. The charge of proselytism among Roman citizens had point only if Paul and his company had made vigorous public efforts to propagate the gospel throughout the city, and specifically among citizens of the colony. The frank appeal to anti-Semitic prejudice—"These men, being Jews . . ."—may indicate an awareness of recent efforts of the emperor Claudius to discourage the spread of Judaism, and his expulsion of the Jews from Rome.[6] But the willingness of the magistrates to accept the accusation without a trial and the hostility of the townsmen suggest that the activity of the Christian leaders had received public notice prior to this incident. Paul and Silas were handed over to the police to be beaten with rods and imprisoned. The case was quickly dropped, however, and in the morning the missionaries were expelled from the city, with apologies from the magistrates for having mistreated Roman citizens without a trial (Acts 16:22–39). The affair recalls the provision for the treatment of itinerant seers or soothsayers in a fourth-century compendium of Roman law, the *Sententiae Pauli*: "The custom is to give them a beating and drive them out of the city."[7] In a letter to the Thessalonians Paul recalled the incident vividly. "As you know," he writes, "we had suffered and been shamefully treated at Philippi"* (1 Thess. 2:2).

From the narrative in Acts 16 we might judge that the church of Philippi consisted of a few women (Lydia and her household; the girl who had been possessed), the Roman jailer and his family (Acts 16:25–34), and some few others ("the brethren" of verse 40). This initial impression is probably mistaken. The work had been advanced sufficiently to merit leaving Luke at Philippi to give leadership to the young church.[8] Continued hostility on the part of significant elements in the city failed to intimidate the believers.

In the weeks that followed, they twice contributed to the support of Paul and his companions in Thessalonica (Phil. 4:15–16). When the apostle moved on to Corinth they sent aid to him again (2 Cor. 11:8–9). Their generosity repeatedly refreshed Paul and sealed their participation in his labors for the gospel. While Paul commends all of the churches of Macedonia for their eager support of the collection on behalf of the poor believers in Jerusalem, what he says was true preeminently of Philippi:

> . . . in a severe test of affliction, their abundance of joy and their extreme poverty have overflowed in a wealth of liberality on their part. For they gave according to their means, as I can testify, and beyond their means, of their own free will, begging us earnestly for the favor of taking part in the relief of the saints—and this, not as we expected, but first they gave themselves to the Lord and to us by the will of God" (2 Cor. 8:2–5).

It is certain that Paul revisited Philippi twice (Acts 20:1–6; 2 Cor. 2:12–13; 7:5–6) before his imprisonments in Jerusalem, Caesarea, and Rome, and it is probable that when he returned to Macedonia in the last years of his life (cf. Titus 3:12) he again made his way to Philippi, fulfilling his intention to visit the church once more (Phil. 1:26; 2:24). Between these two points may be located the communication that we know as Paul's Epistle to the Philippians.

2. WORD OF THANKSGIVING

Philippians is a deeply personal letter, written out of mature affection for a company of believers who had repeatedly encouraged Paul in his labors for Christ. It is essentially Paul's word of thanksgiving, not merely for a gift received and services rendered but for the warm concern the Philippians continued to show for him. Paul saw that the church was anxious concerning two specific matters: they had heard that his circumstances as a prisoner had changed, and they had learned of the severe illness of Epaphroditus, the messenger by whom they had delivered their gift to Paul. To relieve their anxiety Paul determined to send Epaphroditus back to Philippi, fully recovered, with a letter of commendation and assurance (Phil. 2:25–30).

Paul felt a closer emotional bond with the Philippians than with any of his other churches. This is evident from the opening lines of the letter in which, instead of asserting his apostleship, Paul contents himself with the designation "bondslave of Christ Jesus."* He does not hesitate to greet the financial officers who had been responsible for the collection and distribution of gifts, both for him and for the poor of Jerusalem.[9] From other churches Paul had been unwilling to accept for himself even the bare necessities of life (2 Cor. 11:8–11), but he was confident that his integrity was unquestioned at Philippi. He warmly acknowledges his readers' earnest participation in his mission: "I thank my God for all of your remembrance of me . . . for your partnership in the gospel from the first day until now"* (Phil. 1:3, 5). His prayer for the church is always marked by joy, and his thanksgiving is couched in intimate terms: "I hold you in my heart. . . . For God is my witness, how I yearn for you all with the affection of Christ Jesus" (1:4, 7–8). The ground of Paul's confidence for the steadfastness of the believers is God "who began a good work in you and who will mature it until the day of Jesus Christ"* (1:6). At the same time Paul prays that their love—for himself and for each other—may increase yet more, equipping them to participate in the full harvest of righteousness which is granted through Jesus Christ (1:9–11; cf. 2:12–13). One by one Paul touches upon the themes developed throughout this letter: his thanksgiving and affection for the Philippians, his profound confidence in God's sovereign control of all circumstances, the necessity for an increase in love, and Jesus Christ as the source of life and fruitfulness.

The anxiety of the Philippians for Paul's welfare is understandable. His circumstances had changed. He had recently come to trial and was currently in prison awaiting the verdict. The decision, once reached, was beyond appeal; he would either be released or sentenced to death (1:7, 13, 16, 19–26; 2:17). Paul was not deceived about the seriousness of the moment, nor was he unappreciative of the concern of his friends: "It was kind of you to share my trouble," he writes (4:14). Yet the appropriate response to anxiety was a quiet reliance upon God expressed through prayer.

> Yes, and I shall rejoice. For I know that *through your prayers* and the help of the Spirit of Jesus Christ this will turn out for my vindication . . . whether by life or death* (1:19–20).

> Have no anxiety about anything, but in everything *by prayer and supplication with thanksgiving let your requests be made known to God* (4:6).

In the latter passage the anxiety is specifically a concern for Paul in the face of trouble and uncertainty. The apostle assures his friends that the response of God to prayer offered with thanksgiving is peace, as a soldier on watch, standing guard over the hearts and minds of believers (4:7).

Paul possesses this peace, for behind the troubles that have befallen him he can discern the hand and purpose of God. His altered circumstances had actually served to advance the gospel. During the course of his trial it had become known to the whole praetorian guard and to all associated with his case that his imprisonment was for Christ, not for a criminal offense. Moreover, as a direct result of his defense of the gospel, local believers were proclaiming Christ with greater boldness (1:12–18). Their number included slaves and freedmen attached to the emperor's residence (4:22). While Paul is confident that he will be delivered from prison (1:19, 24–26), his ultimate trust is in God, whether he lives or dies. He exclaims triumphantly, "For to me to live is Christ, and to die is gain" (1:21). For Paul, as for the Philippians, Christ is the giver and sustainer of life, and the object of all his hopes.

In the appeals addressed to the church is included a call for steadfastness in the face of conflict (1:27–30). Only to Philippi, proud of the colonial status which conferred Roman citizenship on large segments of its population, does Paul write:

> Only *discharge your obligations as citizens* who are worthy of the gospel of Christ, so that whether I come and see you or am absent, I may hear of you that you *stand firm in one spirit, with one mind striving side by side* for the faith of the gospel, and *not frightened in anything by your opponents.* This is a clear omen to them of their destruction, but of *your vindication,* and that *from God** (1:27–28).

The company of men striving side by side, refusing to be frightened by their opponents, evokes the image of the phalanx, the body of lancers whose close and deep ranks constituted the most formidable military device in antiquity. With the phalanx Philip of Macedon had united Greece, while his son Alexander the Great had brought to its knees the mighty Persian Empire. Philip had founded the city of Philippi, bestowing upon it his name. It is unlikely that the Philippians missed Paul's allusion to their glorious past. Appealing to their pride as Macedonians and Romans, Paul urges their steadfastness as Christians, that they may be vindicated by God in a trial of faith similar in character to his own (1:29–30). Their conflict may have been associated with the imperial cult, for it is known that Philippi was one of the few Greek cities possessing an order of Roman citizens pledged to the worship of the divine Augustus— the *Augustales*—while an inscription at Neapolis refers to a municipal magistrate from Philippi who functioned as a high priest of the divine Claudius. A flourishing imperial cult would bid for the allegiance of all members of the colony. In the face of such pressures, the Philippians must stand firm with an uncompromising loyalty to Jesus Christ.[10]

In a passage contrasting Christians with the men of this world ("enemies of the cross of Christ . . . with minds set on earthly things" 3:18–19), Paul writes, "but our commonwealth is in heaven" (3:20). The term "commonwealth" was used technically to designate self-sufficient and self-governing communities of noncitizens who formed a city within a city. The metaphor came naturally to Paul's mind, for he had seen Jewish "commonwealths" in many of the larger cities of Asia. In Philippians his point is that "the Christians are not citizens, but resident aliens in the cities of the world, and their colony has special rules."[11] In any conflict of authority, their ultimate allegiance is to the heavenly commonwealth, from which they await the divine "Savior, the Lord Jesus Christ, who will change our lowly body to be like his glorious body, by the power which enables him even to subject all things to himself" (3:20–21). Like the designation "Lord," "Savior" was a term applied to the emperor in the imperial cult. Paul reminds the Philippians that the title is appropriate to Jesus Christ alone.

While conflict made unity imperative, it was important for its own sake as that which binds together the church in Christ (1:27; 2:2). This was much upon Paul's mind, not merely because of his experience of disunity in the church of Rome (1:15, 17) but because of a flagrant instance of disaffection that threatened the unity of the church at Philippi. "Therefore my brethren . . . *stand firm thus* in the Lord, my beloved. I entreat Euodia and I entreat Syntyche to have *the same disposition* in the Lord. And I ask you also, true yokefellow, help these women, for they have *contended side by side with me in the* gospel.* (4:1–3). By a sensitive use of language in chapter 2 Paul had prepared for this exhortation to Euodia and Syntyche. His admonition, to "do nothing from selfishness or conceit, but in humility count others better than yourselves" (2:3), finds supreme illustration in Christ Jesus, who refused to grasp selfishly at equality with God but assumed the form of a slave and in deep humility became obedient unto death (2:6–8). Euodia and Syntyche needed to understand that selfish vying for personal rights and honors is inconsistent with advancing the cause of Christ.

So careful has been Paul's preparation for this final entreaty that the somewhat turbulent opening of chapter 3 comes as an unexpected surprise. An abrupt change in tone and subject is apparent in the lack of transition between verses one and two:

Finally, my brethren, rejoice in the Lord. To write the same things to you is not irksome to me, and is safe for you.

> Look out for the dogs, look out for the evil-workers, look out for those who mutilate the flesh. For we are the true circumcision, who worship God in spirit, and glory in Christ Jesus, and put no confidence in the flesh" (3:1–3).

The probable explanation for the rupture in thought is that the apostle had been interrupted in the course of dictating the letter, and before returning had received a report of the renewed activity of the Judaizers—men who were attempting to put Christians back under the law and were boasting in their Jewish pedigree. Paul felt it necessary to warn his friends against such men. His manner of dealing with the issue contrasts strikingly with the careful doctrinal presentation which characterizes Galatians, and suggests that the Judaizers had not actually come to Philippi but were active elsewhere. Paul shows that "according to the flesh" he has more of which to boast than any of them—though to him this is "foolishness" (cf. 2 Cor. 11:19, 21, 23). He boasts of his birth, over which he had no control, and then of his own accomplishments in the law, zeal, and righteousness (Phil. 3:4–6). But he quickly passes to a different kind of "boasting" and a calmer conclusion (3:7–14). He has a new righteousness (3:9) and a new zeal (3:12–14). He who persecuted the church (3:6) now pursues the fulfillment of God's plan for his life (3:12) and the prize of the resurrection, the "upward call" of God in Christ Jesus (3:14). Christ is not merely the beginning of Paul's life but its present reality and its future goal (3:20–21). Having set forth Christ as the supreme object of Christian desire, Paul can make himself a secondary example to the church: "Brethren, join in imitating me, and mark those who so live as you have an example in us" (3:17; cf. ch. 4:9). Only then does Paul return to the matter of agreement, love, and courtesy in the Lord. The style is appropriate to private speech and the deeply personal character of the Philippian letter.

The letter draws to a conclusion as it had opened, with a further acknowledgment of the gifts received through Epaphroditus (4:18–20) and an expression of Paul's deep affection for his friends.

3. SLAVERY AND LIFE IN CHRIST

Paul's willingness to become personally involved in the lives of individuals as well as of churches is evident not only from Philippians but from the Epistle to Philemon as well. When the apostle found himself confronted by a fugitive slave who appealed for his help, he could not refuse it. The fact that the slave had a Christian master raised the larger issue of slavery and life in Christ. While Paul had faced this issue in earlier correspondence, it now forced itself upon him with a new relevance.

The economy of the Roman Empire was sustained on slavery.[12] Not merely the lowest, most degrading tasks but all forms of manual labor were considered beneath the dignity of a citizen and proper only to slaves. The less fortunate were assigned to gangs in the mines, the galleys, or the cattle sheds. The conditions under which they worked were appalling. They were treated like animals. Those who were artisans or who performed domestic and clerical tasks tended to find a more favored existence. Because a social stigma was attached to the conduct of business, such necessary transactions as the arrangement of loans and interest, the sale of goods, the keeping of accounts, and the supervision of other slaves were frequently entrusted to slaves skilled in commerce. Surprisingly, slaves also constituted the professional class of doctors, teachers, musicians, and artists. During the first century the Roman fleet was captained by the emperor's slaves. The support of the official and social life of the city of Rome alone demanded that one third (an estimated 600,000 individuals) of its population be enslaved. These hundreds of thousands of persons were subject not only to social barriers but to severe legal limitations: by Roman law, and in the common view, slaves were accorded no recognized existence in Roman society. They were not persons but chattels, possessing neither rights nor legal recourse against harsh and brutal treatment.

Since many of the early converts to Christianity were slaves, and others owned slaves, it was necessary for the Apostle Paul to define his position on slavery. Of several passages bearing on this issue, two are important for capturing the essence of what he says elsewhere.

1. In A.D. 55 Paul wrote to Corinth:

> Every one should remain in the state in which he was called. Were you a slave when called? Never mind. But if you can gain your freedom, avail yourself of the opportunity. For he who was called in the Lord as a slave is a freedman of the Lord. Likewise he who was free when called is a slave of Christ. You were bought with a price; do not become the slaves of men. So, brethren, in whatever state each was called, there let him remain with God" (1 Cor. 7:20–24).

Paul does not challenge the institution of slavery but deals with the situation as it then existed. He argues that a Christian may serve God in any social status. External circumstances are matters of indifference. While a Christian slave should avail himself of the opportunity for manumission,[13] even if he remains unliberated he may know the dignity of being the Lord's freedman.

2. Several years later the apostle wrote:

> Slaves, obey in everything those who are your earthly masters, not with eye-service, as men-pleasers, but in singleness of heart, fearing the Master. Whatever your task, work heartily, as serving the Master and not men, knowing that from the Master you will receive the inheritance as your reward; you are serving the Master, Christ. For the wrongdoer will be repaid for what he has done wrong, and there is no partiality.
>
> Masters, display justice and fairness to your slaves, knowing that you also have a Master in heaven"* (Col. 3:22–4:1).

Throughout this passage Paul draws a contrast between the earthly masters (*kyrioi*) whom slaves must serve and the Master (*kyrios*) of both slaves and their owners, Jesus Christ. Though conscious of the inequities between slaves and masters, Paul orders the slaves to obey wholeheartedly as an act of reverence to the Lord. In turn, their masters are reminded that they are accountable to a higher authority for the manner in which they treat their slaves. The entire passage furnishes the conclusion to a code in which nearly twice the amount of space (74 words) is allotted to the relationship of slaves and their masters compared with the directives to the free members of the household (42 words). Sufficient reason for this may be found in the fact that when Paul penned Colossians he was wrestling with the question of what he should do with the runaway slave who had sought refuge with him.

Onesimus, a slave owned by Philemon[14] of Colossae, had not only proved unsatisfactory in his work but had fled from his master after robbing him (Philem. 11, 15, 18). How he had discovered Paul, or under what circumstances he had sought refuge with him, are unknown, but his plight was intensely serious. The flight of a slave was one of the most momentous offenses recognized by Roman law. If the renegade was captured, the law permitted the wronged master great latitude in punishing him.[15] Commonly the slave would be branded with the letter F or FVG (for FVGITIVVS) on his forehead, and death by crucifixion was not unknown.[16] The entire legal question is complicated because it is unknown whether his owner was a Roman citizen or a provincial. The provisions of the civil law which deal with the detention of another's slave and the punishment of fugitive slaves pertained only to Roman citizens. If Philemon was a citizen, the *lex Fabia* provided a penalty of 50,000 sesterces to be paid to the owner by any person who concealed a slave who had fled from his master. Moreover, the wages or services owed for the period of the slave's absence were also demanded of one implicated in concealing a runaway. If the master was a provincial, a Roman citizen (like Paul) was not legally obligated to surrender the fugitive.[17]

Whatever the circumstance, the apostle determined to send Onesimus back to his owner. The decision must have been reached with great difficulty. Onesimus had become a Christian during his stay with the apostle and had proven so useful that Paul regarded him as a son and desired to retain him. Nevertheless, he became convinced that it was God's will to restore Onesimus to Philemon. In the company of Tychicus, the bearer of the letters to the churches at Colossae and Laodicea and the more personal note to Philemon, Onesimus returned to the Lycus Valley (cf. Col. 4:8–10).

The reception of Onesimus hinged upon the weight of the Epistle to Philemon. An incomparable model of spiritual direction, tact, and love, it provides a graphic illustration of the quite new way in which the apostle approaches the Christian master and slave relationship. It is Paul's briefest[18] and most personal letter. All of the Pauline letters are personal, in the sense that the apostle bares his concern for his readers even in his most collective and impersonal sections. But the letter to Philemon is more highly personal than the others, for it is solely concerned with a concrete problem in personal relationships. Nevertheless, this personal letter is not a private communication. Although it treats a very delicate question, and in the strictest sense concerns the decision of Philemon alone (see vss. 4–22), it both begins and ends as *a church epistle*. The salutation, in which Timothy is associated with Paul, is addressed to Philemon, Apphia (his wife), Archippus (their son?), and the church gathered in their house (vss. 1–3), while the employment of the plural form of the personal pronoun in the concluding benediction ("grace . . . be with *your* spirit") indicates that the church is again in view. The reason for this is not literary but theological: in the body of Christ personal affairs are no longer private.[19] The new existence in Christ is both personal and communal. What affects one member involves the whole body, the church (cf. 1 Cor. 12:12–27). This explains the peculiar form of the Epistle to Philemon, in which personal address is sandwiched between greetings to the congregation.

Paul's purpose in writing to Philemon is twofold: (1) to assure a favorable reception of Onesimus and (2) to urge Philemon to return to the apostle the formerly useless slave, that Onesimus may give himself to ministry. The first of these purposes is prominently in view, while the second is only delicately suggested.

Paul assumed that Philemon had a claim of ownership on Onesimus. It was for this reason that he had persuaded the slave to return to his master, even though to do so was like tearing out his own heart (Philem. 12). So intimately does Paul identify himself with his new son that he quickly adds he will comply with the Roman and Greek law making the father the financial guarantor for the debts of his child: "If he has wronged you at all, or owes you anything, *charge that to my account. I, Paul, write this with my own hand, I will repay it"* (vss. 18–19).

While Paul assumes the posture of a supplicant, there is an undertone of apostolic authority in all that he says. The question of the fate of Onesimus was opened with a concession: "though I am *bold enough in Christ to command you to do what is required,* yet for love's sake I prefer to appeal to you. . . . I appeal to you for my child, Onesimus" (vss. 8–10).

It is brought to a close with a note of finality: *"Confident of your obedience,* I write to you, knowing that you will do even more than I say" (vs. 21). The "more" that Paul desired was that Philemon would willingly return Onesimus to labor alongside the apostle. "I would have been glad to keep him with me, in order that he might serve me *on your behalf* during my imprisonment for the gospel; but I preferred to do nothing without your consent in order that your goodness might not be by compulsion but *of your own free will"* (vss. 13–14).

Gently Paul reminds Philemon of the debt he owed: "—to say nothing of your owing me even your own self" (vs. 19). The opportunity to acknowledge that debt is provided by the appointment of Onesimus to function with Paul as Philemon's ambassador, assuming the responsibilities that the master would have gladly undertaken if he had access to Paul in prison. Onesimus, when with Philemon, is the representative of the apostle, and when with Paul, he is the representative of Philemon. The return of the slave to his owner allowed Philemon a magnificent opportunity to advance the gospel by directly commissioning Onesimus to serve the Lord with Paul. Paradoxically, by freely yielding his slave to the Christian mission, Philemon will possess him forever (vs. 15).

Paul's appeal to Philemon is based upon an important theological consideration: What happens to Onesimus is to be decided *in Christ.*

Perhaps this is why he was parted from you for a while, that you might have him back for ever, no longer as a slave but more than a slave, as a beloved brother, especially to me but how much more to you, both in the flesh and *in the Lord*. . . . Yes, brother, I want some benefit from you *in the Lord*. Refresh my heart *in Christ* (vss. 15–16, 20).

The reality of union with Christ shatters the traditional conception of the relationship between master and slave. Because Onesimus has experienced life in Christ (vs. 10) Philemon is to recognize in him a member of his own family, a brother.

Where life in Christ exists, justice is to be its expression. In this confidence Paul does not hesitate to challenge the master's right of ownership over his slave (vs. 14). His challenge represents an oblique condemnation of slavery itself. The fact that he did not intend the Epistle to Philemon to be generalized—that it was accompanied by the Colossian letter with its specific admonition for slaves to serve their masters as an act of reverence for Christ—should not conceal the importance of this document. By transforming the relationship between master and slave with his penetrating insights on the meaning of life in Christ, Paul cut deeply into the taproots of a social system which depended upon slavery. The concern of Christ for slaves and freedmen found a response in the personal involvement of his apostle in the plight of a fugitive slave.[20]

NOTES

1. The use of the first person plural in Acts 16:10 introduces the first of the "we" sections where Luke indicates his presence. Since the section extends to verse 17, Luke joined Paul and his companions in Troas and accompanied them to Philippi.

2. On Neapolis and Philippi see W. A. MacDonald, "Archaeology and St. Paul's Journeys in Greek Lands," *Biblical Archaeologist,* 3 (1940), pp. 18–24; F. W. Beare, *A Commentary on the Epistle to the Philippians* (1959), pp. 5–15 and the bibliography listed on pp. 43–44.

3. Dio Cassius li. 4. 6. Much relevant data on the Roman colony in general and Philippi in particular is provided by A. N. Sherwin-White, *Roman Society and Roman Law in the New Testament* (1963), pp. 71–83, 92–100, 176–84.

4. According to Acts 16:16 she had a *python* spirit. Such persons were thought to be inspired by Apollo, the Pythian god, who was supposed to be embodied in a great python at Delphi (also called Pytho). According to Plutarch (*de defectu oraculorum* ix. 414E), individuals like the girl uttered words beyond their control.

5. For the assertion of the principle of incompatibility in the Bacchanalian

scandal of the second century B.C. see Livy, xxxix. 16. 8–9. The legal questions are discussed fully by Sherwin-White, *op. cit.,* pp. 71–83; S. L. Guterman, *Religious Toleration and Persecution in Ancient Rome* (1951), pp. 27–48.

6. Suetonius, *Claudius* xxv. 4. There is much evidence for anti-Jewish prejudice in this general period: cf. Cicero, *Pro Flacco* 28; Juvenal, *Satires* xiv. 96–106.

7. *Sententiae Pauli* v. 21.1, cited by Sherwin-White, *op. cit.,* p. 77, who adds: "but this usage cannot be brought down, in evidence, to an earlier age" (p. 78).

8. This may be inferred from the fact that the first "we" section ends at Acts 16:17 with Luke in Philippi; when the next one begins at 20:5–6, Luke is still at Philippi, where Paul has rejoined him.

9. The term translated "bishops" in Phil. 1:1 commonly designates financial officers for townships and guilds, and probably should be so understood here as well. For the collected evidence see L. Porter, "The Word *episcopos* in Pre-Christian Usage," *Anglican Theological Review,* 21 (1939), pp. 103–12.

10. R. P. Brewer, "The Meaning of *politeuesthe* in Philippians 1:27," *Journal of Biblical Literature,* 73 (1954), pp. 76–83, especially p. 80.

11. Sherwin-White, *op. cit.,* p. 185; cf. Brewer, *op cit.,* pp. 82–83.

12. For a popular presentation see J. Stuart, "A World Built on Slavery," *Life* 60:9 (March 4, 1966), pp. 74–77. Stuart remarks: "All ancient societies were based on slavery. But none exploited slaves more thoroughly, squandered them so wantonly or depended on them so completely as the Romans did." See, further, W. W. Fowler, *Social Life at Rome in the Age of Cicero* (1910), pp. 204–36; R. H. Barrow, *Slavery in the Roman Empire* (1928); J. W. Duff, "Slaves and Freedmen," *Cambridge Ancient History,* IX (1951), pp. 787–89.

13. A master could release his slave either during his lifetime or at his death if he provided for manumission in his will. For the procedure and related matters see W. W. Buckland, *The Roman Law of Slavery* (1908), pp. 437–597, 678–701, 714–23.

14. For an alternate suggestion that Archippus, mentioned in Col. 4:17 and Philem. 2, is the slave owner, see J. Knox, *Philemon Among the Letters of Paul* (1935), pp. 25–34.

15. See especially P. R. Coleman-Norton, "Paul and the Roman Law of Slavery," in *Studies in Roman Economic and Social History in Honor of A. C. Johnson* (1951), pp. 174–77.

16. For branding, see Petronius, *Satyricon* 103.4; for crucifixion, Dio Cassius xlix. 12. 5.

17. Coleman-Norton, *op. cit.,* pp. 173–74, summarizes the Roman law; on Hellenistic law in the East, with particular reference to the law of fugitives and suppliants in Hellenistic Egypt, see E. R. Goodenough, "Paul and Onesimus," *Harvard Theological Review,* 22 (1929), pp. 181–83.

18. Philemon is equal in length to Jude; only 3 John is briefer.

19. Rightly stressed by T. Preiss, "Life in Christ and Social Ethics in the Epistle to Philemon," in *Life in Christ* (1954), pp. 33–34.

20. Fifty years or so after Paul penned his letter to Philemon, the name Onesimus occurs as the bishop of Ephesus, in a letter addressed to the church by Ignatius, the bishop of Antioch. The occurrence of reminiscences from Philemon in the first six paragraphs of Ignatius' letter, in which Onesimus is the real subject (*ad Eph.* 1–6), lends support to the suggestion that the man in question is none other than the former slave whom Paul had introduced to Christian life and service. For a careful presentation of the evidence see Knox, *op. cit.*, pp. 50–56.

SELECTED READING

Barth, K., *The Epistle to the Philippians*. Richmond: John Knox, 1962.

Beare, F. W., *A Commentary on the Epistle to the Philippians*. New York: Harper & Brothers, 1959.

Coleman-Norton, P. R., "Paul and the Roman Law of Slavery," in *Studies in Roman Economic and Social History in Honor of A. C. Johnson*. Princeton: University Press, 1951. Pp. 155–77.

Knox, J., *Philemon Among the Letters of Paul*. Chicago: University of Chicago Press, 1935.

Manson, T. W., "The Date of the Epistle to the Philippians," in *Studies in the Gospels and Epistles*, M. Black, ed. Philadelphia: Westminster, 1962. Pp. 149–167.

Martin, R. P., *An Early Christian Confession: Philippians ii. 5–11 in Recent Interpretation*. London: Tyndale, 1960.

Muller, J. J., *The Epistles to the Philippians and to Philemon*. Grand Rapids: Eerdmans, 1955.

Preiss, T., "Life in Christ and Social Ethics in the Epistle to Philemon," in *Life in Christ*. Chicago: A. R. Allenson, Inc., 1954. Pp. 32–42.

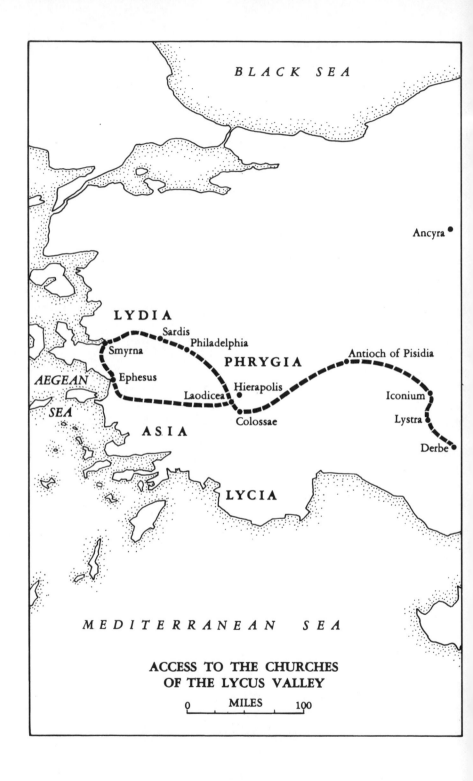

BLACK SEA

Ancyra •

LYDIA
Sardis
Philadelphia
Smyrna
PHRYGIA

Antioch of Pisidia

AEGEAN
Ephesus

Hierapolis
Iconium

SEA
Laodicea
Lystra

Colossae

Derbe

ASIA

LYCIA

MEDITERRANEAN SEA

**ACCESS TO THE CHURCHES
OF THE LYCUS VALLEY**

0   MILES   100

XIV

�֎

COLOSSIANS AND EPHESIANS—
THE THREAT OF SYNCRETISM

THE first century was an age of syncretism. The essence of syncretism is the tendency to fuse deities, rites, observances, and interpretations of one people or region with those of another. Men did not hesitate to alter or modify their religious orientation by adopting elements of belief or expressions of piety originally quite foreign or distinct from their own. This was evident throughout the Hellenistic-Roman period as older and newer forms of religious fervor merged. Changes in political administration or social conditions frequently introduced new cults which appeared to supersede older existing expressions of worship. Yet essential elements of the older cults often were preserved under new names and forms. Even in the cities, ancient folk religion could continue to survive beneath the veneer of a more sophisticated type of devotion.[1]

Judged from the religious and social perspective of the Roman world, Christianity was merely another new cult. Especially in Asia Minor, serious attempts were being made to accommodate it to Hellenistic religious philosophy. Faced with this threat of syncretism, a primary concern of the apostle Paul became the integrity of the gospel. This is pointedly expressed in Colossians, which was written at a time of crisis when the nature of salvation was being obscured by false teaching. It is implemented more broadly in Ephesians, where the apostle is striving for a distinctively Christian outlook on history and religion. The latter epistle marks the high point of Paul's articulation of the sovereign purpose of God—the achievement of unity in the cosmos and in the church.

1. CHRISTIANITY IN THE LYCUS VALLEY

To speak of the Lycus River valley in the old Phrygian region of Asia Minor is to think of three centers whose fortunes were largely intertwined:

Laodicea and Hierapolis, both important and wealthy cities, and the more ancient town of Colossae, whose former glory was now eclipsed by its neighbors.[2] The valley was the gateway to ancient Caria, Lydia, and Phrygia, and in the Roman period the junction point of two important roads which led from the Aegean coast into the hinterland of Anatolia. One followed the Maeander River valley from Ephesus to Laodicea and then turned southeast to follow the Lycus toward Pisidian Antioch, Iconium and through the Cilician gates to Tarsus. A second route eastward followed the Hermus River valley to the north from Smyrna to Sardis and Philadelphia (cf. Rev. 2–3), and then ascended the Phrygian mountains in the direction of ancient Ancyra (the modern Ankara, Turkey). These two main routes were connected by a road from Laodicea to Philadelphia. Laodicea, therefore, marked the first and most important junction in the road system.

The man responsible for bringing Christianity to the Lycus Valley was Epaphras, a native of Colossae (Col. 4:12): it was from him that the Colossians first heard the gospel (1:6–7), and he had labored diligently at Laodicea and Hierapolis as well (4:13). His own initial contact with the Christian message probably can be traced to the time of Paul's Ephesian ministry when the Apostle was teaching daily in the hall of Tyrannus. Luke records: "This continued for two years, so that all the residents of Asia heard the word of the Lord, both Jews and Greeks" (Acts 19:10).

This wide extension of the gospel may have taken place as Paul's disciples were instructed by him and then returned to evangelize their own native towns. This would explain why Paul writes of Epaphras: "he is a faithful minister of Christ *on our behalf*" (Col. 1:7). Epaphras had preached the gospel at Colossae as Paul's emissary. It also explains Paul's dependence upon Epaphras for his information concerning the Christians of the Lycus Valley and the apostle's assumption of authority over a church with which he had little personal acquaintance (cf. 1:4, 8 f.; 2:1). While Paul was unable to visit all of the congregations established during the course of his Ephesian ministry, he had a vital personal interest in them. On this understanding, the church at Colossae must have been established A.D. 52–55.

Perhaps five years after the founding of the church at Colossae, Epaphras sought out Paul, presumably at Rome, to inform him of developments within the congregation. Although the work had advanced, a type of teaching had been introduced which, if unchecked, could only obscure the character of salvation and reduce Christianity to an unwholesome asceticism. To judge from the relative mildness of Paul's response (in contrast to the tone assumed in Galatians), the error had not yet subverted the gospel. Nevertheless the situation was sufficiently serious to call forth a letter from the apostle's pen.[3]

Our only source for reconstructing the false teaching is Paul's letter to the Colossians, and caution must be exercised in interpreting its statement. Certain aspects of the error may be readily identified. From Judaism came an insistence upon circumcision (2:11), legal ordinances (cf. 2:14), food and drink regulations, and observance of the festival calendar (2:16). The rigorous asceticism which found expression in the regulations "Do not handle, do not taste, do not touch" (2:21) may or may not be Jewish in origin. The designation of the teaching as "philosophy," i.e., the "love of wisdom," and the use of such catchwords as "knowledge" (*gnōsis*), "wisdom," and "mystery" suggest a syncretistic religious outlook. The tenor of the Colossian epistle indicates that the error consisted fundamentally in an inadequate view of Christ. But it is the precise nature of this viewpoint which must be carefully defined. The crux of the problem lies in the interpretation of Paul's difficult reference to humility, the worship of angels, and visions (2:18).

Diaspora Judaism accorded a decisive place to angels through whom the law was given (cf. Acts 7:35, 53; Heb. 2:2). It is commonly assumed that at Colossae there was a veneration of angelic power. This interpretation is reflected in the translation of Colossians 2:18 adopted for the Revised Standard Version: "Let no one disqualify you, insisting on self-abasement and worship of angels, taking his stand on visions, puffed up without reason by his sensuous mind. . . ." On this understanding, angels were not merely heavenly beings but "principalities and powers, lords of the planetary spheres, sharers in the plenitude of the divine essence," who must be placated by regular legal observances and a severe asceticism.[4] In his descending to earth, Christ had yielded his power to these guardians of the spheres. Such insights purportedly came from heavenly visions in which the proponents of the doctrine exulted. They represented an advanced type of syncretism which obscured the dignity and deity of Christ.

Serious questions must be entertained before this interpretation may be adopted. Was there, in fact, such a high degree of syncretism in the Colossian church? If this was the case, would not Paul's polemic against the error be more direct? The dominant impression conveyed by the letter itself does not support the interpretation that angels were being worshiped— having usurped the honors which belong to Christ and God alone. If the error was really of the character so often projected, how could Paul write: "For though I am absent in body, yet I am with you in spirit, rejoicing to see your good order and *the firmness of your faith in Christ*" (2:5)? The veneration of angels is incompatible with this statement. In Colossians, Paul is clearly responding to error of a syncretistic nature, but probably not the error that is commonly imagined.

It is possible that in Colossians 2:18 "worship of angels" does not mean the veneration of angelic creatures by men, but rather the worship directed toward God *by the angels*.[5] By rigorous asceticism, the false teachers contended, men could receive in their lifetime a vision of the angelic service into which they would enter—a vision others would behold only after death. This vision of the heavenly liturgy and its attendant glory Paul calls "a shadow of what is to come" (2:17).

In contrast to such submission to ascetic practices in order to qualify for visions, Paul urges thanksgiving "to the Father, who has qualified us to share in the inheritance of the saints in light" (1:12). In contrast to rigid self-denial as a means of attaining perfection during one's lifetime, Paul exults in the God who has already "translated us to the Kingdom of his beloved Son"* (1:13). In this manner the apostle indicates that Christians already experience what the false teachers had argued was available only through a life of vigorous self-denial. Christians did not have to struggle to enter into the inheritance of the saints; God had graciously provided that entrance in his Son.

2. CHRIST: THE WISDOM OF GOD

To introduce the heart of his teaching about Jesus Christ, Paul employs the language of worship by drawing upon fragments of a hymn which may have been familiar to Christians of the Lycus Valley (1:15–20). The hymn consists of two stanzas or strophes, built in a parallel way:

Strophe 1 (1:15–18a)	Strope 2 (1:18b–20)

He is the image of the invisible God,
  the first-born of all creation;
  for in him all things were created. . . .
	He is the beginning,
	  the first born from the dead. . . .
	  for in him all the fulness of God
	    was pleased to dwell. . . .

Long before their application to Jesus Christ, such terms as these had described the divine Wisdom. In the wisdom literature of the Old Testament (especially Proverbs 8:22 ff.) and the Apocrypha (particularly Sirach 24:8–12, 23–29; Wisdom of Solomon 7:21–8:1), God's wisdom is personified and four predicates are ascribed to it:

1. Wisdom was with God in the beginning and functioned as creator.
2. Wisdom sustains the creation, acting in God's behalf upon the earth.
3. Wisdom reveals God to men (with the result that in Sirach divine Wisdom is identified with the law).
4. Wisdom reconciles men and makes them friends to God (a function that elsewhere in the Old Testament is assigned to the Spirit of God).

By speaking of Jesus as the Wisdom of God, Christian missionaries were able to establish a point of contact with the people of the Hellenistic world. Because the Palestinian concept of the messiah was eschatological in orientation and the Gentile had little appreciation for eschatology, Wisdom Christology addressed a real need for effective communication.

The hymnic fragments in Colossians 1:15–20 express two main predicates concerning Jesus Christ:

1. "He is the image of the invisible God, the first-born of all creation" (vs. 15, a statement reflecting upon Jesus' relationship to *God and the world*).
2. "He is the beginning, the first-born from the dead" (vs. 18, a statement reflecting upon Jesus' relationship to *salvation*).

These two statements may be viewed as propositions which were acknowledged in the worship of the church and to which Paul adds his own commentary.

1. Christ is the *image* of God before men. The contrast is between Christ who is seen and God who is unseen, even in the visions of the false teachers. The opening line of the hymn thus anticipates Paul's strong statement that "in him [Christ] the whole fulness of deity dwells *bodily*" (2:9).[6]

2. He is described as *the first-born of all creation*. The term "first-born" stresses *uniqueness* rather than priority in time. Jesus is the first-born in virtue of the fact that he is the agent of creation ("for in him all things were created") and the heir of creation ("all things were created . . . for him"). The relationship of the Son to all created existence is that of the Lord to subjects. The stress falls on the sovereignty of Christ.

In the second strophe Paul is concerned to establish the relationship of the Son to the church. The relationship is that of head over the body, for Paul declares, "he is the head of the body of the church"* (1:18). In Romans and First Corinthians Paul had introduced the image of the body, on the analogy of a common Hellenistic metaphor which compared the state or the empire to a human organism (see below, pp. 228 f.). The new element in Colossians and Ephesians is the description of Christ as the head.

In Colossians 2:19, in which the anatomical terms "joints and ligaments" indicate that Paul is relying on a physiological metaphor, Christ is described as "the head" which sends down life into the whole body. But in 1:18 and 2:10 ("the head of all rule and authority"), the thought is more political. "Head" means properly "leader." The statements which follow also have a political tone, speaking of Christ's preeminence and of his sovereign act of reconciliation and peacemaking (1:18, 20). In view is the primacy of Christ over the whole church. The false teachers, by joining to the gospel an insistence upon human devices for attaining advanced spirituality, have ceased to hold "fast to the Head, from whom the whole body, nourished and knit together through its joints and ligaments, grows with a growth that is from God" (2:19). Failing to submit to Christ as head (in a political sense), they substituted their wisdom for his. As a result they were in danger of becoming truncated, "not holding fast to the Head" (in a physiological sense), and so losing the life that he supplies.

The substance of the Colossian error is pointedly in view in 2:4–3:4. The false teaching had been commended as "wisdom" and "knowledge," but Paul describes their system as "beguiling speech," "empty deceit," and "human tradition" (2:4, 8), a reflection of the demonic, hostile cosmic powers Christ had disarmed, triumphing over them (2:15). In Christ alone, the fullness of deity dwelt bodily, and in him the Colossians had come to the fullness of life which they were seeking (2:9–10; 3:1–4). Their task was now to remain steadfast in Christ (2:6–7). What was promised in the offer of "philosophy" had already been accomplished in Christ! Not new teaching but a return to the tradition is the antidote for the unwholesome situation at Colossae.

The ascetic practices urged to attain visionary entrance into heaven were mere human devices. In contrast to such a negative approach to Christian existence, Paul urges the reality of life in a risen Lord. Since you have experienced resurrection life with Christ, he writes, "seek the things that are above," the concerns of the risen and exalted Christ (3:1). The Christian is free to use the world precisely because Christ has freed him from the world.

3. A WORD OF WISDOM TO THE MATURE

In spite of the traditional heading, relatively little is known about the recipients of the letter designated Ephesians.[7] The letter was delivered to its destination by Tychicus, who in Ephesians 6:21 and Colossians 4:7 is named Paul's emissary. Presumably, the Colossian epistle was delivered at the same time, since in both letters Paul states in similar language that Tychicus will inform the readers concerning his current situation. Paul has had no personal contact with the community addressed in Ephesians, and the tone of the letter is impersonal. He knows of his readers' faith in the Lord Jesus and their love toward other Christians (1:15; 4:21). Therefore, he assumes that they have heard of the stewardship of divine grace which has been granted to him for their sake (3:2). The community appears to have been exclusively Gentile, for the apostle writes:

> Therefore remember that at one time *you Gentiles in the flesh,* called the uncircumcision by what is called the circumcision, which is made in the flesh by hands—remember that you were at that time separated from Christ, alienated from the commonwealth of Israel, and strangers to the covenants of promise, having no hope and without God in the world (2:11–12).

Paul designates himself "a prisoner for Christ Jesus *on behalf of you Gentiles"* (3:1) and exhorts his readers to lay aside the vices of their pagan past (4:17 ff., 25 ff.). This much is explicit. But can anything more be known about the recipients of this letter and of their life situation to which the apostle addressed himself?

It is common knowledge that Ephesians bears a strong relationship to Colossians. Between these two epistles there are closer parallels in content, language, and style than exist between any other New Testament letters. About 70 percent of Colossians is shared by Ephesians, while approximately 50 percent of Ephesians finds its parallel in Colossians. It is a striking fact that when the 50 percent of Ephesians which is common to Colossians is removed, there remain units of tradition which are complete in themselves and distinctive to Ephesians:

1: 3–14—a hymn in praise of God or an expanded benediction, consisting of a single, balanced periodic sentence.

2: 1–10—a confessional summary of the new life, consisting of a single periodic sentence.

3:14–21—a prayer that the readers may understand the mystery of Christ.

4: 1–16—an elaborate exhortation to unity supported by confession and the interpretation of Scripture.

5: 8–14—an exhortation to walk in the light, concluding with a hymnic fragment.

5:23–32—a theological expansion of one section of the household code, developing the mystical marriage of Christ.

6:10–16—an expanded exhortation to put on the armor of God.

The Ephesian letter is far more liturgical than is usual for Paul. Especially these seven units show careful preparation. They have been integrated with the remaining portions of the letter so well that they are recognizable as independent units of tradition only because we possess Colossians. The reconstruction of the mission situation to which the letter is addressed must take account of this material.

One suggestion which lies close to the surface is that the units distinctive to Ephesians were used for instructing converts either prior to or following baptism. Pursuing this clue, it is evident that throughout the letter there are various types of material appropriate to a baptismal context. These include:

1. Formulations appropriate to a baptismal liturgy (1:3–14; 2:11–18). In 1:3–14, for example, a solemn review of the redemptive activity of the triune God is presented. Through verse 12 the first person plural (we/us) is used consistently. The abrupt change to the second person plural in verse 13 is intelligible if the passage is a fragment of a baptismal charge:

> In him, according to the purpose of him who accomplishes all things according to the counsel of his will, *we who first hoped in Christ* have been destined and appointed to live for the praise of his glory. IN HIM YOU ALSO, who have heard the word of truth, the gospel of your salvation, and have believed in him, were sealed with the promised Holy Spirit, which is the guarantee of *our inheritance* until *we acquire* possession of it, to the praise of his glory (1:11–14).

In this connection it is perhaps significant that Jesus is designated "the Beloved" in verse 6, echoing the heavenly voice on the occasion of his baptism, "Thou art my beloved Son" (Mark 1:11). The reference to "the forgiveness of our trespasses" in verse 7, together with the phrase "sealed with the promised Holy Spirit" in verse 13, evokes reminiscence of similar language from contexts which are explicitly baptismal (e.g., Acts 2:38–39).

Ephesians 2:11–18 is suggestive of a charge to candidates for baptism, urging them to remember what their state had been and how that condition has been altered in Christ. The charge is built around an exposition of Isaiah 57:19: "Peace, Peace, to the far and to the near, says the Lord, and I will heal him." The terms "far" and "near" designate the Gentiles and Israel respectively. It is natural to recall Acts 2:38–39 in which "far" and "near" occur in an explicitly baptismal setting. The least that can be said is that the language is appropriate to a baptismal liturgy.

2. There are creedal or confessional formulations. Ephesians 1:20–23

embodies a confession of the sovereign dignity of Christ, who has been exalted "above every name that is named, not only in this age but also in that which is to come." His lordship over cosmic and earthly powers is made visible within the church, "which is his body, the fulness of him who fills all in all." Confession belongs to the heart of Christian worship. The confession of the synagogue is capsulized in the ancient words of the *Shema*: "Hear, O Israel: The Lord our God is one Lord" (Deut. 6:4). The confession of the church, forming an exact counterpart to Israel's acknowledgment, is presented in Ephesians 4:4–6: "There is one body and one Spirit, just as you were called to the one hope that belongs to your call, one Lord, one faith, one baptism, one God and Father of us all, who is above all and through all and in all." The *Shema* is here expanded to speak of the Spirit, the Lord, and the Father. The reference to the "one baptism" is especially appropriate if this confession was recited in a baptismal setting.

3. There appear to be fragments of hymns appropriate to baptism. If it is correct to detect such a fragment in 2:19–22, the thought of incorporation in the new temple which will provide a dwelling for God is especially suitable to such a context. The antithesis "no longer strangers and sojourners" but "fellow citizens with the saints and members of the household of God" recapitulates the note sounded in the charge to the candidates in 2:11–13. The reference to "the Lord, in whom *you also* are built," recalls the abrupt transition from the first to the second person plural in 1:13. The citation in Ephesians 5:14 is a clearer example, with its reference to death and resurrection and the bestowal of light through Christ, shattering the darkness of the pagan past:

> Awake, O sleeper, and arise from the dead,
>   and Christ shall give you light.

4. Finally, there is considerable formulated material of a parenetic character, admonishing the believers to live lives worthy of Christ (4:1–6:9; cf. Col. 3:1–4:6). The language of 5:26, which describes Christ's activity as a sanctifying of the church, "having cleansed her by the washing of water with the word," deserves particular attention. Even when such language is discounted, it has been widely recognized that the life setting of the household code (5:21–6:9) is the instruction of new believers both before and after baptism.[8]

The isolation of these several kinds of material would support the suggestion that Ephesians is a pastoral homily designed to be read at some occasion of importance, such as baptism at Easter.

There are, however, other elements in the letter which also press for recognition. There is in Ephesians a real striving for a theology of history. The primary theme of the letter is that all things are moving toward unity (that is, perfection) in Christ. The key to this theme is provided by 1:9–10: "For he has made known to us in all wisdom and insight the mystery of his will, according to his purpose which he set forth in Christ as a plan for the fulness of time, *to unite all things in him,* things in heaven and things in earth." In developing this theme Paul gives an exposition of God as Father over the whole universe (cf. 3:14–15), of the meaning of sonship (cf. 1:5), and of the reconciliation of the cosmos (1:19–23; 2:20–22).

A secondary theme clarifies how the church relates to the achievement of unity. In developing this secondary theme, the apostle develops a high concept of the church as the pledge of that ultimate and perfect unity which God will achieve. The church is the first manifestation of the unity that shall be. This fact explains the imperative present need for oneness within the church (4:1–6). The unity manifested in the church, however, is far more than an expression of the future. It is the means by which God confronts those hostile powers in history that stand opposed to unity (cf. 3:10, 20–21; 6:11–12). The Christian is one who experiences in history what reconciliation to God means. The church in history must be a dynamic expression of the meaning of Christ's death and resurrection; it must be the place where the alienation and hostility of the world is broken down. The fact that within the church the middle wall of partition separating Jew and Gentile already has been removed (2:14–16) indicates that God is bringing his sovereign purpose to fruition.

Related to the concern for unity is a developed understanding of the church as the body of Christ. Whereas in Colossians Paul's stress falls on Christ as the head of the body, in Ephesians the church is more centrally in view. Paul uses the metaphor of the body on three different levels:

1. The church is like any human body (Rom. 12:3–8; 1 Cor. 12:12–27, in which the advance on the basic Hellenistic metaphor is only slight).
2. The church is like the real body of Christ offered up for us upon the cross (1 Cor. 10:16–17; 11:23–27, in which in each instance the context is eucharistic).
3. The church is like the real body of Christ risen (Eph. 1:19–23).

At each level is sustained a metaphorical use of the statement, "The church is like a body," but the metaphor does not mean the same thing in every case. Only in Ephesians does Paul reflect upon the church as the body of Christ risen and exalted over all things. In the church, Christ is seen not only as the suffering Servant (level 2) but as the triumphant Lord of glory. It is, therefore, not surprising that in Ephesians the exaltation of Christ is described in the highest terms (cf. 1:4–5, 9–10, 20–23; 3:11–12).

Finally, in Ephesians, Paul shows an awareness of the new religious philosophies sweeping the Roman Empire—the Eastern mysteries and incipient Gnosticism. To judge from the vocabulary of the letter, the recipients are keenly alive to the religious syncretism which contributed so much to later Gnosticism.[9] Ephesians has more "syncretistic" vocabulary than does Colossians, though the focus of attention falls upon syncretism less consciously in Ephesians than in Colossians. Paul evidently found himself challenged to crystallize his own thinking over against the new competitors to Christian faith. He recognized that the church must prepare itself to meet a syncretistic religious philosophy bidding for the allegiance of men. Paul was open to new ways of understanding and explaining the person and work of Christ, and in the vocabulary and thought of some of the newer movements he finds a fresh vehicle for addressing the church of Asia Minor.

Seen in the light of such emphases, Ephesians can be regarded as an example of what Paul speaks about in 1 Corinthians 2:6–7—a word of wisdom to the mature: "Yet among the mature we do impart wisdom, although it is not a wisdom of this age or of the rulers of this age, who are doomed to pass away. But we impart a secret and hidden wisdom of God, which God decreed before the ages for our glorification."

Elements of baptismal liturgy in Ephesians are thus not intended primarily for the instruction of catechumens but to recall to the readers the liturgy in which they participated, the confession they made, the hymns they sang, and the exhortations to which they gave heed. Looking back upon their initial commitment to Christ and his church, they are to press on "until we all attain to the unity of the faith and of the knowledge of the Son of God, to mature manhood, to the measure of the stature of the fulness of Christ; so that we may no longer be children . . ." (Eph. 4:13–14). The appropriateness of such a word of wisdom, over against the specious wisdom offered in religious syncretism, is self-evident.

What would have been the occasion for Paul to think and write in this way? What is the life situation which accounts for the distinctive character of the letter? While Paul was in prison in Rome, the need for new materials with which to instruct converts in Asia Minor became acute. It is likely that the apostle had already gathered portions of the tradition, having anticipated this need. In the Corinthian correspondence, reference is made to words of wisdom and knowledge, and to hymns recognized as gifts of the Spirit (cf. 1 Cor. 12:8; 14:26). Some of the hymns and confessional statements may have been adapted from previously existing forms of Jewish or Hellenistic origin. An impetus to bring the material together was provided by the arrival of Epaphras, who informed Paul of the threat to Christian truth in the Lycus Valley. In response, the apostle penned the Colossian letter. At the same time, the epistle that we know as Ephesians may have been sent to Laodicea and an extra copy left at Ephesus, the capital of Asia Minor. This would explain a reference to a Laodicean letter in Colossians 4:16. Paul urges the Colossians to exchange their letter for one that had been delivered to Laodicea.[10]

If this assumption is correct, Ephesians, like Colossians, is a letter addressed to the Lycus Valley region. Its specific destination is Laodicea, and its purpose is to foster Christian maturity. The apostle intends that "Ephesians" will be read at Colossae as well, and perhaps at Hierapolis; the copy left at Ephesus provides assurance that Paul's directive will reach the greater part of the province. The letter was written in response to the newer religious philosophies sweeping the area, the mysteries and incipient Gnosticism, which threatened to obscure the nature of salvation, the significance of the church, and the cosmic dimensions of the sovereign plan of God.

4. THE AUTHENTICITY OF EPHESIANS

The textual tradition that the writer of Ephesians is the Apostle Paul is unbroken (Eph. 1:1; 3:1). The Pauline authorship of the letter was accepted by all the fathers and canonical lists of the early church. In spite of the weight of this historical evidence, the authenticity of the letter has been vigorously disputed since the nineteenth century.

The controversy centers on the interpretations of specific data from the letter itself: its relationship to Colossians and to passages in the other Pauline epistles; its unusual vocabulary and formal style; its distinctive teaching. An often repeated suggestion is that Ephesians was written by one of Paul's disciples some twenty or thirty years after his death to provide a cover letter for the apostle's collected epistles. While the unknown author drew most heavily upon Colossians, it is urged, signs of indebtedness to all the authentic Pauline letters give to Ephesians the character of a "mosaic."[11]

There is a high degree of subjectivity in any such reconstruction. In the absence of new evidence, scholarship has reached an impasse: one group

hears the voice of the apostle while another detects only the echo preserved by one from the Pauline circle. This was well expressed by H. J. Cadbury in an address analyzing the language of Ephesians in relationship to the
other Pauline letters:

> That problem remains a dilemma. Acknowledge as one must the likeness and
> the differences between Ephesians and the others we are confronted with an
> imponderable comparison. We might try to state it statistically something like
> this, though the proportions used to express it are quite arbitrary, and if any-
> one wishes to change them, that will not obscure the nature of the dilemma of
> probability: which is more likely—that an imitator of Paul in the first century
> composed a writing ninety or ninety-five per cent in accordance with Paul's
> style or that Paul himself wrote a letter diverging five or ten per cent from
> his usual style?[12]

While he limited his analysis to the language of Ephesians, Professor
Cadbury rightly adds that "in the psychology of authorship a consideration
of ideas is even more subjective than the consideration of style."

For this reason, a better approach is to examine the nature of a document
as a whole, seeking to understand its intention and the situation in life to
which it is addressed. When Ephesians is seen as an illustration of what
Paul speaks about in 1 Corinthians 2:6–7—a word of wisdom addressed to
the mature—its appropriateness as a letter from his pen is evident. That insight also helps to explain why more extensively and intensively than any
other New Testament epistle, Ephesians has been given the form of prayer.
The entire first half of the epistle (1:3–3:21), and much of the plea for
worthy conduct in the second half (4:1–6:24), is presented in the language of prayer. Within a framework of prayer (cf. 1:3, 16; 3:14, 21;
5:20; 6:18, 23–24), Christ's achievement on behalf of the church is confessed before God and men. When Ephesians is recognized as a word of
wisdom couched in the form of prayer, its language and style is intelligible.
The pastoral concern, the formal liturgical style, and the involved sequence
of thoughts which are such marked characteristics of Ephesians find their
exact parallel in other Pauline letters in which the apostle gives himself
to prayer of adoration, confession, and supplication (e.g., Rom. 8:31–39;
11:33–36; 16:25–27; Phil. 2:6–11).[13]

The recognition of the similarities and differences between Colossians
and Ephesians supports the thesis that Paul is the author of both epistles.
He wrote Colossians to call back to the apostolic tradition a community
threatened with a specific form of religious syncretism. At the same time
he composed Ephesians. Because his mind was full of the matters with

which he dealt in the first letter, there are extensive parallels with Colossians (although identity in language seldom extends beyond five words). But his intention in Ephesians was to synthesize his understanding of the Christian faith in a positive fashion. The apostle accordingly replaces the polemic thrust of Colossians with the language of worship and devotion. There is no valid reason for denying the letter to Paul.

NOTES

1. A helpful introduction to syncretism is provided by F. C. Grant, *Hellenistic Religions* (1953), pp. xiii–xxxix.

2. See S. E. Johnson, "Laodicea and Its Neighbors," *Biblical Archaeologist*, 13 (1950), pp. 1–18, and W. M. Ramsay, "The Jews of the Graeco-Asiatic Cities," *Expositor*, 6th series, 5 (1902), pp. 19–33, 92–109, esp. 95–105, "The Jews of the Lycus Valley Cities."

3. Paul was very conscious of Colossae at this time, for he had with him the runaway slave Onesimus, whom he had determined to send back to his master. Cf. Col. 4:7–9 and see above, pp. 210 ff. For the wide acceptance of the false teaching, note Paul's unrestricted remarks to the congregation as a whole in 2:16–3:11.

4. Citation from F. F. Bruce, *Commentary on the Epistle to the Colossians* (1957), p. 167.

5. See F. O. Francis, "Humility and Angelic Worship in Col. 2:18," *Studia Theologica*, 16 (1962), pp. 109–34.

6. That Paul is employing language descriptive of Wisdom is clear from Wisdom of Solomon 7:26: Wisdom is "the radiance of eternal light, a spotless mirror of the working of God and an *image of his goodness.*"

7. The conclusion that "Ephesians" was not addressed to the community Paul founded in the metropolis of Asia is based on internal evidence and is corroborated by the history of the text. It is generally agreed by textual critics that the two words "in Ephesus" in the initial greeting are not original. They are missing in P[46], the oldest manuscript of the Pauline epistles, and from such excellent witnesses to the original text as Vaticanus (where the words have first been added in the margin by a later hand) and Sinaiticus (where they have been added by a corrector). Origen, the finest textual critic among the church fathers, did not read these words in his text, while Basil informs us that they were missing from old texts. In fact, the oldest witnesses to the words "in Ephesus" in 1:1 are the Latin commentary of Victorinus in the second half of the fourth century and the late manuscripts known to Basil and Jerome. For this reason the Revised Standard Version rightly omits the designation.

8. There is much helpful material in E. G. Selwyn, *The First Epistle of St. Peter,* 2d ed. (1947), Essay II, pp. 365–439, esp. pp. 419–39, "The Social Code."

9. There is an undeniably subjective element in such a judgment, but in view is the language of such passages as 1:20–23 ("above all rule and authority and power and dominion," "above every name that is named," "the *plēroma* of him who fills all in all"*) and 2:2 ("following the Aeon of this world, following the prince of the power of the air"*). Cf. 2:15; 3:2–6, 9 f., 15; 5:32; 6:10. For a discussion of Aeon as a person, see W. L. Lane, "Ages (Aeons)," *Encyclopedia of Christianity,* Vol. I (1964), pp. 100–102.

10. The reference to a Laodicean letter has called forth several conjectures, since it appears incredible that any letter would have been lost to which reference was made in a letter which has been preserved. This is especially true when the reference was accompanied by a command that it should be read in more than one community. As early as the middle of the second century, Marcion identified Ephesians as the letter to the church at Laodicea. The extensive parallel with Colossians lends support to that identification. Moreover, the praise of the congregation (Eph. 1:15) and the mention of the reason for sending Tychicus (6:21–22) would be more fitting in a letter addressed to a single community than in a circular epistle. Alternate suggestions are that Philemon is the letter to which reference is made in Col. 4:16 (see John Knox, *Philemon Among the Letters of Paul,* [1935]) or that reference is made to a letter addressed to Laodicea by Epaphras, who for some reason was detained in prison with Paul (see C. P. Anderson, "Who Wrote 'The Epistle from Laodicea'?" *Journal of Biblical Literature,* 85 [1966], pp. 436–40).

11. E.g., E. J. Goodspeed, "The Place of Ephesians in the First Pauline Collection," *Anglican Theological Review,* 12 (1929–30), pp. 189–212; *idem,* "Ephesians and the First Edition of Paul," *Journal of Biblical Literature,* 70 (1951), pp. 285–91; B. S. Easton, "Post-Pauline Paulinism," in *Munera Studiosa,* M. H. Shepherd, Jr., and S. E. Johnson, eds. (1946), pp. 69–89; Knox, *op. cit.;* C. L. Mitton, "Important Hypotheses Reconsidered: VII. The Authorship of the Epistle to the Ephesians," *Expository Times,* 67 (1955–56), pp. 195–98, among others.

12. "The Dilemma of Ephesians," *New Testament Studies,* 5 (1959), p. 101. The entire article is important.

13. M. Barth, *The Broken Wall: A Study of the Epistle to the Ephesians* (1960), pp. 23–26.

SELECTED READING

Barth, M., *The Broken Wall: A Study of the Epistle to the Ephesians.* London: Collins, 1960.

Bowman, J. W., "The Epistle to the Ephesians," *Interpretation,* 8 (1954), pp. 188–205.

Cerfaux, L., *The Church in the Theology of St. Paul.* New York: Herder & Herder, 1959.

Cross, F. L., ed., *Studies in Ephesians.* London: A. R. Mowbray, 1956.

Hanson, S., *The Unity of the Church in the New Testament: Colossians and Ephesians.* Uppsala: Almquist & Wiksells, 1946.

Johnson, S. E., "Early Christianity in Asia Minor," *Journal of Biblical Literature,* 77 (1958), pp. 1–17.

———— "Laodicea and Its Neighbors," *Biblical Archaeologist,* 13 (1950), pp. 1–18.

Simpson, E. K., and Bruce, F. F., *Commentary on the Epistles to the Ephesians and Colossians.* Grand Rapids: Eerdmans, 1957.

XV

THE PASTORAL EPISTLES—THE EMERGENCE OF THE INSTITUTIONAL CHURCH

FOR more than two centuries Paul's two letters to Timothy and one to Titus have been labeled, with some justification, the Pastoral Epistles. The designation recognizes certain common features of these letters and indicates something of their purpose. But it should not obscure the individual characteristics of each. The simplest and perhaps earliest of the three is the brief letter to Titus, who had remained at Crete to organize the church following the evangelistic labors of the apostle Paul. The letter summons Titus to Nicopolis as soon as Artemas or Tychicus arrive in Crete to relieve him of his responsibilities. He is further instructed to "speed Zenas the lawyer and Apollos on their way; see that they lack nothing" (Titus 3:12–13). The Epistle to Titus is thus a pastoral directive, a letter of recall to one of Paul's associates and a note of commendation for Zenas and Apollos. First Timothy is also a pastoral directive to a trusted lieutenant left at Ephesus to oversee the life of the church in that Asian metropolis. Second Timothy, the final word from Paul, is a personal letter of recall, urging Timothy to come to Rome before winter, before travel becomes impossible.

The value of these epistles is that they depict the continuing life of the church at a time when others were beginning to build upon the foundations which Paul had laid. It had become necessary for the church to establish itself in the world without compromising its distinctiveness from the world. What was required was a more disciplined and structured life in Christ. The community of the Holy Spirit was now beginning to realize and sustain itself in a genuinely institutional church. Several factors fostered this development: conflict over the authority to govern the churches, an internal struggle between true and false teaching, and the external opposition of the Hellenistic-Roman world to the Christian gospel. The delegation of authority to men who had labored closely with Paul and the recognition of the crucial importance of the apostolic tradition served to counteract the forces which threatened to divide and destroy the young churches.

1. THE APOSTLE'S DELEGATES

As early as the second missionary journey Paul adopted the policy of delegating important tasks to members of his company. When he was forced to withdraw from Philippi, he left Luke behind to organize and nurture the new church. Under similar circumstances, Silas and Timothy remained at Berea to consolidate the gains from Paul's preaching mission. Timothy and Titus served as representatives of the apostle in Macedonia, Corinth, and elsewhere. It is proper to view such men as apostolic delegates, whose authority was based upon the specific commission each had received from Paul.

The letters to Timothy and Titus shed light on the nature of the authority conferred and the variety of commissions entrusted in two specific instances. No official title is given to Timothy in Ephesus or to Titus in Crete. They are temporary delegates appointed for an interim period of ministry. Paul urged Timothy to remain in Ephesus to bring order into a chaotic situation created by erroneous teaching (1 Tim. 1:3). The pastoral directive to Timothy is a supplementary word of instruction until the apostle himself comes to assume charge of the church (3:14–15; 4:13). The nature of Titus' commission is defined in terms of amending what is defective and appointing elders in every town as directed by Paul (Titus 1:5). Its temporary character is clear not only from the summons to Nicopolis, once Artemas or Tychicus arrives in Crete (3:12), but from Paul's later word to Timothy that he had sent Titus to Dalmatia (2 Tim. 4:10). Timothy and Titus are thus instruments of the apostle's authority rather than possessors of an inherent authority. It is this element which distinguishes them sharply from the developed monarchical episcopacy championed by Ignatius and others in the early second century.

Timothy, the younger of the two men, was associated with Paul from the beginning of the second missionary journey (Acts 16:1–3). He had been commended to the apostle by the good opinion of Christian believers in both Lystra and Iconium, and perhaps by prophetic utterance as well (cf. 1 Tim. 4:14). With the possible exception of Luke, he proved to be Paul's closest companion, ministering with the Apostle in Macedonia, Achaia, Asia, and Rome. In several of the Pauline letters his name is associated with Paul's in the salutation (2 Corinthians, Philemon, Colossians, 1, 2 Thessalonians, Philemon), while the apostle's references to Timothy are laden with affection (cf. 1 Cor. 4:17; Phil. 2:19–22).

Yet Paul was thoroughly aware of a certain timidity and reticence in Timothy's nature. His earlier words to the Corinthians about this young man ("so let no one despise him," 1 Cor. 16:11) find their echo in Paul's word to Timothy, "Let no one despise your youth" (1 Tim. 4:12). The apostle does not hesitate to remind his son in the faith that "God did not give us a spirit of timidity, but a spirit of power and love and self-control. Do not be ashamed then of testifying to our Lord" (2 Tim. 1:7–8). But in spite of these limitations, Paul had complete confidence that this young apostolic delegate was fully capable of restoring order in Ephesus.

Unlike Timothy, who figures prominently in the narrative of Acts, Titus is known only from incidental allusions in the Pauline letters. He was a Gentile who accompanied Paul from Antioch to Jerusalem and became the center of a heated dispute when the Judaistic wing of the church sought to compel him to be circumcised (Gal. 2:1–5).

While it is probable that Titus continued to travel and labor with Paul, nothing more is heard of him until about a decade later when he is mentioned significantly in Second Corinthians (1:23–2:13; 7:5–15; 8:6, 16–23). A cloak of silence veils Titus' movements for the next eight to ten years until his ministry in Crete. Paul had apparently left there only recently, after a preaching mission in several cities of the island (Titus 1:5). The initial tasks of organization and administration were left in Titus' care. Presumably he rejoined the apostle at Nicopolis in Epirus (3:12), but whether he accompanied Paul from there to Rome is uncertain. Of his ministry in Dalmatia (cf. 2 Tim. 4:10), nothing is known.

2. THE PRESUMED LIFE SITUATION

Early in the fourth century the church historian Eusebius wrote: "Tradition has it that after defending himself the apostle [Paul] was again sent on the ministry of preaching, and coming a second time to the same city, suffered martyrdom under Nero" (*Hist. Eccl.* II. xxii). The Pastoral Epistles find their natural life situation in this period of renewed mission and martyrdom, after the Roman imprisonment described in the Book of Acts. It is important, therefore, to ask whether a sufficient basis for the tradition actually exists.

Luke concludes Acts with Paul a prisoner in Rome, living for two complete years under the conditions of light custody, dwelling in his own hired lodging and having considerable freedom of movement and activity (Acts 28:30–31). His legal position was very favorable. Not only had no basis for capital jurisdiction been found by the provincial governors who had examined Paul (cf. 23:29; 25:18, 25; 26:31 ff.), but the nature of his imprisonment in Rome did not conform to the treatment of prisoners suspected of having committed a capital offense. Paul himself expected to be released and to revisit some of the churches in Asia and Macedonia (Philem. 22; Phil. 1:19, 25–27; 2:24). It is possible that Nero, in a show of clemency, or simply to shorten the court list by dropping cases long overdue for prosecution, in the absence of any proven charge against Paul may have acted as Paul's benefactor. The proposal remains a conjecture, but one for which supporting evidence actually exists.[1]

Beyond the Pastoral Epistles themselves, which presuppose Paul's release and subsequent mission, evidence in late first-century and second-century literature clearly reflects the tradition that Paul was released from his imprisonment and returned to preaching.[2] What is required by the Pastorals is a journey eastward to Ephesus, Crete, and Macedonia. First Timothy implies a recent journey in Asia on which Paul, when proceeding to Macedonia, left Timothy in Ephesus (1:3). Incidental allusions in Second Timothy indicate that he had visited Miletus, Troas, and Corinth as well (4:13, 20). The Epistle to Titus implies a mission in Crete (1:5) and the intention to remain at Nicopolis in Epirus for the duration of the winter (3:12). It is probable that Paul had stopped at Crete before sailing to Ephesus. A reasonable hypothesis is that Paul, released from prison, was determined to revisit the key centers of Asia Minor and Macedonia in the light of developments within the churches during his absence. While traveling in Macedonia and Greece he penned the letter to Titus and the first of the two letters to Timothy. The circumstances under which he was arrested and returned to Rome are now shrouded in obscurity, but Second Timothy sheds considerable light on his situation at that time. In striking contrast to his earlier experience of custody, he was fettered like a criminal (2 Tim. 1:8, 16–17; 2:9). Men sought him out at their own peril. Many of his acquaintances had abandoned him (1:15–18; 4:10). He fully expects to be executed before the winter is over (4:6) and urges Timothy to come

to him before travel becomes impossible with the winter storms (4:21).
Paul's language implies a second and more severe imprisonment in Rome,
ending in the apostle's martyrdom.

3. THE AUTHENTICITY OF THE PASTORALS

Ever since the birth of modern criticism in the nineteenth century, the
dispute over the authenticity of these three letters has been greater than
that concerning any of the other Pauline epistles. The weight of tradition
strongly supports Pauline authorship. That Marcion failed to include the
Pastorals in his canon is not suprising, since they explicitly contradicted
his teaching of abstinence from wine, meat, and marriage (e.g., 1 Tim.
4:1–3; 5:23).[3] For the most part, the three letters were known and accepted
as Pauline throughout the church from the second half of the second century. The language of the *Muratorian Fragment,* which preserves the
earliest list of apostolic writings, purportedly received in the church (*ca.*
A.D. 170–180), crystallizes an already long-established tradition. After listing the Pauline letters to church centers, the list continues: "To Philemon
one and to Titus one and to Timothy two, (being written) through love
and affection, yet they have been held sacred through the esteem of the
universal church for the ordering of ecclesiastical discipline" (lines 59–
63).[4] Parallels to the language of the Pastorals in early second-century
documents almost certainly imply the existence and circulation of these
epistles in the church.[5] The dispute about the authenticity of the Pastorals
did not arise from a lack of strong and early attestation in the church at
large.

The major objections urged against their genuineness hinge on the
interpretation of the data presented by the epistles themselves. These objections may be summarized under four headings:

1. The language and style of the Pastorals betray such marked differences from the other ten Pauline letters that it is inconceivable they can
be from the same hand. Of a total vocabulary of 848 words (and 54 proper
names), 306 do not occur in the other ten epistles. Words, phrases, and
particles characteristic of Paul are absent from the Pastorals, while words
and phrases distinctive of the Pastorals do not appear elsewhere in Paul's
letters.[6]

Moreover, there are marked stylistic differences between the Pastorals
and the other Pauline letters. In most of his letters, Paul's thought soars
beyond its literary resources. It travails for expression, breaking many

of the fixed rules of style so as to produce incomplete sentences, sharp breaks, and abrupt parentheses. The diction of the Pastorals, on the other hand, is unruffled. The force of rhetoric and logical demonstration, so characteristic of Romans, Galatians, and the Corinthian correspondence, is replaced in the Pastorals by instruction and assertion. Small particles, an essential element of personal style that had distinguished the great Pauline letters, occur only rarely in the Pastorals.

2. The Christianity of the Pastorals differs essentially from that of the authentic Pauline Letters. Its chief characteristics are orthodoxy and good works.[7]

3. The organization of the church reflected in the Pastorals is too highly developed to date from Paul's time. Specific attention is given to the offices of bishop and deacon and to the order of widows. The absence of any reference to the charismatically endowed persons suggests that in the time of the Pastorals the cessation of spiritual gifts necessitated a strengthening of the organizational structure of the church.

4. The errors in teaching against which the Pastoral Epistles contend also belong to the post-Pauline age.[8]

It is imperative to consider each of these objections, not neglecting the relationship between interpretation and critical judgment. A proper approach starts with the objective phenomena and then asks how the phenomena may best be explained. If Paul wrote the Pastoral Epistles, under what circumstances would such phenomena appear? If they were written by someone other than the apostle, what factors explain their production?

The presence of unusual vocabulary in the three letters is sufficiently explained by the subject matter treated. Not only does the writer address himself to new subjects, but he says something new in areas he has treated before. Of the 310 words peculiar to First Corinthians, 200 occur in sections treating a special subject; of the 250 words peculiar to Romans, more than two fifths of them occur in 112 lines of the text covering Romans 1:18–3:26; 12:1–21; 14:17–20, contexts dealing with subject material not treated elsewhere. The content of the Pastoral Epistles bears little direct relationship to the earlier epistles, and the vocabulary has been adapted spontaneously to the new situations faced. The degree to which special subjects have called forth unusual vocabulary may be indicated by the following table listing the number of rare words found in one or more of the Pastorals, but not elsewhere in Paul.[9] In the final column words which occurred in more than one of the three letters were deducted.

Subject	1 Tim.	Titus	2 Tim.	Total
1. False teaching	30	20	18	50
2. The ministry and its qualifications	22	12	—	29
3. Functions and character of Timothy and Titus	23	9	32	61
4. Church order and discipline	74	16	—	89
5. The experience and circumstances of Paul	6	13	—	19
6. The Scriptures	—	—	7	7
7. Virtues and vices	8	4	20	30
				285 words

On the matter of vocabulary, the table indicates that of the 306 words found in the Pastorals, but not elsewhere in Paul, 285 of this number may be accounted for by the special subjects treated. The greater number of the rare words occur in First Timothy precisely because it treats the new subject material at greater length.

In order properly to appreciate the relationship of the Pastoral Epistles and the other Pauline Letters, resemblances as well as divergences in vocabulary and expression must be taken into account. Among the nearly 600 words the Pastorals share with the other ten epistles are 38 which are distinctively Pauline and not found elsewhere in the New Testament. Moreover, between the Pastorals and the undisputed letters there are extensive similarities of expression and whole phrases of which the apostle was particularly fond.[10] Of the 148 words in the Pastorals which do not occur elsewhere in the New Testament, 82 are not found either in the Apostolic Fathers or in the Apologists. There is no single word in any of the three letters which cannot be accounted for by the language in vogue in the first century and earlier.[11] While word statistics do not adequately convey a feeling for the language, or answer the objection that stereotyped phrases occur within the Pastorals which have no parallel elsewhere in Paul, they serve as a warning that linguistic phenomena cannot serve as an adequate basis for rejecting the authenticity of these letters.

The difference in style between the Pastorals and the earlier Pauline letters is undeniable. In evaluating the relative importance of this difference it is imperative to take into account the nature and purpose of the letters being compared. This is particularly evident in the matter of particles, as the following table indicates:

	Earlier Pauline	
Particle	Letters	The Pastorals
consequently (*āra*)	15	0
so then (*āra oūn*)	12	0
therefore (*diō*)	21	0
because (*diōti*)	10	0

Since particles are a characteristic element of personal style, it appears evident that the same man could not have written the earlier Pauline letters and the Pastorals. Yet such a conclusion is premature because the statistics provided are based on *debate particles,* the majority of which are concentrated in Romans, Galatians, and First and Second Corinthians. Each of these four letters is highly rhetorical in nature, conforming to what is known as the diatribe style, and it is natural to find within them the use of debate particles. "Consequently" and "so then" occur almost always in the course of pressing argumentation (e.g., 1 Cor. 5:10; Rom. 5:18; 8:1, 12; 14:12); they are found frequently in Galatians, but never in Colossians or Philippians and only once in Ephesians. The special nature and purpose of the Pastorals, which are directives addressed to two of Paul's most intimate associates, explains why they lack the rhetoric that characterizes certain of the earlier letters. If the style of the three Pastoral letters is compared with the more quiet and practical sections of the apostle's earlier epistles (e.g., Rom. 12–15; 2 Cor. 8–9), it will be found to be clearly more like that of Paul than that of any other New Testament writer.[12]

It is true that orthodoxy and good works are prominent in the Christianity of the Pastoral Epistles. Only in the Pastorals does the expression "sound doctrine" occur, together with other phrases containing the root idea of health or wholesomeness (e.g., 1 Tim. 1:10; 6:3; Titus 1:9, 13; 2:1–2, 8; 2 Tim. 1:13; 4:13). In some passages "faith" comes close to meaning "the doctrine of the faith." Tradition is stressed and compared to a valuable deposit that must be carefully guarded (e.g., 2 Tim. 1:14). The sources of tradition include "the words of the Lord Jesus" (1 Tim. 6:3), the gospel (2 Tim. 1:11, 13; 2:8), and the inspired Scriptures (1 Tim. 5:18; 2 Tim. 3:15–17). The deposit of faith is also embodied in hymns (1 Tim. 3:16), "faithful sayings" (1 Tim. 1:15; 3:1; 4:9; 2 Tim. 2:11–13; Titus 3:8), and creedal formulae (1 Tim. 6:13; 2 Tim. 4:1).

This emphasis on tradition, however, is by no means new to the apostle Paul (cf. 1 Cor. 11:2, 23 ff.; 15:3–4; 2 Thess. 2:15; 3:6); as early as

Romans he speaks of "the form of doctrine to which you are committed"*
(Rom. 6:17). The special interest of the Pastorals in these earlier forms
is sufficiently explained by the necessity of combating early heretical movements within the church. The use of medical metaphors for orthodoxy
("sound doctrine," 1 Tim. 1:10; Titus 2:1) and heresy ("gangrene," 2
Tim. 2:17) serves to drive home the writer's point that heresy is a fes-
tering disease which consumes the body of the church. In his struggle
against false teaching he has introduced older confessions of faith and
hymns which exhibit a less developed Christology than the other Pauline
Epistles (e.g., 1 Tim. 3:16; 6:13–16; Titus 2:13–14). The presence of
such earlier forms is consistent with Paul's practice elsewhere (e.g., Rom.
1:3–4; Phil. 2:6–11).

A stress on good works as a revelation of the power of the new life in
Christ is typically Pauline (e.g., 2 Thess. 2:17; 2 Cor. 9:8; Rom. 2:7;
13:3; Col. 1:10; Eph. 2:8–10). The prominence given to good works in
the Pastorals is due to their intensely practical nature. Yet in the sharp
antithesis between grace and works the mind of Paul can be unmistakably
recognized (see, e.g., Titus 3:5; 2 Tim. 1:8 f.). There is nothing in the
distinctive teaching of the Pastorals on these matters which may be construed as a sign of postapostolic origin.

A Pauline emphasis on church organization can be detected as early as
the first missionary journey when Luke reports that Paul and Barnabas
appointed "elders" in the churches of Galatia which they had established
(Acts 14:22–23). The office was familiar from the synagogue. "Elder"
and "bishop" were apparently interchangeable terms in the Pauline churches
(cf. Acts 20:17, 28). The exact significance of the office in Galatia, in
Ephesus, or at Philippi, where "bishops and deacons" were officers in the
congregation (Phil. 1:1), is unclear.[13] No lists defining the function of an
elder/bishop are available for this early period.

The Pastoral Epistles provide the earliest treatment of the qualifications
for the office of bishop and shed considerable light on the functions to be
performed. While experience has undoubtedly served to refine and sharpen
earlier insights on ruling a local congregation, the points of parallel between
the Pastorals and Paul's earlier practice are impressive. Just as Paul and
Barnabas had appointed elders in the new centers of Galatia where they
had labored, Titus is instructed to "appoint elders in every town as I
directed you" (Titus 1:5). The titles "elder" and "bishop" are used inter-
changeably in the text (1:5–7). The elders who are described as governors
of the community (1 Tim. 5:17) form an exact counterpart to the leaders

of territorial communities known from the earliest Pauline letters (e.g., 1 Thess. 5:12; 1 Cor. 16:16–17; Rom. 12:8). Though the elders constituted a distinct and recognizable group within the congregation (1 Tim. 4:14, "the presbytery"*), there is no evidence that one man exercised authority over this group. This is in striking contrast to the evidence of Ignatius and others, that by the beginning of the second century the monarchical episcopate had already emerged within the churches of Syria and Asia. If the Pastorals display a developed ecclesiastical organization, they must be situated somewhere between Paul's earlier letters and the epistles of Ignatius (ca. 110–117). There is insufficient information available on organizational developments to allow anyone to say that the Pastoral Epistles are sufficiently like Ignatius and unlike Paul to deny them to the apostle. Moreover, the first evidence for an order of widows as a distinctive form of ministry within the church is provided by 1 Timothy 5:3–16; the very explicitness of Paul's instructions in this matter indicates that the institution has not been in existence long at Ephesus.

Although there is no *explicit* reference to charismatically endowed individuals in the Pastorals, the text contains no suggestion that spiritual gifts have ceased or that prophets in the congregation have been supplanted by church office holders.[14] Timothy is specifically urged not to neglect "the gift you have, which was given you by prophetic utterance when the elders laid their hands upon you" (1 Tim. 4:14), and Paul solemnly reminds him "to rekindle the gift of God that is within you through the laying on of my hands" (2 Tim. 1:6). Moreover, the formula introducing the prophetic word in 1 Timothy, "Now the Spirit expressly says . . ." (4:1), may attest the existence of prophets in the congregation or the exercise of the prophetic gift by the letter writer himself. It is difficult, therefore, to find any evidence for post-apostolic origin of the Pastoral Epistles, either in the level of ecclesiastical organization reflected or in the purported absence of reference to spiritual gifts.

The charge that the false teaching against which the Pastorals contend must be located in the post-Pauline period cannot be substantiated, precisely because so little is known of incipient Gnosticism and other forms of syncretism in this period. The teaching attacked in Titus had definite Jewish roots (1:10, "they who are of the circumcision"*; 1:14, "Jewish myths"; 3:9, "quarrels over the law"), but whether this was true of the heresy at Ephesus is less certain. Our problem is that Paul was primarily interested not in setting forth the doctrinal system of the rival teaching but in pointing out its dangerous implications for morality. Nevertheless, it is possible to hazard a conjecture as to its actual character.

Men had arisen within the congregation forbidding marriage and commanding abstinence from meats, both of which had their origin in the creation ordinances of God (1 Tim. 4:1–3). Some taught the erroneous conception that the resurrection was already past (2 Tim. 2:18). The resurrection of Jesus had projected the church into the "age to come," and the conditions of life in that age were now in force. Jesus' statement that in the resurrection men neither marry nor give their children in marriage demanded that marriage cease (Matt. 22:30). The risen Jesus had indicated by his own example that the food to be taken after the resurrection was fish (Luke 24:42; John 21:9–14). Against such reasoning Paul insists in 1 Timothy 4:8 that "godliness is profitable in every way, *having promise of the life which now is and of that which is to come.*"* The italicized words distinguish between the present experience of the church and that experience after the consummation of which the present is only a foretaste. The failure of the heretics to make this distinction accounts for their doctrine and provides an early instance of "over-realized eschatology" in the church. It is this which the writer castigates in the larger context of 1 Timothy 4:1–3.[15]

The case for the Pauline authorship of the Pastorals rests on more than simply a set of answers to the objections of critics. It is implied by Paul's constant personal reference to his own life and to his relationship with Timothy.[16] In the light of these personal sections of the letters it is not uncommon for writers who reject the Pauline authorship of the Pastoral Epistles to speak of genuine fragments which have been incorporated into the letters. It is simpler, however, to accept the three letters for what they purport to be, directives from the apostle Paul to Timothy and Titus dating from a period in the middle of the seventh decade when he had fulfilled a preaching mission in the east and was finishing his course of ministry.

NOTES

1. See the careful discussion of A. N. Sherwin-White, "Paul at Rome," in *Roman Society and Roman Law in the New Testament* (1963), pp. 108–19, citing Josephus, *Antiquities* XX. § 215; Pliny, *Epistle* X. 56. 2–3; Tacitus, *Annals* xiii. 11. 2; 23. 50; 27. 6; 43.7; xiv. 45. 4; Suetonius, *Nero* 10. 2.

2. The literature is surveyed by L. P. Pherigo, "Paul's Life After the Close of Acts," *Journal of Biblical Literature,* 70 (1951), pp. 277–84.

3. Cf. Tertullian, *Adversus Marcionem* v. 21. For two opposing views on Marcion and his canon see E. C. Blackman, *Marcion and His Influence* (1948),

and J. Knox, *Marcion and the New Testament: An Essay in the Early History of the Canon* (1942).

4. The discrimination used in compiling the list is evident from the sentence which immediately follows (lines 63–66), which asserts that there are other alleged letters composed in Paul's name (to the Laodiceans, to the Alexandrians, and others) which cannot be received into the universal church. At about the same time Irenaeus cites 1 Tim. 1:4 with the addition, "as the Apostle says," cites 2 Tim. 4:10–11 as the statement of Paul, and introduces Titus 3:10 with the formula, "Paul commanded us."

5. For coincidences with the language of Barnabas, Ignatius, and especially Polycarp's *Epistle to the Philippians,* see *The New Testament in the Apostolic Fathers* (ed. by a Committee of the Oxford Society of Historical Theology, 1905), pp. 12–14, 71–73, 95–98. So convincing are the Polycarp passages (*ca.* A.D. 115–135) that the German historian H. von Campenhausen has argued that Polycarp brought the Pastorals into general use in the church and that they were written either by Polycarp or by one of his clergymen at his direction (*Polykarp von Smyrna und die Pastoralbriefe,* 1951). Cf. Polycarp, Phil. 4:1 with 1 Tim. 6:10, 7; 9:2 with 2 Tim. 4:10; 12:3 with 1 Tim. 2:1–2.

6. Cf. P. N. Harrison, *The Problem of the Pastoral Epistles* (1921); *idem,* "The Authorship of the Pastoral Epistles," *Expository Times,* 67 (1955–56), pp. 77–81. On the basis of primarily linguistic evidence Harrison rejects the Pauline authorship of the Pastorals. Nevertheless, he feels compelled to argue that authentic Pauline fragments have been incorporated into the letters, pointing to such personal passages as Titus 3:12–13; 2 Tim. 4:9–21.

7. B. S. Easton, *The Pastoral Epistles* (1947), pp. 1–29. For orthodoxy see 1 Tim. 1:19; 6:3, 20; 2 Tim. 1:12–14; 2:2; 4:3; Titus 1:9–13; 2:1 f., 8; for good works, 1 Tim. 2:10; 5:10; 6:18; 2 Tim. 2:21; 3:17; Titus 2:4.

8. For the false teachers see 1 Tim. 1:3–11; 4:1–10; 6:3–5, 20 f.; 2 Tim. 2:18, 23; 3:1–9; 4:3 f.

9. These figures are based on lists compiled by R. St. John Parry, *The Pastoral Epistles* (1920), pp. cxviii–cxxiv. His entire treatment of the critical data is worthy of careful consideration.

10. The best treatment is that of C. Spicq, *Les Épitres Pastorales* (Études Bibliques, 1947), pp. cvii–cxviii, with an extensive list of resemblances between the Pastorals and the other ten Pauline letters in vocabulary and expression on p. cxvii (text and note 2).

11. Cf. the analysis of the words peculiar to 2 Tim. by A. E. Hillard, *The Pastoral Epistles of St. Paul* (1919), pp. xxx–xxxi.

12. W. Lock, *A Critical and Exegetical Commentary on the Pastoral Epistles* (1936), pp. xxvii–xxviii.

13. Cf. L. Porter, "The Word *episcopos* in Pre-Christian Usage," *Anglican Theological Review,* 21 (1939), pp. 103–12.

14. Spiritual gifts were in fact much in evidence in the church at Ephesus even as late as the middle of the second century. See Justin, *Dialogue* 82:1: "For even until the present time gifts of prophecy exist among us"; and 88:1: "Now, if you look around, you can see among us Christians, both men and women, endowed with gifts from the Spirit of God."

15. See W. L. Lane, "I Tim. IV.1–3. An Early Instance of Over-realized Eschatology?" *New Testament Studies*, 11 (1964), pp. 164–67.

16. References to Paul's life: 1 Tim. 1:11, 12–16; 2:7; 2 Tim. 1:3, 11, 12, 15–18; 3:10; 4:6–8, 9–18; references to his relationship with Timothy: 1 Tim. 1:3, 18; 3:14; 4:6–16; 5:23; 6:12, 20; 2 Tim. 1:5, 13, 18; 2:1; 3:10, 11, 14.

SELECTED READING

Guthrie, D., *The Pastoral Epistles and the Mind of Paul*. London: Tyndale, 1956.

———— *The Pauline Epistles: New Testament Introduction*. Chicago: Inter-Varsity Press, 1961. Pp. 198–246.

Lock, W., *The Pastoral Epistles*. Edinburgh: T. and T. Clark, 1924.

Pherigo, L. P., "Paul's Life After the Close of Acts," *Journal of Biblical Literature*, 70 (1951), pp. 277–84.

Sherwin-White, A. N., *Roman Society and Roman Law in the New Testament*. Oxford: Clarendon, 1963. Pp. 108–119.

Simpson, E. K., *The Pastoral Epistles*. London: Tyndale, 1954.

XVI

MARK—A NEW LITERARY FORM

IT IS generally recognized that Mark is the earliest of the four Gospels. Synoptic criticism has in the last century and a half produced detailed evidence that Matthew and Luke had before them a document virtually identical with our Gospel of Mark. The remarkable agreements of both Matthew and Luke with Mark in regard to content, order, and wording could be explained only in this way.[1]

If Mark is indeed the first Gospel, it merits careful and serious consideration by any student of history or Scripture. Its author introduced to the Roman world a form of popular literature previously unknown. Of its sixteen chapters, seven are devoted to the last week in the life of its principal subject. Mark is an historical narrative oriented around a crisis —the death of Jesus Christ. There is every reason to believe that the Gospel was written for people who themselves confronted a crisis not unlike the one Jesus had faced.

1. THE GOSPEL AS "JOYFUL TIDINGS"

The language of Mark's opening line, "the beginning of the gospel concerning Jesus the Messiah, the Son of God,"* must have struck a responsive chord among those who encountered these words for the first time. The word "gospel" or "evangel" was not a new word first coined by the Christians. Among the Romans it meant "joyful tidings" and was associated with the cult of the emperor, whose birth, attainment to majority, and accession to power were celebrated as festival days for the whole world. The reports of such festivals were called "evangels" in the inscriptions and papyri of the Imperial Age. A calendar inscription from about 9 B.C., found in Priene in Asia Minor, says of the birthday of the emperor Octavian (Augustus): "The birthday of the god was for the world *the* *beginning of joyful tidings* which have been proclaimed on his account" (*Inscr. Priene,* 105, 40). This inscription is remarkably similar to Mark's initial line, and it clarifies what was essential as the content of an evangel in the ancient world: a historical event which introduces a new situation for the world. In this perspective the Roman would understand Mark's proclamation of Jesus the Messiah. Beginning with the inauguration of Jesus' public ministry, Mark announces Jesus' coming as an event that brings about a radically new state of affairs for mankind.

There is, however, another aspect to the meaning of "gospel." Mark's own understanding of what constituted "joyful tidings" drew heavily on the prophetic tradition of the Old Testament. An illustration of its perspective is offered by Isaiah 52:7, 10. The context depicts the return of the Lord to Zion to comfort and redeem Israel:

> How beautiful upon the mountains are the feet of him
>   who brings joyful tidings
>   who publishes peace,
>   who brings joyful tidings of good,
>   who publishes salvation,
>   who says to Zion, "Your God reigns."
>
> The Lord has bared his holy arm before the eyes of all the nations;
> and all the ends of the earth shall see the salvation of our God.

In this context to announce salvation on God's authority is itself a creative act—in a sense it inaugurates the reality of which it speaks.

In keeping with this usage in Isaiah, Mark's opening verses center attention on both the earliest apostolic preaching about "Jesus the Messiah, the Son of God," and the joyful tidings announced by Jesus himself (1:14 f.). In the initial phrase of Mark's Gospel and in the summary of Jesus' Galilean proclamation, the word "gospel" has not yet come to mean a written document. It refers to a living word of hope from the lips of an appointed messenger.

2. THE FIRST GOSPEL AS "WITNESS DOCUMENT"

The Gospel of Mark represents the church's first attempt to put these "joyful tidings" into written form. In it the words and deeds of Jesus are remembered and proclaimed. Mark is a *witness document* that grew out of the early apostolic preaching of salvation through Jesus Christ. It is intended to be neither a formal historical treatise nor a biography of Jesus. It is essentially proclamation. The evangelist's intention is caught when the opening line of Mark is paraphrased, "The beginning of the preaching of the gospel." To understand Mark properly, one must approach it as if listening to an early Christian sermon. It is full of action and drama; if time permits, it should be read at one sitting. Modern scholarship often describes the structure and content of Mark as kerygmatic. This term is accurate, for it means that the material in the Gospel sustains a close relationship to the earliest Christian proclamation, the *kerygma.*

That Jesus is the Messiah, the Son of God, is not really open to man's judgment. It is something given by God. Mark bears witness to this word of revelation throughout his entire Gospel. The opening verse of Mark dictates the structure of the account which follows. The first half of the Marcan witness reaches its climax in the confession of Peter at Caesarea Philippi: "You are the Messiah"* (8:29). All that has preceded has prepared for this moment of recognition. All that follows, as Jesus turns his face to Jerusalem and the Passion, clarifies what it means for Jesus to be the Messiah. The climax to the second half of the Gospel comes with the confession of a soldier who witnessed Jesus' crucifixion: "Truly this man was the Son of God!" (15:39). Through these two confessions, one uttered by a representative of Israel and the other by a spokesman for the Gentile world, Mark bears witness to the faith which undergirds his document. Jesus is Savior of all the world.

Mark's Gospel may be described as a "passion-narrative with an extended introduction."[2] The reason that almost half of Mark's sixteen chapters describe the final week of Jesus' ministry is that it is in Jesus' suffering, death, and resurrection that the revelation of God in Christ is most clearly seen. Throughout the Gospel the evangelist has prepared for the acceleration of tension and movement which characterizes the passion narrative.[3] The task and destiny of the Son is sharply presented in a series of mission-sayings, through which Jesus clarifies the purpose for which he was sent into the world by the Father: "For the Son of Man also came not to be served but to serve, and to give his life a ransom for the many"* (10:45; cf. 8:31; 9:31; 10:33 f.). Such statements involve Mark's reader in the offense of the cross and prepare him to be left before the silent witness of the empty tomb as interpreted by the word of an angel: "You seek Jesus of Nazareth, who was crucified. He has risen, he is not here; see the place where they laid him" (16:6). Mark records this witness of faith in order to invite men to share this faith. It is this characteristic of the Gospel which sets it off as a witness document.

Mark's work received wide circulation and soon became a model for two other evangelists, Matthew and Luke, who not only appropriated much of the Marcan material but structured their Gospels in a similar manner. Thus the first Gospel became a literary influence, stimulating a new form of popular literature, the "gospel," or book of witness.

3. A GOSPEL FOR ROME

The clear tradition of the church both in the West and in the East toward the end of the second century and the beginning of the third is that Mark's Gospel was written primarily for the Christians in Rome and Italy.[4] Its probable date is within the late sixties of the first century. It should be understood as an address to real persons facing a real crisis. To understand how they could be informed by the tract read in their meetings it is necessary to appreciate their life situation.

The emperor at this time was Nero. Known for his extravagance and feared for his capricious cruelty, he had shown himself recklessly despotic in his relations with the aristocracy of Rome. Heavy taxation on the estates of childless couples, false accusations followed by confiscation of wealth, and invitations to suicide at public banquets had reduced the Senate to abject servility and made of life a reign of terror for men of wealth. Relatively little attention, however, had been given by the imperial authorities to the gatherings of Christians for worship. It is probable that their assemblies appeared indistinguishable from the vast number of religious societies and associations to be found throughout Rome. Christians were occasionally accused of heinous offenses by segments of the populace. Especially were they accused of the hatred of men,[5] a charge based on the reluctance of Christians to participate in pagan guild feasts and other social affairs where idolatrous practices and immorality were common. But there is no suggestion in the extant records that the authorities took these charges seriously or that there had been any police investigation of the Christian gatherings.

The situation was radically altered by the disastrous fire that swept Rome in the summer A.D. 64. The fire began among the cluttered shops near the Circus Maximus but, fanned by a strong wind, quickly spread to other wards of the city. After raging unchecked for more than a week, it was brought under control, only to break out a second time from the estates of Tigellinus, head of the praetorian guard. Of the fourteen wards of the city only four were untouched. Three wards were reduced to ash and rubble; in seven others many of the oldest buildings and monuments were destroyed or seriously damaged.

After the initial shock, popular resentment was fanned by widespread rumors that the fire had been officially ordered. Suetonius charges that Nero "set fire to the city so openly that several ex-consuls did not venture to lay hands on his chamberlains although they caught them on their estates with tow and firebrands."[6] Tacitus is more cautious, stating tersely: "Disaster followed. Whether it was accidental or caused by the emperor's criminal act is uncertain—both versions have supporters." He reports that "no one dared fight the flames; attempts to do so were prevented by menacing gangs. Torches, too, were openly thrown in, by men crying that they acted under orders," but adds, "perhaps they had received orders; or they may just have wanted to plunder unhampered."[7] The emperor did his utmost to aid the homeless and the injured, levying a tax for relief and lowering the price of grain to provide food for the impoverished. He engaged in vigorous urban renewal, clearing the slums, widening the streets, introducing new parks, and insisting that new construction be of fireproof material such as brick or stone. When none of these measures succeeded in allaying suspicion and resentment, a scapegoat had to be found. Blame for the fire was placed squarely upon the Christians. Tacitus, writing a generation removed from these events, expresses himself with strong feeling:

> Neither human resources, nor imperial munificence, nor appeasement of the gods, eliminated sinister suspicions that the fire had been instigated. To suppress this rumor, Nero fabricated[8] scapegoats—and punished with every refinement the notoriously depraved Christians (as they were popularly called). . . . First, Nero had self-acknowledged Christians arrested. Then, on their information, large numbers of others were condemned—not so much for incendiarism as for their anti-social tendencies. Their deaths were made farcical. Dressed in wild animals' skins, they were torn to pieces by dogs, or crucified, or made into torches to be ignited after dark as substitutes for daylight. Nero provided his Gardens for the spectacle, and exhibited displays in the Circus, at which he mingled with the crowd—or stood in a chariot, dressed as a charioteer. Despite their guilt as Christians, and the ruthless punishment it deserved, the victims were pitied. For it was felt that they were being sacrificed to one man's brutality rather than to the national interest (*Annals* XV. 44).

Such erratic behavior by the central government meant that the situation became unpredictable for the Christians in Rome.

Mass arrests and capital punishment upon admission to membership in a Christian group were presumably short-lived and localized excesses, yet they introduced martyrdom as a significant reality to the church. The self-awareness of the Christian community in this charged situation is reflected in 1 Peter, with its word of trial by fire addressed to the Asian churches (see below, pp. 341–343). "Babylon" becomes a cryptogram for Rome, the place where the new Israel now found itself exiled and captive.

The greeting from "Babylon" in 1 Peter is coupled with one from Mark, Peter's companion in Rome: "She who is at Babylon, who is likewise chosen, sends you greetings; and so does my son Mark" (1 Peter 5:13). The Mark in question is the Jewish Christian, John Mark, well known from the New Testament. He was originally from Jerusalem, where his mother, Mary, owned a home in which the nucleus of the original Christian community met; it was to this house that Peter came after his miraculous release from prison (Acts 12:12). Mark had traveled to Cyprus with his cousin Barnabas and Saul of Tarsus on a missionary journey (13:5); but when they turned to go inland to Asia, Mark returned to Jerusalem (13:13). When Paul refused to take him along on a projected second journey, Barnabas and Mark returned to Cyprus for mission activity (15:36 ff.). Later Mark was with Paul during an imprisonment in Rome, and was sent by the apostle on an important mission to Asia Minor (Col. 4:10; Philem. 24). Some years later, when Paul was again in prison and sentence had been passed upon him, he instructed Timothy in Ephesus to bring Mark to Rome, since he would be useful to him (2 Tim. 4:11). When 1 Peter was written, Mark was in Rome laboring with Peter as he had earlier served with Paul (1 Peter 5:13). The Gospel which bears Mark's name is actually anonymous, but an unbroken tradition puts forth as its author John Mark, who would have been in Rome at the time of crisis.

The content of Mark's Gospel, though it does not prove Roman origin, is highly consistent with it. Among the words of Jesus that Mark remembered was one which no other evangelist records: "Everyone will be salted with fire" (9:49). Jesus' statement had found fulfillment in the trial and persecution of Roman Christians under Nero. Their needs appear to have provided a major incentive for the preparation of the Gospel of Mark.

In agreement with Roman reckoning, Mark speaks of four watches of the night rather than the three that were traditional to Judaism. Mark records that Jesus approached his disciples walking on the sea "about the fourth watch of the night" (6:48), or that the master of the house may return "in the evening, or at midnight, or at cockcrow, or in the morning" (13:35). This terminology for the four watches would have been understood immediately by readers in Rome. It is even possible that the evangelist has structured his Passion narrative according to the four Roman night watches, for Jesus entered Jerusalem to share the Passover with his disciples *in the evening* (14:17); the hour of betrayal in the Garden of Gethsemane was very probably *midnight* (14:41); the denial of Peter occurred in connection with *cockcrow* (14:72); and "as soon as it was *morning*" Jesus was brought before Pilate (15:1).[9] If it was Mark's intention to structure his narrative deliberately in this fashion, it was in Rome that the significance of this would be especially appreciated.

It appears, moreover, that Mark prepared his Gospel for Gentile Christians who studied the Old Testament in the Greek Septuagint version[10] and needed an explanation for the Jewish customs and practices to which reference is made (e.g., 7:3, the ablution before meals and washing of vessels; 14:12, the day of the slaughtering of the Passover lambs; 15:42, the Day of Preparation is the day before the Sabbath). The evangelist regularly translates for his readers the Aramaic words and sentences he has used (cf. 3:17; 5:41; 7:11, 34; 9:43; 10:46; 14:36; 15:22, 34), including the simple "Abba," which Paul had used when writing to the church at Rome (Rom. 8:15).

Finally, it is noteworthy that the Gospel of Mark reaches its climax in the confession of a Roman centurion: "Truly this man was the Son of God!" (15:39). This cumulative evidence strongly supports a Roman origin for the first Gospel. If it was not written for Rome, at least there is every likelihood that Roman Christians early adopted it as a Gospel peculiarly appropriate to their life and problems.

4. "HE WAS WITH THE WILD BEASTS"

If Rome is in view, Mark's problem was the pragmatic one of how best to project Christian faith in a context of impending martyrdom. How will the gospel be proclaimed in a climate of uncertainty? Mark selected and grouped his material not merely to tell a story but to present the Christ who *had acted* as he who *continues to act* and speak meaningfully in a context of crisis. What was needed was not merely a past word—what Jesus had done and said—but a present word through which the living Christ might be conceived, known, and heard.

The Marcan account is characterized by simplicity, straightforwardness, and concreteness in detail. Its language and style is less elaborate and more popular than that of Matthew or Luke. Mark's sentences are very simply constructed, strung together generally by the conjunction "and." By frequent use of the word "immediately," a sense of vividness and excitement accompanies the action. Within a narrative, direct speech is preferred. The evangelist is especially fond of using the present tense to speak of past happenings. More than 150 times he employs this "historical present" where other writers would have used the simple past tense. The Marcan style has frequently been labeled "barbarous" or "unrefined." It is better to see it as having a conscious literary or even theological purpose, making Jesus the contemporary of those who read the account. In Mark, Jesus continues to act and speak with authority in the midst of his people.

It is characteristic of the first Gospel that attention is focused primarily on the deeds of Jesus rather than his sayings. Mark frequently reports that Jesus taught the people, without indicating what Jesus said; his primary intention was not to transmit the tradition of Jesus' words. Much of this tradition was probably already familiar in the church of Rome. Mark preserves only two lengthy discourses of Jesus, the parables of the Kingdom (4:1–34) and the Olivet discourse (13:1–37). There is no Sermon on the Mount. In contrast to Matthew, in which the mission instruction to the disciples extends to 38 verses (10:5–42), Mark limits it to four (6:8–11). The Marcan counterpart to Jesus' long denunciation of the scribes and Pharisees in Matthew (23:1–36) is one terse warning (Mark 12:38–40).

Though extended formal discourses are rare in Mark, there are numerous independent fragments of discourse reflecting conflict with the Jewish authorities. Early in the Gospel (2:1–3:6), Mark or his tradition groups five instances of conflict in Galilee, to which correspond five instances of conflict in Jerusalem at the close of Jesus' ministry (11:27–12:37). Between these two points Mark reports the Beelzebul controversy with Jerusalem scribes (3:22–30) and an extended dispute over clean and unclean (7:1–23). Mark's interest in the tradition's reporting instances of conflict is especially meaningful if designed for readers facing analogous situations of conflict in their experience with the imperial authorities.

There are other distinctive features in the form in which Mark presents his material. Brief and lengthy incidents alternate with one another. Many of the accounts, such as the healing of the paralytic man (2:1–12) or the restoring of the possessed man of Gadara (5:1–20), are narrated at greater length and in fuller detail than elsewhere in the synoptic Gospels. Mark can simply state facts, but it is more usual for him to present the narrative in a vivid and concrete manner. The graphic details that are his alone appear to reflect the presence of an eyewitness—Peter or some other apostle. It is only Mark who gives the name of the blind man (10:46), who relates that Jesus labeled James and John "sons of thunder" (3:17), and who reports that during a fierce storm at sea Jesus was asleep on the fisherman's pillow in the stern of the boat (4:38). It is Mark who makes frequent reference to the emotional reactions of the participants in the drama of salvation which Jesus' presence brings. He notes not only the fear and amazement of the disciples (10:24, 32) but the emotions of Jesus as well. The language expresses Jesus' stern anger (e.g., 1:43, "he sternly charged him"; 3:5, "he looked around at them with anger, grieved at their hardness of heart"), exasperation (e.g., 7:34, "looking up to heaven, he groaned and said . . ."*), or compassion (e.g., 8:2, "I have compassion on the crowd . . ."). The result is an account characterized by simplicity, color, and movement.

When the Roman believers received the Gospel of Mark, how did it speak to them? It is instructive to read the Gospel through with this question in mind, putting oneself existentially in the life situation of the Christian community in Nero's Rome. What would be of greater interest to a people reduced to a catacomb existence than to read of the Lord who was driven into the wilderness (1:9–13)? Only Mark records that in the wilderness Jesus was with the wild beasts (1:13). This detail emphasizes the loneliness and terror associated with the wilderness. But it was filled with special significance for those called to enter the arena and stand helpless in the presence of wild beasts. In Mark's Gospel they found that nothing they could suffer in Rome was alien to the experience of Jesus. Were they misrepresented to the people and falsely labeled? This had happened to Jesus as well, as officials from Jerusalem charged that his power was demonic and that he was himself demonic (3:21–22, 30). Did they know what it was to be betrayed from within the circle of intimate friends? One of the Twelve had been "Judas Iscariot, who betrayed him" (3:19).

As Mark was read in the Christian meetings there were notes peculiarly appropriate to the Roman situation. Jesus spoke openly of the persecution that could be expected in the Christian life. In the interpretation of the parable of the sower, Jesus referred to those who "have no root in themselves, but endure for a while; then, when tribulation or persecution arises on account of the word, immediately they fall away" (4:17); he had foreseen that there would be others who had heard the word, "but the cares of the world, and the delight in riches, and the desire for other things" entering in would choke it, preventing it from becoming more fruitful (4:19). Mark records the fulfillment of these sayings in the experience of Jesus when a man of great possessions turned from him as he learned the cost of discipleship (10:17–22), and later when Jesus' own disciples fled from him (14:27–31, 66 ff.). But it would not be strange for the Roman Christians to find such words realized again right in their own midst. When Jesus promised those who followed him "houses and brothers and sisters and mothers and children and lands," he added significantly: "with persecutions" (10:30). Jesus warned of the day when those who followed him would be delivered up to councils to be beaten, when they would stand before governors and kings for his sake, to bear testimony before them. He had not withheld the cruel truth that brother would betray brother to death, and the father his child, and children their parents, and that his followers would be hated by all men for his sake (13:9–13). In crucial statements on discipleship, he had made it clear that what he demanded was a radical abandonment of life in response to a call to martyrdom.

> If any man would come after me, let him deny himself and take up his cross and follow me. For whoever would save his life will lose it; and whoever loses his life for my sake and the gospel's will save it. . . . Whoever is ashamed of me and of my words in this adulterous and sinful generation, of him will the Son of man also be ashamed, when he comes in the glory of his Father with the holy angels (8:34–38).

The language speaks of cross-bearing, which Tacitus makes clear was a literal reality for Mark's readers in Rome. It had been a literal experience for Jesus as well, preceded by trial, scourging with the bone-tipped flagellum, and the cruel mockery of the praetorian guard (15:15–20). It was under the threat of such torture that a man could be moved to deny Jesus, showing shame for his association with the Lord. In so doing he would save his life only to meet rejection by Jesus when he returned at the last day in triumphal procession with his holy angels. This kind of language was charged with relevance for men upon whom was heaped derision and humiliation because they bore the name of Jesus. The Gospel was explicit: to reject suffering and death was to be on the side of men, and not on the side of God—and Jesus was on the side of God.

Mark's Gospel left no doubt concerning the sovereign authority of Jesus. The word remembered in connection with the call of the disciples was brief and urgent: "Follow me" (1:17; 2:14). In response to that word men had left family, home, and profession to be his disciples. Jesus taught with authority (1:22) and commanded even the forces of Satan (1:27). He demonstrated his authority to forgive sins (2:10) and his lordship over the Sabbath (2:28). The issue of Caesar's authority had been raised pointedly when Jesus was questioned concerning payment of taxes to Rome. His response, "Render to Caesar the things that are Caesar's, and to God the things that are God's" (12:17), imposed significant limits to the authority and the dignity of the emperor. There could be no confession that Caesar is Lord from one who rendered "to God the things that are God's."

When Jesus finally stood before Caesar's representative at a Roman tribunal, Pilate marveled at his dignity, then delivered him to be scourged and crucified to satisfy the demands of the crowd. But when his centurion saw how Jesus died, he exclaimed, "Truly this man was the Son of God!" (15:39). God's vindication of his Son was made complete on the third day, in the resurrection of Jesus. Mark's reader is left before the eloquent witness of the empty tomb as interpreted by the word of revelation:

> Do not be amazed; you seek Jesus of Nazareth, who was crucified. He has risen, he is not here; see the place where they laid him. But go, tell his disciples and Peter that he is going before you to Galilee; there you will see him, as he told you (16:6–7).

It is not difficult to imagine the meaning this would have for Christians in Rome. It provided the pledge of their own vindication. In the command to share these tidings with the disciples they found encouragement to continue their activity of mission in spite of imperial opposition. The explicit reference to Peter meant that the way was open for restoration to one who had denied his Lord. Here was a basis for forgiveness for those who had denied they were Christians, and for their persecutors as well. Their situation was too intensely real for them not to read the Gospel in this way.

NOTES

1. A standard statement of the evidence for Mark's priority is presented by B. H. Streeter, *The Four Gospels* (1953), pp. 151–98.

2. The phrase is Martin Kähler's, applied by him to all the Gospels. See *The So-called Historical Jesus and the Historic Biblical Christ* (1964, transl. of 1896 ed.), p. 80.

3. The student who wishes to trace this development in Mark should note the increasing clarity with which Jesus and his opponents speak in the sequence 2:20; 3:5; 8:31; 9:12, 31; 10:33 f., 38, 45; 12:6–8; 14:8, 17–21, 22–25, 27, 34, 36, 37 f., 41 f., 48 f.

4. *The Anti-Marcionite Prologues to Mark and to Luke* (*ca.* A.D. 160–180); Irenaeus, *Adv. Haer.* III. i. 1; cf. III. x. 6; Clement of Alexandria, *Hypotyposes apud* Eusebius, *Hist. Eccl.* IV. 14.

5. E.g., Tacitus, *Annals* XV. 44; cf. Athenagoras, *Legatio pro Christianis* iii; *Letter of the Churches of Lyons and Vienna,* in Eusebius, *Hist. Eccl.* V. 1.

6. *The Lives of the Caesars,* Bk. VI, *Nero,* § 38 (Loeb ed. II, pp. 154 f.).

7. *Annals* XV. 36–38 (Penguin Classics, pp. 351 f.).

8. *Subdidit,* used of fraudulent substitution or false suggestion. Tacitus did not believe the Christians were guilty.

9. Cf. R. H. Lightfoot, *The Gospel Message of St. Mark* (1950), p. 53.

10. The common language of Rome appears to have been Greek, not Latin. Paul's letter to the Romans, for example, was written in Greek. The earliest Latin versions of the Bible were not made until the late second century, and then not in Rome but in North Africa.

SELECTED READING

Bowman, J., *The Gospel of Mark: The New Christian Passover Haggadah.* Leiden: Brill, 1965.

Burkill, T. A., *Mysterious Revelation: An Examination of the Philosophy of St. Mark's Gospel.* Ithaca, N.Y.: Cornell University Press, 1963.

Johnson, S., *The Gospel According to St. Mark.* New York: Harper, 1961.

Lohse, E., *Mark's Witness to Jesus Christ.* New York: Association, 1955.

Mauser, U., *Christ in the Wilderness: The Wilderness Theme in the Second Gospel and Its Basis in the Biblical Tradition.* Naperville: Allenson, 1963.

Robinson, James M., *The Problem of History in Mark.* London: S.C.M., 1957.

Stonehouse, N. B., *The Witness of Matthew and Mark to Christ.* Philadelphia: The Presbyterian Guardian, 1944.

XVII

✠

MATTHEW—BLESSING ON THE NATIONS

THE person who opens his New Testament at its beginning is greeted by the words, "The book of the generation of Jesus Christ the son of David, the son of Abraham" (KJV). He is introduced to an extended genealogy, an account of Jesus' birth and infancy, and an unfolding of the gospel story from the appearance of John the Baptist until that day when the risen Christ stood upon a mountain in Galilee and sent forth his followers to "make disciples of all the nations." Unpromising as the genealogy may seem to the modern reader, the book that follows it is a most impressive piece of work. Very quickly the Gospel of Matthew surpassed its predecessor, Mark, in popularity. The reasons for this are not hard to discover. Matthew reproduces almost all of Mark's content, and in addition supplies the reader with a large body of Jesus' teaching on a number of subjects that were of vital importance to the church. Through the centuries, this Gospel has maintained its prominence and influence in the Christian church. It is doubtful that any set of ethical teachings has had as great an impact upon human life and thought as Jesus' Sermon on the Mount recorded in Matthew. Its formulation of the Lord's Prayer is repeated every day in private and public worship by people representing a wide range of religious beliefs. It is Matthew alone who reveals that Jesus intended to form a church. A text in Matthew became the basis for the doctrine of the primacy of Peter. It was Matthew's "great commission" that contributed such a powerful thrust to the church's great missionary expansion in the last two centuries.

1. MATTHEW'S PURPOSE

The reason for Matthew's success was not that it was a "better" Gospel than Mark, or merely that it was more complete, but that its distinctive purpose and structure made it exceedingly useful to the church, from its own day to the present. Matthew's purpose is best understood from a consideration of its beginning (1:1) and its ending (28:18–20).

A. THE FIRST VERSE

Right at the outset, Matthew establishes Jesus' continuity with two of the great men of Israel's past, Abraham and David. In doing this, he draws upon a feature of the church's earliest proclamation of Jesus that Mark had not developed to any notable extent—the idea of promise and fulfillment. According to the Book of Acts, early Christian preaching had centered on two classic Old Testament promises.[1] The first was made to Abraham in Genesis 12 and reiterated many times to Abraham, Isaac, and Jacob:

> And I will make of you a great nation, and I will bless you, and make your name great, so that you will be a blessing. I will bless those who bless you, and him who curses you I will curse; and in you all the families of the earth shall be blessed* (Gen. 12:2–3).

The second was made to David through the lips of the prophet Nathan:

> When your days are fulfilled and you lie down with your fathers, I will raise up your offspring after you, who shall come forth from your body, and I will establish his kingdom. He shall build a house for my name, and I will establish the throne of his kingdom for ever. I will be his father and he shall be my son. . . . And your house and your kingdom shall be made sure for ever before me; your throne shall be established for ever (2 Sam. 7:12–16; cf. Pss. 89:3 f., 19–37; 132:11 f.; Isa. 55:3; Jer. 33:17).

Though the immediate application of this latter promise had been to Solomon, later passages referred it to a king that was yet to come, while Paul at Antioch saw its fulfillment in David's greater son, Jesus of Nazareth.

As the Abrahamic and Davidic promises merge with one another in the sermons of Acts, so they do also in the first verse of Matthew's Gospel. Matthew's genealogy in 1:2–16, with its summary in 1:17, makes clear that the two promises are really one, and Jesus the Christ is its fulfillment. The fourteen generations from Abraham to David mean the attainment of nationhood and blessing for Israel; the fourteen generations from David to the captivity mean the loss of these gifts; the fourteen generations from the captivity to the Christ mean the regaining of the promises and the dawn of God's kingly rule.

It must be remembered that for Matthew the genealogy has a purely preliminary character. It is not the end of the story but the beginning; the primary significance of Jesus Christ lies not in the people or events that preceded him but in that which followed him and came to pass as a result of his ministry. This can be seen from Matthew's opening phrase, "the book of the generation of Jesus Christ." This heading recalls the formula, "This is the book of the generations of Adam," in Genesis 5:1, and the kindred expression, "These are the generations of. . . ." Ten times in all, this kind of statement occurs in Genesis (cf. Gen. 2:4; 5:1; 6:9; 10:1; 11:10, 27; 25:12, 19; 36:1; 37:2). The Hebrew word for "generations," *toledoth,* is commonly understood as "genealogy," but actually involves more than the mere listing of names. It is perhaps best translated as "history." In each of its uses in Genesis, *toledoth* refers not to what precedes but to what follows.[2]

Against this background, the "generation of Jesus Christ" probably does not refer to Matthew's genealogy, which lists Jesus' ancestors rather than his descendants. Nor is there any reason to limit the phrase to the birth narratives of Matthew 1–2. Instead, "the book of the generation" is best understood as a title for the whole Gospel of Matthew. This Gospel tells us *what came of the event of Jesus Christ.* The evangelist is aware that the happenings he records bear within themselves an abiding significance that reaches to his own time and beyond. He closes his Gospel with Jesus' word of assurance to his disciples, "Lo, I am with you always, even to the close of the age"* (28:20). Jesus of Nazareth is not the end but the beginning. His continuing ministry as the risen and exalted Lord is essential to the completion of the *toledoth* of Jesus Christ. Even as the Gospel of John reopens the Book of Genesis with its "In the beginning was the Word," so Matthew can be regarded as a kind of new Genesis, an eleventh and decisive *toledoth* to crown the ten that Genesis provides, and to witness to Jesus Christ as the progenitor of a new line, the founder of a new kingdom.

B. THE FINAL COMMISSION

The New Testament writers chose to emphasize sometimes the Abrahamic, sometimes the Davidic, promise because of specific practical concerns. The Davidic promise of 2 Samuel 7 was particularly adaptable to Christological teaching because it spoke of an individual "son of David." The Abrahamic promise of Genesis 12 was more suitable to the theme of a mission to the Gentiles because of its assertion that through Abraham and his descendants blessing would come upon all the families or nations of the earth. Matthew makes use of both aspects, but "blessing on the nations" is the one he has chosen for particular development. At the very end of his presentation he cites Jesus' words:

> All authority in heaven and on earth has been given to me. Go therefore and make disciples of all nations, baptizing them in the name of the Father and of the Son and of the Holy Spirit, teaching them to observe all that I have commanded you; and lo, I am with you always, to the close of the age (28:18–20).

For Matthew this is the point at which the promise to Abraham begins to find its fulfillment. Now through Abraham's seed the nations of the earth will indeed be blessed.[3] Even the concluding assurance of Christ's continuing presence with his missionary church is reminiscent of God's ancient words to Jacob as he renewed to him the Abrahamic covenant: "Behold, I am with you and will keep you wherever you go" (Gen. 28:15).

The key to Matthew's immediate purpose in writing a Gospel lies in one particular phrase of Christ's commission, "teaching them to observe all things whatsoever I have commanded you." Presumably, the things commanded are precisely the things recorded in Matthew's own Gospel. This means that Matthew can be regarded not only as a Gospel, following the outline of Mark, but also as a book of the teachings of Jesus, intended primarily for use in the church's task of instructing Gentile converts. In view of the author's strong interest in the Old Testament and in Jewish patterns of thought and expression, the Gospel of Matthew is likely a product of Jewish Christianity, but of a very particular type. Matthew allows no place for the narrow exclusivism of Paul's Judaizing opponents; he represents rather a Jewish Christianity that accepted with utmost seriousness its task of evangelizing the Gentiles, in order to fulfill the ancient promise to Abraham.

The most plausible home for such a missionary-minded Jewish Christianity is Antioch of Syria. According to the Book of Acts, Antioch was the base for the church's first expansion in the direction of the Gentiles. In all probability the Jews of Antioch were Greek-speaking, and correspondingly the Jewish Christians were also Hellenists. Thus, like so many other New Testament writings, Matthew seems to be a product of the churches of the Hellenists. Linguistic analysis indicates that in spite of its Jewishness, Matthew's Gospel was composed in Greek; it is not a translation of a Semitic original. The probable life setting of the Gospel of Matthew is a Hellenistic Jewish Christianity located at or near Antioch, convinced that "the field is the world" (13:38) and characterized by a remarkably broad and unrestricted view of the missionary task.

Ironically, this is exactly the opposite of the impression that many readers of this Gospel have received. It is, for example, Matthew who furnishes the information that Jesus had limited his disciples' initial activity to the "lost sheep of the house of Israel," warning them to "go nowhere among the Gentiles, and enter no town of the Samaritans" (10:5 f.). It is also Matthew who records the saying that their mission to Israel would not be complete "before the Son of man comes" (10:23). But it is clear that the specific limitation of the gospel to Israelites is temporary, coming to an end with the death and exaltation of Christ and being done away with by the universal commission of 28:19–20. Although the mission to Israel continues to the end of the age (10:23), it is really part of a larger task—the proclamation and teaching of the good news of Christ and his Kingdom to the whole world.

2. THE FIVEFOLD PATTERN

If Matthew is a teaching book for the Gentiles, then we have a right to expect this fact to be reflected in its character and content. In contrast to Mark its predecessor, Matthew's Gospel possesses a curious double character, reflected in the fact that it can be outlined in either of two ways. On one level Matthew belongs to the literary form that we have come to call a Gospel; it follows the familiar Marcan outline based upon the recital of Jesus' career found in certain of the speeches in Acts (i.e., John the Baptist, Jesus' baptism, Galilean ministry, journey to Jerusalem, and death and resurrection). If anything, Matthew makes the division even more pronounced with the words "from that time" in 4:17 and 16:21, marking the beginnings of the Galilean Kingdom-preaching and the journey to Jerusalem respectively.

On another level Matthew can be outlined as a catechetical or teaching book, and in this respect it is unique. That teaching manuals were used both in Judaism and in Christianity is evidenced by such works as the Qumran *Manual of Discipline,* and the Christian *Didache* of the second century. The *Didache* in fact seems based to some extent upon Matthew and has as its full title *The Teaching of the Twelve Apostles to the Gentiles.* Matthew's uniqueness, however, resides in its being *both* a Gospel and a teaching manual. The clue to the outline of Matthew along catechetical lines can be found in a formula repeated on five different occasions (with only slight differences in wording) : "And it came to pass when Jesus had finished all these sayings" (7:28; 11:1; 13:53; 19:1; 26:1). Matthew's first use of this summary statement can be roughly paralleled from Luke

7:1, so that its origin may have been Q, but only Matthew has adopted it as a division marker in his overall structure. Each occurrence of the formula signals the end of a discourse of Jesus upon a particular theme:

1. The Sermon on the Mount: Jesus' teaching on the *ethics* of the Kingdom (5:1–7:27).
2. The Charge to the Twelve, as they are sent to the cities of Israel: Jesus' teaching on *mission* (10:1–42).
3. The Parables of the Kingdom: Jesus' teaching on *redemptive history,* the nature of the Kingdom itself (13:1–52).
4. The Discourse on *church discipline* (18:1–35).
5. The Olivet Discourse: Jesus' teaching on *eschatology* (23:1–25:46).

Thus Matthew's Gospel can be divided easily into five blocks of teaching material separated by narrative sections. The fivefold structure makes us think of the Pentateuch, the five books of Moses, suggesting the idea of Jesus as a new Moses, the propagator of a new law upon another Sinai. But there is no correlation in subject matter between Matthew's discourses and the five books of the Pentateuch. It is more likely that Matthew has simply adopted a common Jewish method of structuring his material.[4]

The teaching material found in the five discourses is comprehensive and varied enough to speak to almost every area of Christian faith and life. Most of it comes from common tradition, but by means of his topical arrangement of the material, Matthew has allowed it to express his own distinctive interests. A host of questions which arose in the Christian community become the object of his attention and concern. Many of these questions reflect a rather mature stage in the community's growth and development. They presuppose a self-consciousness as "church," a historical entity in the world with definite organizational structure and particular forms through which worship and instruction were carried on. For example, it was asked: How does the new convert relate himself to his fellow Christians? What is his relation to a hostile world and to persecution? How should the church treat the brother who commits sin? What continuing validity is there to the Jewish law? Why was it that Jesus' ministry met with failure as well as success? Why do not all men receive the witness of the church? Does the element of failure mean that the Kingdom Jesus proclaimed will not come? Has God cast off the Jews forever? Why was Jerusalem destroyed? Does the consummation of the age depend on the church's completion of her task?

To questions such as these, Matthew's five discourses provide answers from the lips of Jesus himself. The Sermon on the Mount sets forth the general principles governing human and Christian relationships and guards against flagrant disregard of God's law in the name of free grace. The reality of persecution and the need for radical commitment and discipleship emerge clearly from the missionary discourse. The parables of chapter 13 show how the Kingdom will still come in spite of its small beginnings and man's persistent rejection of the gospel message. The fact that the church, no less than the world, is a mixture of good and evil need be no stumbling block to the Christian. Jesus foresaw that this would be so, and in fact it was so in his own day. The mixed character of the church is itself a part of God's redemptive plan and a necessary preliminary step to the realization of his rule upon the earth. Jesus himself laid the foundation for his church (16:18 f.) and made mutual forgiveness the governing factor in its discipline (ch. 18). In all of these things it is necessary to keep in mind that life in the Christian community is life lived in the shadow of the consummation. Jesus will one day return as the eschatological Son of man upon the clouds of heaven. He can be compared to a bridegroom arriving for a midnight wedding, or a lord of the manor returning from a journey to reward or punish his servants, or even a thief surprising a sleeping household under cover of darkness (chs. 24–25). A key concept in Matthew's concluding series of eschatological parables is that of stewardship. Jesus addressed himself to those entrusted with authority in the church. To them much has been given; they will be held responsible for their trust when their Lord comes, and they will be rewarded or judged according to their deeds. Thus the bulk of Matthew's discourse material is best understood on the supposition that his book is a manual primarily for Christian teachers and secondarily for those whom they teach, "all the nations," whether in their early missionary contacts with catechumens (i.e., persons undergoing instruction prior to baptism) or with the full-fledged members of the congregation.

3. THE FORMULA QUOTATIONS

When all of this has been said, it still remains true that Matthew is also a Gospel. A threefold division that might serve as Matthew's equivalent to the Marcan outline would be:

1:1–4:16—Preparation for Jesus' ministry.
4:17–16:20—Proclamation of the Kingdom of heaven.
16:21–28:20—Progression of events leading to Jesus' death and resurrection.

This outline can be superimposed upon the fivefold one described above, or the two can be regarded as alternative ways to structure the Gospel. There is some advantage to be gained by subsuming the birth narrative of chapters 1 and 2 and the baptism and temptation accounts of chapters 3 and 4 under one heading. Thus 1:1–4:16 becomes the true prologue of Matthew, bringing Jesus from his birth in Bethlehem to the threshold of his Galilean ministry.[5] This section is bound together by seven Old Testament quotations that focus on the personal and geographical names associated with Jesus' birth and early life. Five of these citations are introduced by a formula particularly characteristic of Matthew: "in order that what was spoken by the prophet might be fulfilled." Today we think of events almost entirely with reference to a temporal sequence of cause and effect. Not so in the world of the Bible. To Matthew, the deeds of Jesus and the circumstances of his life down to the smallest particulars took place not merely in order to accomplish some immediate purpose but that ancient oracles of prophecy might be fulfilled. Just as Matthew's total presentation of Jesus' life is integrated with Israel's past by the theme of blessing on the nations through the Abrahamic promise, so also a wide sampling of specific details within the narrative is linked up with Old Testament references by means of the formula quotations. Altogether, Matthew's Gospel contains ten such quotations. The five set forth in the prologue are:

1:23—"Behold, a virgin shall conceive and bear a son, and his name shall be called Emmanuel, which means, God with us" (from Isa. 7:14).

2:15—"Out of Egypt have I called my son" (from Hos. 11:1).

2:18—"A voice was heard in Ramah, wailing and loud lamentation, Rachel weeping for her children; she refused to be consoled, because they were no more" (from Jer. 31:15).

2:23—"He shall be called a Nazarene" (source unknown, possibly Isa. 11:1 or Judg. 13:5).

4:15–16—"The land of Zebulun and the land of Naphtali, toward the sea, across the Jordan, Galilee of the Gentiles—the people who sat in darkness have seen a great light, and for those who sat in the region and shadow of death light has dawned" (from Isa. 9:1–2).

To these might be added two others of similar character but without the distinctive formula:

2:5-6—"For so it is written by the prophet: 'And you, O Bethlehem, in the land of Judah, are by no means least among the rulers of Judah; for from you shall come a ruler who will govern my people Israel' " (from Mic. 5:1, 3, and 2 Sam. 5:2).

3:3—"For this is he who was spoken of by the prophet Isaiah when he said, 'The voice of one crying in the wilderness: Prepare the way of the Lord, make his paths straight' " (from Isa. 40:3).

Whether we count five or seven, it is clear that these quotations share a common concern to root the events and place names of Jesus' early life in the holy history of the past. When Gentiles or non-Christian Jews would ask, "Who is this Jesus and from where did he come?" Matthew could speak of Bethlehem, Egypt, Ramah, Nazareth, the Judean wilderness, or Galilee and point out correspondences between these places and God's saving acts and promises to Israel in the Old Testament.

The first and the last of this block of quotations are especially noteworthy, since they are programmatic for Matthew in the total development of his Gospel. In 1:23 the evangelist translates the Hebrew of Isaiah's "Emmanuel" as "God with us," an implicit promise that finds its realization at the very end, in the words, "Lo, I am with you always" (28:20). The presence of God with his people begins with Jesus' birth, but it does not end with his death or with his ascension to the Father. Rather, it continues through the time in which Matthew himself lives, and on to the consummation of the age. The last of this early group of citations (4:15 f.) similarly anticipates the final commission. Its key phrase is "Galilee of the Gentiles." Even though Matthew is quite clear that Jesus did not conduct a mission to the Gentiles during his lifetime (10:5), still the Galilean ministry is seen as the first decisive step that is finally to issue in the command to "make disciples of all the Gentiles" (28:19).

Throughout the rest of Matthew's Gospel (from 4:17 to the end), five more formula quotations are distributed through the major blocks of teaching material. These are not, of course, Matthew's only citations of the Old Testament; some others are introduced in different ways or attributed to Jesus (e.g., 13:14 f.). The last five formula quotations are as follows:

8:17—"He took our infirmities and bore our diseases" (from Isa. 53:4). This quotation belongs to the narrative section that follows the discourse on *ethics* (chs. 5–7). It summarizes the ministry of *healing* that Matthew has just described.

12:18–21—"Behold, my servant whom I have chosen, my beloved with whom my soul is well pleased. I will put my Spirit upon him, and he shall proclaim justice to the Gentiles. He will not wrangle or cry aloud, nor will any one hear his voice in the streets; he will not break a bruised reed or quench a smoldering wick, till he brings justice to victory; and in his name will the Gentiles hope" (from Isa. 42:1–4). This quotation forms a part of the series of narratives that follow the *missionary* discourse (ch. 10). Since it accompanies the statement that he "ordered them not to make him known" (12:16), it serves to underline the *secrecy,* or *reserve,* that characterized Jesus' ministry. Notice that this period of secrecy is contrasted to a later time when God's victorious judgment shall be revealed, specifically "to the Gentiles." Thus once again is anticipated the period of the church and its mission when Gentiles shall "hope in his name."

13:35—"I will open my mouth in parables, I will utter what has been hidden since the foundation of the world" (from Ps. 78:2). In this case the quotation does not have a narrative context but falls within the teaching section itself. In the midst of the parables chapter, Jesus' discourse on *redemptive history,* the Psalm citation links his use of parables with the Old Testament while at the same time stressing the newness of the revelation that Jesus brings.

21:5—"Tell the daughter of Zion, Behold your king is coming to you, humble, and mounted on an ass, and on a colt, the foal of an ass" (from Zech. 9:9 and Isa. 62:11). This quotation comes after the *church discipline* section (ch. 18) and identifies Jesus as the Davidic king of Jewish expectation. The three previous citations dealt with general aspects of Jesus' ministry—healing, secrecy, and parabolic teaching—while this one and the one that follows are more like the first seven in that they point to specific incidents, this time leading up to the passion.

27:9–10—"And they took the thirty pieces of silver, the price of him on whom a price had been set by some of the sons of Israel, and they gave them for the potter's field, as the Lord directed me" (though attributed to Jeremiah, these words actually come from Zech. 11:12–13). This last of Matthew's formula quotations falls within the passion narrative and follows the last of the discourses, the one on *eschatology.* It speaks of the disposal of Judas' blood money, the thirty pieces of silver received for betraying Jesus.

Thus it can be seen that the formula quotations have been carefully spaced by the evangelist; seven are assigned to the prologue and one each to the five sections of narrative and discourse that comprise the rest of this Gospel. There is no need to insist that these quotations must bear any special relationship to the teaching discourses that precede or follow them. They simply furnish some concrete examples of how various aspects of the career of Jesus can be connected with Old Testament prophecies. In the life situation of the church of Matthew's day, they served a twofold purpose: (1) for the Jewish Christians who were committed to the task of teaching the Gentiles, the quotations would provide assurance that Jesus in his birth, his words and deeds, and his passion had in fact fulfilled the Old Testament; (2) for the Gentile convert who was learning of Jesus, they would serve as reminders that the Old Testament was a holy book, worthy of continuing study and meditation. The purpose was not so much to introduce Jews to Jesus Christ as to introduce Gentile converts to the Old Testament, thus opening up for them a whole new world—the story of God's ancient dealings with his elect people and his promises to bring blessing through them to all nations.

It is likely that almost from the beginning early Christians "searched the Scriptures" to find foreshadowings of the career of Jesus Christ, and compiled lists of significant messianic proof texts. Such lists, known as testimony books, were kept by the Qumran community, and have been discovered and studied (e.g., the so-called *Testimonia* and *Florilegium* found in Cave Four).[6] Since most of Matthew's quotations were not used by other New Testament writers, Matthew may have been his own compiler of testimonies. It has even been suggested that his Gospel may be the product of a "school" of Christian scribes or teachers rather than the work of one man.[7] The traditional ascription of the Gospel to Jesus' disciple Matthew or Levi, the tax collector (9:9; cf. Mark 2:14), need not be doubted, but the systematic arrangement of the teaching material, the use of the quotations and of specific formulas as aids to learning, suggest that Matthew may have become a kind of Christian rabbi, the head of a catechetical school designed to equip missionary teachers for their job of fulfilling Jesus' great commission.

Jesus himself is the Teacher par excellence. He teaches with authority (7:28), calls followers to himself, and instructs them with true wisdom (11:25–30). They proclaim the good news of the Kingdom (10:7), but they are not ready to be teachers until they are themselves fully taught. Not only must they become "scribes fully instructed as disciples for the Kingdom of heaven"* (13:52), but they must be equipped with Jesus' own teaching authority through the power of his resurrection (28:18 ff.). It is in the belief that these conditions have been met that Matthew forwards the task of teaching all nations the truth of Jesus Christ.

4. THE SHEEP AND THE GOATS

The "school" setting of Matthew's Gospel sheds considerable light on the celebrated Last Judgment passage in 25:31–46. Coming as it does at the very end of the last of the five discourses, this scene possesses a particularly climactic and therefore memorable quality. The righteous and the wicked are separated like sheep and goats; the righteous are invited to inherit the Kingdom while the wicked are sent into everlasting fire.

The heart of the matter is the criterion by which the verdict is reached: Jesus the Son of man has been hungry, thirsty, a stranger, naked, sick, and in prison. The righteous are those who have ministered to him in his affliction, while the wicked are those who turned their backs on him in time of need. When neither group is aware that these things have happened, Jesus explains: "As you did it to one of the least of these my brethren, you did it to me" (25:40). Who are these "brethren" with whom Jesus so closely identifies himself, and who have undergone such harsh privations? The only other place where such an identification is made is at the end of the missionary discourse in chapter ten. There Jesus addresses his disciples whom he has sent out to proclaim the gospel of the Kingdom: "He who receives you receives me, and he who receives me receives him who sent me" (vs. 40). Then he adds, "And whoever gives to one of these little ones even a cup of cold water because he is a disciple, truly, I say to you, he shall not lose his reward" (vs. 42). A comparison of this passage with chapter 25 suggests that the "least" or "little ones," Jesus' brethren, are those commissioned to preach and teach the good news.

Correspondingly, the group being judged and divided into "sheep and goats" is precisely "all the nations" (25:32), the same group that the disciples are commissioned to baptize and teach according to the last words of Matthew's Gospel. The judgment scene in chapter 25 thus looks forward to the close of the age and assumes the completion of the universal task of "teaching all nations." To the teachers of the truth goes the assurance that Christ is "with them always," so their afflictions are his as well; to the Gentiles goes the warning that their eternal destiny hinges on their willing acceptance of the Christian message—and their deeds of kindness toward the messengers.[8]

This interpretation helps to place Matthew's Gospel in a setting in which it was important to reflect upon the ministry of instruction and the mutual obligations of teacher and catechumen. Seen from the perspective of the Abrahamic promise, the final separation of "sheep and goats" in Matthew 25 is simply the ultimate fulfillment of God's statement to the patriarch: "I will bless those who bless you, and him who curses you I will curse" (Gen. 12:3). For Matthew this sobering intimation of eternal judgment qualifies to some degree the glorious hope inherent in the great commission that "in you shall all the nations of the earth be blessed."

5. THE CHRIST OF MATTHEW'S GOSPEL

Beyond its teaching interest, Matthew has also a very specific Christology, more developed than Mark's. He begins with "Jesus Christ, the son of David, the son of Abraham," and ends with the risen and ever present Lord to whom has been given "all authority in heaven and earth."

One purpose of the birth narrative is to reinforce the claim that Jesus is the anointed King of Jewish expectation, the son of David. His father, Joseph, is a "son of David" (1:20); Jesus himself is "king of the Jews," born in Bethlehem, David's city, and like David appointed to shepherd God's people (2:2, 5–6).[9] Again and again through Matthew's Gospel the reader is kept aware of this Davidic type of Christology. Jesus' ability to cast out demons persuades many that he is indeed David's greater son the Messiah, so that in the triumphal entry and again in the temple he is greeted with a "Hosanna to the Son of David!" (21:9, 15). Matthew gives no hint that this testimony represents a mistaken or inadequate conception of Jesus' person. On the contrary, it is said of the shout of Hosanna that "Out of the mouth of babes and sucklings thou hast brought perfect praise" (21:16, from Ps. 8:3, LXX). Without qualification Matthew believes that Jesus was the Jewish Messiah.

Although the Davidic hope is not set aside or transcended, it is caught up into a higher sphere. The son of David is also Son of God, for the full import of the virgin birth is expressed only by the "God with us" of Matthew 1:23. To Matthew, Davidic Messiahship does not mean that Jesus is merely a political ruler of human origin. He is "conceived of the Holy Spirit" (1:20) and bears a unique relation to his Father in heaven. It is no alien intrusion in Matthew's Gospel when Jesus says, "All things have been delivered to me by my Father; and no one knows the Son except the Father, and no one knows the Father except the Son and any one to whom the Son chooses to reveal him" (11:27). The same Father who ordains that

children should say, "Hosanna to the son of David," reveals to Simon Peter
that Jesus is "the Christ, the Son of the living God" (16:16–17; cf.
11:25). The anointed one of Israel can only be the Christ, the God-Man of
the Christian church.

The transcendent claim that "All things have been delivered to me by
my Father" (11:27) is repeated so as to lay a basis in Christology for the
great commission, when Jesus says, "All authority in heaven and on earth
has been given to me" (28:18). Here at the end, which for Matthew is
really the beginning of the "generation of Jesus Christ," several strands
come together: the son of David is now manifest as God's unique Son.
Moreover, Matthew follows Mark in preserving for his readers Jesus' self-
designation as Son of man. The great commission adds another dimension
to this concept even as it does to messiahship. Here the Son of man stands
fully unveiled as the mysterious figure of Daniel's prophecy to whom "*was
given authority, and all the nations* of the earth of various kinds, and all
glory was given to him. And his authority was an everlasting authority
which shall not be taken away, and his Kingdom one that shall not be
destroyed"* (Dan. 7:14, LXX). As Son of man, no less than as the seed
of Abraham and David, Jesus exercises his authority and extends his redemptive rule to "all the nations."

Whether we speak of the Abrahamic promise and the theology of mission that it supported, or whether we trace the Jewish Davidic hope and the
transcendent Son of man concept to their place of meeting and merging,
we can see that Matthew has advanced beyond Mark in his theology.
Written within the framework of established church life, this book is more
than a recital of events, more even than a teaching manual; it is a genuinely
theological work. Matthew's Gospel belongs with the writings of Paul,
John, and Luke as one of the cornerstones on which any total New Testament theology must be built.

NOTES

1. See Peter's sermon at Pentecost (Acts 2:25–36), and again in Solomon's
portico (Acts 3:13, 25 f.), as well as Paul's address at Antioch of Pisidia (Acts
13:17, 22 f., 26, 32 f., 36 f.).

2. Thus the *toledoth* of Adam (Gen. 5:1) includes a list of Adam's *descendants,* not of his ancestors. It tells who or what came from Adam. The *toledoth* of
Noah (Gen. 6:9) names his three sons but devotes more attention to the events
of his life. The *toledoth* of the heavens and earth (Gen. 2:4) tells not how the

heavens and the earth were created but what they brought forth: man, and a garden where man might dwell.

3. At the same time, the Davidic promise has not been altogether forgotten. God had said to his anointed Davidic king in Psalm 2:8: "Ask of me, and I will *give* you the *nations* for your inheritance, and the ends of the earth for your possession."*

4. Note, for example, the fivefold division of the Book of Psalms as marked by doxologies at the end of Psalms 41, 72, 89, 106, and 150.

5. Cf. E. F. Krentz, "The Extent of Matthew's Prologue," *Journal of Biblical Literature,* 83 (1964), pp. 409–14.

6. For English translations of these writings see A. Dupont-Sommer, *The Essene Writings from Qumran* (Meridian Books, 1961), pp. 310–17.

7. Krister Stendahl, *The School of St. Matthew* (1954).

8. For a fuller discussion of this passage see J. R. Michaels, "Apostolic Hardships and Righteous Gentiles," *Journal of Biblical Literature,* 84 (1965), pp. 27–37.

9. Cf. 2 Sam. 5:2, also Matt. 9:36; 10:6; 15:24.

SELECTED READING

Blair, P., *Jesus in the Gospel of Matthew.* New York: Abingdon, 1960.

Bornkamm, G., Barth G., and Held, H. J., *Tradition and Interpretation in Matthew.* Philadelphia: Westminster, 1963.

Davies, W. D., *The Setting of the Sermon on the Mount.* Cambridge: University Press, 1964.

Filson, F. V., *The Gospel According to St. Matthew.* New York: Harper, 1960.

Franzmann, M., *Follow Me: Discipleship According to Saint Matthew.* St. Louis: Concordia, 1961.

Stanley, D. M., *The Gospel of St. Matthew* (New Testament Reading Guides 4). Collegeville, Minn.: Liturgical Press, 1963.

Stonehouse, N. B., *The Witness of Matthew and Mark to Christ.* Philadelphia: The Presbyterian Guardian, 1944.

XVIII

LUKE-ACTS—MISSION IN
HISTORICAL AND THEOLOGICAL
PERSPECTIVE

WITH the author of the third Gospel we are introduced to the most prolific writer in the New Testament. Not only is his Gospel the longest of the four, but the second part of his work, the Acts of the Apostles, is the longest single document in the New Testament. Together these two books comprise more than all the writings of John or of Paul.

The importance of this author cannot, however, be measured by the length of his contribution. Rather, it is the nature of his literary effort that has given him his particular importance. The vital role of Luke in shaping the New Testament is now almost universally recognized—in spite of the fact that his two-part work early became divided so that each of the parts had to win its way into the canon on its own merits. In the process, Luke's account of the life of Jesus came to be recognized as the most beautiful of the Gospels, while Acts is indispensable since it provides the bridge between the Gospels and the Pauline Epistles.

Regardless of this success, Luke-Acts has suffered immeasurably from forced separation. The Book of Acts, for example, depends for its selection of incidents and teachings upon the particular interpretation of Jesus' life presented in the Gospel. By the same token, the Gospel of Luke can only be appreciated when one has read the conclusion of the whole matter as found in Acts. The consistent picking up of motifs from the life of Jesus and their development in Acts makes clear the author's special understanding of Christian truth. Apart from a recognition of the mutual dependence of the two parts, Luke's purpose and the framework of his thought can never be fully understood. In recent years this has resulted in fresh approaches to Lucan studies. There has been an increasing appreciation for the author, not only as an historian of the primitive church but as one of its major theologians.[1]

1. THE QUESTIONS THAT PROMPTED LUKE-ACTS

Luke-Acts is the only major New Testament writing addressed to an individual rather than to a church. It is not a piece of private correspondence, however, for the addressee, Theophilus (Luke 1:3; Acts 1:1), was representative of a sizable group of Gentile converts to Christianity. He was neither uninitiated in the gospel nor unconvinced by its claims, but he lacked detailed knowledge of the historic antecedents of his faith. All that he knew of Palestine, Judaism, and the Old Testament Scriptures he most likely had learned from Christian teachers. That there remained significant gaps in his understanding is a reasonable conjecture.

Although the chief events in Jesus' life were quite clear to him, he was not always certain of their meaning and connection. References to individuals around Jesus also proved confusing. While he recognized some of their names, the specific relationships they sustained to Jesus baffled him.

From the first time Theophilus had heard the gospel, Jesus' death and resurrection had been the subject of his instruction. The subsequent events, however—the advent of the Holy Spirit, the early ministries of the disciples, the varied experiences of the early church—were probably as obscure to him and as little integrated into his thinking as were the details of the career of Jesus. What part had the apostles played in the missionary expansion? Under what circumstances had Paul become involved with the Christian faith? What was the nature of his apostleship in relation to the Twelve? What of the other early heroes of the Christian movement?

The transition through which the church passed as it emerged from its provincial Palestinian context upon the world scene must also have raised questions to Theophilus. How had the geographical center of the church shifted from Jerusalem to Rome? In Jerusalem, the gospel as first proclaimed had been relatively simple. The apostles had appealed to the Jews to acknowledge Jesus as Messiah, to submit to baptism as a sign of repentance, and to live lives worthy of God. By such acts of obedience they would receive the blessing of God promised to their fathers through the prophets. Those who responded did not cease to be Jews when they became Christians. Questions concerning where they should worship, what law they should obey, or what customs they should practice were never raised. As Jews they lived under the rule and word of God, now expressed through the teaching of the apostles. They continued to voice their prayers in the temple, to study the Scriptures in the synagogue, and to attend the great religious festivals in Jerusalem.

In Theophilus' time all this had changed. The composition of the church was now predominantly Gentile. Its adherents lived in Antioch, Corinth, and Rome rather than in Jerusalem. Its theology had grown more complex. The Christian evangelists still proclaimed the sovereign God, but now as the one that could be known only through Jesus Christ his Son. They continued to affirm the messiahship of Jesus, but now as an expression of his lordship over heaven and earth. They announced the Spirit, but now as the one who had come down to energize the lives of believers and unite men of all races in one body. They proclaimed the people of God, but now as a new creation, the church. They were caught up in a divine mission, directed no longer to Jews only but to the whole world.

Like most converts out of paganism, Theophilus studied the Greek Old Testament and was instructed in the words of Jesus and the apostles. He would have no trouble recognizing that in the Gentile world a significant reinterpretation of the gospel had taken place. It was important that he understand how, and under whose authority, this translation had taken place. Beyond this he needed to know to what extent the new developments were supported by the Old Testament Scriptures and were already implied in Jesus' own life and teaching. Every presentation of the gospel carried with it the assumption that the Christian faith and the Hebrew Scriptures belonged together. Was this assumption valid? Did the events of Jesus' life, particularly his suffering and death, belong to biblical revelation? Did the Scriptures actually anticipate the descent of the Spirit, the birth of the church, and the Gentile mission?

Some of the questions facing Theophilus were prompted by difficult practical problems. Wherever the gospel had been proclaimed, it had carried with it a demand for conformity to God's law. In Palestine, where the very law of the land was based on the religious ideals of the Old Testament, this requirement was one thing. For a Christian living in the Roman world it was quite another. His whole society was oriented toward pagan practices and beliefs: idolatry, emperor worship, mystical rites, and sacrifices were the order of the day. Against exposure to such practices the Gentile Christian had little protection. Unlike the Jerusalem Christians, he was accountable for his behavior not to religious authorities but to civil magistrates. Nor did he share in the privileged sanctuary awarded to the diaspora Jew.

who was not required to practice customs alien to his religion. The Gentile Christian, and especially the Roman citizen, found it necessary to come to terms with his society in such a fashion as neither to compromise his faith nor to deny his obligations to the State. Upon his successful resolution of this tension depended his freedom to proclaim the gospel in the Roman world. It was of immediate importance for Theophilus to know how the earliest disciples, and Jesus himself, had regarded the civil authorities who had opposed them.

Most of these difficulties which Theophilus faced were symptomatic of a more basic problem: Since a Gentile Christian possessed no frame of reference by which he could understand his place in the divine economy, how could he be expected to act with understanding in his present situation? What he needed was a total historical and theological perspective, broad enough to encompass all of God's saving action in history and yet specific enough to indicate how he and his times related to the divine plan. If God was truly the Lord of all "times and seasons," what was the meaning of his activity in the past, especially toward Israel? What was the significance of Jesus' time? How long would the present age endure? When would the end come, bringing with it the fulfillment of God's purpose? Answers to such questions as these would help Theophilus stand fast and advance the gospel in a hostile world.

The urgency of these needs may well have provided all the incentive required to induce Luke to give some answer to his friend. Additional stimulus may have come from quite a different quarter. In the preface to Luke-Acts, reference is made to "many" who had undertaken to provide gospel narratives (Luke 1:1-2). We may assume that among the "many" were some who attempted to synthesize Christianity with its environment. Already in the epistles of Paul we are made aware of such activities and of the fact that many divergent ideas, some of them alien to the teaching of the apostles, were competing for a place in the theology of the early church. Much of Paul's time was spent contending against a synthesis in which the gospel would have been subsumed under the larger category of Judaism. This would have required eventually that all Gentile Christians live under the law and express their faith within the religious and cultural confines of Judaism. Although such a synthesis probably owed its origin to Jewish Christians, there were many Gentiles who were open to this possibility, attracted by the ancient character of Judaism, the venerableness of its documents, and the elaborate ritual of its sacrificial system.

In Luke's day an opposing tendency, incipient in form, may have offered an even greater menace. Some Gentiles saw no necessary connection between the gospel and its Jewish antecedents. They failed to locate in the Old Testament and its traditions any relevance to their particular situation in the world. They may even have found it difficult to appreciate the significance of Jesus' own ministry, since it was lived exclusively within a Jewish context. Such persons would be open to a synthesis in which Christian faith could be viewed more as a speculative philosophic system. The orientation would inevitably become Hellenistic rather than Jewish, and the historic character of God incarnate in human flesh would soon be denied. Such a development would tend to discount any connection between the God of the Old Testament and Jesus, the divine Son. We know that such movements did emerge at a later date, and it is probable that their roots trace back to the early conflicts between the gospel and the Hellenistic world.

Out of concern for such problems Luke undertook a unique task—to set forth for Theophilus the details surrounding the redemptive events foundational to the church. To enable his reader to see with clarity the progress and meaning of God's activity in Christ—from Jesus' birth through the universal mission of the new people that confessed his lordship—he would arrange in coherent order the materials gathered by the witnesses and ministers of the word. Such a total view of the career of Jesus had continuing relevance to the life and ministry of the church.

2. THE EVANGELIST'S METHOD

The character of Luke's program inevitably dictates his method.

First: By necessity, his approach is *historical.* In answer to some who questioned the factuality of the momentous events that had created the church, Luke aims faithfully and soberly to set forth what actually took place. Points necessary to establish the historicity of the record had to be fixed so that anyone who desired to check the truth of what he wrote might be able to do so. In Luke-Acts, therefore, chronology is geared to corresponding situations in Roman history. Sites and locations are identified by proper technical designations. In accordance with the standards of the better historians of the day, events are narrated in language appropriate to the time and the people involved. Local color is faithful to prevailing customs. As a historian Luke demonstrates the correctness of his knowledge and the credibility of his account.[2]

Yet Luke has no intention to plow over old ground. There were other accounts, at least of Jesus' life, which aimed at a standard no less high than his own. Nor has he the desire to function simply as a chronicler of sacred history. Because Luke's aim is that Theophilus be instructed by what is presented, his work exhibits a deliberate principle of selectivity and a careful structuring of the material.

Although others might have found such a task impossible or difficult even to conceive, for Luke the situation was by no means hopeless. It was his good fortune to possess certain natural advantages for his undertaking. He had the benefit of a considerable lapse of time through which to view events. To write contemporary history is an extremely precarious task. Only time can furnish the necessary perspective which enables a historian to distinguish what is relatively important. Luke has gained this perspective. Pentecost having taken place, the church having been established, the mission being in process, he is able to view Jesus' words and actions from an advanced position. Later events served to illumine the words and deeds of Jesus, even as these continued to define the meaning of the subsequent events.

Luke had access to excellent sources. Not only did he have intimate connections with apostolic personages and with authoritative accounts, written and oral, but he had time and opportunity in his travels to collect concrete data which were of inestimable help to him. Possessing the instincts of a good historian, he brought to this task the sensitivity, the critical faculties, and the general awareness necessary to accomplish his purpose.

Second: Another characteristic of Luke's methodology is that it is *schematic.* As a historian he is concerned about fitting events into a coherent and logical framework. He is, however, not content to deal with these events simply as secular history, but to understand them as the history of salvation. They are the events by which God's purpose in the affairs of men can be perceived. As divinely ordered, they constitue a sacred pageant, of which God himself is director and producer. Because it is genuine drama, the divine plot can only be understood when the distinct scenes of the pageant have been presented one by one. Luke's task is to treat sacred history in terms of its component parts so that the essential characteristics of each age can be recognized. This necessitates setting forth the links connecting the ages one to the other to make the whole presentation intelligible.

It should not be assumed that Luke's decision to schematize sacred history represented something novel. The Jews long before had realized that their covenant promises demanded some such approach. Although many of God's promises had been strikingly fulfilled throughout Israel's history, each one in retrospect appeared to be a pledge of a yet further and more significant fulfillment. Increasingly this future realization was seen to involve a radical break with the past, one that would revolutionize Israel's relationship to God and to history. As a result sacred history was viewed in two parts. The Jew now participated in the first age. Begun with creation, it would be brought to its conclusion by God's judgment over the whole world. The patriarchs, the monarchs, and the prophets had long since passed from the scene; and Israel believed that this first era was rapidly drawing to a close. Their own duty at the present moment consisted in total obedience to the law of Moses inherited from the past.

The second part of sacred history according to Jewish thought consisted of the "age to come." It was confidence in the certainty of this future age which sustained the people in Israel's most difficult days. Whether through a series of cataclysmic events originating in heaven or through a political reinstitution of the throne of David on earth, the fortunes of God's people would be restored. Frequently prophecies about the new age included the appearance of God's anointed representative, the Messiah. He would deliver Israel from oppression, rule the nations with justice, and effect the rule of God over every heart.

At first the disciples of Jesus shared this Jewish interpretation of the "times of God." But those who retained it uncritically after Jesus' resurrection were quickly beset by serious difficulties. Since the Messiah had now appeared, the golden age must immediately come. The disciples reflected this confusion when they asked the risen Jesus, "Will you at this time restore the kingdom to Israel?" (Acts 1:6). Events demonstrated that the two-age scheme was insufficient and vastly oversimplified. God's saving activity in history had a dimension yet unrecognized. It was Luke who perceived that inherent to the gospel is a uniquely Christian schematization of sacred events. He realized that the central point for such a schematization must be Jesus Christ, whose appearance reveals the purpose of all God's acts and provides the key to the "times of God." Because Jesus is the central figure of sacred history, all that took place in the past must find its significance as an anticipation of him, while all things subsequent to his appearance must derive from and depend upon him.

Luke views sacred history in terms of three ages. The *first epoch* is the period of Israel. It begins with the events recorded in the sacred law and ends with the ministry of John the Baptist. In it God anticipates his decisive saving work in Jesus and prepares for its enactment. The *second epoch,* or the midpoint, of God's time, is the historical career of Jesus, beginning with his baptism and concluding with the ascension. In him is manifest the coming salvation. Jesus alone epitomizes this period and represents its true character. The *third epoch* is that of the church and its witness to the world. It begins with Jesus' ascension and will end when the divine mission is fulfilled.

The special mark of this last period is the activity of the Holy Spirit. Luke's particular insight is that the duration of this age of the Spirit is not necessarily brief. It is, in fact, divided into two rather specific segments, each with its own definable characteristics. The first part of the final age is the time of the apostles and the founding of the church, comprised of the initial events recorded in Acts. Luke considers most of these incidents to be unique and unrepeatable, rather than typical or normative. He never suggests that they should be imitated or reproduced by other churches. They are signs confirming the presence of the church in history, even as Jesus' miracles confirmed that the day of salvation had come. The ministry accomplished in this period is a ministry of the apostles.

To the second part of the church age belongs the later extension and development of the Christian mission. Informed both by the teachings of Jesus and by the activities of the apostles and earliest believers, this period possesses an inner integrity and character of its own. While Luke does not delineate its character in any detail, Paul's address to the Ephesian elders (Acts 20:18–35) best represents the kind of life and activity he believes should characterize the church for the remainder of this last age.

Third: In addition to being historical and schematic, Luke's method is *literary.* He does not write an informal personal letter to his friend Theophilus, but a deliberate literary composition. Because of its length, his work is properly divided into two equal parts in order to facilitate its publication on rolls of papyrus. The address to Theophilus is a normal procedure in such an instance, and it is very little different from the formal dedication page of a modern book. In the ancient world such a dedication might indicate that the person named was the sponsor of the publication.

Since Luke intended his work for general circulation, he followed the prevailing rules for such a production. One of these had to do with the form of the preface. In the first roll the preface was meant to introduce the work *as a whole.* It generally set forth the circumstances under which the composition had been undertaken and the purpose it hoped to accomplish. Because the preface on the second roll had a different function, it was cast in a somewhat different form. Customarily, after offering a summary of what had gone before it would introduce the materials to be covered in the next part of the work. The reasons for this procedure were strictly utilitarian. Prefaces identified the correct order in which the rolls should be read. If rolls became separated (as they frequently did), the prefaces immediately located for the reader the portion of the composition he possessed.

Luke's intention to produce a literary work is also evident from the language and style of his composition, which conforms to the written, rather than to the spoken, language of the day. It is instructive to compare Luke's language, style, and vocabulary with that of Mark. The earliest Gospel presents a simple non-literary form of communication. The material is narrated directly and vividly with many of the normal crudities of vernacular speech and writing. In Luke the opposite is true. Although he depends on Mark's Gospel for much of his material and follows the Marcan outline quite closely, he studiously avoids Mark's overworked vernacular present and imperfect tenses, certain words or phrases that have become clichés by too frequent use, and some of the more obvious redundancies. He frequently improves the transitions between events or changes the order of presentation within a narrative so that the account runs more smoothly. In all of this, his aim is to conform to the accepted literary standards of his own day, especially to those of his particular audience. Luke reveals himself to be a man of culture who is completely at home in the Hellenistic world, the "nearest to a Greek man of letters that the early church provides."[3]

Fourth: Luke also employs a *biblical* methodology. He can be identified as one of the church's earliest biblical theologians. Not content merely to identify fulfillment passages, he seeks to add to the total understanding of biblical revelation by focusing special attention on incidents and situations which allow him to bring together the Old Testament Scriptures and the facts of Jesus' life and ministry. From the gospel tradition he selects incidents that unveil the meaning of sacred history and revelation. When he treats Jesus' ministry, he focuses on the sermon at Nazareth (Luke 4:16–21), because it is here, in an exposition of a passage from Isaiah 61, that he finds the decisive clue to Jesus' life. His concern at this point is not merely to assert that Jesus is the Messiah but to show from the prophetic writings the kind of messiah he was destined to be. In his passion narrative Luke, more than any other Gospel writer, seeks to connect the event with the accomplishment of all that was told by Moses and the prophets (cf. Luke 24:25–27, 44–47).

In Acts, where Luke is breaking new ground, and hence has greater freedom in his presentation, his biblical methodology becomes even more pronounced. The explanation of the events on the day of Pentecost involves a significant use of the second chapter of Joel. Peter's early preaching includes important expositions of Psalms 2, 16, and 110. Stephen's address involves an interpretation of the whole redemptive history of the Old Testament. James in Acts 15 makes a significant application of Amos 9 to the life of the church. In Luke's presentation of each of these incidents we see at work the instincts of a genuine biblical theologian. Whenever he finds in the tradition an important instance of Old Testament exegesis influencing early Christian life and thought, he preserves and develops it so that the reader will be instructed in biblical truth.

Fifth: Finally, Luke's method is *pastoral.* However deep his commitment as a historian and biblical theologian, his abiding concern is to apply Jesus' saving ministry to the lives of individuals. Consistently the narrative emphasizes man's sin, his need for repentance, and the availability of divine forgiveness. The individual's encounter with salvation especially fascinates the evangelist. Luke alone records the incidents involving the sinful woman (Luke 7), the tax collector Zacchaeus (ch. 19), and the penitent thief (ch. 23), and the parables of the lost sheep, the lost coin, and the lost son (ch. 15).

Luke's interest ranges beyond the initial experience of salvation. He gives equally serious attention to the practice of Christianity. His Gospel encompasses materials with strong ethical overtones, designed to instruct the believer regarding his duties in the world. Examples of this are found in the story of the good Samaritan (ch. 10), the parable of the foolish rich man (ch. 12), and the account of the rich man and Lazarus (ch. 16). In the Book of Acts, Luke's pastoral bent expresses itself in the care with which he describes the corporate life of the believers, the place of the Spirit in the church's life, and the nature and necessity of mission.

3. THE EPOCH OF ISRAEL

A. THE BIRTH OF JOHN (LUKE 1:5–80)

Luke begins his Gospel by transporting the reader back into the milieu of the Old Testament. The people involved are those whose lives are blameless before the law of God. The sacred place of revelation is the temple. Those who reveal God's will are the holy angels (Luke 1:9–10). The requirement for blessing is faith toward God and obedience to his will. Visions, prophetic utterances, sacrifices, prayer, and fasting complete the picture (ch. 1).

The event central to the narrative is the birth of John the Baptist, but what is recounted is of more than historical importance. We are confronted here with a historical situation in which there is an idealization of the whole of Israel's life, belief, and expectation. John's parents, Elizabeth and Zechariah, enjoy the favor of God almost in the manner of Old Testament patriarchs. In the blessings which they receive we recognize an expression of God's faithfulness to the remnant in Israel who remain true to his ancient covenant. The joy with which they greet the announcement of the coming salvation, the forgiveness of sins, and the appearing of a Savior represents the ideal response to the messianic age from any true Israelite.

The question must be raised: Why all of this pageantry centered on the birth of John? Why should he be singled out for honor above all others?

Luke answers that John's importance was not a consequence of his personal achievement or exceptional piety. Rather it depended on the fact that his destiny was to stand at the convergence of two ages, the end of the Old Covenant and the appearance of the New. God's counsel was that the New Covenant would be introduced through the witness of the Old. Thus it was fitting that God should raise up a final prophet to herald the new age.

But John was to be far more than a prophet. He would embody in his preaching the total witness of the past and bring it to fruition. The call for repentance (3:1–14) that echoed through Judea was the voice of God summoning men back to his covenant. The command to "Prepare the way of the Lord" was the word of Moses and all the prophets.

Although John appeared in the wilderness, Luke is careful to show that this was not the place of his origin. Like Samuel of old, the womb from which he came was the temple, and in his veins flowed the blood of all those faithful priests who had ministered there in God's presence. If his birth is miraculous, it is not to place him at a distance from the events of the past. Rather it binds him to them. As God gave initial witness to his covenant with Abraham through Isaac's miraculous birth, he now gives witness to the fulfillment of that covenant by the birth of John.

These considerations indicate how Luke fixes the Baptist's place in the divine scheme of things. Precisely because John speaks the final word of revelation under the Old Covenant, he always stands at a distance from Jesus and the gospel. This is the enigma of John. While Jesus says of him that "none greater is born of woman" he also adds that "the least in the Kingdom of God is greater than he"* (7:28).

John and his preaching therefore belong to the past. His message of repentance has no validity for the new age unless it is joined to the gospel proclamation. His baptism has no efficacy unless it is completed by the coming of the Spirit. But when repentance is followed by gospel and baptism by the gift of the Spirit, God's covenant is fulfilled and the true ministry of John maintained. In this fashion Luke preserves for the Baptizer a unique place in the history of salvation. At the same time he cautions any in his own day who might want to identify John as an eschatological figure of the new age that this last of the prophets belongs essentially to the epoch of Israel.

B. THE BIRTH OF JESUS (2:1–40)

The second part of Luke's introduction records the birth of Jesus. Since John's ministry preceded that of Jesus, it was proper that his birth be given first. This order also provided Luke an opportunity to contrast the two men and to demonstrate Jesus' superiority. Whereas John's birth occurred in terms of biblical patterns provided by the past, Jesus' birth was unique. In John's case a miracle had been required so that Elizabeth could conceive, but the conception itself was wholly within the laws of human procreation. Zechariah actually was the father of John the Baptist, and Elizabeth was his mother. With Jesus the miracle is of an entirely different order. Mary alone is responsible for his human parentage. Jesus has no human father. It is the Spirit of God who provides for the conception. The angel Gabriel declares to Mary that he who is so born is shown by this very sign to be holy, the Son of God (1:35).

For Luke the importance of this tradition was that it demonstrated that Jesus was Son of God from the moment of his birth. Consequently, Luke never raises the question of Jesus' "messianic consciousness." The form of the birth narrative renders all such speculation irrelevant. Jesus is born according to the creative activity of God; his sonship, saviorhood, and lordship are determined from this moment. Luke does not mean to deny that Jesus' development was according to human standards and characteristics. He is in fact very careful to assert the opposite. But he insists that the difference between Jesus and John is an essential one which can be traced to their origin.

C. THE "TEMPLE MOTIF"

Luke includes from the tradition an account of an early visit to the temple by Jesus (2:41–52). Although others may have attributed to this boyhood incident only minor importance, passing over it in silence, Luke gives it a central place in his presentation. He makes the episode programmatic for a "temple motif" that he develops throughout his two-volume work in order to set forth the differences between the epochs of God. By its presence and function the Jerusalem temple indicates the direction of God's redemptive purpose.

I. THE TEMPLE AND ISRAEL

It is the temple which furnishes the backdrop against which the birth narratives are presented. Elizabeth and Zechariah are introduced as descendants of priestly lineage who in their devoutness are representatives of the true temple heritage (1:5, 6). Zechariah, while engaged in the faithful performance of his priestly duties *in the temple,* receives a visitation from the angel of God (1:8–20). After Jesus' circumcision, Mary and Joseph present him *in the temple* and offer the appropriate sacrifices according to the laws of purification (2:22–24). Simeon, inspired by the Spirit, prophesies over Jesus *in the temple* and blesses him (2:25–35). Anna, *in the temple,* proves her faithfulness to God with fasting and prayer night and day (2:36–38).

With each of these references, Luke suggests the role of the temple under the Old Covenant. Within its confines true piety is nurtured; the Spirit of God moves in freedom and accomplishes wonderful deeds. From its environs comes forth God's prophetic utterance. Luke shows in this manner how the temple serves as a connecting link between the old and the new, so fulfilling its ministry in relation to Jesus.

II. THE TEMPLE AND THE DAY OF SALVATION

Thirty years later, when Jesus assumed his ministry, the role of the temple had completely changed. Throughout this period the control of the temple rested in the hands of lawless men. The usurpers who controlled the holy place were noted for their resistance to God's Spirit. They not only refused the baptism of John, but they were the bitter opponents of Jesus. Under these circumstances the temple was unable to make any contribution to Jesus' ministry. It was for him a place neither of prayer nor of strength, but loomed as an object for his ministry.

Jesus' journey to Jerusalem had for its purpose his own passion as well as the liberation of the temple. His first act in the city was to take possession of this holy place and cleanse it of its defilement (19:45–48). Henceforth it became his abode for proclaiming the gospel to the multitudes (20:1–8). Although every night he withdrew to the Mount of Olives, every morning he returned to resume his teaching ministry in the temple and maintain his authority over it (21:37–38). By these acts he restored it to its divine service and prepared it for its final functions. When the moment of Jesus' passion arrived, the temple participated symbolically in the mystery of his death as its inner veil was torn in two (23:44–46).

III. THE TEMPLE AND THE CHURCH

Although the temple plays no part in the resurrection appearances of the Lord, it appears to be the place where the disciples gathered on the day of Pentecost (Acts 2:1). They may have understood that Jesus' requirement for them to remain in Jerusalem until they received the Holy Spirit involved their attendance at God's sanctuary (Luke 24:49, 53). Luke seems to regard the temple environs as the place where the Spirit of God descended as tongues of fire and rested on each of the disciples. Immediately the temple became the scene of divine activity. Jesus' ministry in the temple had included no miracles or signs, but now the disciples began to manifest unique powers. They accomplished unusual healings, proclaimed the gospel with boldness, and answered their enemies in the wisdom of the Spirit. All the people gathered at the temple to hear them, and no one was able to resist them. Luke shows that it was the disciples who now "occupied" the sacred precincts (cf. Luke 24:53; Acts 2:46–47); though they did not control it physically, they nonetheless acted as its true priests. Daily they went to the temple for prayer, to offer up sacrifices of praise and blessing, and to preach the word of God. When the high priest arrested them, an angel of the Lord opened their prison doors and commanded, "Go and stand in the temple and speak to the people all the words of this Life" (Acts 5:20).

IV. THE TEMPLE AND THE MISSION

By the time of the church's universal mission the role of the temple had again changed. Although the Jerusalem Christians continued to make the sanctuary their special abode, it no longer had any special function to discharge. Wherever believers gathered, the Spirit of God was present— whether in Jerusalem, Antioch, or Ephesus. The concern of the mission, and hence of the Holy Spirit, was the whole world.

The mission to Israel also continued, nurtured in a peculiar way by the presence of the temple. Yet the destruction of the temple A.D. 70, so catastrophic to Israel, had little effect on the church. Although Jewish Christians must certainly have grieved over its demise, the rest of the church found in this event only a new incentive to complete the Gentile mission (cf. *Barnabas* 16:1–10). In the destruction of the temple the final "sign" for its accomplishment had been given.

V. THE TEMPLE AND JESUS' BOYHOOD VISIT

With the temple motif in mind, it is now possible to understand why

Luke was willing to interrupt the "silent years" of Jesus' life with one incident from his youth which demonstrated Jesus' relationship to the temple long before he began his public ministry. In Luke 2:41–52 two aspects of the temple motif are developed.

First: Luke shows that Jesus' relationship to the temple exceeded that of any typical Jew whose concern was faithfulness to the law. Jesus had been presented to God by his parents in the temple according to the biblical commandment (Luke 2:22 ff.; Exod. 13:2, 12; Lev. 12:2–8). Now, as an expression of his maturity under the law, he and his parents made their pilgrimage to the temple to keep the Passover (2:41–42). Luke's specific reference to Jesus' twelfth year suggests that the boy went to Jerusalem at this time to take the customary vows of obedience to the law in the temple, rather than in his local synagogue. In any case, Luke indicates that Jesus remained in the temple by his own choice. His presence in the temple, even at this early time, was not the expression of a youthful whim or of parental piety but of a special relationship to God. The temple was the house of his Father. Toward it he felt distinctly personal obligations and responsibilities. This is what Jesus was saying to his parents and what they found difficult to understand (2:48–51).

Second: Jesus' questions and answers revealed unusual understanding and caused amazement on the part of the teachers (2:46–47). Luke sees in this a prophetic foreshadowing of another and very different confrontation with the temple authorities near the end of Jesus' life. Although the boy Jesus is not yet ready to assume the seat of instruction from the priests and elders, or to claim, as God's Son, ascendency over the temple, in this early encounter is the promise of what must come.

4. THE EPOCH OF JESUS, OR THE DAY OF SALVATION

A. THE MINISTRY IN GALILEE (LUKE 3:21–9:27)

Luke divides Jesus' ministry into three periods, each of which he describes in terms of (1) a geographical location, (2) a heavenly revelation, (3) a disclosure of messiahship, (4) a special type of mission, and (5) a symbolic meaning. In the first period the locale is primarily Galilee. The heavenly revelation takes place at Jesus' baptism. The messianic disclosure is that Jesus is the Son of God ("Thou art my beloved Son, with thee I am well pleased," 3:22). The mission calls for Jesus to reveal by word and deed the day of salvation and to gather his witnesses. The symbolic meaning suggested is that since Jesus' own ministry was conducted among the outcasts of the Jews (that is, in Galilee rather than in Jerusalem), he anticipated the church's own mission to the Gentiles and provided it chief sanction.

The key episode in this first section is Jesus' visit to his home city Nazareth (4:16 ff.). This incident is of central importance to Luke be cause it serves to introduce Jesus' whole ministry. While ministering in the synagogues of Galilee (4:15), Jesus appeared on the Sabbath day in Nazareth, at his own synagogue. Assuming the place of the public reader of the Scripture, he stood up and unrolled the scroll of the prophets to Isaiah 61:1–2, reading:

> The Spirit of the Lord is upon me,
> because he has anointed me to preach good news to the poor.
> He has sent me to proclaim release to the captives
> and recovering of sight to the blind,
> to set at liberty those who are oppressed,
> to proclaim the acceptable year of the Lord.

Closing the book, he announced before them all, "Today this scripture has been fulfilled in your hearing" (Luke 4:18–21). When the people reacted in unbelief, Jesus left the village. Through this episode Luke introduces three major themes developed throughout Luke-Acts: (1) the presence of the Holy Spirit; (2) the fulfillment of Scripture; and (3) the rejection of the appointed messenger.

Jesus says, "The Spirit of the Lord is upon me" (4:18). Luke's own orientation as a teacher and evangelist is to a church in which the presence of the Spirit in the world is recognized. If the Spirit had not come and created a new people of God, there could be neither church nor mission. Luke knows that only as the Spirit continues to work will the church prosper and the mission endure. For this reason his entire narrative em phasizes the importance of the Spirit's presence and seeks to exhibit the nature and extent of the Spirit's activity in each of the epochs of God's time. Luke's ultimate intention is to instruct and encourage his readers concerning the relationship they may expect to sustain to the Spirit in their own time and place. The underlying assumption of Luke's presentation is that wherever and whenever God acts redemptively on behalf of his people, it is the Spirit through whom he effects his purposes.

Jesus is the man of the Spirit par excellence. Not only was he born of the Spirit (1:35), but at his baptism the Spirit descended in bodily form upon him (3:22). From that moment he effected his ministry by the Spirit's power. More than any other evangelist, Luke preserves from he tradition references to the Spirit's activity in Jesus' life. A fact noted only by Luke is that at the time of his baptism Jesus had been praying (3:21–27); in that context the Spirit had come upon him. Only when Jesus had been filled by the Spirit was he led into the wilderness for his trial by Satan (4:1). After his victory over Satan he had returned "in the power of the Spirit" to undertake his ministry (4:14). Subsequently, when the multitudes came to him sick and diseased, the "power of the Lord was with him to heal" (5:17).

One has only to read the early chapters of Acts to see to what extent Luke saw in Jesus' experience a pattern for the early church. Before Pentecost the disciples also devoted themselves to prayer (Acts 1:14). They too, after being filled by the Spirit (2:4), were put to the test (4:1–18). Having successfully withstood trial, they experienced a further outpouring of the Spirit (4:31). Thereafter, the power of God was with them to proclaim (4:33) and to heal (5:12–16).

Thus it becomes clear why Luke has selected the visit to Nazareth to introduce Jesus' ministry. The words Jesus quotes from Isaiah serve to epitomize his whole ministry. They confirm that what characterizes the Messiah is the presence of the Holy Spirit, who is once more dynamically at work in the world. They show as a consequence of the Spirit's anointing that good news is proclaimed, the sick are healed, and the blind see. Isaiah's words also serve to instruct the church concerning its own mission, a fact demonstrated at greater length in Luke's treatment of the church.

The second theme, fulfillment of the Scriptures, is introduced by Jesus words, "Today has this scripture been fulfilled in your hearing" (Luke 4:21). Although Luke consistently teaches that the Kingdom of God is an event of the future (cf. 21:31; 19:11; Acts 1:6), he is certain that through Jesus salvation is present and effectual in the lives of men. Luke cites Jesus' statement, "If it is by the finger of God that I cast out demons, then the kingdom of God has come upon you" (Luke 11:20). This does not mean that the Kingdom is present spiritually, or mystically, but that in Jesus the saving effects of the Kingdom are already operative. Wherever Jesus is, Satan is bound (10:18). Although ultimate redemption—the Kingdom of God—remains future, the individual has opportunity even "today" to hear Jesus' Kingdom proclamation and be saved.

The third theme introduced in the Nazareth episode is the note of rejection. When Jesus brings the good news to his own village and people, they attempt to destroy him. Nazareth becomes for Luke a symbol of the Jewish rejection of the gospel. One of the real problems that faced the church was the hostility of Judaism. Luke's narrative indicates that the Jewish rejection of the gospel had been expressed already in Jesus' lifetime. Nevertheless, while Jesus is rejected at Nazareth, he is accepted in Capernaum. If he is rejected in Jerusalem, he is accepted in Galilee. Though he is rejected by the Jew, he is destined to be accepted by the Gentile.

B. THE JOURNEY (LUKE 9:28–19:27)

The scene of the second period of Jesus' ministry is a journey to Jerusalem (cf. Luke 9:51; 10:38; 13:22, 33; 17:11; 18:31; 19:11). It is not Luke's intent to furnish an itinerary of Jesus' travels in this period but simply to suggest the background against which the incidents must be understood. Jerusalem is the place of Jesus' suffering and death. The journey to Jerusalem therefore furnishes the prelude to the passion. It also reveals Jesus now acting and teaching out of the context of "his departure, which he was to accomplish at Jerusalem" (9:31). The point of the journey is not that Jesus now travels in a different area but that he "travels in a different manner."[4] He travels in order that he might fulfill his destiny by dying at Jerusalem.

This section, like the previous one, is introduced by a heavenly revelation, a voice from heaven addressed to the disciples: "This is my Son, my Chosen; listen to him!" (9:35). Now that they have confessed Jesus as Messiah (9:18–20), they are to learn from him what messiahship entails. Although he has already told them of his passion (9:21 f.), they do not yet understand (9:44; 13:32 f.; 18:31). Only after the resurrection do they comprehend what he was saying to them and why he had said it. Within the framework of the journey, however, Jesus proceeds to give them detailed instruction. It is this activity with his disciples that constitutes Jesus' special mission during this perod.

The symbolc significance of this section is related to Jesus' teaching on discipleship. He not only exhorts the disciples to follow him (9:23 f.), but he shows to them the "way" they must go. Having himself received the commandment to go to Jerusalem and suffer, Jesus steadfastly sets himself to this task (9:51, 53; 12:50; 13:32 f.). In that he allows nothing to deter him, he manifests what true discipleship means.

Jesus' transfiguration is the key episode for Luke within the section. It not only serves to introduce the journey and to provide the occasion for new Christological disclosures, but it also anticipates the final trial and victory. Luke alone notes that on this momentous occasion the disciples were burdened with sleep—even as they were later at Gethsemane (9:32;

22:45). They had no real understanding of the incident (9:33), even as at first they were unable to understand Jesus' resurrection (24:25). Only afterward did they perceive that in the transfiguration they had seen his glory (9:32), the glory into which he entered at his ascension (24:26).

c. The Jerusalem Ministry (Luke 19:28–24:53)

The third part of Jesus' ministry, which is located in Jerusalem, opens with the triumphal entry and conclues with the ascension. Here, too, Luke's treatment of the traditional materials conforms to his fivefold pattern. Jesus' special mission in Jerusalem is to conduct a teaching ministry within the temple precincts (cf. 19:47; 20:1; 21:1; 21:37). There is a certain "rhythm" to Jesus' activity during the last week of his life: by day he teaches in the temple; by night he prays on the Mount of Olives. Into this rhythm Luke fits the account of Gethsemane (22:39–53). Gethsemane is on the Mount of Olives, and Jesus is there, "as was his custom" (22:39). Luke knows that Jesus' great final mission is to be his own death and resurrection. In preparation for this climax and in the midst of his time of anguish and testing, Jesus receives a final heavenly visitation when an angel of God comes to strengthen him (22:43).[5]

In this final section Jesus also makes a full disclosure of his authority. He publicly acknowledges that the Son of man is Son of God (22:70) and King of the Jews (23:3), who will exercise that power which is at the right hand of God (22:69). In the resurrection narrative, Luke makes it clear that Jesus' "sonship" has as its ultimate frame of reference his deity. The final confession of the disciples is "*The Lord* has risen indeed" (24:34).

Symbolically, attention is focused on Jesus' trial before the Roman authorities. Three times Jesus is officially pronounced innocent of any wrongdoing (23:4, 14, 22). Three different Roman officials join in this verdict (23:4, 15, 47). The final Roman judgment, however, is expressed in the words of the centurion who witnessed Jesus' death: "Certainly this man was innocent!" (23:47). Though innocent, Jesus is crucified, but before he dies he prays for his enemies, "Father, forgive them; for they know not what they do" (23:34).[6]

It seems fairly clear that Luke sees in Jesus' suffering, in spite of his innocence, an anticipation of the church's experience. The disciples, no less than their Master, will undergo trials of their faith. Paul will be examined before three different officials of the Roman Empire, each of whom will pronounce him innocent of any wrongdoing (Acts 23:29;

25:25; 26:31). Nevertheless, persecution will take place which the church must be willing to bear with patience (cf. 14:22). Like Jesus, it must learn to forgive its enemies and pray that its persecutors be not condemned for what they have wrongfully, but ignorantly, done.

4. THE TIME OF THE CHURCH AND ITS MISSION

The third epoch of salvation is the concern of Acts. To unfold the meaning of this era Luke employs a method of schematization not unlike that used for the life of Jesus. He follows a geographical and chronological pattern supported by certain thematic emphases. In this way he exhibits both the internal and the external development of the church. The plan of the whole book is set forth in Acts 1:8, where Jesus tells the disciples "you shall be my witnesses in Jerusalem and in all Judea and Samaria and to the end of the earth." This movement from "Jerusalem" to "the end of the earth" is described by means of six "panels," or vignettes, each of which treats one phase of the church's extension and covers approximately five years. The panels are easily identified: each one is limited to a specific geographical area, and each concludes with a single summary statement describing the success attained in the locality under discussion.

PANEL I: THE ASCENSION, THE SPIRIT, AND THE WITNESSES

The first panel (1:4–6:6) depicts the mission in Jerusalem, from Jesus' ascension and the outpouring of the Spirit to a summation in Acts 6:7. "And the word of God increased; and the number of the disciples multiplied greatly in Jerusalem, and a great many of the priests were obedient to the faith."

A. THE ASCENSION

After the programmatic statement in Acts 1:8, Luke begins with an account of Jesus' ascension (1:9–11). While this event has been described already at the end of the Gospel (Luke 24:50–51), the important relationship it sustains to two different epochs motivates its repetition. As the ultimate witness to Jesus' divine sonship and the climax to the resurrection appearances, it belongs to the time of Jesus. As the event which occasions the sending forth of the Spirit and the creation of the church (Acts 2:33), it initiates a whole new episode in salvation history, and belongs to the final stage of God's redemptive program.

The ascension typifies the relationship of God to the church. It depends solely upon God the Father, who overcame the sentence of death inflicted upon Jesus and elevated the rejected Messiah to his own right hand (cf. 2:32 f.; 5:31). This event had vindicated Jesus before the world and revealed that by him, the Prince of life, men could receive God's gift of salvation (3:14–16). The exalted Lord sent the Spirit from heaven to call into existence the Christian church. The church is not the creation of the Twelve, or a natural consequence of their belief in the resurrection of Jesus. The church comes into existence solely by the will and act of God.

From the very beginning the church's destiny is in the hands of its sovereign Lord.[7] It prospers and multiplies not by human effort but by the grace of God, who "added to their number day by day those who were being saved" (2:47).

B. THE SPIRIT

Significant space in this first panel is devoted to the advent of the Holy Spirit. The narrative of Pentecost explains the changes effected by the Spirit both in the external sphere of God's redemptive plan and in the inward life of the disciples. Luke's premise is that possession of the Spirit by the believer is the chief consequence of God's saving act.

In regard to the external order of salvation, Luke develops the following points:

First: The Spirit is an eschatological gift and sign. His presence in the world is a direct fulfillment of God's promise to his people and culminates God's redemptive activity (2:39; 3:19 f.). All who receive the Spirit participate in the "last times" of God. This does not mean that the time prior to the end is short, but rather that the plan of God is complete as far as its redemptive phase is concerned. The emphasis is no longer on waiting or hoping, as in the past, but on receiving the fulfillment of the divine promise. The age of salvation is not future but "today."

Second: Pentecost demonstrates that the Spirit is for *all* who believe the gospel; the promise is directed "to you and to your children and to all that are far off, every one whom the Lord our God calls to him" (2:39). The devout Jews "from every nation under heaven" gathered in Jerusalem (2:5) ultimately represent the whole world. As the mission proceeds to Samaria and to the Gentiles, everyone who responds to the gospel with faith receives the Spirit without distinction (8:17; 10:43 f.).

Third: Except in unusual circumstances, the normal order for reception of the Spirit is repentance, belief, and baptism (2:37 f.). When this order appeared to be violated, as in the case of the Samaritans, it attracted apostolic attention (8:14–17). In the case of the Gentile Cornelius, the reception of the Spirit came first, followed almost at once by baptism at the command of Peter (10:44–48). Throughout the remainder of Acts it is assumed that bestowal of the Spirit is the natural consequence of belief and baptism in Jesus' name (e.g., 19:5 f.).

Fourth: The Holy Spirit comes to the *church:* only as a member of the believing community does the individual partake of the Spirit. Not even the first disciples received the divine gift as isolated individuals. The Twelve received the Spirit in common with *all* believers gathered in Jerusalem (2:1–4; cf. 4:23–31). This communal aspect of the Spirit's ministry means that deceit against the church is a lie against the Holy Spirit himself (5:3 f.). By the same token the actions of the church, whether in counsel or witnessing, can be regarded as actions of the Holy Spirit (13:2; 15:28). Yet the Spirit of God always acts in sovereign freedom. The church can only submit to God in worship and obedience.

As significant as the change wrought in the external order of salvation is the effect which the descent of the Spirit had upon the disciples. Even their enemies noted the difference it made in their lives (4:13). Prior to the crucifixion, Jesus' disciples had been totally dependent for direction, instruction, and help upon their personal contact with Jesus. They had gone forth in public ministry at his command. Their works had been accomplished only by his initiative and with his authority. When they failed, they returned to him for counsel. The cross and the resurrection changed all of this. Although for a brief period Jesus had appeared to them, their relationship to him had been irrevocably altered. After the ascension they felt themselves cast adrift without the external aid or real comfort which his presence afforded.

At Pentecost the vacuum that Jesus' absence had created was wonderfully filled by a new descent of God. The first evidence of this change was the confidence they now possessed to proclaim the gospel (4:8). They found themselves able to do signs and wonders beyond what they had accomplished during Jesus' lifetime (2:43). The Spirit brought a renewal in the life of the disciples as a community. Whereas Jesus had found it necessary to rebuke their self-seeking, envying, and jealousy, now they graciously supported one another in the common cause (2:43 f.; 4:32). Daily they realized in a fresh way the reality of a shared life: "great grace was upon them all" (4:33). The inward witness to the Spirit in the group was their unity of heart and soul. The external manifestation was a state of sustained joy.

This latter feature represents one of Luke's cardinal interests. It is his conviction that an experience of God's salvation is evidenced by the presence of divine joy. Salvation for Luke is a cause for celebration; everyone who receives the gospel goes on his way rejoicing (8:39). The gift of God, created through his Spirit, is an abiding and eternal joy that neither persecution nor torment is able to suppress (5:41; 13:52; 16:25).

C. THE WITNESSES

This first period in the history of the church is also the time of the "witnesses." The term refers primarily to those previously chosen by Jesus to be his disciples (1:2, 8), who were with Jesus from the beginning and to whom he appeared after his resurrection (1:21, 22). Their experience of the risen Lord qualified them for their task as apostles and provided the chief content of their testimony. They became the official witnesses to the resurrection of Jesus (3:14–16). The witnesses were authorized to promise forgiveness to those who in faith repented and submitted to baptism in Jesus' name (2:32 f.). Works performed in Jesus' name authenticated their witness (3:6, 16). With increasing boldness the apostles bore witness to the only "name under heaven given among men by which we must be saved" (4:12).

The testimony of these appointed witnesses is variously described by Luke as "the word," "the word of God," "the word of the Lord," or "the word of salvation." Although others do in time become "ministers" of this word and many give testimony concerning it (2:4), the apostles alone are "the witnesses." To them belongs the responsibility to maintain the truth of the word and to validate it in each new situation. This explains why Peter proclaimed the gospel at Pentecost, why the Holy Spirit did not fall in Samaria until John and Peter went there to bestow it upon the new converts, and why Peter's mission to Cornelius had to precede the great Pauline outreach to the Gentiles. Luke's first panel thus introduces the key redemptive events of ascension and Pentecost and the apostolic witnesses who declared the good news in Jerusalem and beyond.

PANEL II: THE NEW MESSENGERS IN JUDEA AND SAMARIA

The second panel begins at Acts 6:8 and extends to a summary verse describing the spread of the word throughout Palestine: "So the church throughout all Judea and Galilee and Samaria had peace and was built up; and walking in the fear of the Lord and in the comfort of the Holy Spirit it was multiplied" (9:31). Luke uses this panel to introduce his readers to the new messengers of the word—Stephen (6:8 f.) and Philip (8:4 ff.). Although Paul is also introduced (9:15 ff.), only his conversion is described.

Neither Stephen nor Philip became qualified for their service by any personal past relationship to Jesus of Nazareth. Nor were they among those to whom the risen Lord had appeared. They are characterized simply as men "full of the Spirit and of wisdom" (6:3). "Wisdom" suggests that they had been instructed in the word of the apostles (cf. 2:42) and were competent to speak of the things pertaining to Jesus. These men, and others like them, led by the Spirit, began to proclaim the word of God. It was ultimately through their activities that the gospel moved beyond the environs of Jerusalem. The role of Stephen, and the persecution which followed his death, was crucial in this advance (6:8–8:2; see above, pp. 134 ff.). It is, of course, not possible for Luke to relate the total story of the expansion of the mission. He limits himself to the activities of Philip as an illustration of the kind of activity being undertaken at this time by those who were not apostles (8:4–40).

Luke's purpose in this panel, beyond setting forth the historical tradition, is to show that the apostles were not the only chosen instruments of God. Very early God had effected his purposes through other men. Although the original followers of Jesus did have a unique function as witnesses, God never limited himself to their ministry. This fact is especially important to Luke for two reasons:

1. It helped his readers to understand how Paul, who was not one of the Twelve, could later assume such a prominent place in the evangelization of the Gentiles. God continued to use the original witnesses, but he also enlisted new messengers who extended the mission beyond Jerusalem, most of whom were not apostles. The calling of the apostle Paul demanded an extension of the resurrection appearances of the Lord (9:3–6; 1 Cor. 9:1; 15:8).

2. The emphasis upon those who were not apostles also strengthened the confidence of Luke's readers that in their own day God would raise up men within the churches to do his will. Even if all who were then leaders should be imprisoned or put to death, the mission would continue. The aspect of the mission that depended on the apostles was complete. Now was the day for the evangelists, teachers, and proclaimers of the word. Against such a company persecution had not prevailed in the past, nor would it prevail in the future.

PANEL III: TO THE GENTILES

The third panel begins with Acts 9:32 and ends with the summary verse, "But the word of God grew and multiplied" (12:24). The purpose of this panel is to tell the circumstances under which the gospel came to the Gentiles in Antioch. While the Christians who "scattered because of the persecution that arose over Stephen" traveled as far as Antioch, they preached only to Jews (11:19). But when some Cypriot and Cyrenian Christians arrived, they addressed themselves also to the Gentiles (11:19–20).

Even prior to this, however, Luke shows that God himself took the initiative in preparing the church for the inclusion of the Gentiles. The crucial step was the conversion of a Roman centurion, a Gentile named Cornelius, effected through the ministry of Peter. An index to the importance of the incident is the fact that Luke tells it twice in detail (chs. 10, 11) and refers to it again in chapter fifteen. It not only dominates this panel but assumes a critical position in the whole of the Acts narrative. As a result of divine revelation, both to Cornelius and to Peter (10:1–16), a pious Gentile heard the gospel, received the Holy Spirit, and was baptized in Jesus' name (10:17–48). The church drew the only conclusion possible: God had granted the Gentiles "repentance unto life" (11:19).

Peter's role, therefore, was the decisive one. Not only had he inaugurated the mission among the Jews, and confirmed it to the Samaritans, but through him the door was opened to the Gentiles. In this fashion God preserved the unity of the mission and protected it against serious divisions that might easily have occurred. By showing that the individual efforts of the two great apostles, Peter and Paul, had not been in opposition but had complemented one another, Luke demonstrates how inexcusable it would be for their followers in his own day to engage in partisanship and strife. Luke also shows from the tradition that despite rumors to the contrary, the church at Jerusalem never opposed the extension of the gospel to the Gentile world. Once they recognized God's leading and work among the Gentiles, the apostles rejoiced with Peter and gave God the glory (11:18). On their own initiative they sent Barnabas and certain of their prophets to assist in the work at Antioch (11:22, 27). While some Jewish Christians resisted the inclusion of the Gentiles without circumcision (15:1, 5), the mainstream of the Jerusalem congregation did not support their point of view (15:23–29).

PANEL IV: A NEW BEGINNING IN ASIA

Acts 12:25 introduces the fourth panel, which concludes with the summary: "So the churches were strengthened in the faith, and they increased in numbers daily" (16:5). Whereas the first three panels were dominated largely by the imposing figure of Peter and provide the basis of the world mission, the last three panels shift attention to the Apostle Paul and depict the continuing progress of the mission. The fourth panel features the narrative of how the gospel went into Asia. Acts 13:2–3 reminds the reader that it was the hand of God that initiated and directed the new phase of the mission. Chapters 13 and 14 give samples of Paul's preaching and also something of his labors, while chapter 15 tells the story of the Jerusalem council.

What stands out in this panel is a remarkable similarity between Paul's activities among the Gentiles and those of Peter in Jerusalem. Paul's mission began with an impulse from the Holy Spirit (13:2; cf. 2:4). What follows is an extensive sermon (13:16 ff.; cf. 2:14 ff.), the healing of a lame man in the vicinity of a pagan temple (14:8 ff.; cf. 3:1 ff.), and a persecution in which Paul is stoned and dragged out of the city (14:19 f.; cf. 5:17 ff.). The parallelism with Peter's experiences appears to be more than coincidental. What is its meaning?

It is possible that here we are confronted with God's providential control over the Christian mission. How could God better assure his new messengers, or demonstrate more effectively his own concern for the Gentiles, than by confirming their ministry with signs similar to those granted to the apostles at Jerusalem? It is also possible that when Paul and Barnabas reported to Antioch, and later to the church at Jerusalem, they deliberately singled out those events in their missionary activity which paralleled the experiences of the Jerusalem church. It is equally conceivable that Luke himself selected materials from the tradition so as to emphasize certain similarities and demonstrate that God was concerned for the Gentiles no less than for the Jews. Certainly he had enabled Paul to do great and wonderful things among the Gentiles. A comparison of these events with those which marked the beginnings of the gospel at Jerusalem would assure Gentile Christians of God's commitment to the world mission.

The fourth panel reaches its climax in chapter 15 with a record of the Jerusalem council which resolved the circumcision question and preserved Gentile freedom. The letter of instruction sent to the churches of Syria and Cilicia (15:23–29) is essentially a warning against "lawlessness." Though Gentiles are not to be troubled by the Mosaic requirements that govern the life of Jews, they are nonetheless expected to obey the commandments which the Jewish world held to be binding upon all men. Anything less would be an offense, not merely to Jewish legalists but to the Creator himself.

PANEL V: A NEW BEGINNING IN EUROPE

The fifth panel, treating the extension of the gospel to Europe, begins with Acts 16:6 and ends with the summary, "So the word of the Lord grew and prevailed mightily" (19:20). Again the Holy Spirit determines the area the gospel is to penetrate, and a vision from God confirms it. Among the cities evangelized are Philippi, Thessalonica, Corinth, and Ephesus, familiar to us because of Paul's letters. Part of the importance of this panel lies in valuable background information for study of the Pauline epistles. The same material, however, is interesting from another point of view. Beginning with Acts 16:10, the use of the pronoun "we" suggests that the author is drawing on his own travel notes,[8] while the use of many more proper names suggests that the churches involved are familiar to him.

There are two especially prominent features of this European ministry.

1. The large number of converts required a different strategy: the missionaries found it necessary to spend much more time in a given locality in order to instruct the believers. Paul accordingly lived more than eighteen months at Corinth and some two years at Ephesus.

2. This was perhaps the time of the most remarkable signs confirming Paul's ministry. Throughout the European stay unusual direction was given to the mission by God and striking evidences of divine power were given in Paul's own life. Again there is a noteworthy similarity between certain of these experiences and those of Peter. At Philippi, Paul is delivered from prison (16:25 ff.; cf. Peter's liberation in Jerusalem, 5:19; 12:6 ff.). In Ephesus, disciples of John the Baptist received the Spirit only after Paul laid hands on them (19:1 ff.; cf. Peter's ministry in Samaria, 8:17). The possession of Paul's handkerchief is sufficient to effect cures and exorcisms (19:11, 12; cf. the effect of Peter's shadow, 5:15). When the seven sons of Sceva attempt to usurp the power of God by invoking the name Paul uses, they are publicly humiliated (19:13 f.; cf. Peter's encounter with Simon Magus, 8:18 ff.).

It seems certain that Luke believes God has granted to Paul, as well as to Peter, an apostolic authority. Yet only once does he refer to Paul as an apostle (14:14), and then the designation is not meant technically, since Barnabas is also included. Luke is reluctant to apply the designation of "apostle" to others besides the Twelve. The incident involving the seven sons of Sceva (19:13 ff.) is probably intended to be a warning to anyone attempting unlawfully to employ that power which is solely the prerogative of an apostle. Not even Paul's companions share this power with him. Whatever ability they may have had to effect healings, it appears to have been of an order entirely different from that possessed by Paul himself.

PANEL VI: JERUSALEM AND ROME

The last panel extends from Acts 19:21 to the end of the book, concluding with the summary, "and he [Paul] lived there [at Rome] two whole years at his own expense, and welcomed all who came to him, preaching the kingdom of God and teaching about the Lord Jesus Christ quite openly and unhindered" (28:30–31). This is by far the longest section (almost one third of the book), and it climaxes Luke's presentation. Specifically it sets forth the circumstances that led to the proclamation of the gospel at Rome. The events recounted include Paul's final visit to Macedonia and Achaia, and his final encounter with the Jewish authorities in Jerusalem. His arrest, trials, and subsequent appeal to Caesar resulted in the long voyage to Rome as an imperial prisoner.

Beyond the recital of these historical events, important enough in their own right, Luke has two other concerns in this section: (1) to present an apology, or formal defense, on behalf of the apostle Paul and (2) to make a similar apology for the gospel itself. That Paul needed someone with a wide knowledge of the relevant facts to provide his defense is obvious even from his own letters. His early career as a clever and zealous persecutor of the faith had, by his own admission, caused untold suffering to the church. He had hounded Jewish Christians from synagogue to synagogue, imprisoning and punishing as many as he was able (8:3; 9:1 f.; 26:10, 11). His conversion was not sufficient in itself to allay every suspicion on the part of his brothers in the new faith (cf. 9:26).

If Christians were slow to trust the new apostle, the attitude of most Jews toward him was one of outright revulsion. To them he was a turncoat who had betrayed his own cause. Their one thought was to kill him (9:29) and erase his shame from their memories. Paul's attempt to minister in Jerusalem proved fruitless. He left for Tarsus (9:30), and from there he was brought by Barnabas to Antioch (11:25, 26). In the missionary travels that ensued, Paul faced the enmity of Asian Jews (cf. 21:27; 24:18).

Paul's afflictions stemmed largely from his missionary strategy. Committed to give the Jew first opportunity to hear the gospel, the Apostle began his mission in each new city by going first to the local synagogue or prayer cell. Although some Jews were converted, violent clashes with the Jewish authorities were common. Paul preached the forgiveness of sins through Jesus—that through him a man could be freed from everything over which the law of Moses was powerless to deliver him (13: 38 f.). This emphasis could only result in a depreciation of the importance of the law and the temple cult.

Paul went beyond this. He contended that the Gentile could have direct access to God's grace through Jesus wholly apart from the Mosaic institution. Quite understandably, the "devout" Gentiles, or "god-fearers," heard this news gladly. When the Jewish authorities opposed Paul, many from this group followed him out of the synagogue and into the new fellowship of the church. This in turn gave rise to another problem: How was it possible to maintain in one communion both the ritual law of the Jew, and Gentile freedom? Many of the Jews and Gentiles did the only thing that seemed reasonable under the circumstances. In their table fellowship they agreed to behave simply as brothers in the Lord and sharers of a common life.

Paul's practice of encouraging free association between Jewish and Gentile converts to Christianity was taken as a direct attack on the Mosaic institution. The Asian Jews (21:27; 24:18), who had opportunity to observe at first hand what Paul was doing when he established churches, now became his chief tormentors (20:19–20). Their report to the Jewish authorities at Jerusalem occasioned a mounting spirit of animosity toward Paul in the capital city. It was probably from this source that false rumors began to circulate in the Christian assembly at Jerusalem as well that Paul now taught Diaspora Jews that they no longer needed to circumcise their children or observe the traditional customs (21:21–22).

Paul recognized that the presence of such accusations not only jeopardized his personal ministry in the church, but endangered the whole mission to which he had given his life. He determined to go to Jerusalem and give a full account of his activities in order to silence the false rumors once and for all. Even if he should die at the hands of his enemies, the genuine motivation of his life would be made clear to the Christians at Jerusalem, and his actions, now so grievously misinterpreted and misrepresented, would be set in their true light.

Beyond this, Paul had a warm personal feeling for his Jewish brethren. Luke makes clear how profound was Paul's commitment to his Jewish heritage. Deeper yet was his passionate concern that they should know the truth of the gospel of Jesus Christ. If the price of such knowledge should turn out to be his own life, Paul was more than glad to pay it.

At this point Luke's contribution to the description of events becomes invaluable. He was himself an eyewitness to this final chapter of Paul's life.[9] As Paul's co-laborer, he had personal knowledge of the issues involved, the events that preceded and followed, and particularly the agonizing in the mind of Paul, his colleagues, and his churches over the decision to go to Jerusalem. It is something of this that Luke brings to light in his account, and in so doing he humanizes the apostle for his readers. For the first time we get a glimpse of the warm relationship that existed between Paul and his churches. One does not easily forget the picture of the disciples at Tyre entreating Paul not to go to Jerusalem and, when he remained resolute, accompanying him, with their wives and children, outside the city and kneeling with him for a final prayer and farewell (21:3 f.). Similarly moving is the description of the Ephesian elders embracing and kissing the apostle as he takes leave of them, certain that they will see his face no more (20:37), or the Caesarean church begging Paul with tears to reconsider his decision, and almost breaking his heart by their insistence (21:13).

The larger purpose which Luke carries out in this section is the demonstration of Paul's integrity. In Paul's defense before the various magistrates, he roundly denies and refutes the attacks made against him. He had never repudiated his Jewish heritage, nor blasphemed the law or the temple (24:12; 25:8). Always faithful to Jewish customs, he had visited the temple at Passover and showed himself ready to assume vows consistent with Jewish piety (24:11, 17 f.). Paul insists that the real issue between himself and the Jewish authorities is not custom or practice but the hope of Israel (23:6; 24:15; 26:6; 28:20). The question is whether Jesus of Nazareth really rose from the dead (23:6; 25:19; 26:8), and subsequently appeared to Paul (22:8; 26:15), making him an apostle to the Gentiles (26:16 f.). The issue is whether Paul has the freedom to pursue the will of God and make known the gospel to Gentiles as well as to Jews, that all men might believe. For Paul, there is no alternative. He cannot be "disobedient to the heavenly vision" (26:19). As long as he has the "help that comes from God" (26:22), he will carry this witness to the Gentiles.

The man who records this defense is by no means nonpartisan in his feeling. He writes as a sincere admirer of the missionary to the Gentiles. As Paul's companion, Luke has personally witnessed many of the strange phenomena that accompany his ministry—his power to heal, to perform miracles, and to effect powerful exorcisms. He knows of Paul's mystical communion with God—that God has revealed himself to Paul by visions, spoken to him in dreams, and visited him with angels. Of these things the author attempts no explanation. That he believes Paul implicitly goes without saying. He has seen how much of himself the Apostle is prepared to sacrifice for the truth of the gospel. He knows the kind of self-discipline Paul demands of himself and of his fellow laborers in the tasks that God has given them (cf. 15:38 f.). Although Luke is careful not to romanticize or idealize the apostle, it is obvious by the tone of his writing that he has found in Paul a man unique among men, a servant of God above and beyond any other he has ever known.

Luke also uses these final chapters to present an apology on behalf of the gospel. Against any pagans who might accuse the Christians of being disturbers of the peace or traitors to Caesar, Luke shows that it is the very genius of the gospel to move in an entirely different direction. While the gospel had been associated historically with serious commotions in several cities, Luke shows that these uprisings were caused not by the Christians but by their opponents. *They* had acted contrary to the laws and disturbed the peace. The detractors of the gospel had been motivated by greed and envy. At Ephesus the issue was the vested interest of some wealthy silversmiths (19:23 ff.). In none of the disturbances had Christian missionaries acted sacrilegiously, or incited anyone against Caesar (19:37; 25:9). Rather, they had appealed to the mind and conscience of their listeners with the intention of acting honorably before men even as they did before God (ch. 24:16).

The weightiest defense of the gospel, however, was to be found in the history of its appearances before the courts. In the process of time its servants had appeared before the Jewish council, a tribunal, a proconsul, two Roman governors, and a king. In each instance the civil authorities had completely exonerated the Christians of all charges made against them. Even before the Jewish council, where Paul's testimony was heard, there had been those who had held him innocent of any wrongdoing (23:9).

It is probable that Luke is here recounting history not only to furnish answers to the detractors of the gospel but also to instruct his readers concerning their own behavior. Many of them also would, in time, be tested and tried by their adversaries. In such an eventuality, Luke wants them to follow the pattern established by Jesus and practiced by the Jerusalem disciples and Paul. In each situation they must maintain an attitude of respect toward the law and do nothing to deny the right of authorities to examine their practices and judge their behavior. Under such circumstances in the past the gospel had proven to be self-justifying. Although Christians had occasionally suffered at the hands of the State, it was usually because of ignorance on the part of officials. In many more instances the reverse had proven true, as the State became the church's protector against mob violence. The more the gospel was proclaimed and understood, the less the authorities were concerned to oppose or persecute it.

As the sixth panel comes to a close, Paul is at Rome, "preaching the kingdom of God and teaching about the Lord Jesus Christ quite openly and unhindered" (28:31). Though the apostle's future at this point is rather uncertain, Luke's task is complete: the witnesses have moved out from Jerusalem, Judea, and Samaria "to the end of the earth" (1:8), to Rome, the hub of the universe, a meeting place not only of Jews and Gentiles but of men from every race and nation. The church's mission was far from complete, but the pattern had been set and the principles established which Luke hoped would govern the church's life and strategy of witness even in his own day.

NOTES

1. See especially H. Conzelmann, *The Theology of St. Luke* (1960), and for a survey of trends, C. K. Barrett, *Luke the Historian in Recent Study* (1961).

2. The importance of truthfulness in a historian is demonstrated by a little tract composed not long after the time when Luke was writing, Lucian's "On Writing History": "The one aim and goal of history is to be useful, and this can result only from its truth" (9); "the one task of the historian is to describe things exactly as they happened" (39); "this is the one essential thing in history, to sacrifice to the truth alone" (39).

3. H. J. Cadbury, *The Book of Acts in History* (1955), p. 53.

4. Conzelmann, *op. cit.*, p. 65.

5. Although some ancient manuscripts omit 22:43–44, the recurring motif of heavenly visitation suggests that these verses are original to Luke. It is plausible that some scribes might have suppressed them because they depict Jesus' humanity with such vividness.

6. Again, a few ancient manuscripts omit the crucial words. It may have been an offense to some in the later church that those who were guilty of deicide should be forgiven. But the fact that Luke attributes a similarly forgiving spirit to Stephen (Acts 7:60) makes it likely that the words should be retained here.

7. In the first panel, see especially Acts 4:31 (boldness to witness); 5:20 (the opening of prison doors); and 5:42 (irresistible wisdom). The same principle

governs the later panels as well. God opens the door of salvation to Gentiles by sending Peter to Cornelius (10:20). God chooses Paul and Barnabas to open the mission to Asia (13:2). When these same disciples decide to revisit the Asian churches a second time, God closes the door to Asia and Bithynia and sends them instead to Macedonia and Europe (16:6).

8. See H. J. Cadbury, " 'We' and 'I' Passages in Luke-Acts," *New Testament Studies*, 3 (1957), pp. 128–31.

9. The use of "we," which began in 16:9–18, recurs in 20:4–16; 21:1–18; 27:1–28:16.

SELECTED READING

Barrett, C. K., *Luke the Historian in Recent Study*. London: Epworth, 1961.

Bruce, F. F., *The Acts of the Apostles,* 2d ed. Grand Rapids: Eerdmans, 1953.

Cadbury, H. J., *The Book of Acts in History*. New York: Harper & Brothers, 1955.

Conzelmann, H., *The Theology of St. Luke*. London: Faber & Faber, 1960.

Filson, F. V., *Three Crucial Decades: Studies in the Book of Acts*. Richmond: John Knox Press, 1963.

Leaney, A. R. C., *The Gospel According to St. Luke*. New York: Harper, 1958.

Munck, J., "Jewish Christianity according to the Acts of the Apostles" in *Paul and the Salvation of Mankind*. Richmond: John Knox Press, 1959. Pp. 210–46.

Rackham, R. B., *The Acts of the Apostles*. London: Methuen, 1901.

Sherwin-White, A. N., *Roman Society and Roman Law in the New Testament*. Oxford: Clarendon, 1963.

Stonehouse, N. B., *The Witness of Luke to Christ*. London: Tyndale, 1951.

Williams, C. S. C., *The Acts of the Apostles*. New York: Harper, 1957.

XIX

✻

THE LETTER TO THE HEBREWS—
A WORD OF EXHORTATION

HISTORICAL intuition is necessarily an element in the reconstruction of the life situation which makes a New Testament document intelligible. Nowhere is this more true than in the case of the letter to the Hebrews. The letter itself is distinctive in form, and the tradition concerning its authorship, date, purpose, and readers is conflicting and unreliable. The evidence to be garnered from the document itself is open to divergent interpretations. Consequently, any critical reconstruction must be urged with caution as a tentative proposal. The task is like piecing together fragments of a splintered mirror scattered upon the ground; when the reconstruction is finished, important pieces will still be missing, and the image may well be distorted.

1. THE HOMILY FORM

In the brief personal section which concludes the letter the writer has given his work a descriptive title: "I exhort you brethren to permit the word of exhortation: for I have written a letter to you briefly"* (Heb. 13:22). Hebrews, in the mind of the author, is a "word of exhortation," the exhortation consisting of helpful warning, encouragement and comfort. The description recalls the invitation extended to Paul and Barnabas after the reading of the law and the prophets in the synagogue at Pisidian Antioch: "Brethren, if you have any *word of exhortation* for the people, say it" (Acts 13:15). "Word of exhortation" was the technical term for the homily which followed the reading of the Scriptures. It is this homily form that the writer has given to his work.

The insight that Hebrews is basically a homily does much to explain

308

its characteristic style and structure. The conclusion and personal allusions to the readers mark out Hebrews as a letter, whereas its rhetoric, its method of argument, and various incidental indications (e.g., 11:32, "time would fail me to tell . . .") reveal its character as a homily. Its oratorical nature almost demands that it was originally a spoken address, or at least was prepared for oral delivery to a congregation. This is made very clear by the italicized words in the following statements:

> Therefore we must pay the closer attention to *what we have heard,* lest we drift way from it (2:1).

> For it was not to angels that God subjected the world to come, *of which we are speaking* (2:5).

> About this *we have much to say* which is *hard to explain,* since *you have become dull of hearing* (5:11).

> *Though we speak thus,* yet in your case, beloved, we feel sure of better things that belong to salvation (6:9; see further 8:1; 9:5; 11:32).

The stress falls alternately on speaking and hearing.

The sermonic character of Hebrews explains one of its most distinctive characteristics, the interspersing of doctrinal material with practical application. Unlike Paul, who frequently groups doctrine and exhortation separately,[1] the writer punctuates his theological treatment of the high priesthood of Christ with earnest admonition to his readers. The six initial chapters, preparing for the development of the priesthood theme in 7:1–10:18, are intercalated with exhortation (2:1–4; 4:14–16; 5:11–6:20); the long doctrinal section, 7:1–10:18, is followed by the great exhortation in 10:19–13:17, which in turn is interrupted by two more doctrinal sections (11:1–40; 12:18–24). The theological passages constitute the larger part of the letter and serve the pastoral purpose of the writer. A doctrinal statement like that in 13:8, "Jesus Christ is the same yesterday and today and forever," finds its full explanation only in the light of the larger context of the sermon Likewise, the exhortations are informed by the epistle as a whole. An exhortation like that of 4:16, "Let us then with confidence draw near to the throne of grace," is a message on prayer which becomes relevant in the light of the whole epistle.

Among the New Testament letters only Hebrew and First John lack an introductory greeting designating the name of the author and the recipients. When Hebrews is seen as a homily, both the absence of an introductory greeting and the appropriateness of its majestic opening sentence is understandable: "In many and various ways God spoke of old to our fathers by the prophets; but in these last days he has spoken to us by a Son, whom he appointed the heir of all things, through whom also he created the world" (1:1–2). The personal note at the conclusion indicates that the sermon was composed for a particular occasion and a definite purpose (13:19, 23–24). The proper way to approach Hebrews is to recognize its character as a homily, and to come prepared to listen to what the speaker has to say.

2. "TO THE HEBREWS"

The title "To the Hebrews" presents the traditional view of the destination of the letter. It was not attached to the document by the author but probably by one of his early readers. Whether or not the title reflects reliable tradition we cannot be certain. It may have been suggested by the contents of the epistle, which indicate an audience intensely interested in the Old Testament. In any instance, it offers no help in pinpointing a destination for the letter, since in the ethnic sense all who belonged to the "twelve tribes" were "Hebrews," wherever they lived (cf. Acts 26:7; 2 Cor. 11:22; Phil. 3:5). A community of dispersed Jews of any region might be designated by this name. Two inscriptions in Rome, for example, make reference to a certain Gadia, designated "father of the Hebrews" and "father of the synagogue of the Hebrews."[2] A "synagogue of the Hebrews" is also mentioned in Greek inscriptions from Corinth and Lydian Philadelphia.

It is clear that Hebrews was not addressed to the church in a general way, but has in mind a specific local community with a definite history which is well known to the writer. He identifies himself with this group through the use of the first person plural pronoun. They had come to faith in Christ after having received the proclamation of disciples who had heard the Lord (2:3). The writer refers to "former days" when the group had been subjected publicly to abuse, imprisonment, and confiscation of property (10:32–34). He knows his readers personally and expects soon to revisit them (13:19, 23). He is alert both to their failure to mature as teachers of the truth (5:11 ff.) and to their unselfish generosity in ministering to other Christians (6:10). The statement in 5:12, "by this time you ought to be teachers," implies that the original readers of the letter had been believers for some time and were capable of a teaching ministry. Yet they were not the most prominent members of the larger community, for they are urged to submit to their leaders (13:7, 17, 24).

The admonition not to forsake the general assembly (10:25) suggests that they had dissociated themselves from the main body of the church, probably forming a small house-group. Paul mentions no less than three such house-churches in his letter to the Romans (16:3–5, 14, 15), and there may have been many such gatherings in every large city of the Empire.

Whether the core of the group was Hellenistic, Jewish, or Gentile in character is uncertain. What is clear is that their life was regulated by the Greek Old Testament, which is the version that the writer invariably cites. The imagery and message of the Old Testament are marshaled throughout Hebrews as supporting evidence for the superiority of the Christian faith to life under the Old Covenant. The fact that the writer deals with the Old Testament rather than with Judaism provides no determining evidence in the discussion of destination. Nevertheless, incidental references like those in 2:16, "for surely it is not with angels that he is concerned but with the descendants of Abraham," and 13:13, "let us go forth to him outside the camp," would carry a distinct appeal to Hellenistic-Jewish Christians whose minds were saturated with the Old Testament.

The writer of Hebrews is aware that there may be defection and unbelief among his hearers, and he solemnly urges them to understand what straying from Christian faith would mean. To turn away from Christ and Christian doctrine is to abandon "the living God" (3:12) and yet ultimately to fall into the hands of "the living God," who is the judge of his people (10:30–31). The individuals described do not appear to be in danger of oscillating constantly between Judaism and Christianity but of turning their backs on God entirely.

A common suggestion is that the group addressed in Hebrews is located in Rome, or in an area near Rome in southern Italy. In 13:24 the writer conveys the greetings of "those who come from Italy," which suggests that he wrote outside of Italy, sending greetings from Italian Christians with him to the church at home. It is consistent with this interpretation that the earliest witnesses to the existence and authority of Hebrews come from Rome. Clement of Rome both cites the epistle and adopts it as a model for sections of his own letter to the Corinthians (ca. A.D. 95), while the Shepherd of Hermas (A.D. 148) also makes use of Hebrews. Certainly the reference to Timothy in Hebrews 13:23 would be meaningful to the Christians in Rome.[3] The technical designation of "leaders" in the church (13:7, 17, 24) is paralleled in Roman sources,[4] while the allusion to the generosity of the readers in 6:10 and 10:33 f. is harmonious with the known history of the Roman church.[5]

If the evidence is deemed strong enough to support a Roman destination for the letter, it may be possible to identify something of the prior history of the congregation in view. Hebrews 10:32–34 recalls the former days in which the community had experienced deprivation and indignities for the sake of their commitment to Jesus Christ. This passage may be interpreted in the light of Suetonius' tantalizing reference to the expulsion of the Jews under the Emperor Claudius, A.D. 49: "Since the Jews constantly made disturbances at the instigation of Chrestus, he [Claudius] expelled them from Rome" (*The Deified Claudius* XXV. 4). It is commonly assumed that "Chrestus" is a garbled form for Christ. The reference is apparently to dispute over the proclamation of Jesus as Messiah within the synagogues of the Jewish quarter at Rome. The furor had attracted the unfavorable notice of the imperial authorities. If this reconstruction of the evidence proves accurate, then Hebrews 10:32–34 must be addressed to readers who had constituted the nucleus of the church at Rome. At that time they had experienced exile, imprisonment, loss of property, and suffering, but not martyrdom (12:4). The situation now facing the community appears more serious than the earlier one; they are asked to hold fast their confession unto death, perhaps in the period of Nero or of some later emperor. It is clear that the Epistle to the Hebrews was used in Rome in the first century, and a Roman destination appears more convincing than any other that has been proposed.

3. THE WRITER AND HIS PURPOSE

There is no firm tradition from the earliest period concerning the authorship of Hebrews. The epistle is anonymous; and while the writer was clearly known to his readers, the personal notes in chapter 13 are not specific enough to provide identification. While the writer is within the Pauline circle and expects to travel with Timothy, "our brother" (13:23), it is certain that he is not Paul but one who numbered himself among those to whom the immediate hearers of the Lord had delivered the gospel (2:3). The language of the letter constitutes the finest Greek in the New Testament, far superior to the Pauline standard both in vocabulary and in sentence building. The imagery is also distinctive: a ship missing the harbor, an anchor holding fast, a two-edged sword that penetrates and divides the inmost faculties of the soul, the earth watered by rain and producing useful or worthless growth, the body as a veil. All of these images are foreign to Pauline usage. The epistle glows with the distinctive color of the Levitical priesthood; many of its emphases are alien to those of the apostle to the Gentiles. In antiquity the names of Paul, Barnabas, Luke, and Clement of Rome were mentioned in certain church centers as the author of Hebrews, while in more modern times Apollos, Silvanus, the deacon Philip, Priscilla and Aquila, Jude, and Aristion have found their proponents. This divergence underlines the impossibility of establishing the author's identity. All that can be said with certainty is that Hebrews is the work of a creative theologian, deeply versed in the Septuagint, who shows an alertness both to the tradition reflected in the philosophical writings of Alexandrian Judaism and to the theology of the Hellenistic church.

The purpose of the writer's word of exhortation is an intensely practical one, to call his hearers to hold loyally to their confession of Jesus Christ as the one Mediator of salvation in a time of crisis. The structure of the letter is appropriate to this purpose. In moving language there is set forth the finality of God's revelation in his Son, whose dignity is superior both to the angels who are ministering spirits (1:1–14), and to Moses, whose position was that of a servant in the household of faith (3:1–6). Within this context the writer warns his hearers against indifference to the things they have heard (2:1–14) or blatant unbelief (3:7 4:13). The unique priesthood of Jesus Christ, who was a priest-king after the order of Melchizedek, is treated at length in 4:14–10:18. Three contrasts which demonstrate the superior dignity of Jesus Christ are developed:

1. The temporal character of the Aaronic priesthood is overshadowed by the eternal ministry of Melchizedek's successor (5:1–10; 6:20–7:28).

2. The priestly ministry in the tabernacle under the Old Covenant is superseded by the priestly service of Christ in the heavenly sanctuary establishing the New Covenant (8:1–9:28).

3. The inadequacy of the sacrifices under the law is contrasted with the efficacy and finality of Christ's sacrifice (10:1–18). The theme of Christ's priesthood and sacrifice gives substance to the warnings against an immaturity and apostasy which can be overcome only by faith, endurance, and hope (5:11–6:20). A long hortatory passage bears on the perseverance of Christians (10:19–12:29). Here the warning against apostasy is reiterated (10:26–31) while the hearers are exhorted to steadfast endurance. They are to exercise eschatological faith which appropriates the future and acts in the present in the light of that future (10:19–25, 31–12:29). As incentives to faithful conduct the writer appeals to the great heroes of faith from the past (11:1–40) and to the example of Jesus, "who for the joy that was set before him endured the cross" (12:2). A series of brief

exhortations bearing on personal and social conduct precede the valedictory address which brings the letter to a conclusion (13:1–25).

4. THE CHAMPION OF OUR SALVATION

Throughout the letter there appear to be allusions to the crisis that occasioned the writing of Hebrews:

> But exhort one another every day, as long as it is called "today," that none of you may be hardened by the deceitfulness of sin (3:13).

> Let us hold fast the confession of our hope without wavering, for he who promised is faithful; and let us consider how to stir up one another to love and good works, not neglecting to meet together, as is the habit of some, but encouraging one another, and all the more as you see the Day drawing near (ch. 10:23–25).

> Consider him who endured from sinners such hostility against himself, so that you may not grow weary or fainthearted. In your struggle against sin you have not yet resisted to the point of shedding your blood (12:3–4).

> This phrase, "Yet once more," indicates the removal of what is shaken, as of what has been made, in order that what cannot be shaken may remain (12:27).

The nature of this crisis is difficult to define with precision. Is it possible that the writer has provided an important clue in early introducing what may be identified as "champion" Christology? Chapter 2 reflects on the eighth Psalm, directing the attention of the hearers to the man Jesus, "who for a little while was made lower than the angels, crowned with glory and honor because of the suffering of death, so that by the grace of God he might taste death for every one" (ch. 2:9; cf. Psalm 8:5). The reference to Jesus' death introduces a meditation on the appropriateness of the incarnation and death of the Son. Jesus is depicted as one engaged in single combat with the devil. In 2:10 the writer designates Jesus by the unusual title *archēgos*, which in Hellenistic literary sources, inscriptions, and coins was applied especially to the legendary hero Hercules. An acceptable translation for the title in these instances would be "champion," a term which reflects the exploits of Hercules, including single combat. This translation should be adopted for Hebrews 2:10 as well, since the context is replete with "champion" motifs:

> For it was appropriate that he, for whom and by whom all things exist, in leading many sons to glory, should make the Champion of their salvation perfect through suffering. . . . Since therefore the children share in flesh and blood, he himself partook of the same nature, that through death he might

destroy him who has the power of death, that is, the devil, and deliver all those who through fear of death were subject to lifelong bondage* (2:10, 14–15).

The situation described is one in which sons, whom God intended to be led to glory, actually experienced bondage through fear of death; they were held captive by an evil champion who exercised authority in the sphere of death. What was demanded was another champion of sufficient stature to overcome the devil and release those enslaved by him. For this purpose the Son of God became incarnate, that he might become the champion of their salvation. Through his death he destroyed the antagonist who had the power of death and so brought deliverance to the captives. This unusual formulation reflects the older prophetic depiction of God as champion of his people:

> Can spoils be taken from a champion,
>   or the captives of a tyrant be delivered?
> Surely, thus says the Lord:
> "Even the captives of the champion shall be taken,
>   and the prey of the tyrants be rescued,
> for I will contend with those who contend with you,
>   and I will rescue your sons. . . .
> Then all flesh shall know
>   that I am the Lord your Savior,
>   and your Redeemer, the Champion of Jacob* (Isa. 49:24–26).

What God had promised to do, the writer of Hebrews declares, Jesus has done. There may be deliberate reflection on God's promise to be the champion of the sons of Jacob in 2:16 when the author adds, "For surely it is not with angels that he is concerned but with the descendants of Abraham."

This fruitful approach to the incarnation and death of Jesus is not exploited again until chapter 12, when the writer is concerned once more to encourage his readers to persevere in the Christian life:

> Therefore, since we are surrounded by so great a cloud of witnesses, let us also lay aside every weight, and the sin which clings so closely, and let us proceed with perseverance to the contest that is set before us, looking to Jesus the champion and perfecter of our faith, who for the joy that was set before him endured the cross, despising the shame, and is seated at the right hand of the throne of God* (12:1–2).

The prelude to this second introduction of a champion motif is the roll call of the heroes of faith who contended valiantly in their day, and who constitute the host of witnesses before whom the Christians addressed now contend. Having entered the arena, they are to be encouraged by the presence of their champion, Christ. He who triumphed over a foe who had enslaved men with fear of death will cause them to triumph now.

This language is generally viewed as highly metaphorical. But 10:32–34 recalls "a hard struggle with sufferings" which was intensely real, while 12:4–5 anticipates a time when it will be necessary to "resist to the point of shedding your blood." This suggests that the real situation of the arena is in view. It is because of this that the readers are urged to hold fast their confession unto death. In Rome and elsewhere in the Empire the ancient practice of single combat continued in the contests of the gladiators. It was common practice for criminals and slaves to be forced into the arena. The contest was decided before it had begun, for they were pitted against professional champions and had no defender to fight at their side. If this was the prospect facing the community addressed, the early introduction of "champion" Christology in chapter 2 and the resumption of the champion motif in 10:32–12:4 becomes intelligible.

Between these two points of explicit reference to champion motifs occur repeated exhortations to the readers to hold fast to their confidence, or their confession. They may do so because they know who Jesus is and what he has done. These references are related to the champion motif and constitute the link between 2:10–16 and 10:32–12:4. Is it not possible, accordingly, that the crisis which occasioned Hebrews was the prospect of facing severe persecution and the horror of the arena, where champions contend unto death? The community is assured that they have a champion upon whom they are to fix their eyes—Jesus—who, paradoxically, triumphed through his own death.

5. THE DISTINCTIVE THEOLOGY OF THE HELLENISTIC CHURCH

The writer of Hebrews was a profound theologian who took his stand within the mainstream of Christian tradition as developed by the Hellenistic church. His thought displays both originality and complexity as he reflects on Christian truth. Yet several of his major emphases can be recognized as developments of themes already articulated by Stephen in his address before the Sanhedrin. It was essential to Stephen's reinterpretation of Israel's history that from its inception God's intervention in history had an end in view toward which all of its promises pointed. In developing this thought Stephen made much of the motif of pilgrimage and promise, finding primary examples in Abraham, who was called to be a wanderer; in Joseph, who was carried off to an alien land; and in the events of the Exodus, when Israel became the wandering people of God.

This theme of pilgrimage and promise becomes one of the most distinctive notes in Hebrews, as the writer develops the conception of the Christian life as a pilgrimage to the city of God. It constitutes the substance of Chapters 3 and 4, in which attention is focused upon the wilderness experience of Israel, who failed to enter into God's promised rest because of unbelief and disobedience. In chapter 11 the wanderings of the worthy people of God are presented as the model for a total approach to life. The writer plainly states that in this life Christians have no abiding city; they seek the city which is to come (13:14). Only from this perspective do they resemble the heroes of God, such as Abraham, who dwelt in tents, seeking a city or home (11:10, 14, 16). Pilgrimage is characteristic of the obedient people of God under both the Old and the New Covenants, and it cannot be in vain, for God has prepared for them a city (11:10, 16). Christians, through their conversion, have in one sense already come to this city, for we read, "You came . . . to the city of the living God"* (12:22). But in its essence the city remains a reality "which is to come" (13:14). It will be manifested in the time of consummation, when heavens and earth are shaken (12:26); then only the city whose foundation and builder is God will remain. For this reason the people of God must be a pilgrim generation, ever open to the call and will of God.

The concept of the Christian life as a pilgrimage is derived not merely from the Old Testament tradition, which describes a literal pilgrimage, but from a fresh understanding of those circumstances in which men must respond to God's call. This understanding is implicit in Stephen's speech and informs the theology of the Hellenistic church. In Hebrews it comes to sharp expression in the fundamental proposition that the revelation of God is possessed on earth only as promise. That is why the one form of existence appropriate to the man who has embraced the gospel is pilgrimage. He must pursue the promise and lay hold of it for himself. The wanderings of Abraham or of Israel through the wilderness become a useful vehicle for calling the Christian community to a life of faith and obedience shaped by the promise of God.

In developing the motif of pilgrimage and promise, the writer clarifies his distinctive understanding of faith. For Paul, faith is essentially firm commitment to God's act in Christ, having a backward glance especially to the cross and resurrection. The perspective of Hebrews is different. Faith is both an openness to the future, which finds expression in obedient trust in the God who has promised, and a present grasp upon truth now invisible but expressed through the promise. It was this kind of faith in the power of God which enabled Moses to dare the wrath of Pharaoh and deliver Israel from bondage. Under pressure he endured because through faith he saw the invisible God (11:26–27). The faith to which the writer calls his hearers is a confident reliance upon the future, that they may act in the present in the light of that confidence. This is the eschatological faith which pilgrimage demands.

Like Stephen before him, the writer of Hebrews develops the consequences of Israel's history as a record of rebellion and resistance to the purposes of God (chs. 3–4). His emphasis, however, is different from that of Stephen, who pursued the record of Israel's disobedience to its culmination in the betrayal and murder of Jesus. Hebrews is concerned rather with the Christian group addressed, who are in danger of repeating in their experience the disobedience of Israel. It was a primary tenet of the Hellenistic church that no necessary continuity existed between the people who receive the promises and those who participate in their realization. The distinguishing marks of the true people of God are obedience and faith in the promise. The author calls his hearers back to this fundamental insight as he repeatedly urges them to hold fast their confidence, considering "Jesus, the apostle and high priest whom we confess"* (3:1). The Christian community must not emulate Israel in its disobedience to God but pursue the new access to God provided by the blood of Jesus. To fail to do so, to draw back, to sin deliberately after having received the knowledge of truth, is to invite in a heightened form the rejection and death experienced by Israel in the wilderness. It is to know "a fearful prospect of judgment, and a fury of fire which will consume the adversaries" (10:27), when one is brought face to face with the God who has said, "Vengeance is mine, I will repay" (10:30). In dwelling upon the judgment and its awe (cf. 10:31; 12:28 f.) the writer carries the argument of Stephen to a logical conclusion, applying it to a new community in danger of forgetting the character of the God "with whom we have to do" (4:13).

The parallels and differences in emphasis between Stephen's speech and Hebrews indicate that this letter provides a mature expression of the distinctive theology of the Hellenistic church. A question which remains unanswered concerns the source of the conception of Christ as an eternal priest after the order of Melchizedek. Was this conception an insight first grasped by the writer, or was it already to be found in the thinking of the Hellenistic church? The fact that the writer can refer to Christ as a high priest *before* he has given any theological exposition of this insight suggests that it was the common property of the Hellenistic church (cf. 2:17 f.; 3:1; 4:14–16). But there is little doubt that the development of this theme in 5:1–10:18 bears the marks of original and creative reflection on the part of a teacher who had thought long and meaningfully on the tradition treasured by the Hellenists. One of the significant values of the Epistle to the Hebrews is its continuity with this tradition, preserving and developing insights which have continued to enrich the theology and life of the Christian church.

NOTES

1. Cf. Romans, Galatians, Ephesians, Colossians.
2. E. Nestle, "On the Address of the Epistle to the Hebrews," *Expository Times*, X (1899), p. 422.
3. Cf. Col. 1:1; Philem. 1; 2 Tim. 4:9–13, 21.
4. *I Clement* 1:3; cf. 21:6; Hermas, *Vis.* ii. 2, 6; iii. 9, 7.
5. See Dionysius of Corinth in a letter to Soter, bishop of Rome, found in Eusebius, *Hist. Eccl.* IV. xxiii. 9–10.

SELECTED READING

Barrett, C. K., "The Eschatology of Hebrews," in *The Background of the New Testament and its Eschatology*, W. D. Davies and D. Daube, eds. Cambridge: University Press, 1956. Pp. 363–93.

Bruce, F. F., *Commentary on the Epistle to the Hebrews*. Grand Rapids: Eerdmans, 1966.

Guthrie, D., *The Epistle to the Hebrews in Recent Thought*. London: Tyndale, 1956.

Manson, T. W., "The Problem of the Epistle to the Hebrews," in *Studies in the Gospels and Epistles*, M. Black, ed. Philadelphia: Westminster, 1962. Pp. 242–58.

Manson, W., *The Epistle to the Hebrews: An Historical and Theological Reconsideration*. London: Hodder and Stoughton, 1951.

Tasker, R. V. G., *The Gospel in the Epistle to the Hebrews*. London: Tyndale, 1950.

Vos, G., *The Teaching of the Epistle to the Hebrews*. Grand Rapids: Eerdmans, 1956.

XX

✳

CRISIS AND THE COMMON SALVATION

NEAR the end of the New Testament are four short letters, two attributed to Peter, the chief of the apostles, and two attributed to the "brothers of the Lord," James and Jude. These documents are distinguishable from many of the Pauline epistles in that they are addressed to a group of churches or to all Christians everywhere rather than to one particular congregation. They are therefore called "general" or "catholic" epistles: James is written to "the twelve tribes that are in the Diaspora," and First Peter to "the elect strangers of the Diaspora of Pontus, Galatia, Cappadocia, Asia, and Bithynia." Second Peter and Jude address themselves apparently to an even wider audience: Second Peter "to those who have obtained a faith equally as precious as ours," and Jude "to those who are called and beloved in God the Father and kept for Jesus Christ" (i.e., all Christian believers).

We would expect from the wide audience addressed that these letters deal with the great universals of Christian experience (grace, faith, hope, the cross, the Spirit) rather than with a specific historical situation connected with a particular time and place. This is true only in part. Each of these letters does indeed have an awareness of general Christian truth, but always in relationship to a definite crisis or threat, either present or impending. In the case of Jude and Second Peter the crisis is false teaching within the church; in First Peter the crisis is persecution from without; in James it is a matter of moral laxity and doubt on the part of Christians, and oppression of the poor by the rich. The tension between a specific and a general emphasis becomes clearest in the tiny Epistle of Jude. The author states that his first intent had been to write about "the common salvation" but that a sudden necessity caused him instead to warn his readers against a particular group of heretics (Jude 3–4). He never returns to the original task that he had set for himself, but we do find that "the common salvation" is the dominant theme in the first chapter of each of the Petrine epistles.

Perhaps these four documents are best understood not as letters at all in the usual sense of the word but as "tracts for the times." Partly because of this "emergency oriented" quality, partly because of their late acceptance into our Bibles, and partly just because of their brevity, these books have been neglected by the church. This tendency, however, has been to the church's detriment.

The existence of such tracts bears witness to other trends in the church besides those represented by the Pauline corpus. Precisely because of the uniqueness of his calling and the intensity of his involvement with certain churches, Paul was by no means a typical figure in the first century. Other interests and other types of piety existed alongside the ones that he fostered. Though by no means incompatible with Pauline thought, they supplemented it in important ways. Recent emphasis on the particular theologies of Mark, Matthew, Luke, and the Epistle to the Hebrews has made this clear, but even before these distinctions were recognized, the general epistles stood as an effective warning against an oversimplified reconstruction of early Christian history.

Regardless of what conclusions one may reach as to the dates of these writings, there is no doubt that they embody some material as primitive as anything found in Paul: hymns or creedal formulations, ethical teachings, "household codes," and denunciations of heretics. James and First Peter, for example, differ greatly in their content, and yet at points seem to draw upon a common fund of tradition. Note, for example, this series of brief injunctions on God, man, and the devil:

James	*1 Peter*
But he gives more grace; therefore it says, *"God opposes the proud, but gives grace to the humble." Submit yourselves therefore to God. Resist the devil* and he will flee from you. Draw near to God and he will draw near to you. Cleanse your hands, you sinners, and purify your hearts, you men of double mind. Be wretched and mourn and weep. Let your laughter be turned to mourning and your joy to dejection. *Humble yourselves before the Lord and he will exalt you* (4:6–10).	Clothe yourselves, all of you, with humility toward one another, for *"God opposes the proud, but gives grace to the humble." Humble yourselves therefore under the mighty hand of God, that in due time he may exalt you.* Cast all your anxieties on him, for he cares about you. Be sober, be watchful. Your adversary the *devil* prowls around like a roaring lion, seeking some one to devour. *Resist him,* firm in your faith, knowing that the same experience of suffering is required of your brotherhood throughout the world (5:5–9).

Or again these words on joy in trials:

James	*1 Peter*
Count it all *joy,* my brethren, when you meet *various trials,* for you know that *the testing of your faith* produces steadfastness. And let steadfastness have its full effect, that you may be perfect and complete, lacking in nothing (1:2–4).	In this you *rejoice,* though now for a little while you may have to suffer *various trials,* so that *the genuineness of your faith,* more precious than gold which though perishable is *tested* by fire, may redound to praise and glory and honor at the revelation of Jesus Christ (1:6–7).

In the first instance, both writers have made common use of an Old Testament passage (Prov. 3:34) and a word of Jesus (cf. Matt. 23:12) as well as the general concepts of humility before God and resistance to the devil. But while James makes this material part of a section of warning, even denunciation, Peter uses it to climax his words of consolation and assurance to his readers. In the second instance, James' phrase "the testing of your faith" and Peter's "the genuineness of your faith" are identical in Greek, but the RSV translators rightly saw that the two writers had given the same phrase different meanings. James speaks of the *process* of testing which produces steadfastness, while Peter refers to the genuine or approved portion of faith, the *result* of testing that stands firm until the revelation of Jesus Christ. Moreover, James' emphasis seems to be on joy *because of* trials, Peter's on joy *in spite of* trials. Thus fixed forms of Christian exhortation, either oral or written, could be adapted to a variety of specific situations.

In addition, however, to the matter of primitive sources that may lie behind these tracts, the general epistles and related documents have an intrinsic value of their own. Certain negative judgments that have been made about them need to be subjected to close scrutiny. Sometimes it is urged that a marked trend toward ecclesiasticism is discernible, or a substitution of orthodoxy for spiritual passion, or a flagging of hope in the imminent coming of Christ and his Kingdom. The theology that undergirds these documents is said not to be creative and forward-looking but essentially conservative, aimed more at consolidating gains already made than at bringing the gospel dynamically to bear upon the new challenges of its pagan environment.[1] A term frequently applied to them, often in a derogatory sense, is "incipient Catholicism."

Such criticisms cannot be allowed to stand without qualification. Ecclesisticism is not markedly present in any of these writings. Church officers are not mentioned in Second Peter or Jude; James and First Peter speak of elders but without any indication that their power is on the increase. If James has the elders anointing and praying for the sick, he also urges his readers to "confess your sins *to one another*" (5:16). If Peter charges the elders to "tend the flock" and the younger to submit to them (5: 1–5), he also desires that each believer exercise his spiritual gift for the benefit of all "as good stewards of God's varied grace" (4:10–11). Even though Second Peter makes provision for delay in the Lord's coming (3:3–13), he holds fast to Jesus' insistence that the day will come "like a thief" (3:10), while James and First Peter reiterate the original proclamation that "the coming of the Lord" (James 5:8), or "the end of all things" (1 Peter 4:7), is "at hand."

It is true that these documents manifest a desire to conserve the "faith which was once for all delivered to the saints" (Jude 3). They are interested in guarding what the apostles have handed down (Jude 17; 2 Peter 3:2). Though they do not despise prophecy or the Spirit's utterances (1 Peter 1:10–12), they are convinced that it is the apostles who "have the prophetic word made more sure" (2 Peter 1:19).

None of this, however, means that they are lacking in creativity. This becomes especially clear when we realize the kinship that exists between these general epistles and three other short letters or tracts attributed to the apostle John. There is a common concern for orthodoxy as against heresy and a common desire for purity and righteousness of life. There is, moreover, a shared conviction that "it is the last hour" (1 John 2:18) and that the word which is "from the beginning" (1 John 1:1; 2:7, 24) should continue to dwell in the community of believers.

If the Johannine epistles have a legitimate place among these "tracts for the times," they render exceedingly difficult any blanket indictment of this literature as pedestrian, legalistic, or merely "orthodox." The reason for this is that both in style and in theme the three epistles echo the powerful voice of the Gospel of John. Even those few scholars who do not admit the common authorship of these "Johannine" writings tend to agree that they come from the same school of early Christian thought. If John, the most creative and profoundly theological of all the Gospel writers, can also write to his "little children" to "keep the commandments" or "love the brethren," if he can tell them to "abide in the doctrine of Christ" or confess the verbalized creed "that Jesus is the Christ," then it is indeed hazardous to despise Peter or James or Jude for similarly "practical" concerns. If Paul is the great theologian of the emerging Gentile churches, John is the most impressive voice from among the developing churches of the next generation. It was necessary not only to hold fast to the "common salvation" and relate it to new crises, but also to look back upon that salvation, the redemptive act of Jesus Christ, from a new perspective. This John has done. By reinterpreting the life of Jesus, he has made it possible to see his own world in a new way and to realize afresh the presence of God even in situations of adversity and conflict. The Book of Revelation, also attributed to John, undertakes more directly the problem of a Christian view of history, incorporating past, present, and future into one vast panorama of God's blessing and judgment.

NOTE

1. For this kind of approach, see especially R. Bultmann, *Theology of the New Testament,* Vol. II (1955), pp. 119–236; for a more positive estimate, see L. Goppelt, "The Existence of the Church in History According to Apostolic and Early Catholic Thought," in *Current Issues in New Testament Interpretation,* W. Klassen and G. Snyder, eds. (1962), pp. 193–209; also B. Reicke, *Anchor Bible,* Vol. 37 (1964), pp. xv–xxxviii.

XXI

JAMES—THE ROYAL LAW

THE author of the Epistle of James, or Jacob, identifies himself only as "James, a servant of God and of the Lord Jesus Christ" (James 1:1). The few ancient witnesses that speak of this book connect it with James the Righteous, one of Jesus' brothers, the son of Joseph and Mary.[1] As far as we know, this was the one man of that name in the early church who was well enough known to make a more elaborate introduction unnecessary. Little is known of the apostle James, the son of Alphaeus (Mark 3:18 and parallels), while the other apostle James, the son of Zebedee, was martyred in Jerusalem about A.D. 44 (Acts 12:2).

1. THE CAREER OF JAMES THE RIGHTEOUS

James the brother of Jesus was not an apostle, for Jesus' own brothers did not become his followers during his earthly ministry (John 7:5). He is listed as Jesus' brother in the Gospels only in Mark 6:3 and Matthew 13:55; possibly he is the same as "James the small," whose mother's name was Mary (Mark 15:40).[2]

Paul tells us that Christ appeared to James after the resurrection (1 Cor. 15:7); it was doubtless this experience which brought him to faith. Jesus' brothers joined Mary and the apostles in steadfast prayer in Jerusalem after the ascension (Acts 1:14), and James soon appears as a leader in the Jerusalem church (12:17). Paul regards him as one of the "pillars" there, alongside Peter and John (Gal. 1:19; 2:9, 12). At the Jerusalem Council in Acts 15 it is James who hands down the final decision concerning the conditions under which Gentiles shall be received into the church (15:13–21).

According to the agreed division of labor in Galatians 2:9, Paul was to go to the Gentiles, while the sphere of activity for James, Peter, and

John was to be the world of Judaism. James seems to have been as passion-ately dedicated to this mission as Paul was to his. It is James who sounds the warning that Christians should not be too quick to bypass the old landmarks of the law in the interests of new freedom (Acts 15:21). It is he who insists that Paul demonstrate his loyalty to the ritual law by paying the expenses of four Jewish Christians that had taken a Nazirite vow (21:20–22).[3] James' interest extended beyond Jerusalem to "all the Jews that are among the Gentiles" (21:21), i.e., the Judaism and Jewish Christianity of the diaspora. On one occasion Paul speaks as if the "brothers of the Lord," as well as the apostles, conducted missionary journeys similar to his own (1 Cor. 9:5). Though we know nothing directly of James' travels, we do know that from Jerusalem he sent emissaries to Antioch to determine whether the principle of Gentile freedom was being carried too far (Gal. 2:12).

If Peter and Matthew typified the liberal wing of Jewish Christianity, James represented a more conservative strain. The differences among them however, and between all of them and the apostle Paul, were differences solely of emphasis, not of principle. All agreed that the gospel was ulti-mately for the whole world and that this universal blessing would come through the remnant of Israel. Paul stood face to face with one of God's surprises: "a hardening has come upon part of Israel, until the full number of the Gentiles come in" (Rom. 11:25). James, on the other hand, con-tinued to stress the positive side of Judaism's response; in the Jerusalem church he saw the very "tabernacle of David" being rebuilt (Acts 15:16; cf. Amos 9:11); despite bitter rejection by the majority, thousands of Jews had accepted Jesus as their Messiah (Acts 21:20). For all his con-servatism, James seems not to have ben limited or narrowly circumscribed in his vision. In his own way he was a cosmopolitan man who tried to keep his hand on the pulse of world Jewry. Even the little information that the New Testament supplies indicates he had come a long way from his early village life in Nazareth. He presents his epistle as a kind of "open letter" to the "twelve tribes in the Diaspora" (James 1:1).

2. THE JAMES LEGEND

The New Testament portrait of James the Righteous can be supplemented to some degree from certain extra-biblical accounts, largely Josephus and Eusebius. Within these narratives it is not always easy to distinguish be-tween legend and fact. They should be used with caution while keeping in mind the New Testament material as the primary point of reference.

Josephus gives a simple and probably authentic report that at the beginning of the procuratorship of Albinus (A.D. 62), Ananus, the newly appointed high priest, "convened the judges of the Sanhedrin and brought before them a man named James, the brother of Jesus who was called the Christ, and certain others. He accused them of having transgressed the law and delivered them up to be stoned" (*Antiquities* XX, § 200).

Eusebius cites a more elaborate tradition received from Hegesippus, a second-century Jewish Christian:

> He was called the "Righteous" by all men . . . he was holy from his mother's womb. He drank no wine or strong drink, nor did he eat flesh; no razor went upon his head;[4] he did not anoint himself with oil, and he did not go to the baths. He alone was allowed to enter the sanctuary, for he did not wear wool but linen, and he used to enter alone into the temple and be found kneeling and *praying for forgiveness for the people,* so that his knees grew hard like a camel's because of his constant worship of God, kneeling and *asking forgiveness for the people* (*Hist. Eccl.* II, xxiii, 4–6).

This agrees with the New Testament emphasis on James' great concern for "the people," i.e., the Jewish community in Palestine and throughout the world. Hegesippus goes on to tell of a certain Passover when *"all the tribes, with the Gentiles also,"* had come together (*Hist. Eccl.* II, xxiii, 11). With false humility and in unctuous tones the scribes and Pharisees address James the Righteous:

> We beseech you to restrain the people since they are straying after Jesus as though he were the Messiah. We beseech you to persuade concerning Jesus all who come for the day of the Passover, for all obey you. For *we and the whole people testify to you that you are righteous and do not respect persons.* . . . Therefore stand on the battlement of the temple that you may be clearly visible on high, and that your words may be audible to all the people . . . (II, xxiii, 10 f.).

Instead of restraining the people from belief in Jesus, James responds with a ringing declaration of his own Christian faith. Crying out hypocritically, "Oh, oh, even the righteous one erred," the scribes and Pharisees hurl James down from the temple and stone him to death (II, xxiii, 13 ff.). This legend cannot be accepted uncritically. Its details are interesting but of questionable value. In all likelihood Hegesippus has grossly exaggerated James' prominence within Judaism. Yet the leadership of this man among Jewish Christians and his concern for "the people" as a whole are beyond dispute. What is important is the situation that is presupposed, a situation in which church and synagogue do not yet stand over against each other as two mutually exclusive and hostile camps. Instead, Jewish Christians constitute one group with Judaism and, it can be imagined, worship side by side with their fellow Jews in the synagogues. Such circumstances may have prevailed in Jerusalem until A.D. 70, when the city fell, and in certain other areas until about 90, when Jewish synagogues and Jewish-Christian churches finally assumed separate identities and embarked on different pathways. These also appear to be the circumstances that underlie and most plausibly explain the distinctive teachings of the Epistle of James.

3. THE FOUR HOMILIES OF JAMES

In form, James is a "circular" or "open letter" to the "twelve tribes that are in the Diaspora" (1:1). A typical assembly of the believers to whom James writes is specifically called a "synagogue" (2:2) rather than a church. Though he usually addresses himself to his "brethren" (1:2, 16; 2:1, 5, 14; 3:1; 4:11; 5:7, 9, 12, 19), on at least one occasion he turns to another group, "the rich" (5:1).

We know that some early Jewish Christians came to be called Ebionites, a term that means "the poor,"[5] and that even in the New Testament the Christian believers at Jerusalem were known as "the poor" (Rom. 15:26; Gal. 2:10). Conversely, their Jewish compatriots who scorned the Christian confession may have been known as "the rich." The terminology of poverty and wealth could be used in a way that was only loosely related to actual economic status. The beatitudes of Jesus ("Blessed are the poor. . . .") may well have served as a rallying cry for Jewish Christians in the synagogue. Especially the Lucan formulation, with its four blessings upon the poor and four woes upon the rich (Luke 6:20–26) and its references to being reviled and excommunicated (6:22), lends itself to this suggestion. If such an approach is valid, then James is writing to Jewish communities of the diaspora, beset by deep religious and social cleavages; but he addresses himself primarily to the oppressed Christian faction in each synagogue.

The distinctly Christian element in James rests not upon theological affirmations *about* Jesus Christ (e.g., the cross or the resurrection), but upon the words or teachings *of* Jesus himself as James had received them. This letter is primarily ethical rather than doctrinal.[6] It is notoriously difficult to outline, resembling in some ways the Jewish wisdom writings like the Old Testament Book of Proverbs or the apocryphal books of Sirach or Wisdom. Many readers of James have seen in it only a series of moral maxims joined together by word association. Others have pointed out similarities to certain types of Hellenistic speeches, notably the Stoic or Cynic "diatribe."[7] Though James' rhetorical style may bear the stamp of these influences, the substance of his letter is a series of sermonic expansions of certain sayings of Jesus. This feature makes James unique among the New Testament epistles. There are probably fewer allusions to Jesus' words in the whole body of Pauline letters than in the single Epistle of James. Jesus' sayings are not actually quoted by James, nor are they introduced with any formula such as "the Lord said. . . ." They are simply assumed to be already familiar to the readers; their implications for Christian living are developed at some length, and possible misunderstandings are cleared up. Though James follows no hard and fast outline, a recognition of the centrality of these *logia,* or sayings, of Jesus enables us to arrange the material within a rather loose framework that exhibits the main lines of the writer's thought. Four brief homilies or messages have been merged into one: on temptation (1:2–18), on the law of love (1:19–2:26), on evil speaking (3:1–4:12), and on endurance (4:13–5:20).

A. On Temptation (James 1:2–18)

James' opening discourse is really a commentary on the sixth petition of the Lord's Prayer, "Lead us not into temptation." His point is that the Christian is not spared from all exposure to "temptation" in the sense of trial by suffering, but is enabled by God to withstand the trials of life and indeed to triumph over them. Hence "temptation" is for the believer a positive good, strengthening his faith and producing in him endurance and stability that he might be a man of wisdom, confident in prayer, a complete person in Christ.

At this point James only drops a hint that the temptation may be expressing itself in oppression of "the poor" by "the rich" (1:9–11). This theme he elaborates more fully later. Like a composer of great music, James tersely introduces a number of his prime concepts near the outset; again and again he will gravitate back to them, reiterating and developing what he has said before. Several of his key terms are repeated as "catchwords" in verses 2–8, carrying out the progression of his thought and awaiting further explanation in the rest of the epistle: *endurance* (vss. 3, 4); *work* (as verb and noun, vss. 3, 4); *perfect* or *complete* (vs. 4, twice); *lack* (vss. 4, 5); *ask* (vss. 5, 6); *faith* (vss. 3, 6); *doubt* (vs. 6, twice). In verse 12, James returns full circle to the thought with which he began in verse 2, only now in the form of a beautitude:

verse 2	*verse 12*
Consider it all joy, my brethren, when you fall into various temptations, knowing that the proving of your faith works endurance.*	Blessed is the man who endures temptation, for being proven, he will receive the crown of life which God has promised to those who love him.*

Thus verses 2–12 comprise part one of a homily on temptation and may be entitled "The Benefits of Temptation."

In verses 13–19, James addresses himself to a theological problem: If we pray, "Lead us not into temptation," does this mean that when we are tempted it is God's doing? Since temptation is beneficial, we might expect an affirmative answer; but James' reply is negative. Part two of the homily can be called "The Dangers of Temptation." The testing of our faith does not always lead to endurance and completeness in Christ; sometimes it leads to sin. James insists that temptation as an inducement to sin has its origin not in God but in us. To make this clear, he sets forth two "genealogies," or "family trees," by which he seeks to separate God from all that has the taint of evil. This section is the closest that James comes to expressing a real theology. Like Jewish rabbis of his day, he finds the source of wrongdoing in an "evil desire" or "evil inclination" within the heart of man (1:14).[8] This "evil desire" he personifies as a woman who bears a child, "sin." When the child grows up, he in turn fathers a son called "death" (1:15). God, on the other hand, has established his own line of descent: "He willingly fathered us by the word of truth that we should be a kind of first fruits of his creatures"* (1:18). There are thus two families in the world, living side by side like the wheat and the weeds in Matthew's parable (13:24–30, 36–43). They are completely opposite in origin, destiny, and present character:

James 1:15	*James 1:18*
evil desire	God
sin	Christians (by the word)
death	the new creation[9]

"Temptation" takes place when the evil encroaches upon the good; it can bring the Christian either to defeat and captivity to sin, or to a stronger faith. God is not the author of temptation. He is the holy and changeless one. "Every good gift," all wisdom, every resource for overcoming temptation, comes from him (1:5, 17). Thus James' sermon on temptation ends by laying a theological basis for what follows.

B. On the Law of Love (James 1:19–2:26)

The "word of truth" (1:18) by which men become God's children is further described as an "implanted word" (1:21) that assures salvation. But it does not operate automatically. One must not only hear but *do* the word. This doing of the word is equivalent to fulfilling what James calls the "perfect law of liberty" (1:25; 2:12) or the "royal law" (2:8). It is a "law of liberty" as distinguished from the Jewish law, which Christians regarded as a yoke of bondage. It is "royal" because it carries for the "poor" the promise of a Kingdom (2:5; cf. Matt. 5:3). Its ultimate source is the Old Testament (Deut. 6:5; Lev. 19:18), but its immediate source for James is probably a word of Jesus:

> You shall love the Lord your God with all your heart, and with all your soul, and with all your mind. This is the great and first commandment. And a second is like it, You shall love your neighbor as yourself. On these two commandments depend all the law and the prophets. (Matt. 22:37–40).

The second of the two great commandments is actually quoted in James 2:8, but the mention of promises held out to those who love God (1:12; 2:5) shows that both commandments are in view. Jesus' summary of the law of love, then, is James' text for his second sermon.

The second chapter of James is best known in the church for its discussion of faith and works (2:14–26). The "works" James has in mind are specifically the works of the law of love. This is made clear in his summation of true piety as ministering to orphans and widows (1:27), in his attack on the practice of currying favor with the rich (2:1–9), and in his insistence on feeding and clothing those in need (2:14–16). Even his Old Testament illustrations show Abraham's love toward God (2:21) and Rahab's love of neighbor (2:25). Christian faith, for James as for the other New Testament writers, is a beginning, not an end in itself. It corresponds to a genuine hearing of the word, but it must be perfected in the doing of the word. Unless inward commitment extends itself into the outward realm of practical conduct, it is truncated and useless—"faith without works is dead" (2:26, KJV). Many have concluded that on this matter James contradicts the Apostle Paul, who insisted on salvation by faith alone, apart from the works of the law. But it is Paul who states, "So faith, hope, love abide, these three; but the greatest of these is love" (1 Cor. 13:13). For Paul as for James the completion and validation of faith is love. Faith without the works of love is "nothing"; it is no better than a "noisy gong or a clanging cymbal" (13:1–3).

Thus James' second homily begins to manifest more clearly his social concern. He stands in a long and honorable Jewish tradition that had stressed deeds of charity to the poor and hungry. But he also stands in the line of one who had intensified this demand in the Sermon on the Mount—his own brother, Jesus of Nazareth, who had made all the law to depend upon the two commandments: "Love the Lord your God" and "Love your neighbor as yourself."

c. On Evil Speaking (James 3:1–4:12)

In his controversies with the Pharisees, Jesus had commented on the Jewish laws of purity with respect to food in the form of a pungent and easily remembered riddle: "It is not what goes into the mouth that defiles the man, but it is what goes out of the mouth that defiles the man." When asked for a solution to the riddle, Jesus explained, "Do you not see that whatever goes into the mouth passes into the stomach and hence leaves the body? But the things that go out of the mouth come out of the heart, and those defile the man. For out of the heart come evil thoughts, murders, acts of adultery and fornications, thefts, false testimonies, blasphemies. These are the things that defile the man; but to eat with unwashed hands does not defile the man"* (Matt. 15:11, 17–20).

The point made by this riddle becomes the basis for the third of James' homilies on the sayings of Jesus. Anyone in the church or synagogue who aspires to the office of teacher, says James, aspires to an awesome responsibility (3:1). As one who speaks with authority, the teacher embodies an enormous potential for either good or evil. The tongue of man is a dangerous weapon, a fire raging out of control, an untamed beast.

Corresponding to the two families that are in the world—the spawn of evil desire and the children of God—are two kinds of wisdom: earthly wisdom and the wisdom that is from above (3:15 ff.). Because of "temptation," with its encroachment of the earthly upon the heavenly wisdom, there is a terrible ambiguity in the speech of man, even in the speech of the Christian. Of the tongue James writes:

> With it we bless the Lord and Father, and with it we curse men, who are made in the likeness of God. From the same mouth come blessing and cursing. My brethren, this ought not to be so. Does a spring pour forth from the same opening fresh water and brackish? Can a fig tree, my brethren, yield olives, or a grapevine figs? No more can salt water yield fresh (3:9–12).

The imagery belongs to James, but the thoughts are those of Jesus. The stern denunciations in 4:1–10 indicate that James has in view the whole of the Jewish communities—the disciples of Moses and the disciples of Jesus alike. It is just this fact of a mixed audience that James has in common with Jesus of Nazareth, and it is this that may go far to explain their similarities in content and style.

In conclusion, James turns once more to the royal law of love for his sanction. To speak evil against a brother or to judge him is to speak evil against the royal law and so to usurp the place of the one Lawgiver and Judge (4:11–12). The besetting sin of the strife-torn diaspora synagogues was evil speaking—Jew against Christian, Christian against Jew. To James, the remedy for this situation and the only hope of true unity lay in the keeping of law—not, however, the old law of commandments, but the new law of liberty, the royal law of the King Messiah. Christian faith must be perfected in love of God and, therefore, in love of neighbor.

d. ON ENDURANCE (JAMES 4:13–5:20)

The last of James' homilies virtually returns to the theme of the first —endurance of trials. Instead of reflecting on the theological meaning of temptation, however, he now concentrates on the call for endurance and relates this demand specifically to the eschatological "coming of the Lord" (5:7). It is likely that the word of Jesus most prominently in view is one found in the eschatological discourse on the Mount of Olives: "He who endures to the end will be saved" (Mark 13:13 and parallels). With his customary fondness for the beatitude form, James expresses this thought as: "Blessed is he that endures." Already in chapter 1 he had said: "Blessed is the man that endures temptation"* (1:12), and here he reiterates: "Indeed, we regard as blessed those who have endured"* (5:11). Job and the Old Testament prophets are adduced as examples of such endurance in the face of suffering.

The most striking feature of this last discourse is that the life setting of the call for endurance now comes to the surface. Endurance on the part of the "brethren" is necessary because of social and economic oppression. James addresses first the oppressors (4:13–5:6) and then the oppressed (5:7–20). His sternest words are reserved for those who abuse their hired farmworkers and withhold the rightful payment of wages (5:4–6).[10] One cannot help but wonder if this conflict is not as much religious as social. Jesus himself had likened the task of Christian missionaries to that of farmworkers: "The harvest is great but the workers are few. Pray the Lord of the harvest that he might send forth workers to his harvest"* (Matt. 9:37). He had even applied to missionaries a proverbial saying: "The worker is worthy of his wages"* (Luke 10:7;

cf. 1 Tim. 5:18). The farmworkers of James 5:4 may, therefore, simply be James' way of describing Jewish-Christian proclaimers of the gospel who meet rejection and harsh treatment in the "house of Israel" (cf. Matt. 10:13–31). To persecute them is to persecute Jesus himself, the Righteous One, who speaks through them (James 5:6).[11]

In any event, when James turns to the "brethren" in the following verses, he does depict them as farmers. As the farmer patiently waits for the early and late rains with their resultant harvest, Christian believers wait for the coming of the Lord. The quality of endurance, especially as manifested in faithful prayer, dominates James' presentation from here on. Whether he speaks of physical illness (5:13–16) or of a Christian's affliction and conflict in the world generally (5:7–11), he urges firm confidence in God, who controls the outcome and raises up his people. As Elijah's prayers brought rain and a harvest (vss. 17–18),[12] so the prayers of Christian faith will surely bring the eschatological rain and harvest of the consummation, introduced by Christ's return (vss. 7–8). Christian endurance is vindicated; "he that endures to the end" shall indeed be saved. There is no reason why the synagogues should be any longer disrupted by complaints or accusations or oaths. Not these, but prayers of faith and psalms of joy, should be upon the lips of Christians (vss. 9, 12–13).

Though the Jewish communities of the diaspora were like a world in microcosm, divided into two families—the "rich" and the "poor," the children of evil desire and the children of God—James' counsel is not one of despair. As Christian faith realizes itself in steadfast endurance and in the practice of the law of love, the exact opposite of "temptation" can take place. Instead of evil threatening the good and overcoming it, the good can overcome the evil, so that men may be rescued from sin and from its offspring, death (5:19–20). Nothing less than this is the hope and purpose of James in his four homilies on the words of Jesus.

NOTES

1. See, e.g., Eusebius, *Hist. Eccl.* II, xxiii, 1–25.

2. Cf. Matt. 27:56; also Mark 16:1; Luke 24:10. This James is commonly identified as the son of Alphaeus, but evidence for this is lacking.

3. I.e., a vow to abstain from wine and strong drink, not to cut the hair, and to avoid all defilement from contact with a dead body. Cf. Num. 6:1–21.

4. Cf. Acts 21:23–24 and the preceding note.

5. This name, which comes from Aramaic or Hebrew, first appears about A.D. 175 in Irenaeus, *Adv. Haer.* I, xxvi, 2.

6. This probably explains Martin Luther's distaste for James and his characterization of it as an "epistle of straw." For full references see Feine-Behm-Kümmel, *Introduction to the New Testament,* 14th ed. (1966), p. 285.

7. A "diatribe" was not necessarily a ranting denunciation, as our English word suggests, but rather a kind of moralistic "pep talk," a highly rhetorical appeal to the hearers to live a nobler and more serious life.

8. For a good sampling of rabbinic references to the "evil inclination," see C. G. Montefiore and H. Loewe, *A Rabbinic Anthology* (Meridian Books, 1963), pp. 295–314.

9. This is suggested by the phrase "first fruits of his creatures." "First fruits" anticipates a harvest when God shall manifest his rule over the whole world.

10. His words to the rich are not unlike the "taunt songs" of the Old Testament prophets against the heathen enemies of God's people. See, e.g., Jer. 50: 11–16, 31 f.; Amos 4:1–3; Zeph. 2:5–15.

11. Cf. Matt. 10:40; Luke 10:16; Acts 9:4 f. Also Matt. 25:31–46. (See above, pp. 271 f.

12. Cf. 1 Kings 17 and 18.

SELECTED READING

Mayor, J. B., *The Epistle of James,* 3d ed. London: Macmillan, 1913. (Reprint, 1965.)

Mitton, C. L., *The Epistle of James.* Grand Rapids: Eerdmans, 1966.

Ropes, J. H., *The Epistle of St. James.* Edinburgh: T. and T. Clark, 1916.

Shepherd, M. H., Jr., "The Epistle of James and the Gospel of Matthew," *Journal of Biblical Literature,* 75 (1956), pp. 40–51.

Tasker, R. V. G., *The General Epistle of James.* London: Tyndale, 1956.

XXII

FIRST PETER—A ROYAL PRIESTHOOD

THE four Gospels bear unanimous witness that Peter was the leader and spokesman of Jesus' disciples. He was the great confessor of Jesus as "the Christ, the Son of the living God" (Matt. 16:16). Upon him the church was built as on a rock.[1] To him were committed "the keys of the kingdom" that he might have the right to formulate authoritative rules of doctrine and practice in the church.[2] He was the one commissioned to "feed Christ's sheep" by his ministry of teaching (John 21:15–17). We might, therefore, expect that anything he wrote would immediately have assumed a central place among the New Testament writings, that it would in fact have become the norm by which other documents would be evaluated. Such is far from the case. The two epistles attributed to Peter occupy a surprisingly modest place in the New Testament canon. The reason is not merely that scholars have disputed their authorship, but that they are sharply limited in length and scope, and are not direct witnesses to the life of Jesus. Their length, however, is no index of their true importance. Peter's first epistle is a work of exceptional literary and theological power. It speaks to the twentieth century with special import as it underlines what it means to live for God in a world that is without God.

1. TO THE NEW DIASPORA

First Peter, like James, is written to a diaspora (1:1), and encourages its readers to endure times of testing in the world. It cannot be assumed, however, that Peter's diaspora has any particular connection with the group to which James writes. Not only is it limited geographically to certain districts of Asia Minor, but it apparently refers to Gentiles as well as (or instead of) Jewish Christians. Since at least some of the readers of First Peter have been redeemed out of paganism (4:3–4; cf

1:18, 21) rather than unbelieving Jewry, the word diaspora in 1:1 must be used in a figurative sense. It is one of a number of Old Testament and Jewish terms that Peter has transferred to the Gentile churches for which he writes. An "apostle of Jesus Christ" (1:1), he writes as a leader of the new Israel exiled in a new Babylon (5:13) to Christians who are similarly exiled in the diaspora of Asia Minor. Like the Jews, they are dispersed, but not from Jerusalem or its temple. Their true home is heaven. They are "elect strangers" and "aliens" in the world (1:1, 2:11). Like Israel in the wilderness at the beginning of her life with God, they are "an elect race, a royal priesthood, a holy nation, a distinctive people . . . the people of God"* (2:9–10; cf. Exod. 19:6). Nowhere in the New Testament are the privileges and responsibilities of Israel applied to the Christian community as freely as in First Peter. Far from being inconsistent with a predominantly Gentile destination, this fact is precisely what we might expect. In the face of the world's encroachments Peter wants to give these churches a sense of historical identity and continuity with an ancient people. In Christ he wants them to find not only a "living hope" (1:3) but a heritage. This he has done not that they might live in the past but that they might "stand" in God's grace (5:12) amid the complex demands and dangers of the Imperial Age.

2. THE PLEDGE OF GOOD FAITH

The parallel between the churches of Asia Minor and Old Testament Israel is presupposed almost at the beginning of the epistle when Peter says that they have been chosen "unto obedience and sprinkling of the blood of Jesus Christ" (1:2, KJV). He refers to that incident in Exodus 24 in which Moses delivered to the Israelites the words and commandments of the Lord, and the people said, "All that the Lord has spoken we will do, and we will be obedient" (vs. 7). Oxen were sacrificed, and Moses poured half of the blood onto the altar and sprinkled the other half over the people, saying, "Behold the blood of the covenant which the Lord has made with you in accordance with all these words" (vss. 6–8). Peter's point is that Christians have also made a covenant promise of obedience to God, sealed not with the blood of oxen but "with the precious blood of Christ, like that of a lamb without blemish or spot" (1 Peter 1:19). They are "children of obedience" (1:14), who have purified their souls by "obedience to the truth" (1:22). These passages suggest that in this epistle, "obedience" refers primarily to the covenant pledge of obedience to God made by a convert when he confesses Christ and is baptized. Peter actually describes Christian baptism as a "pledge of good faith toward God"* (3:21).[3] It is that act by which the new believer publicly acknowledges Jesus Christ as "Lord," the one to whom he owes absolute obedience. Baptism is the convert's response to the proclaimed "word of the *Lord*" (1:25), by which he "tastes that the *Lord* is kind" (2:3). For these and other reasons, many interpreters of First Peter have concluded that this document is either wholly or in part taken from a baptismal sermon addressed to new converts.[4] But Christian confession and baptism belong to the groundwork, or presuppositions, of the author's argument, not to its substance. Peter is more interested in the ways in which the pledge of good faith is tested in daily life, and especially in the crisis of persecution. He addresses himself to a spiritual community at odds with a culture that threatens Christian integrity in numerous and subtle ways. Always there is the lingering fear that ridicule and slander will give way to blood and fire and the prospect of martyrdom. In this situation Peter's goal is more than simply the preservation of peace or even the saving of Christian lives, more than that his readers should "hold their own" in hostile surroundings. As the covenant people of God, they have a task to fulfill in the world: to be called to obedience inevitably means to be called to a mission.

3. PRIESTS WITH A MISSION

The command in the Book of Leviticus to the people of Israel to "be holy, for I am holy" (e.g., 11:44), acquires in First Peter a new context and, therefore, a new dimension of meaning (1:15). To most of us, such language suggests some kind of ritual purity or else a moral perfection expressed in withdrawal from the world. Not so to Peter. For him holiness must above all else be manifested in conduct (1:15), in the daily affairs and routine relationships of life. To fulfill their mission, Christians must exhibit a holiness visible even to those who despise the faith.

In the development of this theme, Peter uses to good advantage the Old Testament imagery of temple and priesthood. The doctrinal section in 2:1–10 centers in three Old Testament quotations (vss. 6–8), each containing the word "stone":

Isaiah 28:16—The choice, precious cornerstone.
Psalm 118:22—The stone rejected by the builders.
Isaiah 8:14—The stone of stumbling.

These references appear to be taken from an early collection of Old Testament proof texts, probably arranged topically under the heading

"Stone." The Living Stone, Jesus Christ, is the foundation upon which Christian believers (described as "living stones") are "built up as a spiritual house"* (1 Peter 2:4–5). The image is not of an ordinary house or building but specifically of a temple, a place of worship and sacrifice. Rejected by men, Christ has become the cornerstone of a new temple. His people are built into this temple "for the duties of a holy priesthood, to offer spiritual sacrifices acceptable to God, through Jesus Christ"* (2:5).[5] A few verses later, the Christian community is characterized as a "royal priesthood," while their "spiritual sacrifices" are more clearly defined as "proclaiming the virtues of him who called you out of darkness into his marvelous light"* (2:9). The Old Testament idea of priestly sacrifice has here been reinterpreted in a missionary sense to apply to the church's task of bearing witness to God in the world. Perhaps more than any other New Testament book, First Peter gives us a sense of what it means to live as a Christian in a worldly environment. Here the holy confronts the secular; in fact the holiness of the Christian is itself seen as a secular holiness—not *of* the world but deeply involved *in* the world. Correspondingly, the "royal" or "holy" priesthood is in some sense a secular priesthood.

Peter reasserts the ancient concept that *all* of God's people are priests. In Exodus 19:5–6 God had told the children of Israel: "Now therefore, if you will obey my voice and keep my covenant, you shall be my own possession among all peoples; for all the earth is mine, and you shall be to me a *kingdom of priests and a holy nation.*" Here priests are not a special class of holy men; all Israel is a priesthood by virtue of its obedience to God's covenant. The object of its reconciling activity is "all the earth." A similar self-consciousness is found in the Qumran writings. *The Manual of Discipline* describes the Dead Sea community as:

> . . . the House of holiness for Israel and the Company of infinite holiness for Aaron; they are the witnesses of truth unto judgment and the chosen of Loving-kindness appointed to offer expiation for the earth and to bring down punishment upon the wicked. It is the tried wall, the precious cornerstone; its foundations shall not tremble nor flee from their place. It is the Dwelling of infinite holiness for Aaron in [eternal] Knowledge unto the Covenant of justice and to make offerings of sweet savour . . . (1QS viii. 5–9; cf. ix. 4 f.).[6]

The Dead Sea sectarians realized their calling as priests of God by separating themselves from the mainstream of Jewish life and retreating to the wilderness, there to make reconciliation for man's sin by praising God, studying his law, and practicing righteousness among themselves. Peter, on the contrary, insists that the place where his readers must fulfill their holy priesthood is precisely in the world and in the secular relationships of this life—not in disengagement from Roman society but in constant interaction and conflict with it.

This missionary interest lays the foundation for the "household codes" of human relationships extending from 2:13 to 3:9. Making a play on English words, we might say that the mission expresses itself as *sub*mission—to governments, both imperial and local (2:13-17); slaves to masters (2:18-25); wives to husbands (3:1-6). Christian witness is borne not by hostility or belligerence but by "doing good" (2:14-15, 20; 3:6) even to those who misuse their authority.

At this stage Peter maintains his confidence in the basic justice of Roman magistrates (2:13-14). Even though "foolish men" may bring their accusations, Christians who live as good and decent citizens of the Empire have nothing to fear. The case is different for those who are slaves. Peter knows that not all masters are kind or gentle; many Christian slaves will suffer unjustly at the hands of cruel owners. But here too he counsels submission and "doing good." So too with Christian wives married to pagan husbands. Peter holds out the hope that the pure conduct of the wives will bring the husbands to faith.

Despite the emphasis on subjection to human authority in each of these passages, Peter is no champion of political quietism for its own sake. Nor does he wish to deify the Roman state as the ultimate authority to be obeyed under all circumstances. He is very careful with his vocabulary. Christians are urged to "submit" to society's power structures, not to "obey" them. Peter remembers that he is addressing a covenant people whose exclusive "obedience" is to their Lord (1:2, 14, 22). "Honor" belongs to the emperor, but "fear" only to God (2:17). Should there come a conflict between these two obligations, neither Peter nor his readers could have any doubt as to which had the priority (cf. Acts 5:29). If household servants should have to endure unjust suffering, it is because of their "loyalty to God" (2:19). For them to obey God may sometimes mean to disobey their masters (e.g., if they are asked to prepare or participate in a pagan feast). In such a case submission does not mean obedience, but rather the patient and humble endurance of punishments inflicted for disobedience. This is what he means by "suffering for doing good" (2:20); this is what he enforces by appeal to the sufferings of Jesus Christ (2:21-25). Though opposing militancy and rebellion, he refuses to leave the door open for any compromise of basic convictions. Priests of God must bear their witness with simplicity and humility, yet boldly and without fear.

4. THE FIERY TRIAL

For the most part, the tone throughout the section from 2:13 to 3:9 is optimistic. Though there are enemies of the church in Roman society, the state itself is no enemy to those who live as worthy citizens. Peter sums up the matter by asking, "Now who is there to harm you if you are zealous for what is right?" (3:13). At the same time he is aware that the situation can change very quickly. What if the state should suddenly become the enemy? What if outright persecution should fall to the Christian's lot? He faces this possibility in the latter half of chapter 3: "But even if it should turn out that you suffer for righteousness' sake, you are blessed"* (vs. 14). In such circumstances there is no room for compromise or fear of men any more than for angry retaliation. Peter's counsel is to "keep good faith" (3:16) with the God of their covenant and to remember that baptismal day when they confessed "Jesus Christ is Lord." Only in this way can they withstand the cross-examinations of hostile magistrates in the local civil courts (3:15; cf. Mark 13:9–11).

The grounds of their confidence shall be that very hope about which they are questioned, a hope that transcends their earthly involvement and points to a heavenly inheritance (cf. 1 Peter 1:4). The theme of 3:13 to 4:6 is that of trust in the power of God to vindicate his people in spite of all that man might do to harm them. A persecuted church can look forward to a turning of the tables, a reversal of circumstances: those who harass and interrogate Christians before the tribunals of men (3:15) will themselves be called to account before the tribunal of God himself (4:5). Peter calls his readers to look beyond the first tribunal, realizing the ultimacy of the second. He sees for the church's priestly mission a twofold result: (1) for those who have their eyes opened by the good conduct of Christians, the privilege of glorifying God on the final day of visitation (2:12), but (2) for those who persist in their slander and blasphemy, only a dreadful expectation of being "put to shame" before the bar of God's justice (3:16; 4:5). Better to suffer as a Christian now than as an evildoer on that day (3:17).[7]

The theme of vindication is illustrated by the experience of Christ himself, who was put to death by men in the flesh but justified by God in the Spirit (3:18). So it will be for those who have believed the gospel and armed themselves with the same disposition that their Lord had (4:1).

Though judged by men's standards in the flesh, they shall forever live the life of God in the Spirit (4:6).

This same idea governs the obscure passage about the "spirits in prison" and Noah's flood in 3:19–22. Like most Christians and Jews of his time, Peter perceived evil angels or spirits behind the iniquity that long ago brought God's judgment upon the world in the form of a flood (cf. Gen. 6:1–4). As the evil race was destroyed, so the evil angels were imprisoned (cf. 2 Peter 2:4; Jude 6). Peter regards them as representative of all the forces of evil everywhere, including those behind the slanderers of Christianity in his own day. At the time of his resurrection Jesus had proclaimed God's final victory over these powers of darkness. Angels and all supernatural authorities were made subject to him (1 Peter 3:19–20, 22). Like Noah and his family in the ark, the Christian community, small though it was, could be saved "through water" by holding fast to its baptismal pledge of good faith toward God. Thus despite his confidence that violent persecution will not befall the church, Peter prepares his readers for the worst by directing their ultimate hopes away from the benevolence of the Roman state and toward the God who raised up Jesus Christ.

It has often been noticed that at 4:12 the tone of this epistle changes sharply. Peter begins to speak openly of a "fiery trial" no longer as a remote possibility but now as a grim and immediate prospect. Christians are about to face reproach and actual suffering for the name of Christ (4:14, 16). "The time has come for judgment to begin from the house of God"* (4:17). In chapter 5 he calls upon his readers to "be sober, be watchful. Your adversary the devil prowls around like a roaring lion, seeking some one to devour. Resist him, firm in your faith, knowing that the same experience of suffering is required of your brotherhood throughout the world" (5:8). If 1:1 to 4:11 represents Peter's word to the churches in a setting of *possible* or impending persecution, 4:12 to 5:14 may be understood as a postscript hastily written in the light either of news that Peter had just received or of developments in his own city.[8]

The occasion for adding the postscript may have been specifically the outbreak in Rome of the Neronian persecution in which, tradition tells us, Peter met his death.[9] Peter's assumption is that the bloodbath that had just begun in Rome would quickly spread to the provinces of Asia Minor. But the abrupt break does not come entirely without warning. The "fiery trial" is not utterly "strange" or surprising (4:12), but simply the next step in a developing situation. Even the grammar reflects the fact that the theoretical possibilities of chapter 3 have become the fearful realities of chapter 4: instead of, "If perchance you *should* have to suffer"* (3:14), or, "If it *should* be God's will"* (3:17), Peter now says, "Assuming you *are* being reproached"* (4:14), *"are* suffering as Christians"* (4:16).

Precisely at this point doubts have been raised concerning the traditional Neronian date and the apostolic authorship of First Peter. As late as A.D. 111, it is urged, Pliny the Younger, Roman governor of Bithynia (cf. 1 Peter 1:1), was uncertain as to whether the mere profession of Christianity was to be punished, or only the crimes he believed to be associated with it. Therefore, the experience of suffering for the name of Christ (i.e., facing as a formal accusation the sheer fact of being a Christian) can hardly be earlier than the reign of Trajan.[10] This argument for a late date, however, does not stand. When Peter warns his readers not to suffer as murderers or thieves (4:15), his point is not that it is wrong to be *charged* with these crimes, but rather that one must make sure not to be *guilty* of them. Similarly, to "suffer as a Christian" does not mean that the official *charge* was profession of Christianity. The charge might still be a trumped-up allegation of some crime against society. Suffering as a Christian is simply suffering because one really *is* a Christian and, therefore, hated by many elements in Roman society. This situation corresponds perfectly with that of Nero's day. The wholesale slaughter of Christians could not be justified solely on the grounds that these people worshiped Jesus Christ; only when the blame for the great fire was laid to their account did Nero feel free to carry out his carnival of violence (see above, pp. 251–253).

It is unnecessary to assume that Peter's fears for his readers were literally realized at the very time he wrote. There is no evidence that Nero's persecution did in fact spread to Asia Minor. The lasting value of the latter portion of the epistle lies in the way in which it has spoken to a martyr church in many times and places. When Satan shows his power, the controlling imperative is no longer "submit," but "resist him, firm in your faith" (5:8–9). Yet whether the ultimate conflict is imminent or only impending, the Christian's posture must always be to "stand fast" in the grace of God (5:12).

5. THE AUTHOR AND HIS COMPANIONS

The conclusion of this letter as well as its beginning stamps it as the work of the Apostle Peter. Our last glimpse of Peter in the Book of Acts shows him as one of the pillars of the church at Jerusalem (15:7–11; cf. also Gal. 2:9). In Antioch he becomes involved in controversy with Paul over Gentile freedom (Gal. 2:11 ff.). Though he had partisans at Corinth

(1 Cor. 1:9), it is not certain that he ever visited that city, but we can surmise that he traveled extensively and that he carried out a mission to the Jews (cf. 1 Cor. 9:5; Gal. 2:7 ff.). Since in First Peter (5:13), as in the Book of Revelation, Babylon appears to be a code word for Rome, we may conclude that the apostle's travels finally brought him to that city. The reference to "my son Mark" undergirds the church's tradition that the author of the earliest Gospel was Peter's companion in Rome during the last days of the apostle's life (5:13; see above, p. 253). The scribe who penned the epistle at Peter's direction is said to be Silvanus (5:12). It is noteworthy that both Mark and Silvanus (or Silas) were also companions of the apostle Paul (cf. 1 Thess. 1:1; 2 Thess. 1:1; Acts 15:40 ff.; 2 Tim. 4:11). Their influence, as well as possible direct contact between the two great apostles in Rome, may be responsible for the distinctly Pauline elements often noticed in First Peter—e.g., the similarity between the opening of First Peter and that of Ephesians, the centrality of the cross, the use of household codes, and the image of the church as a building. Those who deny Petrine authorship frequently attribute this letter to some disciple of Paul, but the relative absence of so many Pauline concepts (justification by faith, freedom from the law, life in the Spirit) makes this unlikely. On the contrary, certain characteristic emphases in First Peter (the covenant of obedience, the church as a missionary priesthood, Christ's proclamation to the imprisoned spirits) stamp this document as the work of an essentially independent witness to the Christian message.

The fact that Peter's primary concern had been the mission to Judaism gives this letter to Gentile churches some of its distinctive character. Though Peter had come a long way since his vacillation on Gentile freedom at Antioch, he did not become simply a Paulinist. In distinction from Paul, he addresses the Gentiles not so much as a radically new community (e.g., as the body of Christ), but rather as a people incorporated into Israel, living in solid continuity with the ancient people of God, with her covenant, her priesthood, her holy calling. More than anywhere else in the New Testament, the Christian church is depicted in bold strokes as the "Israel of God." Thus, despite its brevity, First Peter makes a fresh and vital contribution to biblical theology.

NOTES

1. Matt. 16:18. For the view that the rock is Peter himself, not just his confession of faith, see Oscar Cullmann, *Peter: Disciple, Apostle, and Martyr* (1962).

2. Matt. 16:19. The Hebrew and Aramaic equivalents of "binding" and "loosing" are words that mean "forbid" and "allow," respectively. In Matt. 18:18 the promise, "Whatever you bind on earth shall be bound in heaven, and whatever you loose on earth shall be loosed in heaven," is repeated in a context that suggests forgiveness of sins is in view, but notice that here the promise is given to *all the disciples,* not just to Peter.

3. The translation of this phrase is much debated, but see Bo Reicke in the *Anchor Bible,* Vol. 37 (1964), p. 106: "pledge of good will to God."

4. For a review of literature on this subject, see F. W. Beare, *The First Epistle of Peter,* 2d rev. ed. (1961), pp. 196–202.

5. This translation follows Beare, *ibid.,* p. 92.

6. For this translation see A. Dupont-Sommer, *The Essene Writings from Qumran* (Meridian Books, 1962), pp. 91, 93.

7. See J. R. Michaels, "Eschatology in I Peter iii. 17," *New Testament Studies,* 13 (1966/67), pp. 394–401.

8. Chapter 4:7–11 bears the marks of an intended conclusion to the letter: these verses constitute a series of brief, pointed injunctions ending with a doxology (cf., e.g., 1 Thess. 5:16–18).

9. See, e.g., *I Clement* 5:4; *Acts of Peter* 35 ff.; *Ascension of Isaiah* 4:2 f. For the latter two references see E. Hennecke, *New Testament Apocrypha,* Vol. II (1965), pp. 317 ff., 648.

10. Beare, *op. cit.,* pp. 14, 167. For Pliny's statement, see Pliny's letter to Trajan, *Letters* X, 96, in D. J. Theron, *Evidence of Tradition* (1958), p. 13.

SELECTED READING

Beare, F. W., *The First Epistle of Peter,* 2d ed. Oxford: Blackwell, 1958.

Cranfield, C. E. B., *The First Epistle of Peter.* London: S.C.M., 1950.

Cross, F. L., *I Peter: A Paschal Liturgy.* London: Mowbray, 1954.

Cullmann, O., *Peter: Disciple, Apostle, and Martyr,* 2d ed. London: S.C.M., 1962.

Selwyn, E. G., *The First Epistle of St. Peter,* 2d ed. London: Macmillan, 1947.

Van Unnik, W. C., "The Teaching of Good Works in I Peter," *New Testament Studies,* 1 (1954), pp. 92–110.

XXIII

✳

SECOND PETER AND JUDE—
ROYAL PROMISES

THE document known to the Christian church as the Second Epistle of Peter seems to bear little resemblance to First Peter but exhibits its closest points of similarity with a shorter tract attributed to Jude, the brother of James and of Jesus of Nazareth. Jude and Second Peter share a common task of combating heresy within the church, and the heresies they have in view appear virtually identical to one another. Jude's epistle is almost entirely given to this purpose. His content roughly parallels that of the second chapter of Second Peter, while Peter's first and third chapters develop different but related subjects.

1. TWO DISPUTED LETTERS

Perhaps because of this limited scope, but also largely because of critical problems surrounding them, Second Peter and Jude are two of the most neglected writings in the New Testament. The fourth-century church historian Eusebius listed them among the disputed books (*antilegomena*).[1] It is surprising that the shorter Jude seems to have been known earlier and more widely than Second Peter. Jude is listed as being accepted in the general church according to the *Muratorian Canon* (*ca.* A.D. 170–190) and was known to Clement of Alexandria about the end of the second century.[2] Second Peter is not mentioned until Origen (early third century),[3] who said, "Peter . . . left behind one acknowledged epistle, and, it may be, a second one; for it is doubted." It is possible, though not certain, that Clement knew Second Peter as well as Jude, for Eusebius tells us that in his brief commentaries Clement did not omit the disputed books, "Jude and the other Catholic Epistles."[4] The publication in 1959 of the *Papyrus*

Bodmer VII–IX (P^{72}) somewhat strengthens the evidence in favor of these two epistles. Coming probably from third-century Egypt, this little ancient book contains First and Second Peter and Jude. This discovery supports the existing evidence from Clement and Origen, and helps to explain why, when the New Testament was translated about this time into Coptic, the language of Egypt, in the third century, Second Peter and Jude were in fact included with all the rest of the general epistles.

Though evidence prior to Origen for Second Peter and prior to the *Muratorian Canon* for Jude is scanty,[5] the next three centuries saw the church's conviction hardening in favor of the authenticity of these two disputed books until, by 400, little doubt remained.

2. THE FAITH ONCE DELIVERED

Jude or Judah, the brother of Jesus, is such an obscure figure in the Gospel narratives (Mark 6:3; Matt. 13:55) that the tract bearing his name would probably not have been attributed to him had he not actually written it. Like James the Righteous, he avoids laying claim to any special relationship to his Lord. In fact his self-introduction to his readers appears to be built upon that of James:

James 1:1—"James, a servant of God and of the Lord Jesus Christ."

Jude 1—"Jude, a servant of Jesus Christ and brother of James."

Jude's claim to authority is based as much upon his relation to James as to Jesus of Nazareth, suggesting that the sphere in which he ministered may have been Jewish Christianity.

Jude's initial purpose—to expound upon the "common salvation" of the "faith once delivered to the saints"—is quickly changed by the necessity to enter into mortal combat with "certain men" who were deceiving the Christian community (vss. 3–4). These heretics were antinomians—that is, they were "against law." Relying on the fact that they had been saved by grace, they freely indulged in all kinds of immorality, thus denying by their lives if not their words the lordship of Jesus Christ (vs. 4).

The remainder of Jude's tract alternates between denunciation of the false teachers ("these," vss. 8, 10, 12, 14, 16, 19) and exhortations to his readers ("you," vss. 5, 17, 20). It can be simply outlined as follows:

1. Three examples of how God   "I desire to remind *you* . . ." (vs. has judged sin in the past   5).
   (vss. 5–7).

2. Description of the heretics and assertion of similar divine judgment upon them (vss. 8–16).	"In like manner *these* also . . ." (vs. 8).
3. A series of admonitions to the readers on how to respond to this threat (vss. 17–23). Doxology to God's protecting power (vss. 24–25).	"But *you*, beloved . . ." (vss. 17, 20).

Noteworthy among Jude's peculiarities is his tendency to appeal to ancient Jewish tradition embodied not only in the Old Testament but in legendary apocryphal writings as well. Side by side with allusions to Israel's judgment in the wilderness (Num. 14), the angels, or "sons of God," that sinned (Gen. 6), Sodom and Gomorrah (Gen. 18), as well as such troublemakers as Cain, Balaam, and Korah, can be found two non-biblical references. Michael the archangel is said to have disputed with Satan over the body of Moses (vs. 9), while to Enoch, seventh from Adam, is attributed a prophecy of God's judgment upon the ungodly (vs. 14). The latter reference is a direct quotation from the late Jewish *Book of Enoch* (60:8), while the former is unidentified.[6] In none of these cases does Jude cite his sources as Scripture. He is not so much interested in deciding which books belong in the Bible as he is in the traditions and "holy history" of Israel's past. Sheer antiquity, with the lessons it teaches, lends authoritative weight to Jude's warnings (cf. vs. 4, "long ago"). Though there is no evidence that he regarded Enoch as part of the Bible, neither does he indicate that he received these traditions at anything but face value. Jude lived in a much less skeptical age than our own. His range of sources was broader than our Old Testament canon, and of the materials at hand he drew freely from those which he believed accurately conveyed the truth of God.

The last few verses of this tract give us a glimpse of what Jude might have done if he had allowed himself a discourse upon the common salvation. They place him much closer to mainstream New Testament thought than we would expect if we had only his denunciations of the heretics. He tells his readers: "Build yourselves up on your most holy faith; pray in the Holy Spirit; keep yourselves in the love of God; wait for the mercy of our Lord Jesus Christ unto eternal life" (vss. 20–21). These positive exhortations remind us that the "strangeness" which we sense in this little Epistle of Jude is largely illusory. Though he spoke to a specific crisis in

Christian life and morals sometime in the latter part of the first century, Jude dealt in the great universals of Christian faith. The exact circumstances of the crisis remain unknown to us, but the seriousness of his appeal indicates that to him the issues at stake were every bit as decisive as Gentile freedom was to the apostle Paul.

3. THE TESTAMENT OF PETER

The authorship and authenticity of Second Peter is open to more doubt than is that of any other New Testament book, including Jude. Among the chief objections to Petrine authorship are the following:

1. Although this letter claims to be written by an apostle, there is less evidence of its early use and acceptance in the church than for any other New Testament writing.
2. The language and style differs from that of First Peter, and includes a number of Greek religious and philosophical terms unlikely to have come from a Galilean fisherman like Peter.
3. A number of details presuppose a date later than the death of Peter (believed to be in the sixties): e.g., at least some of Paul's letters have been collected and possibly regarded as Scripture (3:15–16); the existence of First Peter is known and, critics say, capitalized upon by the author (3:1); the first generation of Christians has passed and the coming (*parousia*) of Christ been long delayed (3:3 ff.).
4. Second Peter is dependent upon Jude and therefore too late to have been written by the apostle.

The vast majority of critics regard these arguments as conclusive. Second Peter is commonly attributed to an unknown second-century author either perpetrating an outright forgery or else sincerely putting down what he thought Peter would write if he were still alive.

The problems raised by criticism cannot be considered apart from an interpretive question. What precisely is Second Peter?

In form, Second Peter is a *testament,* a farewell discourse of one who is about to die. Examples of this form in biblical and apocryphal literature are abundant: there is the farewell of Jacob in Genesis 49 and of Moses in Deuteronomy 31–33; in the New Testament, Jesus' instructions to his disciples in Matthew 24–25 and in John 14–16 may be regarded as farewell discourses; so may Paul's address in Acts 20:17–38 as he takes leave of the elders of Ephesus, as well as his last letter before his execution, the Second Epistle to Timothy. The usual elements in this form are: (1) a prediction of one's death; (2) reminiscences of the past; (3) predictions of what will happen afterward, generally including "hard times" and widespread apostasy; (4) exhortations to the hearers to stand fast in their faith. All of these elements are present in Second Peter: the apostle foretells his imminent departure (1:13–15), warns against false teachers that will come and bring in destructive heresies (ch. 2 and 3:3–7) and exhorts his readers to remember the promises of God and be diligent in building lives of faithfulness and virtue (e.g., 1:1–12; 3:11–18). An appropriate title for this work, then, would have been "The Testament of Peter."

Obviously the classification of Second Peter under the heading of this literary form says nothing regarding its authenticity. A testament can be a mere artifice, a vehicle by which one clothes his message in words falsely attributed to some famous man of the past. Or it can be the genuine product of that man's last years or days, summing up the most vital concerns of his life. Several considerations help us to make a choice between these two alternatives with regard to Second Peter:

1. Although the author speaks clearly of Peter's approaching death and early tradition states almost unanimously that Peter died as a martyr in the Neronian persecution, there is no development at all of the theme of martyrdom. Christian literature of the second century tended more and more to glorify the martyrs. Their heroism and firm adherence to their confession of Christ in the face of threats, imprisonments, and the most exquisite tortures the Roman mind could devise served as vivid and moving examples to strengthen the faith of Christians everywhere. About A.D. 100 Clement of Rome could write specifically of Peter's martyrdom: "Let us set before our eyes the good apostles: Peter, who because of unrighteous jealousy suffered not one or two but many trials, and having thus borne witness as a martyr went to the glorious place which was his due" (*I Clement* 5:3–4). In view of this it would be exceedingly strange for a second-century tract pretending to be a testament of Peter to forego all reference to his glorious martyrdom. But this is exactly what Second Peter has done, and essentially what we would expect in a genuine writing of the apostle.

2. The references in Second Peter to Jesus' prediction of Peter's death (1:14) and to the transfiguration (1:16–18) appear to be independent of the Gospel tradition. Although they *could* be explained as allusions to John 21:18 ff. and Mark 9:2–8 respectively, they are just as naturally understood as genuine personal reminiscences. None of the vocabulary of John 21 is carried over into Second Peter, while the wording of the voice

from heaven at the transfiguration does not agree verbally with any one Gospel account. This evidence is adequately explained by the traditional view that Peter remembered these incidents independently of any written account.

3. It is highly unlikely that the mention in 3:1 of the testament as a "second" epistle implies any allusion to First Peter. The author clearly indicates that *both* epistles in view are reminders of apostolic warnings about heresy in the church. This characterization does not at all describe First Peter, which never refers back to the apostles and does not deal with heresy. This passage does not lend credence to the view that Second Peter is taking advantage of First Peter's reputation to bolster its own authority.

4. Although the author of Second Peter calls himself "apostle" (1:1) and refers to Paul as "our beloved brother" (3:15), he does not model his apostolic claim upon that of First Peter. His use of the Jewish designation Symeon Peter (1:1) is hard to explain as a later fiction; it is a rare form, occurring elsewhere in the New Testament only on the lips of James (Acts 15:14). It seems far more akin to the usage of the primitive Jerusalem community than to that of a second-century "ghost writer" falsifying an apostle's testament.

These considerations support the idea that Second Peter is a real testament, not an artificial one. Most of its content is perfectly credible as early tradition, oriented primarily to the apostle's own lifetime. The more one studies Second Peter, the more it appears that the case against authenticity has been overstated and has tended to build up and solidify over the years without any new evidence. The cautious and sober criticisms of one generation[7] become the negative dogmas of another.

In spite of this there are some hints within the writing itself that Peter's testament has not a single but a double time perspective. Precisely in the section in which the author indicates that his work is a testament he makes two parallel statements:

a. "I think it right, *as long as I am in this body,* to arouse you by way of reminder . . ." (1:13).

b. "And I will see to it that *after my departure* you may be able *at any time* to recall these things" (1:15).

The contrast between Peter's lifetime and the period after his death is striking. The possibility has been raised that the future provision in 1:15 may refer to the Gospel of Mark or to some other document that Peter intended to write later and never did.[8] But since Second Peter is the only testament of the great apostle that we possess, it is just possible that it embodies within itself both stages of the work of bringing to remembrance —"as long as I am in this body," and "after my departure . . . at any time." This seeming paradox could be explained if Second Peter were regarded as a compendium or anthology of genuine Petrine material put together in testamentary form by one or more of the apostle's followers after his death. The relation of Second Peter to the historical Peter would then be somewhat analogous to the relation between the Gospel writers and Jesus, who promised that after his death the Holy Spirit would bring to their remembrance the things he had taught them (John 14:26). Such an approach would recognize some truth in the critical assertion that Second Peter brings the apostle's authority to bear upon certain problems that became more acute after his death.

Posthumous publication in Peter's name does not necessarily imply any intent to deceive. If the tradition behind Second Peter is genuinely Petrine, then the only kind of compiler of the material who might be guilty of deception would be one who presumptuously signed *his own* name to the apostle's teaching. This testament, however, frankly calls itself a "second" or "secondary" epistle (3:1), a designation that perhaps glances back not at First Peter or at a lost epistle but precisely at the traditional Petrine teachings out of which Second Peter is built. In any case the text goes on to urge the readers to "remember the predictions of the holy prophets and the commandment of the Lord and Savior through your apostles" to the effect that "scoffers shall come in the last days" (3:3–4). It must be admitted that such language is more appropriately understood as citing Peter and his fellow apostles in retrospect than as coming from Peter's own hand.

Thus the compendium theory attempts to do justice both to those elements that seem to come from Peter himself and to those that suggest a later viewpoint.

4. THE THREE WORLDS

The message of this short tract is a distinctive one, largely because of a theology of history that is in some ways unique among New Testament writings. An element in chapter 2 that distinguishes Second Peter from Jude is the use of Noah and Lot as illustrations of God's concern to deliver his people in time of judgment (2:5–9). Here can be seen Peter's awareness of a principle that Jesus himself had stated: "As it was in the days of Noah, so will it be in the days of the Son of man" (Luke 17:26 f.; Matt. 24:37 ff.), and "likewise, as it was in the days of Lot . . ." (Luke

17:28 f.). Like Noah and Lot, Christians live in an age of corruption and a world ripe for judgment. Negatively they are characterized as those who have fled or escaped (2 Peter 1:4; 2:18, 20). Positively they are those who have received "very great and precious promises" that they might one day "become partakers of the divine nature" (1:4) as they enter the "eternal kingdom," (1:11), the "new heavens and a new earth in which righteousness dwells" (3:13).

History, according to Second Peter, is divided into three ages or "worlds," as follows:

"the ancient world" (2:5)	"the present heavens and earth" (3:7)	"the eternal kingdom" (1:11)
"the world that then was" (3:6)		"the new heavens and new earth" (3:13)

The two dividing lines are Noah's flood and the *parousia,* or "coming of the day of God" (3:12), respectively. Noah in his day was a "herald of righteousness" (2:5), even as Christians are heralds of a new world "in which righteousness dwells" (3:13). The reference to Noah as one among eight (2:5) may also be intended to designate him as a harbinger of the new world that was to emerge from the waters of universal judgment. As seven was to the early Christians a number of completeness, eight was often used to symbolize a new beginning.[9] As Noah escaped a doomed world and anticipated a new beginning of things, so Christians have fled from a world now grown old and have laid claim to God's mighty promises.[10] They look for a day parallel in its import to the day of Noah's flood, but parallel in kind to the judgment on Lot's city of Sodom, a day when "the heavens will pass away with a loud noise and the elements will be dissolved with fire" (3:10).

A remarkable feature of Second Peter's world-historical outline is its lack of emphasis on the cross-resurrection event as the clearly delineated midpoint of the ages. This has led to grave indictments of Second Peter for suppressing the very core of the Christian message[11] Such criticisms miss the point of what the writer is doing. He divides history by means of outward physical events that change the course of nature rather than by invisible, purely spiritual realities such as redemption or the Holy Spirit. The reason for this is connected with the problem he faces. Mockers were insisting that in spite of its "precious and very great promises," Christianity had brought about no tangible changes in "the way things are." It appeared that all things did indeed continue as they had always been, since

the beginning of creation (3:3 ff.). In Peter's own day this objection must
have been frequently voiced by Jewish objectors to the Christian faith.
The Jewish concept of a messianic age involved a marvelous transformation
of the course of nature—the wolf and the lamb would lie down together
and the desert would blossom like a rose. Christians said the messianic
age had dawned, yet none of these things had happened. Because nothing
had changed since the days of the "fathers" (e.g., Abraham, Isaac, and
Jacob),[12] the Christian claim must be false. Later this argument could have
been taken up by doubters even within the church who wanted to give
up the primitive eschatology and live as in a world that would go on for
ever. For them the "fathers" could well have included first-generation
Christians. But the basic idea of this passage is at least early enough to be
found in an anonymous source quoted as "the Scripture" by Clement of
Rome before A.D. 100 and, therefore, traceable at least as far back as Peter's
time.[13] It is in fact an attitude which always confronts those who cling to
the Christian promise. Whether one says "all things remain the same,"
or "God effects no changes in the world," or even "God is dead," the net
result is much the same—the eternal promises of God become empty, and
hope vanishes. In answer to such a threat, most of the New Testament
writers appeal to the experience of faith. Second Peter appeals instead to
God's *visible* acts in the world, the flood and the coming universal holocaust.

There is one event, however, in Jesus' life that does receive special attention in Second Peter. Instead of the cross or resurrection, it is a related
event, the transfiguration. This was Peter's proof that God's promises are
not "cleverly devised myths" (1:16 ff.). It was no isolated bit of play-
acting but a genuine enthronement. Critics have urged that the phrase in
2 Peter 1:18, "the holy mountain," expresses a veneration of sacred sites
and ways that is foreign to the New Testament and that stamps this epistle
as a late document. But since the words of the heavenly voice have been
largely shaped by the great messianic Psalm 2 ("You are my son, today
I have begotten you," vs. 7), it is far more likely that Peter is alluding
to the royal decree of Psalm 2:6, "I have set my king on Zion, my holy
mountain."* He writes as one who has seen Jesus enthroned in royal power
before his very eyes. The transfiguration, with all its majestic splendor,
provides a foretaste of the second advent, the *parousia* that is yet to come.
It also serves to illustrate the great privilege held out to those whom God
calls—e.g., "his divine power" (1:3), participation in the "divine nature"
(1:4), and "entrance into the eternal kingdom" (1:11). Though mocker

might not be convinced by this, nor by the example of the flood, nor by Peter's firm reassertion of the final judgment, still Christian would be encouraged to continue to lay hold of God's promises by faith. Their calling is not merely to wait but to fill up the time of God's longsuffering by raising upon their faith a whole ladder of virtues, eight in all (1:5–7), culminating in love (*agapē*). Along with the grim warning of chapter 2, these virtues make up the real substance of Peter's testament; they are his positive legacy to the church. Again and again he repeats that "these things" are essential (1:8, 9, 10 f., 12, 15). Thus, for all of its emphasis on God's visible might and on world catastrophe by water and fire, for all of its orientation toward a particular crisis of faith and morals, Second Peter, like First Peter, still anchors itself in the common salvation. Its focus is on the knowledge of God and of Jesus Christ, on God's call, his gifts, his glory and virtue (1:3). Superimposed on the distinctive "three worlds" outline is the common Christian pattern that does center on God's act in Jesus Christ, the cleansing of the former sins (1:9) and the revelation of the divine glory (1:16 ff.). Regardless of the particular date of its final composition, Second Peter belongs not on the fringe of the New Testament canon but close to the very center.

5. HERESIES OF DESTRUCTION

The question remains: Who were the heretics described in Jude and Second Peter? Opponents of Petrine authorship usually hold that Second Peter was written long after Jude and was dependent upon the shorter epistle. Defenders have correspondingly felt compelled to insist that Peter's work was prior and that Jude abstracted from it. Insufficient attention has been given to a third possibility—that both of these tracts depend upon a common source, an anti-heresy tract of apostolic origin, perhaps from the hand of Peter himself. Both Jude 17–18 and 2 Peter 3:2 suggest that something of this kind has taken place. Such a theory would explain why in some places Jude and in other places Second Peter gives the clearer impression of being original.[14]

If both epistles depend on such a source, there is no need to suppose that they are greatly separated in time or that the situations they faced were essentially different. They agree in describing their heretical opponents in the following ways:

1. These false teachers are advocates of immorality, and are themselves immoral (2 Peter 2:2, 13 f., 19; Jude 4, 8).

2. They put forth boastful and extravagant claims (2 Peter 2:18; Jude 16).
3. They are greedy for gain (2 Peter 2:14 f.; Jude 16).
4. They blaspheme angelic beings (2 Peter 2:10 ff.; Jude 8 ff.).
5. They are doomed to destruction (2 Peter 2:1, 3, 9, 12; Jude 11, 13 f.).

Little is said of specific doctrinal deviation except (in Peter) denial of Christ's return. The heretics' denial of "the Master who bought them" (2 Peter 2:1) probably refers more to their conduct than to their words. Jude accuses them of "perverting God's grace into sexual license"* (vs. 4). Their watchword was freedom from law or regulation of any kind, but this "freedom" served only as an excuse to satisfy their own lusts. Thus they became "slaves of corruption" (2 Peter 2:19).

We know that in the first and second centuries there were a number of Gnostic groups that broadly corresponded to this description. But can we go any further than this toward identifying Peter and Jude's antagonists? In the church's later tradition the father of all heresies was believed to be Simon Magus, the sorcerer mentioned in Acts 8 who unsuccessfully tried to buy the gift of the Holy Spirit. We meet Simon only briefly in the Lucan account. He comes into contact first with Philip and then with Peter. The apostle speaks to him a word of condemnation, and Simon, apparently well chastened, says, "Pray for me to the Lord, that nothing of what you have said may come upon me" (Acts 8:24). Whether Simon repented or continued in his evil way we never learn from the New Testament. Later tradition, however, adorned the figure of Simon Magus with a wealth of legend. In the second- and third-century narrative cycles found in the *Acts of Peter* and the Pseudo-Clementine *Recognitions* and *Homilies*, he becomes Peter's constant foe, both in philosophical debate and in contests of miraculous power—and, of course, the apostle always wins. Simon Magus meets his death as an indirect result of a fall induced by Peter's superior magical power when Simon tries to fly (*Acts of Peter* 32)!

Fantastic as these legends are, they do hint at some kind of traditional connection between Peter and the sorcerer Simon. It is instructive to compare the heretics of Second Peter and Jude with certain things that are said about Simon Magus:[15]

1. *Immorality.* There is nothing of this in Acts 8, but Irenaeus, whose late-second-century account is more or less free of legendary features,

speaks of the "profligate lives" of Simon's followers and of how "as being free, they live as they please; for men are saved through grace . . ." (*Adv. Haer.* I, xxiii, 3 f.).

2. *Extravagant claims.* According to Acts 8:9–10, Simon "amazed the nation of Samaria, saying that he himself was somebody great" so that people said he was "that power of God which is called Great."

3. *Greed.* Acts 8:18 ff. tells us that Simon's guilt involved money, as he tried to gain spiritual power by bribery (thus giving his name to the practice of simony).

4. *Blasphemy of angels.* Irenaeus says that, according to Simon, ". . . since the angels ruled the world ill because each one of them coveted the principal power for themselves, he [Simon] had come to amend matters. . . ." By means of laws and precepts, the angels are those who have "sought to bring men into bondage" (*Adv. Haer.* I, xxiii, 3).

5. *Doomed to destruction.* This element so prominent in Peter and Jude also stands out in Acts 8, where Peters says, "May you and your money go to destruction"* (vs. 20), and, "I see [i.e., foresee] you in the gall of bitterness and the bond of iniquity"* (vs. 23).

This comparison raises the interesting possibility that Second Peter and Jude may have been written against an early type of Simonian Gnosticism. When we think of Peter combating heresies, we cannot help but think of Simon Magus, especially when a number of features of the heresies do coincide. Yet if Second Peter were a late forgery, it is hard to see how the forger could have missed an opportunity to speak of Simon directly, as so much of the Pseudo-Petrine literature does. An anti-heretical tract would have been the perfect vehicle for such reflection. If on the other hand we are dealing with essentially genuine material, the parallels are natural. If Simonian Gnosticism was, an many believe, the earliest heretical Christian Gnosis, and if Jude and Second Peter are first-century documents, then this could well have been the threat they faced. Though there is little likelihood that Peter really had any continuing contact with Simon Magus himself, as the legends say, he could have had considerable contact with false teachers who (legitimately or not) claimed Simon as their founder. This, along with Acts 8, would then be the nucleus of fact that underlies the later apocryphal traditions.

Problems obviously remain. There is, for example, no necessary connection between Simon Magus and the scoffers who denied the eschatological hope. Irenaeus, in fact, says that Simon himself looked forward to the dissolution of the world.[16] But traditions can easily become modified or confused even within a few decades. In any case, it is at least within the bounds of plausibility that Second Peter and Jude may have a common base in an early anti-heretical tract drawn up by the apostles, perhaps a specifically anti-Simonian tract by Peter himself.

6. CONCLUSION

When all has been said, it is clear that the case for a traditional view of authorship is by no means so weak as some critics assume. Still, there remain several considerations that should give pause to the traditionalist:

1. Although First and Second Peter have some common features, the very distinctiveness of Second Peter's theology of history sets it somewhat apart from the First Epistle.
2. The language and style of Second Peter are very different from those of First Peter and of New Testament language generally. Greek terms of popular philosophy and examples of almost overexalted rhetoric are present in abundance.[17]
3. There are, as we have seen, some passages which seem oriented to a time after Peter's death.
4. Most important, it is hard to understand why, if Second Peter came from the apostle's own hand, it was so slow to become known and received in the church. But if essentially authentic material was put together after Peter's death and published in his name, this fact would be more easily explained.

For these reasons, it is wise for those who would defend the authenticity of this testament of Peter not to close themselves up to just one possible theory of how the material took shape. The door should be left open to the view that Second Peter *may* represent a compendium of important features of Peter's teaching compiled posthumously as a testament in accordance with his own wishes as expressed in 2 Peter 1:15. The epistle might then be regarded as virtually an extension of Peter's personality into the increasingly complex problems of Christian faith and life in the generation that followed him.

In any case, justice must be done to the most pertinent fact of all: The Christian church did eventually overcome its doubts and accept Second

Peter into the canon. Thus it expressed its confidence that the substance of this brief tract was the work of "Symeon Peter, servant and apostle of Jesus Christ."

NOTES

1. *Hist. Eccl.,* III, xxv, 3.

2. *Ibid.,* VI, xiv, 1.

3. *Ibid.,* VI, xxv, 8.

4. *Ibid.,* VI, xiv, 1.

5. There are a few questionable literary allusions in such writings as the *Apocalypse of Peter* (*ca.* 125–150), Justin Martyr's *Dialogue with Trypho* (*ca.* 150–160), and the *Letter of the Churches of Lyons and Vienne* (*ca.* 177).

6. Clement of Alexandria said that it came from an apocryphal *Assumption of Moses,* but the incident is not found in the existing document of that name. See Clement's fragmentary comments in *The Ante-Nicene Fathers* (ed. A. Roberts and J. Donaldson, 1896), Vol. II, p. 573.

7. E.g., F. H. Chase in Hastings' *Dictionary of the Bible,* Vol. III (1908), pp. 796–818, and J. B. Mayor, *The Epistle of St. Jude and the Second Epistle of St. Peter* (1907).

8. Mayor, *ibid.,* pp. cxlii ff., 102 f.

9. The so-called *Letter of Barnabas* in the second century speaks of the Christian Sunday in opposition to the Jewish Sabbath as "the beginning of an eighth day, that is the beginning of another world" (15:8). The early apologist Justin Martyr relates this idea to Noah and his family, who, "being eight in number, were a symbol of the eighth day, wherein Christ appeared when he rose from the dead . . ." (*Dialogue with Trypho,* § 138).

10. The comparison between Christian experience and the experience of Noah is the most striking of the features that First and Second Peter have in common. The similarities extend even to the use of the number eight and the mention of God's longsuffering (cf. 1 Peter 3:19–22).

11. See, e.g., E. Käsemann, "An Apologia for Primitive Christian Eschatology," *Essays on New Testament Themes* (1964), pp. 169–95.

12. In the New Testament, "the fathers" generally refers to Old Testament saints (e.g., Rom. 9:5; Heb. 1:1). It is the fathers who have received the promise (Acts 13:32), and yet the fathers also who, even in ancient days, rejected the coming of the Righteous One (Acts 7:15 f.).

13. *I Clement* 23:3 f.; the same citation is given in a second-century sermon falsely attributed to Clement (*II Clement* 11:2 f.).

14. Cf. B. Reicke, *Anchor Bible,* Vol. 37 (1964), pp. 189 f.

15. For some of these parallels, see Mayor, *op. cit.,* pp. clxxviii f.

16. *Adv. Haer.,* I, xxiii, 3.
17. Cf. Reicke, *op. cit.,* pp. 146 f.

SELECTED READING

Chase, F. H., "Second Epistle of Peter," in *A Dictionary of the Bible,* J. Hastings, ed., Vol. III. New York: Scribner's, 1908. Pp. 796–818.

Foerster, W., "Peter, Second Epistle of," in *Dictionary of the Bible,* J. Hastings, ed., rev. ed. by F. C. Grant and H. H. Rowley. New York: Charles Scribner's Sons, 1963. Pp. 757–59.

Green, E. M. B., *2 Peter Reconsidered.* London: Tyndale, 1961.

Mayor, J. B., *The Epistle of St. Jude and the Second Epistle of St. Peter.* London: Macmillan, 1907. (Reprint, 1965.)

Robson, E. I., *Studies in the Second Epistle of St. Peter.* Cambridge: University Press, 1915.

Wand, J. W. C., *The General Epistles of St. Peter and St. Jude.* London: Methuen, 1934.

Warfield, B. B., "The Authority and Canonicity of Second Peter," *Southern Presbyterian Review,* 33 (1882), pp. 45–75.

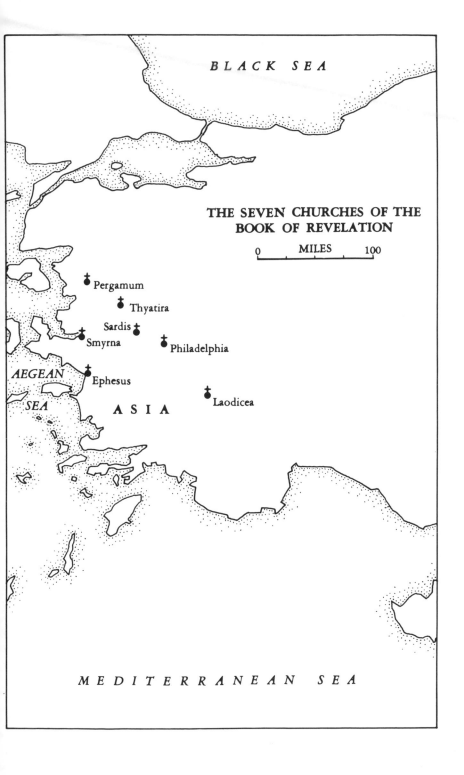

THE SEVEN CHURCHES OF THE
BOOK OF REVELATION

0   MILES   100

BLACK SEA

Pergamum

Thyatira

Sardis

Smyrna

Philadelphia

AEGEAN

Ephesus

SEA

ASIA

Laodicea

MEDITERRANEAN SEA

XXV

✳

REVELATION—THE NEW PROPHECY

TO MOST people, the last book of the Bible is also the most difficult and obscure. The modern reader who has schooled himself to think along with the other New Testament writers is scarcely prepared for what he finds in the Revelation of John. Although this book introduces itself as an apocalypse (1:1), or unveiling of truth, and draws to a close with a command: "Do not seal up the words of the prophecy of this book" (22:10), for the churchman and the unchurched alike it is today largely a closed book. It is hidden from us by vivid, almost fantastic imagery and symbols far more ancient than the book itself—heavenly letters, angels, trumpets, bowls of wrath, nameless beasts from the pit, demonic locusts and horses, fire from the sky . Therefore, in a practical sense many people have a New Testament of twenty-six books that ignores the troublesome Apocalypse.

Others, however, have mixed feelings; repelled by Revelation's strangeness, at the same time they are drawn to it with an absorbing fascination. When they look at the book more closely, it imposes itself upon them as the very word of God, asking to be understood: its source is God himself through Jesus Christ (1:1); its words are "trustworthy and true" (21:5; 22:6); those who read and obey are pronounced happy (1:3), while curses and eternal loss are reserved for those who add to or detract from the completed prophecy (22:18–19). At certain points (13:18; 17:9), the reader is challenged to use his God-given wisdom to interpret correctly the symbolism of this book. All of these things make it essential for the student sooner or later to address himself to this last word from God in the canon of the New Testament.

1. APOCALYPSE OR PROPHECY?

The author of Revelation calls himself John. Exiled from his home in Asia Minor on the lonely Mediterranean island of Patmos, he writes to seven mainland churches that he has known and loved, encouraging them and relating to them a series of visions of "the things that must come to pass." By calling his book "the Revelation of Jesus Christ" (1:1), John designates Jesus as the true author of what is written. John is merely a servant; he belongs to that group known in the Old Testament as God's "servants the prophets" (22:9; cf. Amos 3:7).

In the Old Testament the task of the prophets had been to declare the "word of the Lord."[1] These men were preachers who laid no claim to having composed their own sermons. Their only words were the words that God had given them. Such human ideals as genius, originality, or creativity were far from their thinking. Paradoxically, their claim to authority lay precisely in their passivity and humility toward God. Because their words were not theirs but God's they commanded a hearing. The Old Testament ideal of the prophet is clearly stated in Deuteronomy 18:18–20, where God tells Moses, his first prophet:

> I will raise up for them a prophet like you from among their brethren; and I will put my words in his mouth, and he shall speak to them all that I command him. And whoever will not give heed to my words which he shall speak in my name, I myself will require it of him. But the prophet who presumes to speak a word in my name which I have not commanded him to speak, or who speaks in the name of other gods, that same prophet shall die.

After Malachi the skies were silent for four hundred years. No one was sure that he had a new word from God, until in Luke 3:2 the classic formula of prophetic inspiration reappeared: "the word of God came to John the son of Zechariah in the wilderness." Jesus also bore the unmistakable marks of the prophet, and it was by his resurrection that the prophetic gift came in an unprecedented way upon the whole community of believers (Acts 2:17 f.). That the New Testament is characterized by a fresh outburst of prophetic activity is seen in Acts and Paul and the fourth Gospel,[2] but nowhere more clearly than in the Book of Revelation. Here the author's political exile is "because of the word of God and the witness of Jesus"* (1:9; cf. 1:2). "The word of God" is, of course, the familiar stamp of a prophet; but "the witness of Jesus" is something new. It is the specific form that the word of God takes now that Jesus has come. Jesus Christ, risen from the dead, is both the source and the object of Christian prophecy. Near the end of his visions John is told by an angel that "the witness of Jesus is the spirit of prophecy"* (19:10).

It is, therefore, a misnomer to speak of the Book of Revelation as "the Apocalypse" as if it were merely a Christian equivalent to Jewish apocalypses such as *Enoch*, *Fourth Ezra*, or the *Assumption of Moses*. Apocalyptic is a well-known and identifiable literary genre that flourished in Israel from Maccabean times until the final defeat of Bar Kokhba in A.D. 135. As a rule these revelations about the future or about the structure of heaven were not signed by their true authors but were fictitiously attributed to some great man of Israel's past. This method may have been adopted because of the common idea that prophecy had ceased—no one would believe that the author had a word from God if he wrote in his own name. Accordingly, an ancient patriarch or prophet became the vehicle of the revelation. Whether there was any intent to deceive we do not know. But such were the features that constituted the "rules of the game." Often the pretended ancient author was one who according to legend had had some unique experience with God that allowed him to escape death (e.g., Enoch, Moses, Elijah). In any case the patriarch or at least the spirit of his teaching was regarded as in some sense "alive," so that he could speak to a day far distant from his own. This outlook stands in marked contrast to that of the Book of Revelation, where the source of the message is no ancient patriarch but Jesus Christ, the center of every Christian's faith. Jesus' encounter with God was no unverified legend from a remote age. It was a comparatively recent event; his resurrection from the dead was the heart and core of Christian preaching. Jesus was indeed alive, as he told John: "Fear not, I am the first and the last, and the living one; I died, and behold I am alive for evermore" (Rev. 1:18). Therefore, the author does not need to hide behind a false name to enhance his own authority—not even the name of Jesus; though he professes to write only what Jesus reveals, he freely lets his identity be known. He is simply John, a prophet, one of the servants of God.[3] His book is not an "apocalypse" in the technical sense but a "prophecy" (1:3; 22:7, 10, 18, 19).

2. LORD OF THE CHURCH

Because this book is a prophecy, the one who really speaks is Jesus Christ, but his primary theme is not himself. Just as in the Gospels, Jesus speaks of God the Father and the coming of God's Kingdom— "the things that must come to pass." Still, in revealing the shape of present and future, he inevitably reveals himself as well. To see him as the prophet did, we must shift our thinking from the categories of formal theology to those of worship. Several of the most meaningful portraits of Christ in this book are found within formulas of praise and adoration.

To appreciate Revelation's lyrical presentation of Christ, we should understand that it is not only a prophecy; it is also a letter. Like the letters of Paul it begins with a salutation (1:4–6) and ends with the words: "The grace of the Lord Jesus be with all"* (22:21). Just as Paul weaves into his correspondence a number of doxologies and hymns of praise, John expresses in poetic form the response of men and angels to God's acts in Jesus Christ. But because of the dramatic, pictorial character of his book, John is able to go further than Paul in this respect. Right at the outset, instead of Paul's standard greeting, "Grace to you and peace from God our Father and the Lord Jesus Christ," John expresses his faith in the Trinity with a remarkable formula: "Grace to you and peace from him who is and who was and who is to come, and from the seven spirits that are before his throne,[4] and from Jesus Christ the faithful witness, the first-born of the dead, and the ruler of kings on earth" (1:4–5). Instead of the familiar order—Father, Son, and Holy Spirit—this early Trinitarian statement speaks of Father, Spirit, and Son. Thus it is Jesus who is the climax and the focus of John's interest. He it is who "loves us and has freed us from our sins by his blood and made us a kingdom" (vss. 5–6).

Like Matthew in his Gospel, the prophet John describes Jesus first of all as the Jewish Messiah, the anointed king of David's line. Of this one to come the psalmist had written:

He shall cry to me, "Thou art my Father, my God, and the Rock of my salvation." And I will make him the *firstborn,* the *ruler of the kings of the earth.* . . . Once for all I have sworn by my holiness; I will not lie to David. His line shall endure forever, his throne as long as the sun before me. Like the moon it shall be established forever; the *witness* in the skies is *faithful*"* (89:26–27, 35–37).

The italicized words are the ones picked up in John's salutation (Rev. 1:5), fulfilled in a new and deeper sense that goes beyond the Old Testament expectation. Jesus is firstborn now specifically "of the dead" by virtue of his resurrection. The later chapters of Revelation tell in detail how Jesus comes to be acknowledged as world ruler, "the King of kings and Lord of lords" (cf. Rev. 17:14; 19:16). And for John, the "faithful witness" is no longer a sign in heaven like the sun or the moon, but Jesus himself in his earthly life of obedience even to death. The traditional Davidic categories of Jewish expectation are retained, but raised to a higher level of significance and filled with a content that is as wide in scope as the Christian gospel itself—the death, resurrection, and lordship of Jesus the Son of God.

The same thing occurs in chapter five. In the prophet's vision of the throne room of heaven, only one person is found worthy to open the sealed scroll that will introduce the prophecies that are to follow. Of this one John is told:

> "Weep not; lo, the Lion of the tribe of Judah, the Root of David, has conquered, so that he can open the scroll and its seven seals." And between the throne and the four living creatures and among the elders, I saw a Lamb standing, as though it had been slain, with seven horns and with seven eyes, which are the seven spirits of God sent out into all the earth (vss. 5–6).

In this dramatic scene, "the Lion of Judah, the Root of David" has been combined with the slain Lamb of sacrifice[5] and at the same time given a place of divine majesty equaled only by that of God himself.

A survey of four hymns of praise found in chapters 4 and 5 shows that this phenomenon is part of a larger and carefully worked-out pattern. The first of these occurs in 4:10–11, where John sees twenty-four heavenly beings or "elders" prostrate themselves before "the one seated upon the throne" and cast their crowns before him saying:

> *Worthy art thou,* our Lord and God,
> *to receive* glory and honor and power,
> *because* thou hast created all things,
> and on account of thy will they were created.*

The second hymn is found in 5:9–10. The Messiah from David's line has been introduced as the slain Lamb and has taken the scroll with the seven seals. The elders and four other "living creatures" of heaven sing of him:

> *Worthy art thou*
> *to receive* the book and to open its seals,
> *because* thou wast slain and hast redeemed men to God by thy blood
> from every tribe and tongue and people and nation,
> and hast made thee unto our God and kingdom and priests,
> and they shall reign upon the earth.*

The key words, "Worthy art thou . . . to receive . . . because," bind the two hymns together, while the verbs "created" in 4:11 and "redeemed" in 5:9 sum up the distinctive emphasis of each. The first hymn is a hymn of creation to God the Father, while the second hymn is a hymn of redemption to Jesus the Messiah.

In 5:11–12, "the voice of many angels" combines some features of each of these first two hymns to produce a third:

Worthy is the Lamb who was slain,
to receive power and wealth and wisdom and might and honor and glory and
  blessing.

Again it is the Lamb that is worshiped, but what he "receives" is now
more than the sealed scroll. To him are ascribed the very predicates (glory,
honor, and power) which in 4:11 were reserved for God himself. Indeed
the list has more than doubled in length. God and the Lamb are the
recipients of precisely the same kind of homage from the heavenly court.

This equality between God and Christ reaches a crescendo in the fourth
and last hymn, a paean of praise from "every creature in heaven and on
earth and under the earth and in the sea, even all things that are in them"*
(5:13):

To him who sits upon the throne
and to the Lamb
be blessing and honor and glory and might for ever and ever.

Thus, using the vocabulary of worship rather than of speculative thought,
the Book of Revelation has succeeded in elevating the familiar Davidic
Messiah to the level of deity.

The call of the prophet in chapter 1 takes the form of a visible encounter
with the glorified Christ. To express what he has seen, John momentarily
sets aside the Davidic categories in favor of a more transcendent picture.
With the visions of the prophet Daniel in mind, he speaks of:

. . . one like a son of man, clothed with a long robe and with a golden girdle
round his breast; his head and his hair were white as white wool, white as
snow; his eyes were like a flame of fire, his feet were like burnished bronze,
refined as in a furnace, and his voice was like the sound of many waters; in
his right hand he held seven stars, from his mouth issued a sharp two-edged
sword, and his face was like the sun shining in full strength (vss. 13–16).

Not Jesus of the Galilean hills, but the almighty Lord of earth and sea and
sky confronts the awestruck prophet. And yet it is the same Jesus as he
stands in the midst of seven golden lampstands, symbolic of the seven
churches of Asia Minor.

The details of the vision are picked up individually in chapters 2 and 3
to identify Christ as the speaker in the seven letters (e.g., "the one who
holds the seven stars," "the first and the last," "the one who has the
sharp sword"). He functions as a kind of divine attorney—now an advocate for defense and encouragement of believers, now a prosecutor

bringing reproof and warning of God's wrath. Though the circumstances of each church vary, all the letters have five of the same features in common:

1. Christ's self-identification ("Thus says . . .").
2. His sketch of the church's situation in the world ("I know . . .").
3. An imperative to the church ("remember . . . repent . . . be faithful," etc.).
4. A promise to the faithful Christian ("To him that conquers . . .").
5. A final appeal ("He that has ears to hear, let him hear").

The threats to these churches are twofold: (1) from outside, the encroachments of Roman society, and (2) from within, false teaching and coldness of heart.

A. THE EXTERNAL THREAT

Early Christian tradition dates the Book of Revelation near the end of the reign of the emperor Domitian (A.D. 81–96), and makes of Domitian a cruel oppressor, a mass destroyer of Christians, comparable only to Nero. There is no reason to question the date, but early evidence is lacking for any general religious persecution during Domitian's reign. Though the emperor was a violent man, his violence was directed not against Christians or any other group but against carefully selected individuals whom he suspected of undermining his authority. Among his victims were his cousin Flavius Clemens and Clemens' wife, Flavia Domitilla, who were executed on charges of "atheism" (i.e., disloyalty to the Roman gods).[6] But other Christians, such as the grandchildren of Jude and brother of Jesus, escaped unharmed when Domitian found that they were without wealth or power.[7]

This helps to explain the surprising lack of references to open persecution in the seven letters. Though the church at Pergamos dwells "where Satan has his throne" and has known the death of a martyr (2:13), the very fact that one martyrdom can be singled out suggests that this is not yet a common experience. At Smyrna and Philadelphia, endurance through trial is a prominent theme, but the trials in view are impending rather than present. Certain forces, however, were already at work in maneuvering the church and imperial society toward a collision course. Non-Christian Jews, for example, eager to strengthen their own precarious position in the cities of Asia Minor, were bringing to the civil magistrates false accusations against Christians (2:9; 3:9 f.). Many scholars think that Domitian introduced some kind of compulsory emperor worship, making life virtually unbearable for the Christians. Evidence for such a policy is scanty, though emperor worship may have been instituted in some cities on a purely local basis. In any case it is well to remember the prophetic character of John's book. Its descriptions of the ultimate conflict of good and evil, and its call to endurance and martyrdom, are not sober recitals of historical reality but visions of the future—an eschatological future alien in many ways to the history that John knew. The state of "the things that are" (1:19) is a sign to the prophet—but no more than a sign—that the great crisis is on its way. It is this sign that we can read for ourselves in the seven letters.

B. THE INTERNAL THREAT

The real pressure of Roman culture upon the churches did not take the form of direct persecution. Rather, it exerted itself as a subtle inducement to Christians to modify their exclusiveness by accommodating their moral and religious principles to those of the society at large. Corresponding to this external pressure was a movement from within the churches to make things easier all around by means of certain concessions. At Ephesus, Pergamos, Thyatira, and possibly elsewhere were the so-called Nicolaitans, who, like Balaam or Jezebel in ancient Israel, taught God's people to "eat food sacrificed to idols . . . and to practice sexual immorality"* (Acts 15:28–29; cf. vs. 20). The Jews believed that such rules as these antedated the Mosaic law and originated with Noah.[8] They were for all men, not for Israel alone, and Gentile Christians could be no exception. It was these Noachian commandments that the Nicolaitans rejected, not necessarily out of sheer apostasy or lust, but out of a desire to be accepted in Roman society. The kind of "freedom" they urged would have allowed Christians to participate in pagan feasts and in the quasi-religious activities of the urban trade guilds, and so to enter more fully into the mainstream of their culture.

This attitude, whatever its motivation, is roundly condemned in the seven letters. If the provincial government could be called "Satan's throne" (2:13), if hostile Jews were "a synagogue of Satan" (2:9; 3:9), the things that these professed Christians taught deserved to be known as "the deep things of Satan" (2:24). On the other hand, John knew that even those who successfully warded off these temptations could still slip into a callous lack of love (Ephesus, 2:4), or a spiritual lethargy (Sardis, 3:1–2), or lukewarmness (Laodicea, 3:15 ff.). All of these attitudes stand under the fearful judgment of the "one like a Son of man." To those ruled by them Jesus will come "and remove your lampstand from its place" (2:5), or make "war . . . with the sword of my mouth" (2:16); he will "come like a thief, and you will not know at what hour I will come upon you" (3:3). He is Lord of the church, but those who by their conduct put themselves outside the church will find that he is also Lord of the world, that he bears the sword and rules with a rod of iron. The final words of the seven letters show, however, that he longs to come first in mercy to a repentant people: "Behold, I stand at the door and knock; if any one hears my voice and opens the door, I will come in to him and eat with him, and he with me" (3:20). Those who receive him as he comes thus in grace have nothing to fear when, at the end of all the visions, he comes in judgment:

> Then I saw heaven opened, and behold, a white horse! He who sat upon it is called Faithful and True, and in righteousness he judges and makes war. . . . He is clad in a robe dipped in blood, and the name by which he is called is The Word of God. . . . From his mouth issues a sharp sword with which to smite the nations, and he will rule them with a rod of iron; he will tread the wine press of the fury of the wrath of God the Almighty. On his robe and on his thigh he has a name inscribed, King of kings and Lord of lords (19: 11–16).

Spread out between these two vivid images of the coming one we have the heart and core of the Book or Revelation: there Jesus reveals himself not only as Lord of the church but as Lord of history; there he unfolds to the prophet "the things that must soon come to pass."

3. THE LORD OF HISTORY

The whole Book of Revelation is a prophecy—or in another sense a letter—written and sent to all of the seven churches. What is said to each church is said to them all. Moreover, the visions of chapters 4 to 22 are also a prophetic message to the churches. The seven letters are really open-ended or incomplete in themselves. The issues they raise are solved only in the remainder of the prophecy, with its ringing demonstration that God is victorious in history. Their sevenfold character is mirrored in three more series of seven—the seven seals (6:1–17; 8:1), the seven trumpets (8:2–9:21; 11:14–19), and the seven bowls (16:1–21).

A major question is whether these sequences are to be regarded as parallel descriptions of the same course of events or as following chronologically one after the other. The breaking of the seven seals is the work of Jesus the Messiah on the basis of the victory won in his death and resurrection (5:5 f.; cf. 3:21). As each seal is broken, a brief scene of meaningful events, a vignette of what is going on in the world, passes before the prophet's eyes:

First Seal: A rider on a white horse, *"conquering* and to conquer."
Second Seal: A rider on a red horse, bringing *war.*
Third Seal: A rider on a black horse, bringing *famine.*
Fourth Seal: A rider on a pale horse, bringing death by *pestilence.*
Fifth Seal: At the foot of the altar the souls of those slain "for the word of God and for the witness they had borne," crying, "O Sovereign Lord . . . how long before thou wilt judge and avenge our blood. . . ."
Sixth Seal: A great earthquake, the darkening of the sun and falling of the stars, the great day of the wrath of God and the Lamb.
Seventh Seal: "Silence in heaven for about half an hour."

One should not too hastily assume that these scenes represent the *content* of the sealed scroll. Although we are dealing with a vision, we must assume that its details are patterned after reality. If the scroll is sealed in a normal fashion, it cannot, of course, be opened until *all* of the seals are broken. Therefore, the seven seals cannot represent the content of the scroll, but rather preliminary events, the things that must take place *before* the scroll is opened. This suggests that the content of the scroll is the *Kingdom of God,* the eternal inheritance of the saints. Those who have suggested that the scroll is a last will and testament are probably not far from the truth. By his death Jesus has made the will possible and at the same time become its executor. Normally a will would consist of two parts—a description of the inheritance and a list of the heirs. Just such a document seems to be the image employed in several passages that speak of a scroll or book of life. For example, "I will not blot his name out of the book of life" (3:5); "every one whose name has not been written in the slain Lamb's book of life"* (13:8; cf. 17:8); "those who are written in the Lamb's book of life" (21:27). If the Lamb's scroll of chapters 5 and 6 is identified with the Lamb's scroll of life, then its content is not revealed until the final judgment upon all men, when "books were opened [and] another book was opened, which is the book of life" (20:12), and "if anyone was not found written in the book of life, he was cast into the lake of fire"* (20:15).

Thus the seven seals are essentially *preliminary signs,* characteristic events that must take place before the Kingdom comes: Christ's victory in his first coming, but then war, famine, and pestilence. To a church facing the prospect of suffering these images convey a strong word of consolation. Christians can take heart, knowing that when fearful things happen to them God is not taken by surprise. On the contrary, these hardships are intrinsic parts of his redemptive plan, necessary precursors of his final victory. Every seal that is opened brings the Kingdom a step closer. At most they are *signs of the end,* not the end itself. As Jesus had told his disciples on the Mount of Olives, "Do not be alarmed; this must take place, but the end is not yet" (Mark 13:7). Here a caution must be observed. These signs do not form a chronological sequence of datable happenings that can be ticked off one by one so as to enable the curious to predict the future. The first five at least have always been with us; they characterize John's age and our own. The point of the opening of the seals is simply to demonstrate Christ's sovereignty over them. The prophetic viewpoint allows us to see them in the widest possible scope, to get the "big picture." From this perspective they are Christ's deeds; they belong to his timetable, not ours.

The sixth seal is different. It tallies with nothing that we have experienced, only with what we can imagine. We have no categories for the stars falling or the sky rolling up like a scroll. This is no part of our past or present; it can only belong to the future. Here the focus moves beyond the events of this age to those catastrophic signs that immediately precede the advent, or *parousia,* of Jesus Christ as he comes to rule the world (cf. Mark 13:26–27). With the seventh seal, we expect the book to be opened and the Kingdom to be revealed, but here the prophet (and the reader!) is kept in suspense; he is greeted with nondisclosure—"silence in heaven for about half an hour" (8:1). Not until much later in the prophecy is the silence broken by God's triumphant Word (19:13). In the meantime, the reader is taken over the ground covered by the vision of the seals again and again. He is allowed "close-ups" of various details and is able to examine the significant events and themes from many angles. Slowly and indirectly, the veil is drawn aside, revealing not the chronological sequence, not the names and dates, but more important than these the awesome, glorious reality, the shape of God's future.

The trumpets and the bowls cannot be simply paralleled with the seals nor is it likely that they represent something wholly subsequent to them. They are perhaps best understood as a close-up of the sixth seal. Like the latter, they do not belong to the world we know, but to the consummation, the world to come, seen not as blessing but as judgment. Here the imagery of Revelation is at its most extravagant and fantastic. Even when all due allowance is made for the extensive use of symbols, it remains true that the reality symbolized is beyond present human understanding or experience. It is here a matter of eschatological judgment, of the wrath of God, not the petty quarrels of man.

Certain signals are used to inform the reader when this climactic period of wrath is in view. These are chiefly drawn from the Old Testament account of the manifestation of God's power on Mount Sinai just prior to the giving of the law:

> On the morning of the third day there were *thunders and lightnings,* and a thick cloud upon the mountain, and a very loud *trumpet blast.* . . . And Mount Sinai was wrapped in smoke, because the Lord descended upon it in *fire;* and the smoke of it went up like the smoke of a kiln, and the whole mountain *quaked greatly* (Exod. 19:16–18).

John's first use of this imagery connects it with the heavenly throne room, with the overwhelming and immediate presence of God:

> From the throne issued flashes of lightning, and voices and peals of thunder (Rev. 4:5).

This sets the tone for several of the scenes of judgment that are to follow. For example, at the beginning of the seven trumpets,

> there were peals of thunder, loud noises, flashes of lightning, and an earthquake (8:5).

And at the end,

> Then God's temple in heaven was opened . . . and there were flashes of lightning, loud noises, peals of thunder, an earthquake . . . (11:19).

Again, when the seven bowls of wrath have been poured out upon the world,

> there were flashes of lightning, loud noises, peals of thunder, and a great earthquake such as had never been since men were on the earth . . . (16:18).

The image of the earthquake also dominates the prophet's description of the climactic sixth seal (6:12 ff.), while the trumpet blast of Sinai reappears as seven trumpets heralding the divine wrath.

The close correspondence between John's two visions of climactic judgment, the trumpets and the bowls, can best be seen by putting them down in parallel columns. In each case the italicized words show where the similarities lie:

The Seven Trumpets	The Seven Bowls
1. Hail and fire, with blood, cast to the *earth*. A third of the earth is burned (8:7).	1. Poured out upon the *earth*—evil boils appeared on men who had the beast's mark (16:2).
2. A mountain of fire is cast into the *sea*. A third of the sea is turned to *blood* (8:8–9).	2. Poured out upon the *sea*—it became *blood,* and all life died (16:3).
3. A burning star called Wormwood falls on a third of the *rivers and wells of water* (8:10–11).	3. Poured out upon *rivers and wells of water*—they became blood because men shed the blood of saints and prophets (16:4–7).
4. A third of the *sun, moon, and stars* are darkened (8:12).	4. Poured out upon the *sun*—it burned men, but they did not repent or give glory to God (16:8–9).
5. A demonic locust plague. The sun was *darkened.* Locusts were given authority to injure men as from the sting of scorpions (9:1–12).	5. The kingdom of the beast was *darkened*—although in great pain, men blasphemed the God of heaven and did not repent of their works (16:10–11).
6. Loosing of angels at the *great river Euphrates.* An army of two hundred million horses with tails like serpents with power to kill men. Men did not repent (9:13–21).	6. The *great river Euphrates* was made bitter. A way was opened for the kings of the east. Froglike spirits gathered all kings to the great war of Armageddon (16:12–16).
7. "The kingdom of the world has become the kingdom of our Lord and of his Christ" (11:14–19).	7. "It is done." The final judgment upon Babylon, with giant hailstones. Yet men still blasphemed God (16:17–21).

Two main points emerge from this outline. First, regarding the *imagery:* an awareness of the biblical origin of most of John's language reduces the element of strangeness and helps the reader to understand what is being said. Most of these judgments are reminiscent of the plagues of the Exodus, by which the Egyptian Pharaoh was "persuaded" to give the Israelites their freedom (Exod. 7–12). The waters turn to blood; the sun is darkened; there are hail and fire from heaven, ugly boils upon men, and evil forces comparable to locusts and frogs. In Revelation, the bowls are even referred to specifically as "the seven last plagues" (15:1).

This analogy between God's eschatological judgment on human history and the deliverance of Israel from Egypt shows that through all of the "blood and thunder" the purpose of God continues always to be a saving purpose. John prefaces his chapter on the seven bowls with a picture of the triumphant people of God, "singing the song of Moses, the servant of God, and the song of the Lamb, saying:

> Great and wonderful are thy deeds,
> O Lord God the Almighty!
> Just and true are thy ways,
> O King of the ages!
> Who shall not fear and glorify thy name, O Lord?
> For thou alone are holy.
> All nations shall come and worship thee,
> for thy judgments have been revealed" (Rev. 15:2–4; cf. Exod. 14 and 15).

As in the Exodus, the plagues come as God's reply to the prayers of his suffering people crying out for vindication against their persecutors (cf. Exod. 2:24 f.). Just before the sixth seal, the persecuted saints cry, "How long before thou wilt judge and avenge our blood on those who dwell upon the earth?" (6:10). And when the trumpets begin to sound, it is in response to the "prayers of the saints" (8:4 ff.). The burden of John's prophecy is that Christians will suffer, even as he himself, "for the word of God and the witness of Jesus," but that God will redeem his people; he will put them in the right, as he has always done, and overthrow their tormentors.

Second, an *intensification* or progression in the judgments can be seen. The first four of each group of plagues show God's sovereignty over all the realms of his creation—earth and sky, sea and fresh water. At another point in the prophecy, a heavenly messenger heralds this eschatological time with an "eternal gospel" (14:6–7):

> Fear God and give him glory,
> for the hour of his judgment has come;
> and worship him who made the *sky* and the *earth,* and *seas* and *wells of water.**

But like Pharaoh of old, the unbelieving world hardens its heart and refuses to believe this message or to repent even at the most conclusive proofs of God's infinite might (9:20 f.; 16:9, 11). Under the last three trumpets, the plagues are intensified so as to strike directly at man himself (8:13). The seven bowls, while describing the same sequence of events, exhibit this greater intensity from the very beginning,[9] yet like the trumpets build up in their own sequence to increasingly terrible scenes of judgment.

The seventh trumpet and the seventh bowl, like the seventh seal, bring us to the ultimate completion of God's purposes in history. But now instead of "silence in heaven," there is at least a hint of the fuller disclosure that is to come later. The fact of consummation as positive triumph, not merely as judgment, comes to expression in the resounding cry of 11:15: "The kingdom of the world has become the kingdom of our Lord and of his Christ," and more briefly in the voice from God's temple in 16:17, saying, "It is done!"

4. THE TWO CITIES

The activity of Jesus Christ as Lord of the church and his activity as Lord of history cannot be divorced from one another. By the time Revelation was written the church had become a distinct historical entity; it could not retreat from history, nor could it avoid direct confrontation with secular institutions. Therefore, the church is inevitably caught up in the maelstrom of conflict and judgment that lies at the heart of this book. With the Psalmist the prophet would ask, "Why do the nations conspire, and the peoples plot in vain?" (Ps. 2:1). With other New Testament writers he would answer that behind the political forces that threaten Christian existence are supernatural forces of elemental evil. Behind the church's struggle against civic and religious cults in the cities of Asia Minor is an eternal warfare between light and darkness, God and Satan.

This becomes abundantly clear in chapter twelve. John sees in heaven a great sign: a woman clothed with the sun, with the moon under her feet, brings forth a male child who is to "rule the nations with a rod of iron." A dragon cast out of heaven attempts to devour the child, but the child is caught up to God's throne while the woman is kept safe in the wilderness. The main thrust of this passage is clear, even though some of the details are puzzling. The child is Jesus of Nazareth, the Messiah of the line of David (cf. Ps. 2:9); the woman is an idealized picture of Zion, the nation of Israel, from which Jesus had come;[10] the dragon is identified as Satan, "the ancient serpent" of Genesis 3. Revelation 12 is virtually a commentary on God's primal curse against the serpent: "I will put enmity between you and the woman, and between your seed and her seed; he shall bruise your head, and you shall bruise his heel" (Gen. 3:15). The "seed" of the woman, however, is plural as well as singular. Failing to destroy either the Messiah or the woman, the dragon goes off "to make war on the rest of her seed, on those who keep the commandments of God and have the witness of Jesus"* (Rev. 12:17). Though defeated by Jesus Christ, Satan continues the ancient struggle by turning his evil genius against the Christian church.

Carrying out his ungodly purpose, the dragon spawns a beast that comes out of the sea (13:1). The beast deceives the human race into worshiping him and the dragon, and he undertakes persecution and bloodshed against the Christian community which refuses to do so. It is quite apparent that here we are dealing no more with a supernatural entity but with a historical one. John leaves with the readers—and with the Roman authorities in Asia Minor—a riddle: to the beast is assigned a number, "the number of a man,"* six hundred and sixty-six (13:18).

This number has challenged the ingenuity of the curious ever since John's day. There may never be full agreement as to its interpretation, but it is helpful to remember that in the ancient world numerical values were assigned to letters of the alphabet. Thus every personal name had a corresponding number: the total of the numerical value of the letters that composed it. Among the many names that can be made to equal 666 is one that on other grounds is somewhat plausible—Nero Caesar, written with the letters of the Hebrew alphabet. If this is the answer, then all that is being said is that the "beast" will be a tyrant after the fashion of Nero, the terrible persecutor of the church. The inquisitions, the bloodbath, the lighting of human torches in the emperor's garden—these were still fresh in the minds of Christians a generation after Nero himself had passed from the scene. How could the prophet have given a better impression of the awful conflict to come than by analogy with Nero? Moreover, some superstitious Romans believed in the legend of Nero redivivus —i.e., that although he had committed suicide, he still lived and would return with hordes of Persians to conquer Rome and regain his crown.[11] Of the beast, John writes, "One of its heads seemed to have a mortal wound, but its mortal wound was healed" (13:3). In one sense the beast appears to be the Roman Empire, but in another sense its prime manifestation is this "wounded head," a particular king that shall deceive the nations and terrorize the church. This king, says John, will be a "second Nero," apparently more ruthless and terrible than the first. In the seventeenth chapter, John becomes more explicit as he speaks of a series of seven

Roman emperors, "five of whom have fallen, one is, the other has not yet come, and when he comes he must remain only a little while. As for the beast . . . it is an eighth *but it belongs to the seven*" (17:10–11). Again he alludes to Nero redivivus.

The other major characteristic of the beast is that he is a kind of counterfeit or hideous parody of God and of Christ. Like the Lamb of chapter 5, he has a mortal wound and is yet alive. Whereas God is "the one who is and who was and who is to come" (1:4, 8), the beast "was, and is not, and is to ascend from the bottomless pit and go to perdition" (17:8). Christian thought commonly uses the term Anti-Christ, which suggests not only one opposed to Christ but also one who takes the place of Christ. In calling him an "eighth" (17:10 f.), John uses a number that elsewhere denotes something beyond perfection (one more than seven), a number of rebirth and new beginnings (see above, p. 353). But the appearance is deceptive: he is actually "one of the seven"; in fact he is 666, three times short of perfection. Contrast John's bit of numerology with that of an anonymous Christian prophecy a century or so later, in which the number of Christ is 888:

> Yea, then shall the Son of the great God come to man,
> clothed in flesh, like unto mortals on earth.
> And now will I declare to thee also the whole number:
> Eight monads, and to these as many decads,
> and eight hundreds also his name will show
> to unbelieving men (*Sibylline Oracles* I, 326 ff.).

Thus the complexities of Revelation 13 and 17 make a very simple point: The "beast," the coming world ruler, will be a new Nero and at the same time a false Christ, a cheap imitation of God's anointed. Thus, whoever this Anti-Christ may turn out to be, he is known by his character, not by some secret formula. And yet we may still take to heart the words of 1 John 2:18: "Many antichrists have come," and of 2 Thessalonians 2:7: "The mystery of lawlessness is already at work." The satanic element in history is not confined to the very end. Misguided as their procedures may have been, those who saw the beast of Revelation in the tyrants of their own day were only partially wrong.

The twin elements of church and state seem to be an inevitable part of world history, so it is not surprising when in Revelation 13:11–17 we meet a second beast "with two horns like a lamb" that compels the world to worship the first beast. If the first beast is a political authority, the second is a religious one. Elsewhere he is called the "false prophet" (16:13; 19:20; 20:10). The material for this picture seems to come from the emperor cult which may have been already in existence in John's day; though it had not yet forced a showdown with the Christian claim that Jesus was Lord and God, the prophet foresaw that some day it would. "Satan's throne" was at Pergamos, and soon every believer would have to decide: Christ—or Caesar?

Later in the prophecy John introduces a woman allied with the beast, a prostitute seated upon seven hills (17:9), whose name is "Babylon the great, mother of harlots and of earth's abominations" (17:5). The woman represents a city built on seven hills, the city of Rome, the new Babylon, oppressor of the people of God (17:18). It is Rome that exalts herself in armed rebellion against God (ch. 16); it is Rome that goes down to defeat and destruction at the hands of the victorious Christ (18:10).

Against this city is arrayed another—Jerusalem, the city of God. The suffering Christians are vindicated as Christ appears, riding upon a white horse and striking the nations with the sharp sword of his word. The enemies are punished in the reverse order of their appearance upon the scene—first the city itself (16:19; 17:16–18:24); then the two beasts (19:17–21); finally the dragon, the source of all the evil (20:1–10). Then Jerusalem is disclosed in her splendor as God's dwelling place, as the "beloved city" (20:9) where Christ and his people are said to reign for a thousand years (20:4–6) and where at last, in a new world, God's will is perfectly done (21:1–8).

Two cities—Jerusalem and Rome, the place of light and the dwelling of darkness—are the twin focal points of the prophecy. They are most easily seen in poetic contrast by comparing chapters 17 and 18 with 21:9–22:5. The introductions of these visions are strikingly similar, as shown by the italics:

17:1 ff.—*Then one of the seven angels who had the seven bowls came and said to me, "Come, I will show you* the judgment of the great harlot. . . ." *And he carried me away in the Spirit* into a wilderness, and I saw a woman sitting on a scarlet beast . . . [she] was arrayed in purple and scarlet, and bedecked with gold and jewels and pearls. . . .

21:9 ff.—*Then one of the seven angels who had the seven bowls* full of the seven last plagues *came and spoke to me, saying, "Come, I will show you* the Bride, the wife of the Lamb." *And he carried me away in the Spirit* to a great, high mountain, and showed me the holy city Jerusalem, coming down out of

heaven from God, having the glory of God, its radiance like a most rare jewel,
like a jasper, clear as crystal.*

Each of the cities is portrayed as a woman: one a prostitute, the other a
pure bride adorned for her husband. Each is seen in retrospect: John is
allowed to look back, as it were, from God's eternal perspective to see
the transient splendor that was Rome contrasted with the glory of God
and of the Lamb shining in the holy city of Jerusalem.

The extended description of Jerusalem in 21:9–22:5 seems to take up
and develop in detail the reference in 20:1–10 to the thousand-year reign
of Christ on earth and the "beloved city." Though the language is almost
totally symbolic, the setting is recognizably this earth, not what we think
of as "heaven." There is still a world of "the nations" outside the city
(21:24; 22:2), and the city is closed against uncleanness and falsehood.
God is victorious within history as well as beyond history; the reign of
God for a limited period, symbolized by a thousand years, is for the
prophet a kind of "sign" or "model" of the eternal Kingdom. Only in
21:1–8, it seems, does John venture to speak of the eternal state, and here
as elsewhere in the Bible only with great reserve and caution. He tells
little of what the new heaven and earth *is,* mostly what it *is not*—"no
more sea . . . no more death, or sorrow, or mourning, or pain, for the
former things have passed away"* (21:1, 4). The longer, positive description that follows in 21:9–22:5 refers to a historical fulfillment.
God's victory is first manifested on its present battlefield, the world in
which we live.

5. ISRAEL AND THE CHURCH

The history of man's salvation is memorialized in the new Jerusalem
by the names of the twelve tribes of Israel inscribed upon its gates, and the
names of the twelve apostles of the Lamb upon its foundations (21:
12–14). In giving to his readers the "big picture," John will not let them
forget that the people of God are twofold—Israel of the Old Testament
and the Christian church. Like Paul, he knows of a "Jewish problem" and
attempts to answer the question: What will happen to Israel now that
she has rejected her Messiah? At Smyrna and Philadelphia were "those
who say that they are Jews and are not" (2:9; 3:9). They had become
fomenters of persecution against the church. More true than ever were the
words of Isaiah, quoted by the apostle Paul: "All day long I have held out

ny hands to a disobedient and contrary people" (Rom. 10:21; Isa. 65:2).
Paul had concluded that in the end "all Israel will be saved" (Rom.
11:25), and conducted his own mission in this confidence.

In the Book of Revelation, one aspect of the church's witness is to
'Israel according to the flesh." This mission is depicted symbolically in
chapter eleven. For "forty-two months" (i.e., from Jerusalem's destruc-
ion until the coming of Christ), the Gentile nations are to dominate the
holy city (11:2). During this time the Christian church, symbolized by
two prophets like Moses and Elijah, bears its testimony to a paganized
Jerusalem. The "holy city" has become "the great city," a term elsewhere
applied to wicked Babylon (cf 18:21); she is likened to "Sodom and
Egypt," for she is a rebellious city, the place where the Lord was crucified
(11:8). Here Revelation sets forth the ambiguity of the people of God and
exposes the two faces of Jerusalem. The two witnesses are rejected and
killed, and their bodies left on the streets of the city. Even in Israel, the
power of the beast is supreme. The words that Jesus had uttered decades
before take life again: "O Jerusalem, Jerusalem, killing the prophets and
stoning those who are sent to you! . . . Behold, your house is forsaken
and desolate. For I tell you, you will not see me again, until you say,
Blessed is he who comes in the name of the Lord' " (Matt. 23:37–39).
The episode of the two witnesses ends with the direct intervention of
God. The resurrection of Christians and the coming of Christ are depicted
symbolically as the witnesses come alive, a voice calls them up to heaven,
and the great earthquake introduces the eschatological wrath of God (Rev.
11:11–13). John adds that "a tenth of the city fell . . . and the rest were
terrified and *gave glory to the God of heaven."* This repentance in the
face of divine wrath is unique in the Book of Revelation; in all other
such crises men "did not repent" or "give glory to God" (9:20 f.; 16:9,
11). Only in Israel, paganized as it has become, do men turn again to
their Creator and Redeemer. The faith of the prophets that "a remnant
shall return" and of Paul that "all Israel shall be saved" is maintained
in the Book of Revelation. The new element is that this salvation comes
by God's eschatological act, not by the church's missionary activity. There
is a short-term pessimism here that is covered over by an ultimate optimism.
In raising up a new messianic people, God has not forgotten his ancient
promises to Israel.

Through many students have gone to extremes in discovering throughout chapters 4 to 19 of Revelation always a Jewish remnant and never

the Christian church, our understanding of the book is enhanced if we recognize that the one community of faith does have two historical aspects —Israel as well as the church. This is why in chapters 12 to 13 God protects the woman who brings forth the Messiah no less than "the rest of her seed . . . who keep the commandments of God and bear testimony of Jesus"* (12:17). And it is why in chapter 7 the prophet sees two multitudes of those whom God delivers—not only a "great multitude which no man could number, from every nation" (vs. 9), but also "a hundred and forty-four thousand sealed out of every tribe of the sons of Israel" (vs. 4). The Book of Revelation teaches us that the people of God have a checkered history. They are not always obedient; they become at times secularized so that their face is indistinguishable from that of the world. But God's promises are not made void; his people who by unbelief have become "not-his-people" (cf. Hos. 1:10) are restored in grace to become once more his sons and daughters (Rev. 21:3, 7).

This faithfulness of God, whether to the church or to Israel, undergirds the prophetic demand for a corresponding faithfulness on man's part. The thrust of the whole Book of Revelation may be summed up in the pronouncement, "Here is a call for the endurance and faith of the saints" (13:10; cf. 14:12), or in the command to the church of Smyrna, "Be faithful unto death, and I will give you the crown of life" (2:10). Though the church of Asia Minor in John's day was not yet a martyr church, Revelation is in a way the forerunner of a great body of Christian literature on martyrdom. But unlike some of the later Acts of the martyrs, this book attaches no particular merit to the experience of violent death as such. The Greek word *martyria* simply means witness. The "martyrs" of Revelation do not become martyrs by being slain; they are slain because they are already *martyrs* (i.e., witnesses to Jesus Christ). Those who bear witness in the proper sense are the Christian prophets like John himself, but alongside them are the "saints," the entire community of those who confess the name of Jesus irrespective of the cost.[12]

The Book of Revelation is the great New Testament book of victory. It proclaims the victory of Jesus Christ the Faithful Witness[13] and invites the reader to share in that triumph. The repeated promise of the seven letters: "To him who overcomes . . . ," finds its realization at the end of the book, after all the trials and sufferings, when Christ reigns with his saints as "King of kings and Lord of lords." The cry of an anguished and oppressed community "How long, O Lord . . . do you not judge and avenge our blood?"* (6:10) is answered specifically when "the verdict is handed down in their favor"* (20:4) and they reign for a thousand years. Here indeed is a call to endurance and faithfulness.

NOTES

1. See Jer. 1:2; Ezek. 1:3; Hos. 1:1; Joel 1:1; Jonah 1:1; Mic. 1:1; Zeph. 1:1; Hag. 1:1; Zech. 1:1, Mal. 1:1, etc.

2. See, e.g., Acts 11:27 f.; 13:1 f.; 21:10 f.; 1 Cor. 12 and 14; for John, see the next chapter.

3. Though later tradition identifies this John with the Apostle, the son of Zebedee and author of the fourth Gospel and three epistles, he makes no such claim for himself. He writes with authority not because he has seen Jesus of Nazareth in the flesh or been commissioned by him but because he has seen the Risen Christ and is inspired by the Holy Spirit (1:10; 4:1). The strong prophetic consciousness of the author cannot, however, be used to prove that John was *not* an apostle. Paul, for example, seems to have been both apostle and prophet. Here we shall listen to John on his own terms simply as a Christian prophet much like the prophets of the Old Testament.

4. I.e., the Holy Spirit seen in a sevenfold way as ministering to the seven churches.

5. This connection is not as paradoxical as it may seem to the modern reader. Already in Judaism the conquering Messiah could on occasion be symbolized as a lamb or young ram, powerful to subdue the wild beasts that threatened the flock (*Testament of Benjamin* 19:8; *Enoch* 89:46; 90:9). See C. H. Dodd, *The Interpretation of the Fourth Gospel* (1953), pp. 230–38.

6. See the Roman historian, Dio Cassius, *Hist.* LXVII, 14.

7. Eusebius, *Hist. Eccl.* III, xx.

8. On the Noachian commandments, see W. D. Davies, *Paul and Rabbinic Judaism* (1955), pp. 114–21.

9. Notice that under the first four trumpets one third of creation is affected, while under the bowls no such limitation is made.

10. Cf. Isa. 26:17 f.; 66:7 ff.; in the Qumran Hodajot psalms, 1QH iii. 7 ff.; and in the second-century Christian *Apocalypse of Ezra, IV Ezra* 2:1–40.

11. See the Roman historians Suetonius, *Nero;* Tacitus, *Hist.* I. 2; II. 8–9; Dio Cassius, *Hist.* XLIV, 9; and among Jewish sources the *Sibylline Oracles* IV, 119–24, 137–39; V, 137–54, 361–85.

12. See Rev. 16:6, "the blood of saints and prophets"; 17:6, "the blood of saints and witnesses of Jesus"*; and 18:24, "the blood of prophets and saints."

13. See Rev. 3:21; 5:5; 6:2.

SELECTED READING

Beckwith, I. T., *The Apocalypse of John.* New York: Macmillan, 1922.

Caird, G. B., *The Revelation of St. John the Divine.* New York: Harper and Row, 1966.

Feuillet, A., *The Apocalypse.* Staten Island, N.Y.: Alba House, 1964.

Ramsay, W., *The Letters to the Seven Churches of Asia and Their Place in the Plan of the Apocalypse.* New York: G. H. Doran, 1905. (Reprinted, 1965.)

Rissi, M., *Time and History: A Study on the Revelation.* Richmond: John Knox, 1966.

Tenney, M., *Interpreting Revelation.* Grand Rapids: Eerdmans, 1957.

XXV

�֍

THE GOSPEL AND EPISTLES OF JOHN—
THE WORD AMONG US

T IS fitting that a volume entitled *The New Testament Speaks* should draw to a close with a consideration of the Gospel of John. It is John, more than any other New Testament writer, who presents God as Speaker and Jesus as the one through whom the Father addresses his word to man. Not only is Jesus himself introduced as "the Word" (*logos*) in John's prologue (1:1, 14), but throughout the Gospel he comes speaking not his own words but the words of the Father.[1]

Christian readers in every generation have sensed a remarkably contemporary quality in the words of Jesus as found in the fourth Gospel. Jesus' sayings virtually take wing and soar beyond the particular historical framework in which they stand recorded. They seem to express not what Jesus *said,* but what he *says*—to us, right now. Who can read and quickly forget such declarations as these?

For God so loved the world that he gave his only Son, that whoever believes in him should not perish but have eternal life (3:16).

Truly, truly, I say to you, he who hears my words and believes him who sent me, has eternal life; he does not come into judgment, but has passed from death to life (5:24).

I am the way, and the truth, and the life; no one comes to the Father, but by me (14:6).

Abide in me, and I in you. As the branch cannot bear fruit by itself, unless it abides in the vine, neither can you, unless you abide in me (15:4).

Invitations and promises like these require no long explanations by preachers or scholars in order to effect their purpose. In them the New Testament speaks to us with all of its elemental power and simplicity.

In view of such positive considerations, it seems strange to talk of a Johannine "problem"; yet such a problem undeniably exists. A person who turns from Mark, Matthew, and Luke to the Gospel of John finds himself breathing a very different atmosphere. Nothing is said of Jesus' birth, temptation, or transfiguration. There is no Sermon on the Mount, no teaching in parables, no words of institution of the Lord's Supper. Jesus' baptism and his agony in the garden of Gethsemane are alluded to only indirectly. Instead of one simple movement from Galilee to Jerusalem, the itinerary of John's Gospel takes Jesus back and forth several times between these two focal points of his ministry. Jesus cleanses the temple not in the last week of his life but much earlier, apparently even before the death of John the Baptist. Fewer miracles are told, and many of those that do appear have gone unmentioned in the other Gospels.

Several of the miracles become the occasions for long discourses through which Jesus reveals himself—he heals a lame man and presents himself as the giver of life (ch. 5); as Bread of life he feeds the multitude (ch. 6); giving sight to a blind man he shows that he is the Light of the world and the Good Shepherd (chs. 9–10). In such discourses, Jesus' style of speech is very different from that of the synoptic sayings. Instead of the Kingdom of God, his theme is himself and his relation to the Father. Salvation is almost entirely a present rather than future reality. Short, pithy sayings that give point to a miracle or debate have given way to long, connected dialogues or monologues that ring the changes on several key Johannine themes—eternal life, knowledge, light, truth, all the gifts of God the Father through Jesus the Son.

Anyone approaching the fourth Gospel without a predisposition in its favor may at first be irritated by a repetitiousness, an almost monotonous quality, that characterizes this work. The student who would overcome this impression so as truly to hear John's witness should remember two things: (1) that all the repetitions and refrains in this Gospel contribute to the fullness and depth of expression of the one true word of God; (2) that in John the word of God has a history, a coherent development from the creation of the world through its individual embodiment in the life of Jesus of Nazareth, to its present manifestation in the ministry of the Holy Spirit.

1. THE BEGINNING WORD

The first book of the Old Testament had opened with: "In the beginning God created the heavens and the earth" (Gen. 1:1), and continued

with the refrain: "And God *said* . . . and God *said* . . . and God *said* . . ."
(1:3, 6, 9, etc.). John, believed to have been the last surviving apostle of
Jesus Christ, took up the ancient proclamation again in a new key as the
New Testament era hastened to its conclusion:

> In the beginning was the Word,
> and the Word was with God,
> and the Word was God.
> He was in the beginning with God.
> All things were made through him,
> and apart from him not one thing was made.
> In him was life, and the life was the light of men* (John 1:1–4).

The reader of Mark, Matthew, and Luke who comes to these words will
find this a strange opening indeed for a Gospel. The Gospel form, as we
have encountered it, consists of an extended narrative of the circumstances
of Jesus' death preceded by a concise summary of his ministry and teaching.
The starting point is either his birth or his baptism. Although anticipations
of Jesus' career are sought in the Old Testament, there is no attempt to
project Christian beginnings back to the beginning mentioned in Genesis.
Only John brings together the totality of God's revelation under the
comprehensive heading of "the Word." For him the gospel of Jesus Christ
begins with God's first creative command, "Let there be light."

A survey of the opening sentences of several New Testament books,
however, shows that it is not unusual to refer to the "beginning" of the
word of God. Mark, of course, introduces his account with the phrase "The
beginning of the gospel of Jesus Christ" (1:1). Luke speaks of "those
who *from the beginning* were eyewitnesses and ministers of the *word*"
(1:2). In both cases the beginning stands within the lifetime of Jesus of
Nazareth. Matthew's language is different. In his first verse he mentions
no "beginning," no "word" or "gospel." At the most it might be said
that he assumes as his beginning the Old Testament promise to Abraham
in Genesis 12. The First Epistle of John speaks in a way that is reminiscent of the fourth Gospel, but without specifying clearly how far back
his beginning reaches:

> That which was from the beginning,[2]
> which we have heard, which we have seen with our eyes,
> which we beheld and our hands handled,
> concerning the *word of life* . . .* (1:1).

It is the Epistle to the Hebrews that offers the most fruitful comparison
with the first lines of the prologue of John's Gospel, even though its

similarity rests upon the thought expressed rather than the exact vocabulary used:

> In many and various ways *God spoke* of old to our fathers by the prophets; but in these last days *he has spoken* to us by a *Son,* whom he appointed the heir of all things, through whom also he *created the world* (1:1–2).

The word spoken through Jesus the Son is here closely connected with the "word of the Lord" (*d^ebar Yahweh*) that had come upon the Old Testament prophets, enabling them to prophesy,[3] and by which the heavens had been made (Ps. 33:6).

The word of God was no alien or mysterious concept to the early Christians. It was equivalent to what Paul called "the gospel that I preached to you, which you also received and in which you stand and through which you are saved if you hold it fast"* (1 Cor. 15:1–2). It was the good news that Christ had lived and died among his people, delivering them from their sins, and had been raised from the dead to become Lord of all. At the same time there was an awareness that this new word was in reality a very old word. The apostle Paul could write: "For it is the God who said, 'Let light shine out of darkness,' who has shone in our hearts to give the light of the knowledge of the glory of God in the face of Christ" (2 Cor. 4:6) Whether we think of Jesus' words, or the church's words about Jesus, or God's creative and prophetic words in the Old Testament, it is ultimately the same word of God.

This is why the opening verses of the Gospel of John are not as strange to the world of the New Testament as they may seem at first. Edwyn C Hoskyns, author of one of the great commentaries on John, aptly summed up the truth of the matter when he said, "The workshop in which the Word of God was forged to take its natural place among the great theo logical descriptions of Jesus and His work is a Christian workshop: the tools are Christian tools."[4] Countless efforts have been made to explain John's prologue from the abstract speculations of Greek philosophy or from Hellenistic-Jewish teaching on the divine Wisdom, or from rabbinic legends about the eternal Torah, or from Gnostic mythology with its series of aeons or supernatural powers standing between God and the world None of these sources of extra-biblical knowledge contributes as much to our understanding of John's language as does the parallel material in the New Testament itself.

There is one aspect of the prologue, however, that does seem uniquely Johannine—the *personification* of the word in the man Jesus Christ

Hebrews had come close to this with its statement, "God has spoken to us by a Son," but to say that God's word *is* his Son represents a bold step forward. It is only at the *end* of his prologue that John comes out with the more conventional formulation:

> No man has ever seen God;
> it is God the only Son, ever at the Father's side,
> who has revealed him* (1:18).[5]

Two factors, one in the Old Testament and Judaism, and one in John's own Gospel, help to account for John's startling personification of the word.

a. *The personification of wisdom.* In the Old Testament, the wisdom of God is extolled and sought after as the key to life and fellowship with God. It has given its name to a body of wisdom literature, including Proverbs, Job, Ecclesiastes, and Song of Solomon in the Old Testament, and Sirach and the Wisdom of Solomon in the Apocrypha. The eighth chapter of Proverbs illustrates how wisdom can be personified as a woman:

> Does not wisdom call,
>   does not understanding raise her voice?
> . . . beside the gates in front of the town,
>   at the entrance of the portals she cries aloud:
> "To you, O men, I call,
>   and my cry is to the sons of men.
> O simple ones, learn prudence;
>   O foolish men, pay attention (vss. 1, 3–5).

Later, wisdom describes her role in creation:

> The Lord created me at the beginning of his work,
>   the first of his acts of old.
> Ages ago I was set up,
>   at the first, before the beginning of the earth. . . .
> When he marked out the foundations of the earth,
>   then I was beside him, like a master workman;
> and I was daily his delight,
>   rejoicing before him always,
> rejoicing in his inhabited world,
>   and delighting in the sons of men.
> And now, my sons, listen to me:
>   happy are those who keep my ways. . . .
> For he who finds me finds life
>   and obtains favor from the Lord . . . (vss. 8:22–23, 29–32, 35).

It is easy to see how this cosmic language could have been adopted by the early Christians to express their wonder at Jesus Christ in his unique relation to God the Father. But at most it provides only a point of comparison with John's imagery, not the primary background. As Hebrew poetry had personified God's wisdom in the form of a woman, so John personified God's word as Jesus of Nazareth.

b. *Other personifications in John's Gospel.* More important than the Old Testament wisdom background is John's practice of equating *what Jesus does* with *who he is.* A number of examples will make this clear: Jesus provides bread to feed the multitudes because he *is* the Bread of life that came down from heaven (6:35, 48, 51). He gives light and vision to the man born blind because he *is* the Light of the world (9:4). He raises Lazarus from the dead because he *is* the Resurrection and the Life (11:25). He shows men the way to God and he *is* the Way; he speaks the truth and he *is* the Truth (14:6). All of the mighty works of Jesus are performed by the power of his words, which are the words of God. Hence, behind all these identifications is one which is basic: Jesus *speaks* the word of God as he does because in his own person he *is* the Word of God.

Even though the particular designation Word or *logos* is not applied to Jesus again after the prologue, it governs John's total presentation of Jesus throughout his Gospel. His prologue cannot be severed from the Gospel as something extraneous; it expresses the very heart and core of the Johannine witness. On the one hand, it helps us to understand the fourth Gospel as a whole; on the other hand, it is only when we have read the Gospel through that we can fully appreciate the prologue.

2. THE WORD MADE FLESH

It is conceivable, however, that John has adopted the poetic introduction to his book from an already existing hymn to the *logos*. Pliny the Younger, Roman governor of Bithynia in Asia Minor, wrote to the emperor Trajan about A.D. 111 that Christians "were in the habit of meeting on a certain fixed day before it was light, when they sang in alternate verses a hymn to Christ, as to a god."[6] Though it probably can never be proved, there is an intriguing possibility that all or part of the Johannine prologue is the hymn of which Pliny speaks. In any event, certain stylistic features of the prologue set it somewhat apart from the rest of John's Gospel and give credence to the theory that it once stood by itself as a Christian hymn. Word repetitions carry the thought along from verse to verse in chainlike fashion.

Singling out the key words in several verses, we can set forth a sample pattern as follows:[7]

    1:1—Word . . . Word . . . God . . . God . . . Word

    1:4–5—life . . . life . . . light . . . light . . . darkness . . . darkness

    1:6–8—witness . . . witness . . . light . . . light . . . witness . . . light

    1:11–12—his own . . . his own . . . receive . . . received

This technique lends a certain stately or deliberate quality to the prologue's cadences.

When the word duplications abruptly cease in the middle of verse 12, the effect upon the reader or hearer is a marked speedup in the author's train of thought. Thus the passage moves swiftly to its climax:

> "He gave them authority to become children of God,
> even to them who believe in his name;
> who were born
> not of blood,
> nor of the will of the flesh,
> nor of the will of the male,
> but of God"* (vss. 12b–13).

By the end of verse 13 the gospel story has been told. The ancient beginning at creation and the new beginning when the true Light came are caught up together in a common poetic structure.

Even though the prologue may be based on an early hymn, it has been fully integrated into John's total plan and purpose. Throughout verses 6 to 13 he is clearly looking back on the event of Christ from a point of view after the crucifixion and resurrection. The Light, who is the very Word of God, has come. Men have been making their choice. Some have "believed in his name" and had their lives so radically changed that only the phrase "born of God" can describe their experience. As far back as verse 5, there is good reason to believe that "the light is shining in the darkness"* *now* because of Christ's exaltation, and that "the darkness did not overcome it"* specifically in that historic conflict that reached its climax at Calvary.[8] If this is true, then verse 5 is a general statement of what has happened, while verses 6 to 13 tell how it came about that "the light is shining": first there was John the Baptist, who heralded the light (vss. 6–8); then it is said that "the true light that enlightens every man was coming into the world" (vs. 9); finally the whole Christian revelation is unfolded in a few eloquent words (vss. 10–13). This means that the famed pronouncement of verse 14 is not a startling new insight that brings the reader up short, but a simple resumé of the preceding eight verses. It may be translated, "*So* the Word became flesh and dwelt among us."*

Such evidence from the prologue indicates that the fourth Gospel is written to *Christians*, not to unbelievers. Too much prior knowledge of the Christian message is assumed in John 1:6–14 for these verses to have been addressed to pagans. A classic form of Christian confession was, "Jesus Christ has come in the flesh"* (1 John 4:2; 2 John 7), and in John 1:14 ff. it is the believing community that remembers this central truth: "the Word became flesh and dwelt among *us* . . . *we* have beheld his glory . . . from his fulness have *we all* received." John's purpose is not primarily evangelistic; he is not writing in order to convert unbelievers but, like the other Gospel writers, to deepen the faith of Christians. This is expressed at the close of chapter 20 by a summary statement, paraphrased as follows: ". . . these things are written that you might be strengthened in your conviction that Jesus is the Christ, the Son of God, and that being thus strengthened you may have life in his name"* (vs. 31).[9] Similarly, the point of the prologue is not to start where the pagans are, with a philosophic concept of the *logos*, so as to lead them to the Christian truth that "the *logos* became flesh." It is rather to remind *Christians* that the word of preaching which they have received is an eternal word. Through it God called the world into being and gave life and light to men. Now it has come into our midst, into our history, in the person of Jesus Christ, the Son of God.

Understood in this way, the prologue is not only consistent with the remainder of John's Gospel but provides a key to unlock much of its meaning. As the prologue is written for Christians, so is the Gospel account that follows. As the prologue looks back on "the Word made flesh" from a point of observation after the event, so too does the Gospel of John from beginning to end. Clement of Alexandria called John a "spiritual" Gospel in distinction from the synoptics, which confined themselves to the purely "physical" facts about Jesus.[10] Oversimplified and exaggerated as this opinion may be, there can be no dispute that John's Gospel is highly symbolic in its portrayal of Jesus. Many of its episodes are told not for their own sake, or even as evidences of Jesus' authority; they become "signs" or pointers to eternal, spiritual truth. Statements that seem commonplace in their historical settings take on an added dimension of meaning for those who know Christ as the Risen One. It is assumed that words of Jesus which were enigmas to their original hearers will be understood by the readers of the Gospel. The Christian reader knows, as Nicodemus did not (3:4), how a man "can be born when he is old"—by believing in Jesus and being baptized. He knows, as the Jews did not (6:53), how one can "eat the flesh of the Son of man and drink his blood"—by partaking of the Lord's Supper. He knows that the spring of "living water" that Jesus gives does not come from a well (4:10 ff.). He knows what kind of temple Jesus will raise up (2:20 f.), and why Jesus must "go away" for a time (7:35, 13:33). In short, he is initiated into the mystery of Jesus Christ. The veil over the meaning of Jesus' words and deeds, a veil drawn to some extent in the synoptics, is pulled aside in John to disclose the unique Son of God, the self-revealing Word in all of his fullness. Reading John, we are allowed to behold "his glory, glory as of the only Son from the Father" (1:14).

3. THE PROPHETIC WORD

It is no accident that the fourth Gospel is able to involve its readers so deeply in the drama that it unfolds. Profoundly interested as he is in the life of Jesus, the author has an equally great concern for his own time and world. In some ways it is a very different world from the Palestinian one that Jesus knew, and the difference inevitably affects John's presentation. Therefore, the fourth Gospel, even more than the synoptics, must be viewed from a double time perspective—that of the author and that of Jesus. The evangelist drops several specific hints that his own vantage point is "afterward":

When therefore he was raised from the dead, his disciples remembered that he had said this; and they believed the scripture and the word which Jesus had spoken (2:22).

His disciples did not understand this at first; *but when Jesus was glorified, then they remembered* that this had been written of him and had been done to him (12:16).

He came to Simon Peter; and Peter said to him, "Lord, do you wash my feet?" Jesus answered him, "What I am doing you do not know now, but *afterward you will understand*" (13:6-7).

Harking back to Jesus' words from a later time, John hears them as holy words. Like the words of Old Testament Scripture, they can even be cited with a formula of fulfillment. At Jesus' arrest he insists that his disciples be set free; John adds, "*This was to fulfil the word which he had spoken,* 'Of those whom thou gavest me I lost not one' " (18:9; cf. 6:39). Again, when it becomes clear that Jesus' executioners will be the Romans and hence that he will be crucified (a Roman method of execution), John tells us, *"This was to fulfil the word which Jesus had spoken* to show by what death he was to die" (18:32; cf. 3:14; 8:28; 12:32).

These clues suggest that John is undertaking nothing less than a reinterpretation of the ministry of Jesus from the standpoint of later church life. Precisely how late remains to be determined. It appears, however, that the author has access to an extensive body of early tradition of the acts and sayings of Jesus. Some of this material, such as the feeding of the multitude or the triumphal entry, parallels what we have in Mark, Matthew, and Luke. Some of it is unknown to the synoptic writers, such as the raising of Lazarus or the words about none of the disciples being lost, or about Jesus being "lifted up." All of the material is carefully molded by the Evangelist into a coherent structure and expressed by him in a characteristically Johannine style.

What sets John apart from the synoptics is not so much that he has reinterpreted the life of Jesus and virtually made it contemporary with his own situation and that of his readers. As we have seen, the other evangelists proceed in somewhat the same way, though to a lesser degree. The uniqueness of John consists rather in the theological self-awareness, the deliberate intent, with which he has gone about this task. The key to his purpose is found in several passages where Jesus promises "another Counselor" (14:16), or Paraclete,[13] the Holy Spirit, who will come and instruct the disciples after Jesus' departure:

> But the Counselor, the Holy Spirit, whom the Father will send in my name, he will *teach* you all things, and *bring to your remembrance* all that I have said to you (14:26).

> But when the Counselor comes, whom I shall send to you from the Father, even the Spirit of truth, who proceeds from the Father, *he will bear witness to me; and you also are witnesses, because you have been with me from the beginning* (15:26–27).

> When the Spirit of truth comes, *he will guide you into all the truth;* for he will not speak on his own authority, but whatever he hears he will speak, and he will declare to you the things that are to come. *He will glorify me,* for he will take what is mine and declare it to you (16:13–14).

The italicized words show us the twofold aspect of the Paraclete's ministry:

1. He is a teacher whose prime role it is to convey truth. Hence he is called the Spirit of truth, the one who guides the church into all the truth.

God's revelation is not static, but an ongoing dynamic reality throughout the church age.

2. At the same time, the Spirit's witness is not open-ended or vacillating, subject to change without notice. It is rooted in the once-for-all historic act of God through the man Jesus of Nazareth. The Paraclete leads the church into no other truth than the historic truth of Jesus Christ. He brings to the disciples' remembrance the things that Jesus has said. Parallel to the Spirit's witness is the testimony of the eyewitnesses who have been with Jesus from the beginning.

Among these eyewitnesses is the author himself. His conviction is that the Paraclete is instructing and guiding the church in that very Gospel which he has written. The "Spirit of truth" passages explain why the disciples "remembered" certain events after Jesus' resurrection. What is meant is not simply the recall of facts, but remembrance with understanding. The function of the Paraclete is to work creatively with the tradition—"the facts"—in order to put them in a total perspective and so convey the whole truth of God. This involves selecting some events and sayings while omitting others (20:30), structuring these according to certain historical and theological considerations, and in some instances perhaps even re-formulating and rephrasing the words of Jesus handed down in the tradition.

This last feature may disturb those who assume that the Bible presents a verbally exact record of what was actually said and done on every occasion of which it speaks, much like a tape recorder. But tapes can be spliced and edited so as to use the exact words of the speaker and yet leave a totally false impression. Paraphrase often expresses the truth of what was said better than an exact but partial reproduction of the original words. It all depends, of course, on who is doing the paraphrasing. In one sense John's authority for his interpretive paraphrase is the Paraclete, the Spirit of truth sent from God to complete the witness of Jesus. In another sense the authority is Jesus himself, now glorified and risen from the dead. It is he who continues to speak to his people through the Spirit. Just before the last of his promises of the Paraclete, Jesus declares: "I have yet many things to say to you, but you cannot bear them now" (16:12). Near the end of the same discourse with his disciples, he adds: "I have said this to you in figures; the hour is coming when I shall no longer speak to you in figures but tell you plainly of the Father" (16:25). This "plain speaking" that Jesus promises occurs precisely in the Gospel of John. Interwoven with what Jesus said in a variety of historical settings is the truth of what the risen Jesus *says* to the church of John's day and of our own. The contemporary quality that even the casual reader senses is no accident. It is theologically based. If John were asked to justify the freedom he has exercised in handling the tradition of Jesus' words and deeds, he could appropriately reply, "Who but Jesus has the authority to interpret Jesus? The risen Lord is not another Jesus; he is the same one who lived among us in the flesh. He taught us once and he still teaches us through the Spirit." This, of course, is a theological assertion, a kind of confession of faith. It is not open to proof or disproof. The reader of today, like the reader of John's day, must decide whether or not he will stand with the evangelist and accept the witness as a true witness of the Spirit.

There is, however, in the First Epistle of John a crucial test to be applied to those who presume to speak, as John does, in the Spirit:

> Beloved, do not believe every spirit, but test the spirits to see whether they are of God; for many false prophets have gone out into the world. By this you know the Spirit of God: every spirit which confesses that Jesus Christ has come in the flesh is of God, and every spirit which does not confess Jesus is not of God (1 John 4:1–3).

"Spirit" must be tested by "flesh"; this is a cardinal Johannine principle. A "spiritual" movement that cuts itself off from the "flesh," from the historical reality of Jesus, is false prophecy.

If a spirit that denies Jesus is an aspect of false prophecy, the Spirit that affirms him belongs to true prophecy. Though John does not use this terminology, his Gospel can be characterized as a prophetic Gospel. The creative Word from the beginning that came into history as the incarnate Word completes his task as the prophetic Word in the church. The Paraclete is none other than the Spirit of Christian prophecy. A recognition of this fact helps to establish a basic kinship between the Johannine Gospel and Epistles on the one hand and the Book of Revelation on the other. In none of these works is prophecy confined to the matter of predicting the future; it refers more generally to inspired utterance in the task of making known the very words of God. In John's Gospel, the prophetic function consists in introducing a particular divine perspective on a series of historical events. Prophecy becomes essentially interpretation, and the prophet an inspired interpreter of what Jesus has said and done.

Like all Christian prophets, the author of the fourth Gospel has as his purpose the edification of the church. His ministry, like that of the Paraclete and that of Jesus himself, is not to thrust himself forward. As

Jesus testifies of the Father and the Spirit testifies of Jesus, the author's task is to bear his witness concerning all three. So successfully has he kept himself in the background that his identity has been subject to continual debate through the centuries. If he is the same prophet who penned the Book of Revelation, he has not signed himself "John," as in Revelation 1:1. We find in his Gospel no signature, but a series of cameolike portraits, five vignettes bearing the designation "the disciple whom Jesus loved."

4. THE BELOVED DISCIPLE

When the fourth Gospel was published, the church that put it forth appended a note at the end: "This is the disciple who is bearing witness to these things, and who has written these things; and we know that his testimony is true" (21:24). The disciple in question is contrasted in the four preceding verses with Peter. Peter will be martyred, but this disciple will live such a long life that the rumor will circulate that he is immortal. All that Jesus states, however, is that whether he lives until the *parousia* or not is none of Peter's concern. This anonymous follower is identified as one who had been closest to Jesus at the Last Supper (21:20). Thus the closing reference to the "disciple whom Jesus loved" leads us back to the first such reference, in chapter thirteen.

The reason that this mysterious individual is not introduced earlier in the Gospel may be that only in chapter 13 does Jesus turn his attention specifically to his disciples and to the question of discipleship. The previous chapters had been taken up with miracles and controversy, but 13:1 initiates a new emphasis: "Now before the feast of the Passover, when Jesus knew that his hour had come to depart out of this world to the Father, *having loved his own who were in the world, he loved them to the end.*" Typical of this group whom Jesus loved is one disciple in particular. As they recline at the table for their last meal together before Jesus' arrest, he lies closest to Jesus, and his relation to his Master is described in remarkable terms: "One of the disciples, whom Jesus loved, was reclining *at Jesus' side*"* (13:23). With this, compare the statement about Jesus that summarizes John's prologue: "No man has ever seen God; it is God the only Son, *ever at the Father's side,* who has revealed Him"* (1:18).[12] The closeness between Master and disciple parallels the closeness between the divine Son and his Father.

We meet this beloved disciple again in chapter nineteen. In his last moments upon the cross, Jesus brings together his mother and the disciple whom he loved: ". . . he said to his mother, 'Woman, behold, your son!'

Then he said to the disciple, 'Behold, your mother!' And from that hour the disciple took her to his own home" (19:26–27). Aside from its historical importance, this word of Jesus makes a theological point: By Jesus' declaration the disciple becomes the "brother" of his Lord. Jesus' mother becomes his mother. It is not surprising that in John 20:17, when Jesus sends Mary Magdalene to tell his disciples what she has seen, he speaks of them (for the first time in John) as "my brethren."

In John 20:2–10, the beloved disciple runs with Peter to see the empty tomb. His personal confession of faith is given as he enters the tomb, "and he saw and believed" (20:8)—believed, apparently, that Jesus had gone to be with the Father, even as he had promised (14:28 f.).

In 21:7 the beloved disciple, fishing with his companions on the Sea of Tiberias, is the first to recognize that is it Jesus who has appeared to them and to tell Peter, "It is the Lord!"

These short sketches portray the witness and author of the fourth Gospel in strongly theological colors. In some sense what is said of him is true of all the disciples: Jesus loves them all; they are all "at his side," united to him as brothers by the new life they have received; they all have "seen and believed"; they all confess him as Lord. These things are true not only of the original disciples but of all Christians. Therefore, the view that characterizes the beloved disciple as an ideal figure, as the archetype of true discipleship, is correct as far as it goes. It does not, however, justify the conclusion sometimes drawn that no real historical person is being described. Too many graphic details weigh heavily against this assertion— e.g., the beloved disciple's immediate acceptance of responsibility toward Jesus' mother, and his close association, even perhaps rivalry, with Simon Peter. An incident such as the footrace to the empty tomb (20:3–8) is absurd and pointless if the beloved disciple is not a real person. Who then is it that stands hidden behind this description?

We have been calling the fourth Gospel the Gospel of *John* and with good historical precedent. Christian tradition has uniformly maintained that the beloved disciple is John the son of Zebedee.[13] The reasons are simple. The disciple's presence at the Last Supper indicates that he is one of the Twelve. His place of honor next to Jesus suggests that he belongs to an inner circle within the larger group. The synoptics single out three—Peter and the two sons of Zebedee, James and John—as the privileged witnesses to the transfiguration (Mark 9:2), to Jesus' agony in Gethsemane (14:33), and with Peter's brother Andrew, to certain miracles (1:29) and discourses (13:3). Peter is obviously not the beloved disciple. Andrew, who is twice mentioned by name in the fourth Gospel (John 1:40; 6:8), can probably also be eliminated. James, martyred about A.D. 44 (see Acts 12:2), might conceivably have been the source of the Gospel's witness, but he died too early to have been its author. This leaves John as by far the most plausible candidate. The tradition of the church and the internal evidence of the Gospel itself converge on him so definitely that in the strictest sense it is perhaps misleading to call this an anonymous work. It is true there is no signature, but the five little snapshots of the beloved disciple point so unmistakably to John that no signature is needed.[14] The use of the name John in Revelation 1:1, and the common interest in prophecy and the Spirit shared by John's Gospel and the Book of Revelation suggest that in spite of the difference in subject matter the same personality, John the son of Zebedee, stands behind these two works.

Several qualifications regarding the literary composition of John's Gospel must still be made.

1. Little doubt exists that the ending of chapter 20 ("these are written that you may believe . . .") was originally the ending of the Gospel. If so, then chapter 21 is a postscript. Its content and style are not so distinctive as to indicate different authorship from the rest of the Gospel. The last two verses, however, do come from another hand (21:24, "*we* know that *his* testimony is true"), and it is conceivable that the elders of the church from which or to which John wrote may have appended to his Gospel this additional chapter. Their purpose would have been to incorporate one more resurrection appearance and to clarify the respective roles of Peter and the beloved disciple in the church. Though verses 22 to 23 do not necessarily assume that the beloved disciple has died, it is more likely that so open a comparison of him with Peter would have been made by his followers than by himself (21:18–23).

2. This theory raises another possibility that must be advanced with more caution. In view of the fact that the five portraits of the beloved disciple glorify him in the sense of making him the ideal disciple, it may be that these are not self-portraits of John, but like the appended chapter 21, the work of his followers. For example, a variant textual tradition at Luke 24:12 tells of Peter's visit to the empty tomb: "But Peter rose and ran to the tomb; stooping and looking in, he saw the linen cloths by themselves; and he went home wondering at what had happened" (RSV footnote). The narrative parallels John 20:3–8 except that it mentions only Peter. There is no hint that he is accompanied by the beloved disciple. This,

however, is just the way the beloved disciple himself might have been expected to tell the story, assuming the role of a mere observer and making Peter the center of attention. But the churches that knew John would have realized that their teacher was also a participant in the action. In telling the whole story, they would then have wanted to give him his rightful place. It is possible that here and elsewhere the evangelist's disciples have borne their testimony to him by incorporating into their edition of his Gospel the five specific allusions to the "disciple whom Jesus loved."

5. THE FIRST CONFESSOR

One of the chief differences between the beloved disciple's narrative and that of the synoptic writers is that John assigns an early beginning to Jesus' ministry. Matthew, Mark, and Luke testify that it was after John the Baptist was arrested that Jesus began his Kingdom preaching in Galilee (Mark 1:14; Matt. 4:12; Luke 3:20 ff.) The fourth Gospel, however, unveils an earlier period largely passed over in silence by the synoptists, a period in which the ministries of Jesus and the Baptist ran parallel to one another. Even after a miracle at Cana, after the temple cleansing and the conversation with Nicodemus, John's Gospel tells us that John the Baptist "had not yet been put in prison" (3:24). His disciples and the disciples of Jesus were baptizing concurrently, even to the extent of becoming involved in a kind of potential rivalry (3:25 f.; 4:1). From this awkward situation Jesus fled into Samaria and finally to Galilee (4:3 f.), but the so-called "early Judean ministry" (2:13–4:42) remains a large block of material of which we would know nothing except for the fourth Gospel.

A noteworthy feature of this section, and of the introductory material that precedes it, is its new perspective on the figure of John the Baptist. Over and over again we find an insistence that he is not the Messiah, but only a forerunner. "He was not the light, but came to bear witness to the light" (1:8). John becomes the first Christian confessor of Jesus as "Lamb of God" (1:29, 36) and "Son of God" (1:34), but his confession begins with a negative note regarding himself: "He confessed, he did not deny, but confessed," that he was not the Messiah, or Elijah, or the expected prophet like Moses (1:20–21). Jesus is the bridegroom, while John is merely "the friend of the bridegroom who stands and hears him" (3:29), and he concludes his testimony of Jesus with the declaration, "He must increase, but I must decrease" (3:30).

This constant reiteration of the secondary place of John the Baptist has suggested to many scholars that there were those in the first century who revered John highly and even proclaimed him, rather than Jesus, as the Messiah. A later Jewish Christian tradition asserted: "Yea, some even of the disciples of John, who seemed to be great ones, have separated themselves from the people, and proclaimed their own master as the Christ."[15] If there was such a group as early as the time of the fourth Gospel, they would have felt they had a plausible case. After all, the Baptist had preceded Jesus in time; he had baptized Jesus, and it could be argued that the lesser is baptized by the greater, particularly when the baptism is for the forgiveness of sins and when it apparently makes the person baptized a disciple of the baptizer.[16]

If Jesus was under the shadow of John the Baptist for a time, it is easy to see why the synoptics would have bypassed this early period and dated the official beginning of Jesus' ministry from John's imprisonment. In the face of the counterclaims of the Baptist's later adherents, the fourth evangelist breaks the silence and opens this controversial segment of Jesus' career to the light of day. There was no disputing the fact that Jesus had submitted to John's baptism. It is not even outside the bounds of possibility that Jesus was once a disciple of the Baptist. The phrase "he who comes after me" (1:15, 27, 30) can mean "a disciple of mine."[17] But, the evangelist insists, John the Baptist himself had recognized that this was no ordinary disciple, not just another candidate for baptism. He recognized Jesus as someone extraordinary. Though the Baptist had appeared first on the scene historically, he knew that this man in his company had actually existed before him (1:15, 30). John not only hailed a Coming One who would initiate God's judgment of the world (cf. Matt. 3:11 f.), but he identified Jesus with this one—the Lamb of God and the Son of God. There was therefore no historical basis for any subsequent claim that the Baptist, rather than Jesus, was the Messiah. John had pointed his own disciples to Jesus (John 1:35 ff.), and Jesus had not hesitated to gather disciples of his own (ch. 1:43 ff.). Jesus and his disciples had conducted a baptizing ministry in Judea parallel with John's (3:22 ff.), so that Jesus seems to have been for a time John's associate in an extensive "Baptist movement."

It may have been in the framework of this reform movement in Israel that Jesus' early cleansing of the temple (2:13–22) took place. If so, it is no accident that when, according to the synoptics, he cleanses the temple on his own messianic authority near the end of his life, he answers the challenge of the Jewish priests with a reminder of "the baptism of John" (Mark 11:27–33). The association of Jesus with the Baptizer could also explain why, in his early dialogue with Nicodemus, Jesus mentioned water along with the Spirit as characterizing the new birth into the Kingdom of God (3:1 ff.).

Thus, alongside the primary purpose of deepening the faith of Christians, at least one probable secondary purpose in John's Gospel can be detected —to establish the primacy of Jesus' claims against sectarians who exalted John the Baptist. In carrying out this purpose, the fourth evangelist makes an important contribution to our historical understanding of Jesus by introducing us to an otherwise unknown chapter in his life. As always, however, John's Gospel interprets these events in the light of the full revelation that came with Jesus' death and resurrection. The ultimate meaning of the things that Jesus said and did and of the tribute paid to him by John the Baptist were not completely grasped until "afterward."

6. JESUS THE SON

Very early in the Gospel the thought is introduced that Jesus is the Messiah, the long-expected heir to the throne of David. Andrew announces to his brother Peter, "We have found the Messiah" (1:41). Nathanael acclaims Jesus as "Son of God" and "King of Israel" (1:49).[18] The latter designation echoes back in the Hosanna cry of the crowds at the triumphal entry: "Blessed is he who comes in the name of the Lord, even the King of Israel!" (12:13). When the Samaritan woman mentions the Messiah, Jesus tells her plainly, "I who speak to you am he" (4:26). When the Jews at the Feast of Dedication demand a forthright messianic claim, Jesus responds, "I told you, and you do not believe" (10:25).

Despite these occasions, it is clear that "Messiah" as understood in the framework of Judaism or even Jewish Christianity, fell far short of expressing all that John perceived in Jesus of Nazareth. Instead of praising Nathanael for his messianic confession, Jesus had hinted mysteriously of "greater things": "Truly, truly, I say to you, you will see heaven opened, and the angels of God ascending and descending upon the *Son of man*" (1:51). The language recalls Jacob and his vision of the ladder at Bethel (Gen. 28:12), except that now it is Jesus instead of Jacob who has become the focal point of God's revelation and presence among men. This vivid image of the ladder at the end of John's first chapter sets the pattern for the Christology that is to emerge in the rest of his Gospel. The familiar synoptic term "Son of man" retains its importance, but exists now side by side with a distinctly Johannine theme—union with God.

The most conspicuous title of Jesus in the fourth Gospel is neither Son of man nor Son of God but simply the Son, without any modifying phrase. Jesus refers to himself in the third person as the Son in the same mysterious way that he uses Son of man as a self-designation. This suggests that "Son" and "Son of man" may come from the same tradition of Jesus' sayings; "the Son" may in fact be only a shortened form of "Son of man."[19] If so, then this lofty expression of Jesus' unity with the Father lays strong claim to having originated with Jesus himself rather than the later church.[20]

In any case, it is clear that from the evangelist's point of view no particular distinction was made among "Son of man," "Son of God," and "the Son." Within John 5:19–30, a section in many ways programmatic for the Christology of the fourth Gospel, the three terms are woven together in one fabric:

> Truly, truly, I say to you, the hour is coming, and now is, when the dead will hear the voice of the *Son of God,* and those who hear will live. For as the Father has life in himself, so he has granted *the Son* also to have life in himself, and has given him authority to execute judgment, because he is the *Son of man* (5:25–27).

No matter which of the three titles is used, the most profound Johannine teachings about Jesus appear in connection with his sonship.

At the same time, a surprising amount of evidence suggests that the central figure in John's Gospel is the Father. Only with reference to God the Father is it meaningful to present Jesus as the Son. The Son of God is not an independent supernatural entity, John insists, not some kind of a "second god." In answer to the Jewish charge that he was "making himself equal with God" (5:18) in this fashion, Jesus replied: "Truly, truly, I say to you, the Son can do nothing of his own accord, but only what he sees the Father doing; for whatever he does, that the Son does likewise. For the Father loves the Son, and shows him all that he himself is doing . . ." (5:19–20).

After describing the works of the Father performed through the Son, Jesus returns in verse 30 to the same theme, rounding out 5:19–30 as a unit: "I can do nothing on my own authority; as I hear, I judge; and my judgment is just, because I seek not my own will but the will of him who sent me" (5:30).

This becomes the refrain of John's Gospel: the Son never speaks or acts independently but always in total submission to the Father who sent him. His words and deeds, precisely because they are not his own but his Father's, are of ultimate significance to those who see and hear them.

The son does not seek his own glory, but that of his Father; conversely, it is the Father who glorifies the Son and validates his ministry. Just as the Paraclete testifies not to himself but to Jesus, so Jesus testifies principally to the Father. His "equality with God" is not like the equality of two allied but separate partners in a business venture. Jesus says, "I and the Father are *one*" (10:30)—not two! God acts only in and through Jesus; it is Jesus who uniquely reveals the Father. He is God's final Word to man, and apart from him God cannot be known. At one point Jesus says, "Have I been with you so long, and yet you do not know me, Philip? *He who has seen me has seen the Father*" (14:9). Here, as in the prologue, the ancient principle that "no man has ever seen God" is superseded by the good news that now the only Son "has revealed him" (cf. 1:18). The Johannine confession, "Jesus is the Christ, the Son of God," thus hails more than the coming of a Messiah. It means that God the Father has made himself visible; he has taken human flesh as the man Jesus of Nazareth in order that man might know him and receive life through his name.

7. FROM GLORY TO GLORY

The student who begins to read the Gospel of John soon discovers that the revelation of God takes place according to a coherent plan. He will profit greatly from an awareness of the landmarks that lead him from one section to the next and sometimes point him backward to programmatic statements made earlier.

One statement in the prologue, for example, affords a key to two of the Gospel's major divisions.

1. *The public ministry* (chs. 2–12), in which Jesus presses his claims upon Israel in general, *corresponds to* 1:11 ("He came to his own home, and his own people received him not").

2. *The private ministry* (chs. 13–17), in which "his own" (13:1) are defined more narrowly as his disciples and in which the disciples become the focus of interest, *corresponds to* 1:12 ("But to all who received him, who believed in his name, he gave power to become children of God").

In a more theological vein, a heading under which several of the Gospel's divisions may be considered is that of *glory*. The heart of the believing community's response to the coming of the Word in the flesh is the confession: "we beheld his glory" (1:14). This manifestation is not confined, as in the synoptics, to a single event, such as the transfiguration. Rather it governs the progression of thought and action virtually from beginning to end.

Prior to Jesus' public ministry is a period of preparation (1:19–2:11), consisting of the witness of John the Baptist and the gathering of Jesus' disciples. The Baptist comes in order that Jesus might be "revealed to Israel" (1:31). After he points his disciples to Jesus, their faith is established by the first miracle, the changing of the water into wine at a wedding in Cana of Galilee (2:1–11). It is a relatively private miracle; neither the steward of the feast nor most of the guests even know what has happened. Only the steward's servants and Jesus' group of followers realize that water has become wine. At the conclusion we read: "This, the first of his signs, Jesus did at Cana in Galilee, and *manifested his glory;* and his disciples believed in him" (2:11). Clearly, he has been "revealed to Israel"—a new Israel. This first glimpse of Jesus' glory establishes his disciples' faith and climaxes the period of preparation. But the reader recognizes the act as only a "sign" of a fuller manifestation to come. Before the miracle, Jesus cautions his mother, Mary, with the words, "O woman, what have you to do with me? My hour has not yet come" (2:4). The "hour," we soon learn, is the hour of Jesus' death.

The public ministry of Jesus (2:13–12:50) moves toward this "hour." The cleansing of the temple indicates that Jesus' zeal for his Father's house will ultimately consume him, that the temple which is his body will be destroyed (2:17–19). The twin themes of life and light dominate most of the episodes that follow. Jesus speaks to Nicodemus of new birth and a new life (3:1–10). He tells the Samaritan woman of a spiritual "spring of water welling up to eternal life" (4:14). He heals an official's son at Capernaum with the twice-repeated word of grace, "Your son will live" (4:50, 53), and a lame man at the pool of Bethesda as a sign of his power to give life (see, e.g., 5:21). In chapter 6, after providing bread for the multitude to sustain their life, Jesus makes it plain that paradoxically his gift of himself as Bread of life for the world involves his own violent death (6:51, 53).

Chapters 7 and 8 together constitute another preliminary manifestation of his glory at the Feast of Tabernacles.[21] He goes on to the feast in secret, but he gradually makes his identity known (7:10, 14 f., 24 ff.). The result is sharper and sharper conflict with the Jerusalem authorities. On two occasions, as they try to arrest him, he eludes their grasp *"because his hour had not yet come"* (7:30; 8:20). The self-disclosure at the feast comes to an end as Jesus "hid himself, and went out of the temple" (8:59).

The ultimate demonstration of Jesus' power to bestow life comes in chapter eleven. Previously he had healed the sick or provided food; now he was to raise a man from the dead. Across the narrative of the raising of Lazarus, however, falls the shadow of Jesus' own impending death. Here is the supreme irony: the one who alone has the power to grant eternal life to men must himself die. Hearing of Lazarus' illness, Jesus looks into the near future: "This illness is not unto death; it is for the *glory of God,* so that the Son of God may be *glorified* by means of it" (11:4). Just before he calls Lazarus from the tomb, Jesus says to Martha, the dead man's sister, "Did I not tell you that if you would believe you would see the *glory of God?*" (11:40). Gradually the startling fact is disclosed: beyond all the preliminary displays of "glory" in Jesus' ministry, the final "glorification" toward which they all point is Jesus' death upon the cross. The Lazarus miracle precipitates a decision by the Jewish high court, the Sanhedrin, that "it is expedient . . . that one man should die for the people, and that the whole nation should not perish" (11:50).

In chapter 12 the long-anticipated dramatic climax is finally reached at the Feast of Passover. In response to some Greeks who desire to speak with him, Jesus declares:

> *The hour has come for the Son of man to be glorified.* Truly, truly, I say to you, unless a grain of wheat falls into the earth and *dies,* it remains alone; but if it dies, it bears much fruit (vss. 23–24).

A few verses later, he continues:

> *Now* is my soul troubled. And what shall I say? "Father, save me from this hour"? No, for this purpose I have come to this hour. Father, *glorify thy name* (vss. 27–28).

As the public ministry comes to a close, Jesus adds:

> *Now* is the judgment of this world, now shall the prince of this world be cast out; and I, when I am lifted up from the earth, will draw all men to myself." He said this to show by what death he was to die (vss. 31–33).

Although the actual "lifting up" of Jesus on the cross does not take place until chapter 19, the climax of the drama is here in chapter twelve. From this point on, the crucifixion is inevitable; events will move swiftly to their denouement, and Jesus' main concern will be to prepare his disciples for what is coming.

The emphasis on judgment in this passage underlines another major theme of the public ministry. If Jesus' "glorification" means life for those who believe in him, it also means judgment for those who do not. The works of the Father, said Jesus in his first major discourse, are two in number: the giving of life and the executing of divine judgment (5:21, 22, 26–27). If the former is demonstrated by particular "signs" during the public ministry, so also is the latter. Judgment comes into focus near the end of chapter 6, when Jesus' words are found to have a divisive effect upon his hearers.

Again in chapters 9 and 10 (which form a unit), judgment is the ruling concept. After giving sight to a man born blind, Jesus says to the Pharisees who drove the man from their synagogue, "For judgment I came into this world, that those who do not see may see, and that those who see may become blind" (9:39). The miracle exposes the Pharisees as "blind guides" (cf. Matt. 15:14) and false shepherds of the people. It is against the background of such false shepherds that Jesus presents himself as the Good Shepherd who lays down his life for his sheep (ch. 10). Again his self-disclosure ends in division (10:19) and judgment, as he withdraws himself from those who would put him to death (10:39).

Thus the "glorification" of Jesus settles the issues raised by his public ministry by separating men into two groups—believers and unbelievers: the heirs of life and the recipients of judgment. In his private ministry (13:1–17:26), as Jesus turns his attention to the disciples, he keeps before them this theme of "glorification." For example:

Now is the Son of man glorified, and in him God is glorified (13:31).

Father, the hour has come; glorify thy Son that the Son may glorify thee (17:1).

And now, Father, glorify thou me in thy own presence with the glory which I had with thee before the world was made (17:5).

At a junction in Jesus' life that bore the deepest possible overtones of tragedy, the narrative glows with joy and triumph.

It is clear that a profound reinterpretation of Christ's death has taken place. Other New Testament writers can depict the cross as a temporary defeat that is reversed by the victory of the resurrection. Such was the thrust of Peter's preaching in the Book of Acts: "This Jesus . . . you crucified and killed by the hands of lawless men. *But* God raised him up" (Acts 2:23–24). In his first epistle, Peter recalled that the Old Testament prophets had predicted "the *sufferings* of Christ and the subsequent *glory*" (1 Peter 1:11). According to Luke, Jesus himself had stressed the necessity "that the Christ should *suffer* these things and enter into his *glory*" (Luke 24:26). John boldly merges these two aspects of Christ's experience into one. Glory is no longer seen as something that follows suffering as a kind of compensation; it has become inherent in the suffering itself. The irony of the crown of thorns and of the inscription on the cross, "king of the Jews," has given way to a serious affirmation of faith. That which human judgment can only call a defeat Christian faith celebrates as a victory. The lifting up of Jesus on the cross of shame ultimately signifies his lifting up to universal lordship with the Father (John 12:32; cf. Acts 2:33; 5:31). John could apply to the suffering Savior what Isaiah had predicted for the suffering Servant: "Behold, my servant shall have understanding, and he shall be *lifted up* and *glorified* exceedingly"* (Isa. 52: 13, LXX). What prompted John's triumphant perspective on the death of Jesus Christ? The answer seems clear: the cross is the hour of glory and victory for Jesus because of its *redemptive* significance. As John confesses in his first epistle, Christ "is the expiation for our sins, and not for ours only but also for the sins of the whole world" (1 John 2:2). Though John has not wrestled as Paul has with all the ramifications of how God and man are reconciled, it is nonetheless the atonement that governs his outlook on Jesus' passion and the events leading to it.

A major question remains. If the cross is already Jesus' moment of triumph, what meaning remains for the resurrection? What further glorification is possible or necessary? Reinterpretation of the one redemptive event virtually demands reinterpretation of the other. John's new perspective on the familiar proclamation that Jesus rose from the dead on the third day is crucial, for it becomes the governing factor in his total outlook on the new life in Christ.

8. THE GREAT RETURN

Twice in his public ministry and two more times in his last hours with the disciples, Jesus foretells his own resurrection. When the temple of his body is destroyed, he says, "in three days I will raise it up" (2:19). As Good Shepherd, he promises: "I lay down my life, that I may take it again" (10:17). In neither of these passages is John's emphasis different from that of most other New Testament writers. The resurrection is a conquest of death and a reassertion of life. Its significance is not unlike that which elsewhere in John is assigned to the crucifixion (12:23 f., 31 ff.).

The two other resurrection predictions, however, are different. The theme of the last discourse is twofold: Jesus is "going away" to the Father, and he will "come again" to his disciples. As he prepares his followers for the anguish of this separation, he promises them: "I will not leave you desolate; I will come to you. Yet a little while, and the world will see me no more, but you will see me; because I live, you will live also" (14:18–19). The last seven words reiterate the familiar theme of resurrection life, but the preceding utterances contribute a new dimension to the subject. This distinctively Johannine thrust is that Jesus' resurrection means *reunion*—the renewal of fellowship with his disciples. After he goes away for a time, he will come back to them. They will see him and once more know the joy of his presence (cf. 16:16, 20, 22).

The account of the resurrection itself in chapter 20 exhibits the same characteristics found in the "last discourse." Even in terminology there is a remarkable correspondence between 20:19–29 and the key predictions of chapters 14 and 16:

1. "I will come to you" (14:18, 28); "we will come to him" (14:23).

1. "Jesus came" (20:19, 26).

2. "Peace I leave with you; my peace I give to you" (14:27); "that in me you may have peace" (16:33).

2. "Jesus said, 'Peace be with you' " (20:19, 21, 26).

3. "Your sorrow will turn into joy . . . your hearts will rejoice, and no one will take your joy from you" (16:20, 22).

3. "Then the disciples rejoiced when they saw the Lord"* (20:20).

4. "And I will pray the Father, and he will give you . . . the Spirit of the truth" (14:16–17; cf. 14:26; 15:26; 16:7–15).

4. "He breathed on them, and said to them, 'Receive the Holy Spirit.' " (20:22)

The reader is expected to understand that the promises made after the Last Supper have begun to be fulfilled in the resurrection appearances to the eleven disciples.

The interview of the risen Jesus with Mary Magdalene, however, contains some features that seem at first not to fit the pattern. After revealing his identity to Mary, Jesus warns: "Do not hold me, for I have not yet ascended to the Father; but go to my brethren and say to them, I am ascending to my Father and your Father, to my God and your God" (20:17). Mary's fellowship with her Master cannot be complete because he has "not yet ascended to the Father." By contrast, the gathered disciples experience the full reality of Jesus' presence (20:19 ff.). Mary was forbidden to lay hold of him, while Thomas is specifically invited to touch the wounds in Jesus' hands and side (20:27). The startling implication of all this is that between verses 17 and 19 of John 20 *the ascension has taken place.* In all likelihood it is signaled by the words, "I am ascending to my Father," in verse 17. This means that the ascension is not understood by John as a movement in space but as a change in a relationship. Jesus the Son had been sent into the world to fulfill the plan and purpose of the Father; this mission had necessitated a certain separation between Father and Son. Now the moment had come for the two to be reunited. Jesus himself had summed it up concisely a few chapters earlier: "I came from the Father and have come into the world; again, I am leaving the world and going to the Father" (16:28). The paradox inherent in the resurrection experiences of Mary Magdalene, Thomas, and the other disciples is this: *Only when Jesus has been reunited with the Father can he be fully reunited with his loved ones on earth.* The laws of physics dictate that a person cannot be in two places at the same time, but Jesus' resurrection means that he is no longer subject to the limitations of time and space. When he goes to the Father, he leaves the world, yet in the Spirit, he is closer to his disciples than ever before. Because he is risen, they can "abide in him," united to him by faith. His union with the Father means that *they* have become united with both the Father and the Son. This new relationship of union with God sounds very mystical, but to John it is simply the inevitable consequence of Jesus' resurrection and the privilege of every Christian.

The keystone of John's theology comes just after Jesus' promise that he will rise from the dead and that his disciples will see him and live: "In that day you will know that I am in my Father, and you in me, and I in you" (14:20). This is what the resurrection day means to John. A kind of "telescoping" process is accomplished, whereby the Son dwells "in" the Father as he has done from all eternity and the Christian believer, for his part, dwells "in" the Son and hence also "in" the Father. The imagery of the vine and its branches (15:1–18) points to this same reality of believers dwelling in Christ (with the Father as the vinedresser) and receiving a common life from the Father and the Son. Jesus' prayer for his disciples is "that they may all be one; even as thou, Father, art in me, and I in thee, that they also may be in us. . . . I in them and thou in me, that they may become perfectly one" (17:21, 23). This prayer for unity and mutual indwelling can be realized, according to John, only on the basis of Jesus' return to his Father *and* to his disciples that he accomplishes on Easter day. It is not his outward form that is essential, for only a handful of disciples saw him on that day. What is essential is rather the contact with him which is open to every Christian by faith, through the Holy Spirit. Though John knows as well as Luke that the resurrection appearances finally ceased and Jesus' visible presence was withdrawn, he records no departure of Jesus from the earth. With Matthew, he prefers the truth expressed by the words, "lo, I am with you always, to the close of the age" (Matt. 28:20). As Jesus tells Thomas, "Blessed are those who have not seen and yet believe" (John 20:29). The physical proofs of the resurrection—the empty tomb, the locked doors through which Jesus came to his disciples, the wounds in his hands and sides— are on the one hand presented as literal facts, but on the other hand serve the evangelist as signs of a reality that is more than physical. They point to a union with Christ that is not confined to a single day or room or group of people. It is for all time and every place; it is for all who "believe that Jesus is the Christ" and "have life in his name."

9. LIFE IN GOD

The resurrection in John confirms what has been suggested earlier: that the fourth Gospel is preeminently the Gospel of the *Father*. If for Paul the Christian dwells "in Christ," John's even larger perspective locates the believer's abiding place "in God" or "in the Father and the Son." The goal of man is to know God as Father and to be united to him by faith. John's proclamation is that only in the Son can this goal be achieved. That is why readers of the fourth Gospel have always looked at Jesus as revealed there and said, "He is God." It is not surprising that to John is attributed the "highest" Christology in the whole New Testament. Here the New Testament comes closer than anywhere else to the later formulations of Nicaea and Chalcedon on the deity of Jesus Christ. The beginning and end of the Gospel come together with almost perfect symmetry: the announcements, "The Word was God" (1:1), and, "God the only Son . . . has revealed [God]"* (1:18), find their fitting answer in the joyous outcry of Thomas at the resurrection, "My Lord and my God!" (20:28). It is Jesus' return to the Father and to his disciples that makes possible this ultimate confession.

At the same time, the veil is lifted from a set of mysterious utterances made by Jesus at several points in the Gospel. After washing the disciple's feet at the Last Supper, Jesus had looked into the near future to speak of his passion: "I tell you this now, before it happens, that when it happens you may believe that *I am*"* (13:19). The apparently unfinished "I am" is striking. After Jesus died and rose again and Thomas became convinced of his identity by his wounds, he indeed "believed" and supplied his own predicates for the "I am"—"Lord" and "God." Three times in chapter 8 Jesus had used the puzzling "I am" in disputing with the Jews:

You will die in your sins unless you believe that *I am** (8:24).

When you have lifted up the Son of man, then you will know that *I am** (8:28).

Truly, truly, I say to you, before Abraham was, *I am* (8:58).

The Old Testament background of this term shows why it anticipates Thomas' confession, "My Lord and my God!" and serves as John's profoundest expression of Jesus' consciousness of deity. In the Old Testament, God is the I AM. In revealing himself as Yahweh, "the Lord," who makes a covenant with his people, God tells Moses,

"I AM WHO I AM." And he said, "Say this to the people of Israel, 'I AM has sent me to you.' " (Exod. 3:14).

In the Greek Old Testament, I AM becomes virtually a name for God. The Septuagint translation of the words of Isaiah, as he turns Israel's thoughts again to their covenant, preserves the relevant terminology:

Become my witnesses, as I am a witness, says the Lord God, and my servant whom I have chosen, that you may know and believe and understand that I AM. Before me no other God was made, and there will be none after me* (Isa. 43:10).

I AM, and there is no other. . . . I am I AM, the Lord, speaking righteousness and announcing truth* (45:18–19: note that the second "I AM" is the predicate).

Therefore my people shall *know my name* in that day that I AM myself the one who is speaking. Here am I* (52:6).

These Old Testament parallels to John's Gospel indicate that when Jesus says "I AM" he is revealing God. In all likelihood, "I AM" is the divine name that is in mind when Jesus prays "Holy Father, keep them in *thy name, which thou hast given me, that they may be one, even as we are one*" (John 17:11). On Jesus' lips the name is I AM; in the mouth of a confessor such as Thomas it is "Lord" or "God."

Once the absolute I AM of Jesus is understood from the perspective of his deity as made known in the resurrection, it can be seen as governing those "I am" statements which occur with a predicate ("I am the Bread of life," "I am the Good Shepherd," "I am the Light of the world," etc.). In a very real sense Jesus is revealing *God* as Bread, Shepherd, Light, etc. The uncompromising monotheism of the passages cited above from Isaiah is not weakened in John. He who says "I AM" insists at the same time that there is "no other God" (Isa. 43:10; 45:18). Despite the misgivings of staunch Jewish monotheists, Jesus was no new deity to be added to_an incipient pantheon. To John, Jesus and the Father are, paradoxically, *one God* (10:30; 17:11, 22). Thus Christian experience is indeed life in God; though it is realized only through the Son, the Word who became a man of flesh, it is not exhausted in him. Its goal is fellowship also with the Father.

This theme of life in God supplies a helpful framework in which to view the Johannine epistles. More than any other New Testament writer, John offers the material for a total picture of what the Christian revelation means. Only he has given us both a Gospel and a set of teaching epistles, probably in addition to the prophecy of Revelation. Thus we can gain from him not only a profound and impressive portrait of Jesus of Nazareth but an almost full-orbed view of the Christian life.

10. JOHN'S THREE "EPISTLES": THE MARKS OF DIVINE LIFE

First John, the longest of the three Johannine "letters," has few of the characteristics of a real letter. There is no identification of the writer or of the addressees, no greeting at the beginning, no word of farewell at the end. But popular tradition, based on the occasional use of such clauses as, "I am writing to you, little children," or, "Beloved, I am writing you" (1 John 1:4; 2:1, 7–8, 12–14, 26; 5:13), has led most people to the assumption that this document is a typical New Testament letter from an apostle to some church that he knows well. For convenience, First John has been grouped in the canon with two shorter communications, both of which are unquestionably letters. Second John comes from "the elder to the elect lady" (vs. 1), contains a typical epistolary salutation ("grace, mercy, and peace," vs. 3), and closes with some personal words and a greeting from "the children of your elect sister" (vss. 12–13). In Third John "the elder" writes to "the beloved Gaius," expressing his best wishes for Gaius' health and faith (vss. 1–2). Again he closes with a warm, personal greeting (vss. 13–15). The contrast between these two letters and First John could hardly be greater in this respect, and yet, because they have been placed together, the title of epistle has become attached to all three.

In actuality, First John is more a doctrinal and ethical treatise than a letter in any normal sense of the word. It may have in view a group of churches rather than a single church. Its theology is built securely on the "life in God" theme of the fourth Gospel. At the very outset John writes: ". . . that which we have seen and heard we proclaim also to you, *so that you may have fellowship with us; and our fellowship is with the Father and with his Son Jesus Christ*" (1 John 1:3). This statement is crucial for two reasons:

1. The "fellowship" (*koinōnia*) of which it speaks is not simply conviviality or social "togetherness" in the sense that the word "fellowship" is sometimes used today. Rather, it is an expression of that union with God realized in Jesus' resurrection according to John's Gospel. In his resurrection Jesus returns to the Father and also to his disciples, thus uniting them in himself with the Father. This experience is best understood as communion, the sharing of a common life. Just as in the Gospel, it is ultimately a communion both with the Father and with the Son.

2. The "we" of this introductory statement refers to the eyewitnesses of Jesus' life and deeds. Presumably they are the apostles, here represented by John, one of the last of their number to survive. From the beginning they had heard and seen and even touched Jesus (1:1). Most vivid perhaps was the memory of that Easter day when Thomas had been invited to touch the wounds of the risen Lord. First John is written in order to extend this immediate perception of Jesus from the apostles alone to all Christians everywhere. Thus the readers would be able to participate in the *koinōnia* which the apostles had experienced with the Father and the Son. First John aims at the realization of Jesus' final words to Thomas, "Blessed are those who have not seen and yet believe" (John 20:29).

Such factors as these indicate that the thought of this treatise runs closely parallel to that of the fourth Gospel. Whether First John circulated with the Gospel as a kind of postscript designed to point up the same truths in a more didactic form, or whether it embodies a compendium of John's oral teachings in the churches before he wrote the Gospel, we do not know. What is clear in any case is that we are justified in using each of these Johannine writings to shed whatever light it can upon the other.

The special contribution of the "epistle," however, is its proposal of several practical, concrete tests by which the presence of divine life in a man may be discerned. To speak of dwelling in God or enjoying communion with him is not very significant unless it produces results in the way one actually behaves. Just as a prophetic interpretation of Jesus' life and words in terms of their present significance must be solidly anchored in the historic tradition of what Jesus really said and did, so also spiritual assertions about a person's life in Christ must be proven by the creed he recites and by the actions he performs. Flesh not quickened by the Spirit is profitless; Spirit not manifested in human flesh is meaningless. For the sake of convenience, we may designate these two sides of essential Christianity as the *metaphysical* and the *practical*. The term "metaphysical" is here used in a non-philosophical sense simply to denote what (or where) Christians *are*: they are, for example, "in God," or "in the light"; they have communion with God and with one another; they "abide in him"; they are "of God," or "of the truth"; they are "children of God," or "born of God"; they "know God" and "have eternal life." The term "practical" refers to what Christians *do*: they love God and one another; they "keep the commandments"; they "walk in the light"; they confess specific beliefs about Jesus Christ.

A remarkably high percentage of the sentences in First John can be bisected into precisely these two divisions. They are both metaphysical and practical, put together in such a way as to show that the two aspects of Christian experience are inseparable. Each depends mutually upon the other. A few statements are sufficient to illustrate what is meant: ·

	Practical	Metaphysical
2:10	"He who loves his brother	*abides in the light."*
3:7	"He who does right	*is righteous"*
3:24	"All who keep his commandments	*abide in him, and he in them."*
4:15	"Whoever confesses that Jesus is the Son of God,	*God abides in him, and he in God."*

Sometimes the point is made negatively, but the basic elements are the same:

	Practical	Metaphysical
3:8	"He who commits sin	*is of the devil."*
3:14	"He who does not love	*remains in death."*

To John, the practical marks of divine life can be reduced to three essentials: <u>righteousness, love, and belief</u>.[22] These criteria are applied to Christian experience several times in a cyclical or spiral fashion. While John's thought seems to go over the same ground again and again, there is in reality a definite progression. The tests of love and righteousness recur throughout the treatise, while the test of belief is concentrated especially toward the end. The whole of First John is, however, organized around three doctrinal affirmations which also belong, in the proper sense, to the test of belief:

1. "God is light and in him is no darkness at all" (1:5).
2. "Children, it is the last hour" (2:18).
3. "Jesus Christ has come in the flesh" (4:2).

Ultimately these three propositions reiterate a single message. It is the message of the prologue to John's Gospel and of the Gospel itself as a whole. Each of the three affirmations expresses in its own way the good news of the decisive redemptive event that took place in Jesus Christ. Taken together they constitute the "word of life" which was "from the beginning" and which John declares to his readers (1:1). Each proposition begins a cycle of Johannine thought in which the tests of righteousness and love are applied. These cycles may be used to form a broad outline of First John in terms of *walking in the light* (1:5–2:17), *living for the future* (2:18–3:24), and *believing the truth* (4:1–5:21).

First Cycle: Walking in the Light (1:5–2:17)

To those who have become familiar with the New Testament formulations of the Christian gospel, "God is light" comes as a strangely abstract and speculative way of stating "the message we have heard from him and proclaim to you" (1:5). It is a proposition to which a Hellenistic Jew or even an educated pagan could give assent just as readily as could a Christian apostle or prophet. The existence of evil in the world is a problem which haunts virtually every known religious and philosophical system. The aim of many such systems in John's day was to account for evil without imputing its origin to God. In such a framework, the maxim "God is light and in him is no darkness at all" would be both natural and pertinent.

Many statements in First John suggest that one of its purposes was to combat heresy within the church. It has often been suggested that this heresy was an incipient form of Gnosticism. This is a broad term covering

a number of ancient mythical or philosophical systems that radically separated the true God from the created world as we know it. Gnostics
believed that originally there was only the true God who existed in
perfection. He was the true Light. He created secondary "gods" (e.g.,
Mind, Wisdom, or Primal Man) as reflections of himself. But by a series
of defections or "emanations" that which the true God had created became
more and more estranged from him. The world was not his creation at all,
but the handiwork of alienated and fallen deities. Hence the world of
matter is darkness. Man belongs to this world, yet also possesses within
him sparks of the true light. When a call comes to him from without,
from the world of light, he is initiated into the secrets of that world, the
secrets of his own origin and existence. He becomes a *gnostic*, one who
knows or understands. Thus he is delivered from the material world of
darkness and reunited with the ultimate source of his being.[23] Certain
similarities between these Gnostic systems and New Testament Christianity
are, of course, apparent. As soon as some ventured to identify the Gnostic
revealer, the messenger of the decisive call, with Jesus Christ, there came
into being a Christian Gnosticism that was to plague the church for
centuries. It may be against early examples of such tendencies that John
is contending. If so, two considerations must be kept in mind with respect
to his use of the "God is light" terminology:

1. The declaration that "God is light" derives its force from the corollary
that John attaches to it: "If we say we have fellowship with him while
we walk in darkness, we lie and do not live according to the truth" (1:6).
Frequently the Christian Gnostic, believing that he had been delivered
from the evil physical world, concluded that he was also free from all
moral laws that governed human life in this world. What he did with his
body was of no import; only the soul counted for anything in God's sight.
Against this mentality, John urges that a person's "walk," his practical
daily behavior, is crucial. To say "God is light," as some Gnostics did,
while walking in the darkness of sin was to live a lie. First John, like Second
Peter and Jude, stands firmly opposed to all such antinomianism. A metaphysical assertion that does not pass muster in the realm of personal conduct is worthless.

2. John's rather philosophic formulation of the gospel in 1 John 1:5,
defining God in terms of light, should not be interpreted apart from a
different formulation of the same truth in 2:8. There John articulates the
message more in the language of redemptive history: "the darkness is
passing away and the true light is already shining." Just as in the pro-

logue of the fourth Gospel, it is the *coming* of the light in the historic ministry of Jesus Christ that is decisive (cf. John 1:5, 9). Only on the basis of this once-for-all dawning of the light in history can it be said with conviction that "God is light and in him is no darkness at all." Thus "the message we have heard from him" (1 John 1:5) belongs to the orthodox Christian, not to the Gnostic. For all their accent on revelation, the Gnostics fell short of a true appreciation of what it meant for God to reveal himself in human flesh. That John has not similarly cut himself off from this historic revelation is apparent from his references to the blood of Jesus (1:7) and to the commandments that Jesus gave (2:3 f.), as well as the necessity "to walk in the same way in which he walked" (2:6).

John's first cycle follows a coherent and well-defined pattern. After the initial doctrinal affirmation, the test of *righteousness* is applied in 1:6–2:6. First, a series of five conditional sentences spell out the ethical implications of fellowship in the light (1:6–10). These statements alternate back and forth between the negative (vss. 6, 8, 10) and the positive (vss. 7, 9), confronting the readers with a radical and ultimate choice. In 2:1 the tone changes to one of assurance with the phrase, "My little children." The readers' confidence rests on two facts: their sins are forgiven through the work of Jesus their advocate,[24] and they know God. But the test of righteousness is still being applied. They have this assurance only because they keep Christ's word and walk as he walked.

In 2:7–17 John administers his second test: *love.* The "commandments" (2:3) come to a focus in one commandment which is at the same time both old and new (2:7 f.). It is old because it is a corollary of the "word of life" which was "from the beginning" (cf. 1:1), the gospel message that started with Jesus. Yet it is new because it means the passing away of the old world of darkness and the dawning of a new order (2:8). The context indicates that the commandment John has in mind is the one recorded in 13:34 of his Gospel: "A new commandment I give to you, that you love one another; even as I have loved you, that you also love one another." The application of this test of love follows the same pattern that characterized the test of righteousness; first the doctrinal statement is reiterated (2:8); then the ethical implications are spelled out in alternately negative and positive statements (2:9–11); finally there are assurances to the readers (again addressed as "little children") that "your sins are forgiven" and that "you know the Father" (2:12–14).[25]

The warnings in 2:15–17 serve as a transition to the next cycle of the author's thought. The announcement that "the world passes away" (2:17) looks both backward and forward: backward to the good news proclaimed in 2:8 that "the darkness is passing away and the true light is already shining," and forward to the doctrinal formulation that introduces the next cycle: "Children, it is the last hour" (2:18). The Christian message, even when couched in terms like these, is not world-denying like Gnosticism, but essentially world-affirming. In Christ the darkness that men call their world has been put to flight, John says. It is "passing away," and a new world of light and love and righteousness is upon us. To "love the world" (2:15) is to attempt to live in the past and in the darkness; to have "love for the Father" is to open oneself to the light and live for the future.

Second Cycle: Living for the Future (2:18–3:24)

If the theme of the first cycle was light, the theme of the second is *life*. This time John develops the doctrinal affirmation at some length (2:18–3:3); then he points out the ethical implications of the doctrine in terms of *righteousness* (in a series of alternating negative and positive statements, 3:4–10), and *love* (3:11–17); finally he adds his customary words of assurance (3:18–24).

In the Jewish world to which John had originally belonged, "eternal life" meant "the life of the age to come."[26] His reference to "the last hour" (2:18), therefore, leads him naturally to a discussion of life. But John had told in his Gospel how Jesus shifted the tense of this eternal life from the future to the present. Jesus' promise was that the person who heard and believed his word would receive divine life as a present possession. Jesus had described this experience to Nicodemus the Pharisee as being born all over again, not by natural procreation, but "from above" (John 3:3–10). Here John speaks of being "born of God" (1 John 2:29; 3:9), of being therefore "children of God" (3:1–2, 10). The "last hour" for the world is not "last" for the child of God. He faces the future with confidence, not because he knows in detail what it will bring but because he is sure of his present relationship to the Father (3:2). In early Christian expectation this final appearing of Jesus Christ was to be preceded by times of trouble and stress for the church. There would be persecutions from the outside, while even within the household of faith many would turn from Christ to follow false prophets and teachers.[27] These calamities were frequently expected to cluster around one man or one world system that would come upon the scene as the virtual embodiment of ultimate evil—a "desolating sacrilege" (Mark 13:14), or a "man of lawlessness" (2 Thess.

2:3, 8–9), or a "beast rising out of the sea" (Rev. 13:1), or a counterfeit Christ—an anti-Christ. In this section of First John, the life situation of the author and his readers comes vividly to life as the concept of "anti-Christ" is boldly applied to a group of teachers that has very recently been in their midst: "They went out from us, but they were not of us; for if they had been of us, they would have continued with us; but they went out, that it might be plain that they all are not of us." (2:19). This is the primary clue to a very important fact: *The church or churches to which John writes have been torn by a schism.* A sizable group has left the church, and John addresses himself to those who remain. The hints within the first cycle that some kind of Gnosticism threatens the church here assume a more definite shape. The schismatics have been guilty of lying; they have sinned against the truth by denying that Jesus is the Christ (2:21–22). They have been guilty of murder, through hatred of their brethren. To violate the commandment of love is to disdain the life that God gives and to dwell in the realm of death (3:14–15). To rend the church by such apostasy and hatred is to commit "mortal sin" for which there is no forgiveness (cf. 5:16). He who is truly born of God does not sin in this way. He who commits mortal sin thereby proves that he is not a child of God but belongs to the devil (3:7–10).

The tendency of Gnostic teaching was to lay claim to an esoteric body of knowledge that went far beyond the basic tenets of the gospel. Those who professed such knowledge exalted themselves above ordinary Christians, whom they relegated to "second-class citizenship" within the church. They themselves were the "knowers"; the rest of the church, mere "believers." In response to such a divisive doctrine, John assures his readers that "you have been anointed by the Holy One, and you *all* know" (2:20); "the anointing which you received from him abides in you, and you have no need that any one should teach you; as *his anointing teaches you about everything,* and is true, and is no lie, just as it has taught you, abide in him" (2:27). All who have been baptized and anointed by the Holy Spirit of truth possess the only knowledge that matters, the knowledge of God, both Father and Son, that means eternal life. In this sense there are no differentiated levels of spiritual attainment. All Christians are the children of God; all share a common life and a common hope in him. Anyone, whether inside or outside the church, who repudiates this unity of God's family, identifies himself as no Christian at all, but an anti-Christ. In attempting to exclude his brothers from the knowledge of God, he succeeds only in excluding himself from the divine life.

Thus John speaks harshly against those who would tamper with the essentials of Christian truth. Relentlessly he brings to bear against them the tests of righteousness and love. This treatise of First John lacks most of the qualifying clauses and lists of extenuating circumstances that usually go with ethical instruction. In the crisis faced here, everything is either light or darkness, truth or error, life of death, good or evil. Few gray areas exist to shade these contrasting zones of white and black. One fact above all, however, should be remembered: The righteousness and love which mark the child of God do not mean that he is perfect or altogether without sin —at least not until that day when "we shall be like him [i.e., Christ], for we shall see him as he is" (3:2). Though the Gnostic may have indulged themselves in extravagant pretension of sinlessness, John warns his readers against self-deceit of this kind: "If we say we have no sin, we deceive ourselves, and the truth is not in us" (1:8). Jesus himself was the only sinless one (3:5). "All wrongdoing is sin" (5:17), and there are many sins which are not mortal. As these continually afflict the child of God, they must be confessed and forgiven (1:9). John closes out his second cycle with a word of assurance: "If our heart condemn us, God is greater than our heart and knows all things"* (3:20). The righteousness that God requires is summed up in the twofold commandment "that we should believe in the name of his Son Jesus Christ and love one another" (3:23). This formulation sets the "new commandment" of love into its true perspective. It is not only the highest expression of righteousness but also a corollary of the gospel message that God sent his Son into the world to take away sin—a message that demands faith as its proper response. Thus the three strands of righteousness, love, and faith become interwoven into a strong cord that sustains and assures the child of God, giving him the victory that John celebrates in his third cycle.

Third Cycle: Believing the Truth (4:1–5:21)

The theme of this last section of First John is *faith*. The practical tests of "abiding in God" are doctrinal as well as ethical. He who claims to know God must demonstrate the life that is within him not only by loving his brother and keeping God's commandments but also by assenting to a creed. The Johannine creed is short and specific. It is embodied in the doctrinal affirmation that introduces this last cycle: "Jesus Christ has come in the flesh" (4:2).

Several times through the last two chapters of First John the creed reappears in different forms:

"God sent his only Son into the world" (4:9).
"The Father has sent his Son as the Savior of the world" (4:14).
"Jesus is the Son of God" (4:15; 5:5).
"Jesus is the Christ" (5:1).
"The Son of God has come" (5:20).

This is the event of which John testifies. This is what every Christian must believe and confess. Its fullest development is found in 5:6–7, in which the whole Johannine witness to Jesus' career is epitomized in remarkably few words:

> This is he who came by water and blood, Jesus Christ, not with the water only but with the water and the blood. And the Spirit is the witness, because the Spirit is the truth.

Here is the "Gospel According to John" reduced to its essentials: the ministry of Jesus from his baptism to his death upon the cross, revealed and interpreted by the Holy Spirit of truth. Nowhere else does the thought of the First Epistle of John run as closely parallel to that of the fourth Gospel as it does here.

The distinctive contribution of the epistle to the task of understanding Johannine thought, however, lies in the clearer picture it gives of the life situation that called it forth. While the purpose of John's Gospel can only be defined as that of introducing Christians into a fuller comprehension of the Christ event, the purpose of the epistle is a more specific one: to defend this understanding of Christ against a serious doctrinal deviation. The Gnostics did not content themselves with neglecting the moral life (1:6) nor even with cutting themselves off from the Christian community (2:18 ff.). They also denied that Jesus Christ had come in the flesh (4:1–6). Their doctrine of God did not allow them to accept the idea that God had really become a man. A human Jesus was conceivable to them; so was a divine Christ as revealer of God. But that the two could be united in one historical personality—this was inconceivable. Hence John's distinctive terminology: "in the *flesh*," "*Jesus* is the son of God," "*Jesus* is the Christ." In describing the spirit of anti-Christ, John emphasizes that it does not confess *"Jesus"* (4:3), not that it denies "Christ" or "God" or "the Son." We know that the church of John's day was already threatened by a Docetic teaching [28] that denied the reality of Christ's human nature and of his sufferings. The divine Christ, it was taught, came upon the human Jesus at his baptism but left him before his violent death upon the cross. Jesus was a man; Christ was God. Jesus suffered, but Christ was incapable of experiencing pain.

A late-second-century document, that ironically bears John's name, exemplifies this point of view:

> And my Lord stood in the middle of the cave and gave light to it and said, "John, for the people below in Jerusalem I am being crucified and pierced with lances and reeds and given vinegar and gall to drink. But to you I am speaking, and listen to what I speak" (*Acts of John*, 97).

> "This Cross then (is that) which has united all things by the Word and . . . has also compacted all things into [one]. But this is not that wooden Cross which you shall see when you go down from here; nor am I the (man) who is on the Cross . . ." (*ibid.*, 99).

It is perhaps against speculations of this kind that John insists Jesus came "not with the water only but with the water and the blood" (1 John 5:6). Similarly, in the fourth Gospel, such phrases as "the Word became flesh" (1:14), the references to "eating the flesh" and "drinking the blood" of the Son of man (6:53 ff.), and the deliberate mention of the blood and water from Jesus' side at the crucifixion (19:34) may exhibit a parallel awareness of the Docetic danger.

John develops his third cycle along much the same lines as the first two. Following the basic statement of belief in 1 John 4:1–6, the ethical implications of *love* (4:7–5:2) and *righteousness* (5:3–21) are developed, each section drawing to a close on a strong note of assurance and confidence in God (4:16–18; 5:13–21).

When the tests of life have been applied over and over again, John ends the treatise as he began. Having started by inviting his readers into that communion with the Father and the Son that he had known as an apostle, he concludes that "we are in him who is true, in his Son Jesus Christ. This is the true God and eternal life" (5:20). It is this central reality of "life in God" that binds together the Gospel and the First Epistle of John.

11. SECOND AND THIRD JOHN

Second and Third John are true letters in a sense in which First John is not.[30] Virtually all of the content of *Second John*, however, is paralleled somewhere in the longer First Epistle. The mutual interrelation of right-eousness and love, for example, is summed up concisely in verses 5–6: the new commandment is "that we love one another" (vs. 5); love is then defined as following his commandments, and once more John reiterates that "this is the commandment, as you have heard from the beginning, that you follow love" (vs. 6). Thus John's thought moves in a never-ending circle: love, righteousness, and again love. The doctrinal test recommended to uncover the anti-Christs is "the coming of Jesus Christ in the flesh" (vs. 7). The only new feature introduced in Second John is that these things are specifically summed up, perhaps for brevity's sake, as "the doctrine of Christ" (vss. 9–10). This becomes the test of life and fellowship: "Any one who goes ahead and does not abide in the doctrine of Christ does not have God; he who abides in the doctrine has both the Father and the Son" (vs. 9). A teacher who comes without this doctrine is not even to be greeted or received into one's house, much less into a place of authority in the church (vs. 10). The situation clearly parallels that of the First Epistle, in which "Many false prophets have gone out into the world" (1 John 4:1). Discernment is needed, and John supplies a practical, if simplified, rule to follow in the matter of receiving mission-aries.

Second John thus appears to be a brief précis or abstract of First John written for one particular church. The "elect lady" (vs. 1) is clearly a church, and "her children" are its individual members, while "the children of your elect sister" (vs. 13) are the members of John's own church—tradition suggests Ephesus.[31] If this tradition is correct, Second John may have been sent from Ephesus to another church in Asia Minor, while First John, like the Book of Revelation, may have been a circular distributed to all of Asia Minor. Perhaps Second John was written first, and briefly, because John hoped to explain things more fully in person (2 John 12). Then, when he was unable to come, and found that the problem of heresy was widespread, First John was written in lieu of a personal visit "so that our joy may be complete" (2 John 12; 1 John 1:4).

Third John is not written to a church but to a certain Gaius, otherwise unknown. Its tone is friendly and intimate. Superficially, it seems to contra-dict the second epistle in that emphasis is laid not on rejecting false teachers but on receiving the true messengers of God. John remembers Jesus' words to his disciples after the washing of their feet: "Truly, truly, I say to you, he who receives any one whom I send receives me; and he who receives me receives him who sent me" (John 13:20).

Gaius is to do good to fellow Christians who come to him as traveling strangers, for itinerant missionaries were dependent upon the Christian hospitality that John commends: "You will do well to send them on their journey as befits God's service. For they have set out for his sake and have accepted nothing from the heathen. So we ought to support such men, that we may be fellow workers in the truth" (3 John 6–8).

Not everyone in the church exhibited this attitude. A certain Diotrephes, "who likes to put himself first" (vs. 9), has not only denounced John and denied his authority but "refuses himself to welcome the brethren, and also stops those who want to welcome them and puts them out of the church" (vs. 10). Though Diotrephes is not accused of a specific doctrinal error, he is characterized here as a schismatic. His sin, like that of the Gnostic teachers in First John, is against the unity of the church. It is the sin of hatred and division among the brethren. Diotrephes seems to fall under the condemnation of Cain, a condemnation that John has already pronounced elsewhere: "Any one who hates his brother is a murderer, and you know that no murderer has eternal life abiding in him" (1 John 3:15). The life that Christians have in God is not to be regarded lightly. As Jesus was reunited with the Father, John says, we his disciples have been united to the Son and the Father. The very life of the Christian depends upon this relationship; to deny it is to forfeit one's own life. This is what Diotrephes and the Gnostics have done. But those who maintain this relationship, who "abide in God," are friends of God and of Jesus Christ. Jesus had declared to his disciples: "No longer do I call you servants, for the servant does not know what his master is doing; but I have called you *friends*, for all that I have heard from my Father I have made known to you" (John 15:15).

John's closing word to Gaius echoes this word "friends" and applies it to the people of God with confidence in Jesus' promise: "Peace be to you. The *friends* greet you. Greet the *friends*, every one of them" (3 John 15). It would be hard to find a more appropriate expression for the new way of life made possible because the Son of God has come.

The witness of John in his Gospel and three epistles is perhaps the fullest expression of the New Testament message. The good news is that God's Word has come into our midst. God has spoken in his Son Jesus, and because he has spoken, a new situation confronts the world. Since the Son has finished his work, men can know God as children and as "friends." This is the unique gift, and the awesome responsibility, of which the New Testament speaks.

NOTES

1. See, e.g., John 3:34; 7:16 f., 28 f.; 8:26 ff.; 12:49 f.; 14:24; 17:7 f.

2. Some parallels with John 1 (e.g., the statement that the word was "with the Father," 1:2) suggest that creation is in view, but comparison with passages such as 1 John 3:11 ("the message you heard from the beginning") points rather to Jesus' ministry as the time that John means.

3. E.g., Jer. 1:4; Ezek. 1:3; Hos. 1:1; Joel 1:1; Jonah 1:1; Mic. 1:1; Zeph. 1:1; Hagg. 1:1; Zech. 1:1, etc.

4. *The Fourth Gospel,* rev. ed., F. N. Davey, ed., 1947, p. 162.

5. For this translation, see R. E. Brown, *Anchor Bible,* Vol. 29 (1966), p. 4.

6. *Letters* X, 96. For text and translation, see D. J. Theron, *Evidence of Tradition* (1958), p. 15.

7. The word order is based on that of the Greek text.

8. Cf. 1 John 2:8, "the darkness is passing away and the true light is already shining."

9. The basis for this paraphrase is the fact that the Greek present tense for "believe" suggests "go on believing" rather than "start to believe" or "come to faith." Cf. the *New English Bible:* "that you may hold the faith."

10. Quoted in Eusebius, *Hist. Eccl.* VI, xiv, 7.

11. There is disagreement as to how this term should be translated. Therefore, some scholars prefer simply to transliterate the Greek *paraclētos* as Paraclete and let the context determine the meaning.

12. Brown's translation, see above, note 5.

13. The tradition begins as early as Irenaeus, *Adv. Haer.* III, i, 1.

14. We have purposely left out of consideration two references to anonymous disciples who *may* be identifiable with the beloved disciple: one who along with Andrew was first to be called to follow Jesus (John 1:40), and one who accompanied Peter to the high priest's court (18:15 ff.). No conclusive evidence connects these or the anonymous witness of the spear thrust in Jesus' side (19:35) with the beloved disciple. Though the fourth Gospel is based primarily on the testimony of one eyewitness, there is no reason why he might not have drawn also on the personal experiences of others.

15. Pseudo-Clementine, *Recognitions* I, 54, as translated in *The Ante-Nicene Fathers,* Vol. VIII, p. 92.

16. Note that in Matthew this problem comes up; John objects, "I need to be baptized by you, and do you come to me?" Jesus answers that this is the way that "all righteousness" must be fulfilled (3:14–15).

17. Jesus said elsewhere, "If any man would *come after me,* let him deny himself and take up his cross and *follow me"* (Mark 8:34).

18. That "Son of God" could refer to the Messiah of Jewish expectation is

shown by 2 Sam. 7:14, where God says of David's son, "I will be his father and he shall be my son" (This verse was interpreted messianically at Qumran; see above, p. 261).

19. Admittedly the Aramaic term for "Son of man," which Jesus would have used, means simply "the Man" (e.g., the heavenly man of Dan. 7:13), but the New Testament writers could have used "Son" as an abbreviation for "Son of man" in its Greek form in order to communicate more forcefully to the Greek world Jesus' unity with the Father. Note that in Mark 8:38 the Son of man comes "in the glory of his *Father"* and that in John 6:27 the Son of man is the one upon whom "God the *Father* set his seal." Even in Daniel 7:13 the Son of man comes to "the Ancient of Days" (i.e., to God).

20. The firm tradition that Jesus addressed God simply and directly as "Abba" (Father) without any qualification, as a beloved child would do, makes it entirely plausible that he regarded himself as "the Son." See the Lord's Prayer (Luke 11:2, "Father"), also Mark 14:36; cf. Rom. 8:15; Gal. 4:6. On this see J. Jeremias, *The Central Message of the New Testament* (1965), pp. 9–30.

21. The Revised Standard Version correctly omits 7:53–8:11, an incident which, though probably historical, is not found in the most ancient manuscripts of John.

22. Cf. the three tests proposed by Robert Law, *The Tests of Life* (1914), esp. pp. 7–24. His analysis is most useful, and it served as a stimulus to our own, though with numerous modifications.

23. See the texts in English translation collected by R. M. Grant, *Gnosticism* (1961), pp. 21–61; also the discussion of H. Jonas, *The Gnostic Religion* (1958), Parts I and II.

24. The Greek word is *paraclētos,* the same term that the fourth Gospel applies to the Holy Spirit. As the Spirit addresses man on behalf of God, so Christ addresses God on behalf of man.

25. "Little children," or "children," appears to be the general term for all Christian believers. They are then divided into two subgroups, the "fathers" and the "young men," and addressed separately (2:12–14).

26. See C. H. Dodd, *The Interpretation of the Fourth Gospel* (1953), pp. 144 ff.

27. Cf. Matt. 24:10–12; 1 Tim. 4:1 ff.; 2 Peter 3:3; Rev. 2–3.

28. From the Greek verb *dokeō,* meaning "seem" or "appear." See Ignatius, *Trallians* 10:1, *Smyrnaeans* 2:1; 4:1.

29. Quoted from E. Hennecke, *New Testament Apocrypha,* W. Schneemelcher, ed., Vol. II (1964), pp. 232 f.

30. See R. W. Funk, "The Form and Structure of II and III John," *Journal of Biblical Literature,* 86 (1967), pp. 424–30.

31. E.g., Irenaeus, *Adv. Haer.* II, xxii, 5; III, i, 1 f.; Polycrates, bishop of Ephesus *ca.* A.D. 200 in Eusebius, *Hist. Eccl.* III, xxxi, 3.

SELECTED READING

Barrett, C. K., *The Gospel According to St. John.* New York: Macmillan, 1955.

Brown, R. E., *The Gospel According to John.* Garden City, N.Y.: Doubleday, 1966.

Dodd, C. H., *The Interpretation of the Fourth Gospel.* Cambridge: University Press, 1953.

————— *Historical Tradition in the Fourth Gospel.* Cambridge: University Press, 1963.

————— *The Johannine Epistles.* New York: Harper, 1946.

Hoskyns, E., *The Fourth Gospel,* rev. ed., F. N. Davey, ed. London: Faber and Faber, Ltd., 1947.

Howard, W. F., *Christianity According to St. John.* London: Duckworth, 1943.

Law, R., *The Tests of Life.* Edinburgh: T. and T. Clark, 1914.

Westcott, B. F., *The Gospel According to St. John.* Grand Rapids: Eerdmans, 1950 (from 1881 ed.).

INDEX OF PASSAGES

OLD TESTMAENT

NEW TESTAMENT

APOCRYPHA

PSEUDEPIGRAPHA

QUMRÂN

JOSEPHUS & PHILO

RABBINICS

GREEK AND ROMAN AUTHORS

APOSTOLIC FATHERS

LATER CHRISTIAN WRITINGS

INDEX OF SUBJECTS

�֍

447

76 77 9 8 7